WORKBOOK

S
N
A
P

Student Notes and Problems

MATHEMATICS 31
Alberta Edition

Castle Rock
Research Corp

Canadian Cataloguing in Publication Data

Rao, Gautam, 1961 –
STUDENT NOTES AND PROBLEMS – Math 31 – Workbook

1. Mathematics – Juvenile Literature. I. Title

Published by
Castle Rock Research Corp.
2410 Manulife Place
10180 – 101 Street
Edmonton, AB T5J 3S4

6 7 8 MP 13 07 06

Printed in Canada

Publisher
Gautam Rao

Contributor
Nadine Molnar
Ken Kulka
Bob Frizzell

Dedicated to the memory of Dr. V. S. Rao

STUDENT NOTES AND PROBLEMS WORKBOOKS

Student Notes and Problems (SNAP) workbooks are a series of support resources in mathematics for students in grades 3 to 12 and in science for students in grades 9 to 12. SNAP workbooks are 100% aligned with curriculum. The resources are designed to support classroom instructions and provide students with additional examples, practice exercises, and tests. SNAP workbooks are ideal for use all year long at school and at home.

The following is a summary of the key features of all SNAP workbooks.

UNIT OPENER PAGE

- Summarizes the curriculum outcomes addressed in the unit in age-appropriate language
- Identifies the lessons by title
- Lists the prerequisite knowledge and skills the student should know prior to beginning the unit

LESSONS

- Provide essential teaching pieces and explanations of the concepts
- Include example problems and questions with complete, detailed solutions that demonstrate the problem-solving process

NOTES BARS

- Contain key definitions, formulas, reminders, and important steps or procedures
- Provide space for students to add their own notes and helpful reminders

PRACTICE EXERCISES

- Include questions that relate to each of the curriculum outcomes for the unit
- Provide practice in applying the lesson concepts

REVIEW SUMMARY

- Provides a succinct review of the key concepts in the unit

PRACTICE TEST

- Assesses student learning of the unit concepts

ANSWERS AND SOLUTIONS

- Answers and solutions for the odd-numbered questions are provided in each student workbook.

CONTENTS

Pre-Calculus

Limits

Derivatives and Derivative Theorems

Derivatives of Trigonometric, Logarithmic, and Exponential Functions

Extreme Values and Curve Sketching

Applications of Derivatives

Antiderivatives and Area

Methods of Integration and Applications

Answers and Solutions

PRE-CALCULUS

When you are finished this unit, you should be able to. . .

- factor expressions containing a sum or difference of cubes
- factor expressions containing rational exponents
- factor expression that do not contain perfect squares as a difference of squares
- rationalize numerators and denominators of expressions that contain radicals
- describe and graph the transformations of functions including reflections, stretches, and translations
- combine operations using the four basic operations
- find composite functions of two functions
- use interval notation
- solve quadratic inequalities
- solve rational inequalities
- solve absolute value inequalities
- use trigonometric identities to simplify trigonometric expressions

PREREQUISITE SKILLS AND KNOWLEDGE

Prior to beginning this unit, you should be able to . . .

- factor expressions using a greatest common factor
- factor quadratic expressions
- understand and use function notation
- solve linear and quadratic equations
- solve linear inequalities
- use the quadratic formula to solve quadratic equations
- calculate exact trigonometric values

Lesson 1 FACTORING

The ability to simplify expressions is essential when working with the limits and derivatives that we will be evaluating in future chapters.

You are already familiar with the concept of factoring as well as with several factoring methods. In this lesson, three factoring methods will be presented.

FACTORING SUMS AND DIFFERENCES OF CUBES

$a^3 + b^3$ and $a^3 - b^3$

$$a^3 + b^3 = (a+b)\left(a^2 - ab + b^2\right)$$

$$a^3 - b^3 = (a-b)\left(a^2 + ab + b^2\right)$$

Factoring the sum of cubes or the difference of cubes requires that the values $a = \sqrt[3]{a^3}$ and $b = \sqrt[3]{b^3}$ be determined and then substituted into the appropriate pattern illustrated above.

Example 1

Factor the expression $x^3 + 27$.

Solution

$$a^3 = x^3$$
$$a = \sqrt[3]{x^3}$$
$$a = x$$
$$b^3 = 27$$
$$b = \sqrt[3]{27}$$
$$b = 3$$

Substitute into $a^3 + b^3 = (a+b)\left(a^2 - ab + b^2\right)$

$$x^3 + 3^3 = (x+3)\left(x^2 - x(3) + (3)^2\right)$$
$$x^3 + 27 = (x+3)\left(x^2 - 3x + 9\right)$$

Example 2

Factor the expression $8x^3 - y^3$.

Solution

$$a^3 - b^3 = (a-b)\left(a^2 + ab + b^2\right)$$
$$(2x)^3 - (y)^3 = (2x - y)\left((2x)^2 + (2x)(y) + (y)^2\right)$$
$$8x^3 - y^3 = (2x - y)\left(4x^2 + 2xy + y^2\right)$$

FACTORING EXPRESSIONS WITH RATIONAL EXPONENTS

When an expression has rational exponents with variables in its terms, the variable with the smallest exponent should be factored out of each term.

Example 3

Factor the expression $x^{\frac{5}{2}} + 3x^{\frac{3}{2}} + 2x^{\frac{1}{2}}$.

Solution

The smallest power of x is $x^{\frac{1}{2}}$. Factor $x^{\frac{1}{2}}$ out of each term.

$$x^{\frac{5}{2}} + 3x^{\frac{3}{2}} + 2x^{\frac{1}{2}} = x^{\frac{1}{2}}\left(x^{\frac{4}{2}} + 3x^{\frac{2}{2}} + 2\right)$$

$$= x^{\frac{1}{2}}\left(x^2 + 3x + 2\right)$$

This can be factored further as:

$$= x^{\frac{1}{2}}(x+2)(x+1)$$

Example 4

Factor the expression $x^{\frac{1}{2}} + 7x^{\frac{-1}{2}} + 12x^{\frac{-3}{2}}$.

Solution

The smallest negative power of x is $x^{\frac{-3}{2}}$. Factor $x^{\frac{-3}{2}}$ out of each term.

$$x^{\frac{1}{2}} + 7x^{\frac{-1}{2}} + 12x^{\frac{-3}{2}} = x^{\frac{-3}{2}}\left(x^{\frac{4}{2}} + 7x^{\frac{2}{2}} + 12\right)$$

$$= x^{\frac{-3}{2}}\left(x^2 + 7x + 12\right)$$

$$= x^{\frac{-3}{2}}(x+3)(x+4)$$

Example 5

Factor the expression $a^{\frac{-1}{2}} - 2a^{\frac{-3}{2}} - 35a^{\frac{-5}{2}}$.

Solution

Factor $a^{\frac{-5}{2}}$ out of each term.

$$a^{\frac{-1}{2}} - 2a^{\frac{-3}{2}} - 35a^{\frac{-5}{2}} = a^{\frac{-5}{2}} \left(a^{\frac{4}{2}} - 2a^{\frac{2}{2}} - 35 \right)$$

$$= a^{\frac{-5}{2}} \left(a^2 - 2a - 35 \right)$$

$$= a^{\frac{-5}{2}} (a-7)(a+5)$$

With many of the questions that will be encountered in future units, the factors that have the rational exponents are binomial factors.

The procedure is the same: factor out the factor with the least rational exponent.

Example 6

Factor the expression $(x+1)^{\frac{3}{2}} - 2(x+1)^{\frac{1}{2}}$.

Solution

Factor out the $(x+1)^{\frac{1}{2}}$ because $\frac{1}{2}$ is the smaller exponent.

$$(x+1)^{\frac{3}{2}} - 2(x+1)^{\frac{1}{2}} = (x+1)^{\frac{1}{2}} \left[(x+1)^{\frac{2}{2}} - 2 \right]$$

$$= (x+1)^{\frac{1}{2}} \left[(x+1)^1 - 2 \right]$$

Now simplify $\quad = (x+1)^{\frac{1}{2}} (x+1-2)$

$$= (x+1)^{\frac{1}{2}} (x-1)$$

Example 7

Factor the expression $(x-5)^{\frac{-1}{2}} - 6(x-5)^{\frac{-3}{2}}$.

Solution

$$(x-5)^{\frac{-1}{2}} - 6(x-5)^{\frac{-3}{2}} = (x-5)^{\frac{-3}{2}}\left[(x-5)^{\frac{2}{2}} - 6\right]$$

$$= (x-5)^{\frac{-3}{2}}(x-5-6)$$

$$= (x-5)^{\frac{-3}{2}}(x-11)$$

$$= \frac{(x-11)}{(x-5)^{\frac{3}{2}}}$$

DIFFERENCE OF SQUARES

Factoring expressions of the form $x^2 - a$, where a is a number but not a perfect square, requires the same procedure as the familiar factoring of the difference of perfect squares.

Recall that

$$x^2 - y^2 = (x-y)(x+y)$$

Students will recognize this equation from examples where y is an integer. For example:

$$x^2 - 9 = (x-3)(x+3)$$

This equation can also be applied where y is not an integer. For example:

$$x^2 - 3 = (x-\sqrt{3})(x+\sqrt{3})$$

Example 8

Factor: $x^2 - 5$

Solution

$$x^2 - 5 = (x-\sqrt{5})(x+\sqrt{5})$$

Example 9

Factor: $25x^2 - 8$

Solution

$$25x^2 - 8 = (5x-\sqrt{8})(5x+\sqrt{8})$$

$$= (5x-2\sqrt{2})(5x+2\sqrt{2})$$

PRACTICE EXERCISE

Factor each of the following expressions using an appropriate method.

1. $8x^3 - 125y^3$

2. $64x^3 + 1$

3. $2a^{\frac{5}{2}} + a^{\frac{3}{2}} - 3a^{\frac{1}{2}}$

4. $5a^{\frac{3}{2}} - 20a^{\frac{-1}{2}}$

5. $(x+2)^{\frac{5}{2}} - 3(x+2)^{\frac{3}{2}}$

6. $(x+4)^{\frac{7}{2}} - 4(x+4)^{\frac{-1}{2}}$

7. $\dfrac{(2x-5)^{\frac{1}{2}} + 4(2x-5)^{\frac{-1}{2}}}{2x-1}$

8. $x^2 - 20$

Lesson 2   RATIONALIZING NUMERATORS AND DENOMINATORS

The ability to simplify an expression by rationalizing it is important in problems involving limits.

Recall that the conjugate of any expression of the form $x + \sqrt{a}$ is $x - \sqrt{a}$, and vice versa.

Rationalizing often involves multiplying the numerator and denominator by the conjugate of the expression that is being rationalized.

Example 1

Rationalize the denominator of the expression $\dfrac{2x}{\sqrt{x} - 2}$.

Solution
Multiply the expression (on the top and bottom) by the conjugate.

$$\frac{2x}{\sqrt{x} - 2} \times \frac{\left(\sqrt{x} + 2\right)}{\left(\sqrt{x} + 2\right)}$$

$$= \frac{2x\sqrt{x} + 4x}{x - 4}$$

Example 2

Rationalize the numerator of the expression $\dfrac{\sqrt{x} - 2}{x - 4}$.

Solution
There are 2 different methods that can be used for this rationalization.
Method I: Multiply by the conjugate

$$\frac{\sqrt{x} - 2}{x - 4} \times \frac{\left(\sqrt{x} + 2\right)}{\left(\sqrt{x} + 2\right)}$$

$$= \frac{x - 4}{(x - 4)\left(\sqrt{x} + 2\right)} \ (expand)$$

The denominator was not expanded in anticipation of the cancelling to follow.

$$= \frac{1}{\left(\sqrt{x} + 2\right)} \qquad (cancel)$$

Method II: Factor the denominator as a difference of squares

$$\frac{\sqrt{x}-2}{\left(\sqrt{x}+2\right)\left(\sqrt{x}-2\right)}$$

$$\frac{1}{\left(\sqrt{x}+2\right)} \qquad (cancel)$$

With practice, you can begin to anticipate which method may be more advantageous. It is often just a matter of personal preference.

Example 3

Rationalize the numerator of the expression $\dfrac{\sqrt{x+5}-3}{x^2-16}$.

Solution

$$=\frac{\sqrt{x+5}-3}{(x+4)(x-4)}$$

$$=\frac{\sqrt{x+5}-3}{(x+4)(x-4)}\times\frac{(\sqrt{x+5}+3)}{(\sqrt{x+5}+3)}$$

$$=\frac{x+5-9}{(x+4)(x-4)\left(\sqrt{x+5}+3\right)}$$

$$=\frac{x-4}{(x+4)(x-4)\left(\sqrt{x+5}+3\right)}$$

$$=\frac{1}{(x+4)\left(\sqrt{x+5}+3\right)}$$

Further expansion of the denominator in this case is not helpful.

Example 4

Rationalize the numerator of the expression $\dfrac{\sqrt{x^2+4x-9}+2\sqrt{x}}{x+3}$ and then simplify it.

Solution

$$\frac{\sqrt{x^2+4x-9}+2\sqrt{x}}{x+3}\times\left(\frac{\sqrt{x^2+4x-9}-2\sqrt{x}}{\sqrt{x^2+4x-9}-2\sqrt{x}}\right)$$

$$=\frac{\left(x^2+4x-9\right)-4x}{(x+3)\left(\sqrt{x^2+4x-9}-2\sqrt{x}\right)}$$

$$=\frac{x^2-9}{(x+3)\left(\sqrt{x^2+4x-9}-2\sqrt{x}\right)}$$

$$=\frac{(x+3)(x-3)}{(x+3)\left(\sqrt{x^2+4x-9}-2\sqrt{x}\right)}$$

$$=\frac{x-3}{\sqrt{x^2+4x-9}-2\sqrt{x}}$$

Example 5

Rationalize the numerator of the expression $\dfrac{\dfrac{1}{\sqrt{x}}+3}{\dfrac{5}{6\sqrt{x}}}$.

Solution

$$\frac{\dfrac{1}{\sqrt{x}}+3\left(\dfrac{\sqrt{x}}{\sqrt{x}}\right)}{\dfrac{5}{6\sqrt{x}}}$$

$$=\frac{\dfrac{1+3\sqrt{x}}{\sqrt{x}}}{\dfrac{5}{6\sqrt{x}}}$$

$$=\frac{1+3\sqrt{x}}{\sqrt{x}}\times\frac{6\sqrt{x}}{5}$$

$$=\frac{6\left(1+3\sqrt{x}\right)}{5}$$

$$=\frac{6\left(1+3\sqrt{x}\right)}{5}\times\frac{\left(1-3\sqrt{x}\right)}{\left(1-3\sqrt{x}\right)}$$

$$=\frac{6\left(1-9x\right)}{5\left(1-3\sqrt{x}\right)}$$

PRACTICE EXERCISE

1. Rationalize the denominator in each of the following expressions and then simplify each.

   a) $\dfrac{1}{x - 2\sqrt{x}}$

   b) $\dfrac{x - 5}{\sqrt{x} + \sqrt{5}}$

   c) $\dfrac{4x}{\sqrt{2 - x} + \sqrt{2}}$

2. Rationalize the numerator in each of the following expressions and then simplify each.

   a) $\dfrac{\sqrt{2x - 5} - \sqrt{7}}{x - 6}$

   b) $\left(\sqrt{x^2 + x - 11}\right) - 1$

   c) $\dfrac{\dfrac{1}{\sqrt{x}} - 4\sqrt{x}}{4x - 1}$

Lesson 3   OPERATIONS WITH FUNCTIONS AND COMPOSITION OF FUNCTIONS

Often complex functions are created by combining simpler functions by using the four basic operations or by using methods of composition of functions.

You need to be able to perform the four basic operations on functions and to be able to recognize the more basic functions that make up a more complex function.

USING THE OPERATIONS $+$, $-$, $\times$ AND $\div$

Example 1

Given the functions $g(x) = x^2 - 2x + 1$ and $h(x) = x^2 + 3x - 4$, solve each of the following equations.

a) $f(x) = g(x) + h(x)$

Solution

Substitute the functions for $g(x)$ and $h(x)$

$$f(x) = \left(x^2 - 2x + 1\right) + \left(x^2 + 3x - 4\right)$$

Combine like terms (simplify)

$$f(x) = 2x^2 + x - 3$$

b) $f(x) = g(x) - h(x)$

Solution

Substitute the functions for $g(x)$ and $h(x)$

$$f(x) = \left(x^2 - 2x + 1\right) - \left(x^2 + 3x - 4\right)$$

Combine like terms (simplify)

$$f(x) = -5x + 5$$

c) $f(x) = g(x)h(x)$

Solution

Substitute the functions for $g(x)$ and $h(x)$

$$f(x) = \left(x^2 - 2x + 1\right)\left(x^2 + 3x - 4\right)$$

Expand using the distributive property

$$f(x) = x^4 + x^3 - 9x^2 + 11x - 4$$

14

d) $f(x) = \dfrac{g(x)}{h(x)}$

Solution

Substitute the functions for $g(x)$ and $h(x)$

$$f(x) = \frac{\left(x^2 - 2x + 1\right)}{\left(x^2 + 3x - 4\right)}$$

It is often useful to leave expressions in factored form when further simplifying is required.

$$f(x) = \frac{(x-1)(x-1)}{(x-1)(x+4)}, \ x \neq -4, 1$$

$$= \frac{(x-1)}{(x+4)}, \ x \neq -4, 1$$

The restrictions (nonpermissible values) are established for the original function, before any simplification.
They are retained for the function after the $x-1$ is cancelled.

Example 2

Given the functions $g(x) = \dfrac{1}{x+5}$ and $h(x) = \dfrac{1}{x^2 - 25}$, solve each of the following equations.

a) $f(x) = g(x) + h(x)$

Solution

Substitute the functions for $g(x)$ and $h(x)$

$$f(x) = \frac{1}{x+5} + \frac{1}{x^2 - 25}, \ x \neq \pm 5$$

Simplify by finding the common denominator

$$f(x) = \frac{(x-5)}{(x+5)(x-5)} + \frac{1}{(x+5)(x-5)}, \ x \neq \pm 5$$

$$f(x) = \frac{x-5+1}{(x+5)(x-5)}, \ x \neq \pm 5$$

$$f(x) = \frac{x-4}{x^2 - 25}, \ x \neq \pm 5$$

b) $f(x) = g(x) - h(x)$

Solution

Substitute the functions for $g(x)$ and $h(x)$

$$f(x) = \frac{1}{x+5} - \frac{1}{x^2 - 25} , \ x \neq \pm 5$$

$$f(x) = \frac{(x-5)}{(x+5)(x-5)} - \frac{1}{(x+5)(x-5)} , \ x \neq \pm 5$$

$$f(x) = \frac{x-6}{x^2 - 25} , \ x \neq \pm 5$$

c) $f(x) = g(x)h(x)$

Solution

Substitute the functions for $g(x)$ and $h(x)$

$$f(x) = \left(\frac{1}{x+5}\right)\left(\frac{1}{x^2 - 25}\right) , \ x \neq \pm 5$$

$$f(x) = \frac{1}{(x+5)(x^2 - 25)} , \ x \neq \pm 5$$

d) $f(x) = \dfrac{g(x)}{h(x)}$

Solution

Substitute the functions for $g(x)$ and $h(x)$

$$f(x) = \frac{\dfrac{1}{x+5}}{\dfrac{1}{x^2 - 25}} , \ x \neq \pm 5$$

$$f(x) = \frac{x^2 - 25}{x+5} , \ x \neq \pm 5$$

$$f(x) = \frac{(x+5)\,\cancel{(x+5)}}{\cancel{x+5}} , \ x \neq \pm 5$$

$$f(x) = x - 5 , \ x \neq \pm 5$$

Example 3

Given the functions $g(x) = \sin^2 x$ and $h(x) = \cot x$, solve each of the following equations.

a) $f(x) = g(x) + h(x)$

Solution

Substitute the functions for $g(x)$ and $h(x)$

$$f(x) = \sin^2 x + \cos x \,, \ x \neq n\pi, n \in I$$

$$= \sin^2 x + \frac{\cos x}{\sin x} \,, \ x \neq n\pi, n \in I$$

$$= \frac{\sin^3 x + \cos x}{\sin x} \,, \ x \neq n\pi, n \in I$$

b) $f(x) = g(x) - h(x)$

Solution

Substitute the functions for $g(x)$ and $h(x)$

$$f(x) = \sin^2 x - \cos x \,, \ x \neq n\pi, n \in I$$

$$= \sin^2 x - \frac{\cos x}{\sin x} \,, \ x \neq n\pi, n \in I$$

$$= \frac{\sin^3 x - \cos x}{\sin x} \,, \ x \neq n\pi, n \in I$$

c) $f(x) = g(x)h(x)$

Solution

Substitute the functions for $g(x)$ and $h(x)$

$$f(x) = \left(\sin^2 x\right)(\cos x) \,, \ x \neq n\pi, n \in I$$

$$= \left(\sin^2 x\right)\left(\frac{\cos x}{\sin x}\right) \,, \ x \neq n\pi, n \in I$$

$$= \sin x \cos x \,, \ x \neq n\pi, n \in I$$

d) $f(x) = \dfrac{g(x)}{h(x)}$

Solution

Substitute the functions for $g(x)$ and $h(x)$

$$f(x) = \frac{\left(\sin^2 x\right)}{\left(\cos x\right)} \ , \ x \neq n\pi, n \in I \ , \ x \neq \frac{\pi}{2} + n\pi, n \in I$$

$$= \frac{\left(\sin^2 x\right)}{\left(\dfrac{\cos x}{\sin x}\right)} \ , \ x \neq n\pi, n \in I \ , \ x \neq \frac{\pi}{2} + n\pi, n \in I$$

$$= \sin^2 x \cdot \frac{\sin x}{\cos x} \ , \ x \neq n\pi, n \in I \ , \ x \neq \frac{\pi}{2} + n\pi, n \in I$$

$$= \frac{\sin^3 x}{\cos x} \ , \ x \neq n\pi, n \in I \ , \ x \neq \frac{\pi}{2} + n\pi, n \in I$$

Example 4

Given $g(x) = x + 2$ and $h(x) = x^2 - 4$, find and sketch a graph of $f(x)$ for each of the following equations.

a) $f(x) = g(x) + h(x)$

Solution

$$f(x) = (x+2) + \left(x^2 - 4\right)$$
$$= x^2 + x - 2$$

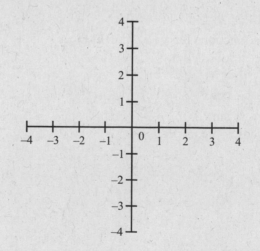

Use a graphing calculator to assist with the sketching of analytic curves will be covered later in the course.

18

b) $f(x) = g(x)h(x)$

Solution

$$f(x) = (x+2)(x^2-4)$$
$$= x^3 + 2x^2 - 4x - 8$$

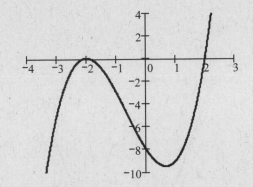

COMPOSITION OF FUNCTIONS

In function composition, a second function takes the place of a variable in the first function. Recall that variables are place holders waiting for a value to be inserted. With composition of functions, the value to be inserted is itself a function.

When the function $g(x)$ is substituted in place of the variable in the function $f(x)$, the composite function is written as $f(g(x))$.

Another common notation for the composite function is $(f \circ g)(x)$.

Example 5

Given $f(x) = x^2$ and $g(x) = x + 4$, find each of the following composite functions and sketch a graph of the new function.

a) $f(g(x))$

Solution

$$f(g(x)) = \left[g(x)\right]^2$$
$$= (x+4)^2$$
$$= x^2 + 8x + 16$$

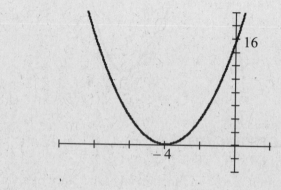

b) $g(f(x))$

Solution

$$g(f(x)) = f(x) + 4$$
$$= x^2 + 4$$

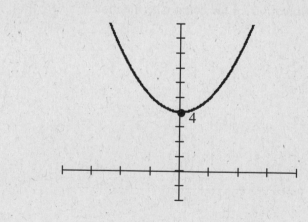

Example 6

Given $g(x) = \dfrac{1}{x}$ and $h(x) = x - 2$, find each of the following composite functions and sketch a graph of the new function.

a) $g(h(x))$

Solution

$$g(h(x)) = \frac{1}{h(x)}$$

$$= \frac{1}{x - 2}, \; x \neq 2$$

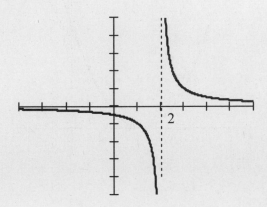

b) $h(g(x))$

Solution

$$h(g(x)) = g(x) - 2$$

$$= \frac{1}{x} - 2, \; x \neq 0$$

$$= \frac{1 - 2x}{x}, \; x \neq 0$$

PRACTICE EXERCISE

1. Given $g(x) = x^2 - 2x - 8$ and $h(x) = x - 4$, find and sketch the graph for each of the following equations.

   a) $f(x) = g(x) - h(x)$

   b) $f(x) = \dfrac{g(x)}{h(x)}$

   c) $g(h(x))$

2. Given $g(x) = \sin x$ and $h(x) = x^2$, evaluate each of the following expressions.

   a) $\dfrac{h(x)}{g(x)}$

   b) $g(h(x))$

   c) $h(g(x))$

3. Given $g(x) = \dfrac{1}{\sqrt{x}}$ and $h(x) = x^2 - 1$, rationalize the denominators of the resulting functions of each of the following equations.

a) $f(x) = g(x) + h(x)$

b) $g(x)h(x)$

c) $h(g(x))$

Lesson 4 TRANSFORMATIONS OF FUNCTIONS

NOTES

In this lesson, we'll review the topic of transformations of functions, which is covered very thoroughly in Pure Math 30. In function transformation, the equation of a function is changed –or transformed– which also causes the graph of the function to change.

The following is a list of transformations and the effect that each has on the graph of the function, for any function $y = f(x)$.

Equation of the Transformation	Effect on the graph
$y = f(-x)$	– reflects $y = f(x)$ horizontally in the y-axis
$y = -f(x)$	– reflects $y = f(x)$ vertically in the x-axis
$y = f^{-1}(x)$ or $x = f(y)$	– reflects $y = f(x)$ in the line $y = x$ (known as the inverse)
$y = af(x)$	– vertical stretch about the x-axis by a factor of a
$y = f(bx)$	– horizontal stretch about the y-axis by a factor of $\dfrac{1}{b}$
$y = f(x) + d$	– vertical translation by d units; when $d > 0$, the graph moves up; when $d < 0$, the graph moves down
$y = f(x - c)$	– horizontal translation by c units; when $c > 0$, the graph moves right; when $c < 0$, the graph moves left

$y = f^{-1}(x)$ can only be used if the inverse is a function

Example 1

Describe in words the transformation applied to the function $y = x$ that produce the function $y = -2f(x) - 3$.

Solution

The function has undergone the following transformations

– vertical stretch in the x-axis by a factor of 2

– vertical reflection in the x-axis

– vertical translation down 3 units

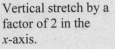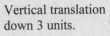

$$y = -2f(x) - 3$$

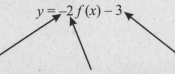

| Vertical reflection in the x-axis. | Vertical stretch by a factor of 2 in the x-axis. | Vertical translation down 3 units. |

Example 2

Describe in words the transformation applied to the function $y = x$ that produce the function $y = -f(2x - 10) + 7$.

Solution

First factor the equation of the transformed function.

$$y = -f(2(x - 5)) + 7$$

horizontal stretch in the y-axis by a factor of $\dfrac{1}{2}$

– vertical reflection in the x-axis

– translation right by 5 units

– translation up by 7 units

Example 3

Given the graph of the function $y = f(x)$ as shown below on the left, write the equation of the transformed function graphed below on the right.

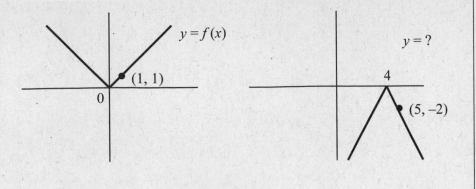

Solution

The graph on the right has been:

– stretched horizontally by a factor of $\dfrac{1}{2}$ about the *y*- axis

– reflected in the *x*-axis
– translated right by 4 units

$$y = -f\big(2(x-4)\big)$$

The function could also be written as having been stretched vertically by a factor of 2 and written as $y = -2f(x-4)$.

Example 4

Given the graph of the function $y = f(x)$ as shown below on the left, write the equation of the transformed function graphed below on the right.

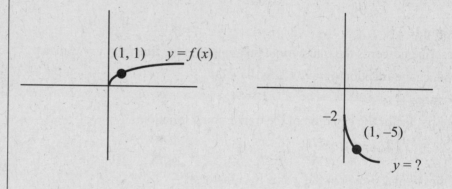

Solution
– stretched vertically about the *x*-axis by a factor of 3
– vertical reflection in the *x*-axis
– translated down by 2 units

$$y = -3f(x) - 2$$

TRANSFORMATIONS OF $y = \sin x$ AND $y = \cos x$

Transformations apply to sine and cosine functions in the same way that they apply to all other functions. There are special terms that we use when referring specifically to these trigonometric functions.

For $y = a\sin(b(x-c))+d$ and $y = a\cos(b(x-c))+d$

Amplitude: (vertical stretch factor) Amplitude $= |a|$

Period: number of radians or degrees that it takes to complete a full cycle.

$$\text{Period} = \frac{2\pi}{|b|}$$

Note: When working with degrees rather than radians, use

$$\text{Period} = \frac{360°}{|b|}.$$

When using calculus, it is uncommon to use degrees.

Phase shift: horizontal translation. (c)

Vertical displacement: vertical translation. (d)

Example 5

Give the amplitude, period, phase shift, and vertical displacement of the function $y = -4\cos(3x-\pi)+10$.

Solution

First, remove a common factor from the binomial $3x-\pi$:

$$y = -4\cos(3x-\pi)+10$$
$$= -4\cos\left(3\left(x-\frac{\pi}{3}\right)\right)+10$$

$$\begin{aligned}\text{Amplitude} &= |a|\\ &= |-4|\\ &= 4\end{aligned}$$

$$\begin{aligned}\text{Period} \quad &\frac{2\pi}{|b|}\\ &= \frac{2\pi}{|3|} = \frac{2\pi}{3}\end{aligned}$$

$$\begin{aligned}\text{Phase shift} &= c\\ &= \frac{\pi}{3}\end{aligned}$$

$$\begin{aligned}\text{Vertical displacement} &= d\\ &= 10\end{aligned}$$

Example 6

Give the amplitude, period, phase shift, and vertical displacement of the function $y = 15\sin\left(4x - \dfrac{\pi}{3}\right) + 3$.

Solution

First, factor the function:

$$y = 15\sin\left(4\left(x - \frac{\pi}{12}\right)\right) + 3$$

$$\text{Amplitude} = |a|$$
$$= |15|$$
$$= 15$$

$$\text{Period} \quad = \frac{2\pi}{|b|}$$

$$= \frac{2\pi}{|4|} \qquad = \frac{\pi}{2}$$

$$\text{Phase shift} \quad = c$$

$$= \frac{\pi}{12}$$

$$\text{Vertical displacement} \ = d$$
$$= 3$$

Example 7

Sketch each of the following functions and their indicated transformations on the same set of axes.

a) $f(x) = x^2$ and $y = 2f(x-4)+3$

b) $f(x) = 2^x$ and $y = 3f(x)-2$

c) $f(x) = \sin x$ and $y = -2f(2x)$

d) $f(x) = \cos x$ and $y = \dfrac{1}{2}f\left(x - \dfrac{\pi}{2}\right)$

Solution

a)

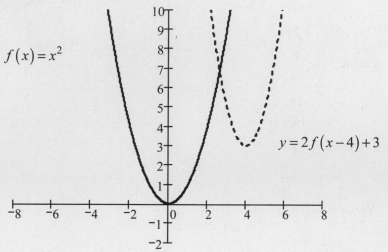

b)

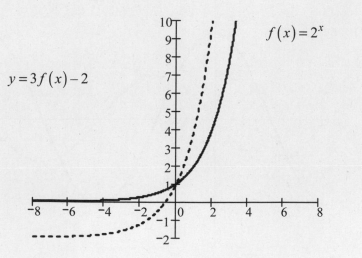

c)

$y = -2f(2x)$

$f(x) = \sin x$

d)

$y = \cos x$

$y = \dfrac{1}{2} f\left(x - \dfrac{\pi}{2}\right)$

PRACTICE EXERCISE

1. Complete the following chart to describe the effect of each of the given transformations to the graph of $y = f(x)$.

	Equation of Transformation	Line that the Graph is Reflected In	Vertical Stretch Factor about the x-axis	Horizontal Stretch Factor about the y-axis	Vertical Translation	Horizontal Translation
a)	$y = -5f(2x) + 1$					
b)	$y = f(3x - 6)$					
c)	$y = -f(-x) - 2$					
d)	$y = f^{-1}(x) - 7$					
e)	$y = -7f\left(-\frac{1}{3}x - 3\right) + 8$					

2. Complete the chart below for the graph of each of the given functions.

		Amplitude	Period	Phase Shift	Vertical Displacement
a)	$y = 3\sin(2x)$				
b)	$y = -5\cos(x + \pi)$				
c)	$y = -\cos\left(3x - \frac{\pi}{2}\right) - 11$				
d)	$y = 10\sin(4x - 3\pi) + 6$				

3. Write the equation of the transformation that was applied to each of the graphs on the left to produce the graphs on the right.

a)

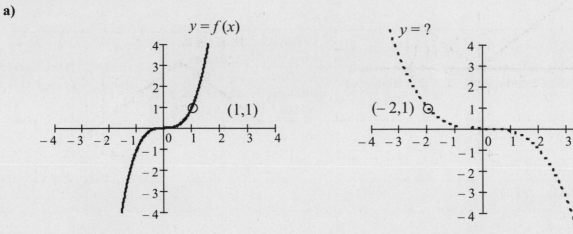

b)

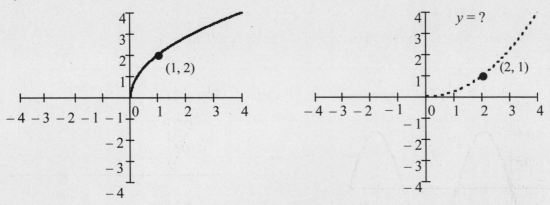

c)

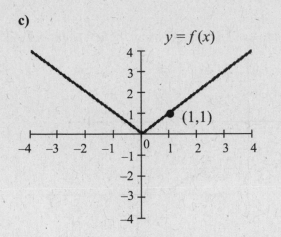

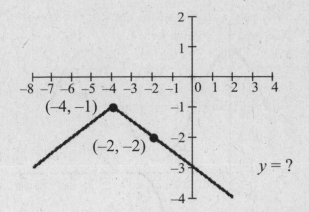

$y = f(x)$

$(1,1)$

$(-4,-1)$

$(-2,-2)$

$y = ?$

d)

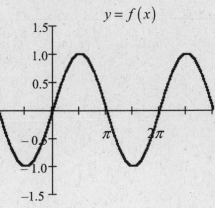

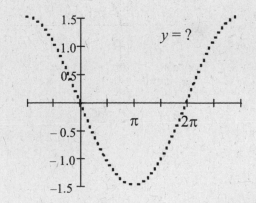

$y = f(x)$

$y = ?$

e)

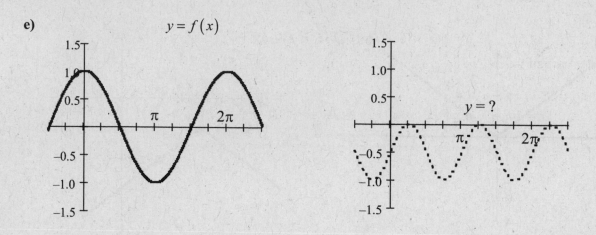

$y = f(x)$

$y = \,?$

PRACTICE QUIZ

1. Factor each of the following expressions.

    a) $x^3 - 125$

    b) $(x-7)^{\frac{3}{2}} + 3(x-7)^{-\frac{1}{2}}$

2. Rationalize the numerator of the expression $\dfrac{\sqrt{x+6} + \sqrt{10}}{x^2 - 16}$.

3. Describe the transformations that are applied to $y = f(x)$ in order to get the function $y = -5f(2x-6)+1$.

4. Given $g(x) = 2x^2$ and $h(x) = 6x - 4$, solve each of the following equations.

a) $f(x) = \dfrac{h(x)}{g(x)}$

b) $f(x) = g(x) - h(x)$

c) $f(x) = g(h(x))$

Lesson 5 INTERVAL NOTATION

In your study of mathematics, you will have seen intervals of values on a function expressed on a number line or as inequalities. In this lesson, you will learn how to use and interpret something known as interval notation.

Interval notation involves two types of brackets. Square brackets [ ] are used to represent a *closed* interval that includes the end values of the interval. Round brackets ( ) represent an *open* interval for which the end values are not included.

In interval notation, the inequality statement $2 \leq x \leq 6$ is written as [2, 6]. The use of the square brackets indicates that x can equal the end values of 2 and 6.

The inequality $2 < x < 6$ is written as (2, 6), using the round brackets to indicate that the 2 and the 6 are *not* included in the interval.

Any interval extending to infinity uses the $\pm \infty$ symbol and the round (open) interval brackets. For example, the inequality statement $x \leq -2$ is written as $\left[(-\infty, -2) \right]$, since it contains both an open and closed interval.

A combination of two or more intervals can be indicated using the $\cup$ symbol, which represents the union of the intervals. For example, the interval $0 < x < 5$ or $x > 7$ is indicated by $(0, 5) \cup (7, \infty)$.

Example 1

Write each of the following intervals using interval notation.

a) $1 < x < 4$

Solution

(1, 4)

b)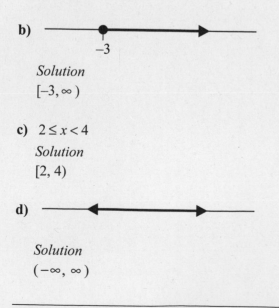

Solution

$[-3, \infty)$

c) $2 \leq x < 4$

Solution

[2, 4)

d)

Solution

$(-\infty, \infty)$

PRACTICE EXERCISE

1. Write each of the following inequality statements in interval notation.

   a) $-5 < x < 8$

   b) $x \geq 2$

   c) $x < 1$ or $x \geq 10$

   d) $x < -1$ or $0 \leq x \leq 10$

   e) $x \leq 7$ or $12 < x \leq 15$

   f) $x \neq 0$

2. Write and expression that represents the values of the following number lines.

a)

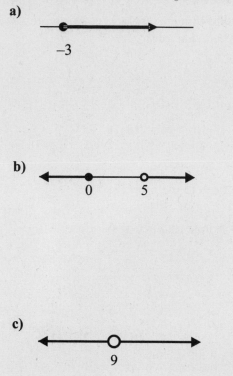

-3

b)

0   5

c)

9

Lesson 6   QUADRATIC INEQUALITIES

NOTES

Recall that if a problem has a definite number of solutions, it is represented by an equation, as in the following two examples.

$$3x - 4 = 11 \quad \textbf{or} \quad x^2 - x - 6 = 0$$

$$3x = 15 \qquad\qquad (x - 3)(x + 2) = 0$$

$$x = 5 \qquad\qquad\quad x - 3 = 0 \text{ or } x + 2 = 0$$

$$\qquad\qquad\qquad\qquad x = 3 \text{ or } x = -2$$

In both cases, there are unique solutions to the problem.

For an inequality, there may be an infinite number of solutions.
For example:

$$3x - 4 < 11$$

$$3x < 15$$

$$x < 5$$

This can be shown as: $\{x \mid x < 5, x \in \mathbb{R}\}$

The solution can also be shown on a number line:

Number lines are used for illustrative purposes here, but are not generally expected for the solutions. Interval notation should be used for all solutions.

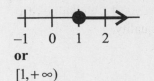

And, it can be shown using interval notation:

$$(-\infty, 5)$$

Example 1

$$2x + 5 \geq 7$$

$$2x \geq 2$$

$$x \geq 1$$

Solution

This can be shown as: $\{x \mid x \geq 1, x \in \mathbb{R}\}$

Or

or
$$[1, +\infty)$$

Example 2

Solve: $x^2 - x - 12 > 0$

Solution

Step 1

First, solve the corresponding equality.

$x^2 - x - 12 = 0$

$(x-4)(x+3) = 0$

$x - 4 = 0$ or $x + 3 = 0$

$x = 4$ or $x = -3$

4 and –3 are called "critical values" because the function may change from positive to negative or from negative to positive at these points.

Step 2

Mark the critical values on a number line.

These critical values divide the number line into regions.

The numbers in each region will either

– all satisfy the original inequality

– all not satisfy the original inequality

Step 3

Check each region by selecting a number in the region.

Here, check $x = 5$ (for the region of $x > 4$)

$5^2 - 5 - 12 > 0$

$8 > 0$ (True)

Thus, all values of x where $x > 4$ will satisfy the original inequality.

Check $x = 0$ (for the region $-3 < x < 4$)

$0^2 - 0 - 12 > 0$

$-12 > 0$ (False)

The original inequality is not satisfied for $-3 < x < 4$. No value of x where $-3 < x < 4$ will satisfy the original inequality.

Check $x = -4$ (for the region $x < -3$)

$(-4)^2 - (-4) - 12 > 0$

$8 > 0$ (True)

All values of x where $x < -3$ will satisfy the original inequality.

NOTES

Therefore, the solution is $x > 4$ or $x < -3$.

Using interval notation, this is shown as $(-\infty, -3) \cup (4, +\infty)$.

The solution could also be shown as:

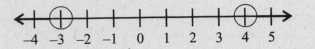

Example 2

Solve: $x^2 - 2x - 8 \leq 0$

Solution

First, solve $x^2 - 2x - 8 = 0$

$(x - 4)(x + 2) = 0$

$x = 4$ or $x = -2$

(Mark the critical values on a number line.)

Check using: $x = 5$, $x = 0$, $x = -3$ (One value for x from each region)

Here, you will find that $x = 0$ is the only value that satisfies the original inequality.

Thus, the solution is: $-2 \leq x \leq 4$.

Using interval notation, the solution is $\left[-2, \ 4\right]$

Using a number line, the solution is:

Example 3

Solve: $x^2 - 6x + 9 > 0$

Solution

$x^2 - 6x + 9 = 0$

$(x-3)(x-3) = 0$

$x = 3$

(Mark the single critical value on a number line.)

Check using: $x = 4$, $x = 0$ (One value for x from each region)

Here, both $x = 4$ and $x = 0$ satisfy the original inequality.

The solution is $x > 3$ or $x < 3$, or simply $x \neq 3$.

Using interval notation, the solution is $(-\infty, 3) \cup (3, +\infty)$.

Using a number line, the solution is:

PRACTICE EXERCISE

1. Solve each of the following quadratic inequalities. State the solution using interval notation.

a) $x^2 - 2x - 15 < 0$

b) $2x^2 + 13x - 7 \geq 0$

c) $x^2 - 9 \leq 0$

d) $x^2 - 6 > 0$

e) $-x^2 + 3x + 10 \leq 0$

f) $x^2 + 4x - 7 \geq 0$

44

Lesson 7 RATIONAL INEQUALITIES

Consider the following rational inequality:

$$\frac{x+3}{x-1} < 2$$

One method to solve this type of inequality is to use critical values.

Here, critical values are the solution(s) to the corresponding equation plus any values for x that make the rational expression(s) undefined.

When $x-1=0$, $x=1$ is a critical value.

To solve this inequality, start by solving the corresponding equation:

$$\frac{x+3}{x-1} = 2$$

$x+3=2x-2$ (multiplying both sides by $x-1$)

$3=x-2$

$5=x$

This is a second critical value.

Graph these critical values on the number line.

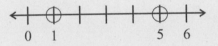

Check using $x=6$, $x=2$, and $x=0$ (one value for x from each region). You will find that when $x=6$ or when $x=0$, the original inequality is satisfied.

Thus, the solution is $x>5$ or $x<1$.

This can also be shown as $(-\infty,\ 1) \cup (5, +\infty)$

or

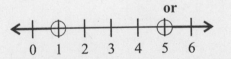

Example 1

Solve the inequality: $\dfrac{4x+3}{x^2-x-12} < 0$

Solution

Step 1

First find the undefined values.

When is $x^2-x-12=0$

$(x-4)(x+3)=0$

$x=4$, $x=-3$

Thus, $x \neq 4, -3$

4 and -3 are critical values.

Step 2

Now, solve the equality: $\dfrac{4x+3}{x^2-x-12}=0$

$4x+3=0$ (multiplying both sides by x^2-x-12)

$4x=-3$

$x=-\dfrac{3}{4}$

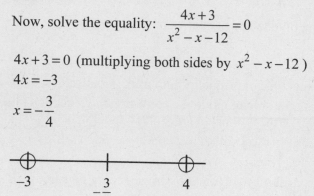

Mark all critical values on a number line.

Step 3

Check using $x=5$, $x=0$, $x=-1$, and $x=-4$ (one value from each region).

Here, you will find that when $x=0$ or $x=-4$, the original inequality is satisfied.

Thus, the solution is $-\dfrac{3}{4}<x<4$ or $x<-3$

This can be shown as $(-\infty,-3)\ \cup\left(-\dfrac{3}{4},4\right)$

or

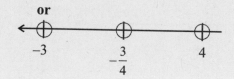

Example 2

Solve the inequality: $\dfrac{2x-1}{x^2-x-2}\ge 0$

Solution

Step 1

First, find the undefined values.

x^2-x-2

$(x-2)(x+1)=0$

$x=2$ or $x=-1$

46

Step 2

Now, solve the equality: $\dfrac{2x-1}{x^2-x-2}=0$

$2x-1=0$

$2x=1$

$x=\dfrac{1}{2}$

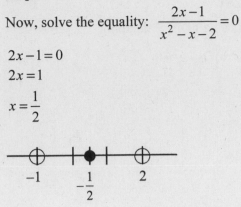

Step 3

Check using $x=3$, $x=1$, $x=0$, and $x=-2$ (one value from each region).

Here, you will find that when $x=3$ or $x=0$, the original inequality is satisfied.

Thus, the solution is $x>2$ or $-1<x\le\dfrac{1}{2}$.

This can be shown as $\left(2,+\infty\right)\cup\left(-1,\dfrac{1}{2}\right]$

or

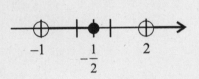

PRACTICE EXERCISE

1. Solve the following rational inequalities. State the solutions using interval notation.

a) $\dfrac{x-2}{x} < 0$

b) $\dfrac{x}{x+5} > 0$

c) $\dfrac{x^2}{x-3} \le 0$

d) $\dfrac{x^2-x-6}{x+1} \ge 0$

e) $\dfrac{3}{x^2+4} > 0$

f) $\dfrac{x}{x^2-x-5} > 0$

48

Lesson 8   ABSOLUTE VALUE INEQUALITIES

Definition of absolute value:

$|x| = x$ if $x \geq 0$

$|x| = -x$ if $x < 0$

You can use this definition to solve equations and inequalities involving absolute value.

Example 1

Solve the absolute value equation: $|x| = 5$

Solution

Case (1): If $x \leq 0$: then $|x| = 5$ becomes $x = 5$

Case (2): If $x < 0$: then $|x| = 5$ becomes

$-(x) = 5$

$x = -5$

Thus, for $|x| = 5$, $x = 5$ or $x = -5$

Example 2

Solve the absolute equation: $|3x + 4| = 13$

Solution

Case (1): If $3x + 4 \geq 0$:

$x \geq -\dfrac{4}{3}$

Then $|3x + 4| = 13$ becomes:

$3x + 4 = 13$

$x = 3$

Note: $x = 3$ is a solution because it satisfies the original condition of

$x \geq -\dfrac{4}{3}$

Case (2): If $3x + 4 < 0$:

$x < -\dfrac{4}{3}$

Then, $|3x + 4| = 13$ becomes:

$-(3x + 4) = 13$

$3x + 4 = -13$

$3x = -17$

$x = \dfrac{-17}{3}$

Note: $x = \dfrac{-17}{3}$ is a solution because it satisfies the original condition

of $x < -\dfrac{4}{3}$

Example 3

Solve the absolute value inequality: $|2x + 5| < 7$

Solution

Step 1

Case (1): If $2x + 5 \geq 0$:

$x \geq -\dfrac{5}{2}$

Then $|2x + 5| < 7$ becomes:

$2x + 5 < 7$

$2x < 2$

$x < 1$

Thus, for case (1), we get: $-\dfrac{5}{2} \leq x < 1$

Note: This solution combines the original condition $x \geq -\dfrac{5}{2}$ and the

solution $x < 1$.

This can also shown by:

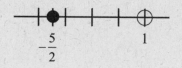

Step 2

Case (2): If $2x + 5 < 0$:

$x < -\dfrac{5}{2}$

Then $|2x + 5| < 7$ becomes:

$-(2x + 5) < 7$

$2x + 5 > -7$ (multiplying both sides by -1 changes the direction of the inequality)

$2x > -12$

$x > -6$

Thus, for case (2), we get: $-6 < x < -\dfrac{5}{2}$

This solution combines the original condition of $x < -\dfrac{5}{2}$ and the

solution of $x > -6$.

This can also be shown as:

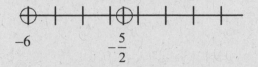

Combining case (1) and case (2), we get:

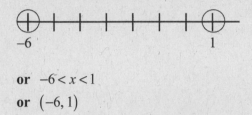

or $-6 < x < 1$

or $(-6, 1)$

This problem can also be solved by studying critical values and the behaviour of the corresponding absolute value function.

Step 1

Solve the equation $|2x+5| = 7$ to determine the x-intercepts of the function $y = |2x+5| - 7$.

$$|2x+5| = 7$$
$$2x+5 = 7 \quad or \quad 2x+5 = -7$$
$$2x = 2 \quad\quad or \quad 2x = -12$$
$$x = 1 \quad\quad or \quad x = -6$$

Step 2

The original inequality, $|2x+5| < 7$, or $|2x+5| - 7 < 0$, can be solved by determining where the graph of the function $y = |2x+5| - 7$ lies below the x-axis.

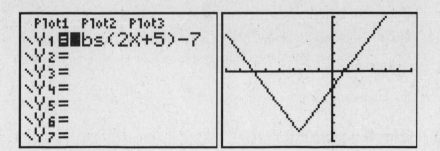

This occurs in the interval $(-6, 1)$

Example 4

Solve the absolute value inequality: $|3x+1| \geq 8$

Solution

Step 1

Case (1): If $3x+1 \geq 0$:

$$x \geq -\frac{1}{3}$$

Then $|3x+1| \geq 8$ becomes:

$$3x+1 \geq 8$$
$$3x \geq 7$$

$$x \geq \frac{7}{3}$$

Thus, the solution for case (1) is $x \geq \frac{7}{3}$, since it satisfies the original

condition of $x \geq -\frac{1}{3}$.

This can be shown as:

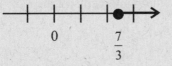

Step 2

Case (2): If $3x+1 < 0$:

$$x < -\frac{1}{3}$$

Then $|3x+1| \geq 8$ becomes:

$$-(3x+1) \geq 8$$

$$3x+1 \leq -8$$

(Multiplying both sides by -1 changes the direction of the inequality)

$$3x \leq -9$$

$$x \leq -3$$

Thus, the solution for case (2) is $x \leq -3$, since it satisfies the original

condition of $x < -\frac{1}{3}$.

This can be shown as:

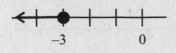

Combining case (1) and case (2), we get

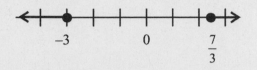

This is the same as: $x \leq -3$ or $x \geq \dfrac{7}{3}$

This problem can also be solved by studying critical values and the behaviour of the corresponding absolute value function.

Step 1

Solve the equation $\left|3x+1\right| = 8$ to determine the x-intercepts of the function $y = \left|3x+1\right| - 8$.

$\left|3x+1\right| = 8$

$3x+1 = 8$ or $3x+1 = -8$

$3x = 7$ or $3x = -9$

$x = \dfrac{7}{3}$ or $x = -3$

Step 2

The original inequality, $\left|3x+1\right| \geq 8$, or $\left|3x+1\right| - 8 \geq 0$, can be solved by determining where the graph of the function $y = \left|3x+1\right| - 8$ lies above or on the the x-axis.

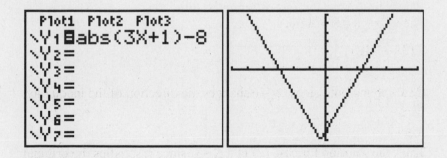

This occurs in the intervals $(-\infty, -3) \cup \left(\dfrac{7}{3}, \infty\right)$.

Example 5

Solve the absolute value inequality: $|2x+5| \leq 7$

Solution

Step 1

Case (1): If $2x+5 \geq 0$:

$x \geq -\dfrac{5}{2}$

Then $|2x+5| = 7$ becomes:

$2x+5 = 7$

$2x = 2$

$x = 1$ (Note: This satisfies the original condition of $x \geq -\dfrac{5}{2}$)

Step 2

Case (2): If $2x+5 < 0$:

$x < -\dfrac{5}{2}$

Then $|2x+5 = 7|$ becomes:

$-(2x+5) = 7$

$2x+5 = -7$

(Multiplying both sides by −1 changes direction of the inequality)

$2x = -12$

$x = -6$ (Note: This satisfies the original condition of $x < -\dfrac{5}{2}$

Thus, the critical points are −6 and 1.

Place these critical points on a number line:

Step 3

Check using $x = -7$, $x = 0$, and $x = 2$.

(One value for x from each region)

Here, you will find that $x = 0$ is the only value that will satisfy the original inequality.

Thus, the solution is $-6 < x < 1$

or $(-6,\ 1)$

This problem can also be solved by studying critical values and the behaviour of the corresponding absolute value function.

Step 1

Solve the equation $|2x+5| = 7$ to determine the x-intercepts of the function $y = |2x+5| - 7$.

$$|2x+1| = 7$$
$$2x+5 = 7 \quad \text{or} \quad 2x+5 = -7$$
$$2x = 2 \quad \text{or} \quad 2x = -12$$
$$x = 1 \quad \text{or} \quad x = -6$$

Step 2

The original inequality, $|2x+5| \leq 7$, or $|2x+5| - 7 \leq 0$, can be solved by determining where the graph of the function $y = |2x+5| - 7$ lies above or on the x-axis.

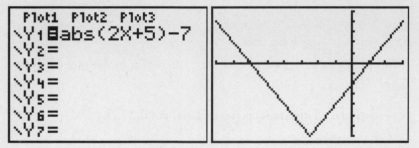

This occurs in the intervals $(-6, 1)$.

RATIONAL INEQUALITIES WITH ABSOLUTE VALUE

Solve: $\dfrac{|x|}{|x-1|} > 1$

One method to solve a rational inequality with an absolute value is to use critical points. Again, that means to find the undefined values(s) for x along with the solution(s) to the equality.

First, find the undefined value(s) for x.

Here, this will be when $x-1=0$

$x=1$

$\therefore x \neq 1$

Thus, 1 is a critical point.

To solve the equality, $\dfrac{|x|}{|x-1|}=1$, consider all cases:

Step 1

Case (1): If $x \geq 0$ and $x-1 > 0$:

$x > 1$

Thus, for case (1), when combining these two restrictions for x, we get $x > 1$.

If $x > 1$, then $\dfrac{|x|}{|x-1|}=1$ becomes:

$\dfrac{x}{x-1}=1$

$x = x-1$ (Multiplying both sides by $x-1$)

$0 = -1$ (Impossible)

Thus, case (1) does not have a solution to the equality.

Step 2

Case (2): If $x \geq 0$ and $x-1 < 0$:

$x < 1$

For case(2) when combining these two restrictions for x, we get $0 \leq x < 1$

If $x > 1$, then $\dfrac{|x|}{|x-1|}=1$ becomes:

$\dfrac{x}{-(x-1)}=1$

$x = -x+1$ (Multiplying both sides by $-x+1$)

$2x = 1$

$x = \dfrac{1}{2}$

Since $\dfrac{1}{2}$ satisfies the original restriction of $0 \leq x < 1$, $\dfrac{1}{2}$ is a critical point.

Step 3

Case (3): If $x < 0$ and $x - 1 > 0$:

$x > 1$

When combining these restrictions, we see that no values for x will satisfy $x < 0$ and $x > 1$.

Thus, case (3) does not have a solution to the equality.

Step 4

Case (4): If $x < 0$ and $x - 1 < 0$:

$x < 1$

When combining these two restrictions, we get $x < 0$.

For $x < 0$, $\dfrac{|x|}{|x-1|} = 1$ becomes:

$$\frac{-x}{-(x-1)} = 1$$

or

$\dfrac{x}{x-1} = 1$, which is the same as case (1).

Now, place the critical points on a number line:

Check using $x = 0$, $x = \dfrac{3}{4}$, and $x = 2$ (one value for x from each region).

Here, we find that $x = \dfrac{3}{4}$ and $x = 2$, which both satisfy the original inequality.

The solution to the original inequality $\dfrac{|x|}{|x-1|} \geq 1$ is, therefore,

$\dfrac{1}{2} \leq x < 1$ or $x > 1$ **or** $\left[\dfrac{1}{2}, 1\right) \cup (1, \infty)$.

PRACTICE EXERCISE

1. Solve each of the following inequalities. State solutions using interval notation.

    a) $|x+1| < 5$

    b) $|x+2| > 6$

    c) $|x-4| - 3 \leq 0$

    d) $|5x-2| < 6$

    e) $\left| \dfrac{x-5}{x} \right| \geq 0$

Lesson 9   USING TRIGONOMETRIC IDENTITIES

An identity is an equation that is true for all values of the variable for which both sides of the equation are defined.

The following list of Trigonometric Identities can be used to simplify expressions, as needed, in order to prove other identities or solve equations.

QUOTIENT IDENTITIES

$$\tan x = \frac{\sin x}{\cos x}, \ x \neq \frac{\pi}{2} + n\pi, \ n \in I \qquad \cot x = \frac{\cos x}{\sin x}, \ x \neq n\pi, \ n \in I$$

RECIPROCAL IDENTITIES

$$\sec x = \frac{1}{\cos x}, \ x \neq \frac{\pi}{2} + n\pi, \ n \in I$$

$$\csc x = \frac{1}{\sin x}, \ x \neq n\pi, \ n \in I$$

$$\cot x = \frac{1}{\tan x}, \ x \neq n\pi, \ x \neq \frac{\pi}{2} + n\pi, \ n \in I$$

PYTHAGOREAN IDENTITIES

$$\sin^2 x + \cos^2 x = 1$$

$$\sec^2 x = 1 + \tan^2 x, \ x \neq \frac{\pi}{2} + n\pi, \ n \in I$$

$$\csc^2 x = 1 + \cot^2 x, \ x \neq n\pi, \ n \in I$$

SUM AND DIFFERENCE IDENTITIES

$$\sin(A + B) = \sin A \cos B + \sin B \cos A$$
$$\sin(A - B) = \sin A \cos B - \sin B \cos A$$
$$\cos(A + B) = \cos A \cos B - \sin A \sin B$$
$$\cos(A - B) = \cos A \cos B + \sin A \sin B$$

DOUBLE ANGLE IDENTITIES

$$\sin(2x) = 2 \sin x \cos x$$
$$\cos(2x) = \cos^2 x - \sin^2 x$$
$$\cos(2x) = 2 \cos^2 x - 1$$
$$\cos(2x) = 1 - 2 \sin^2 x$$

Example 1

Simplify the following trigonometric expression:

$\sin x \cot x \sec x$

Solution

$\sin x \cot x \sec x$

$= (\sin x)\left(\dfrac{\cos x}{\sin x}\right)\left(\dfrac{\sin x}{\cos x}\right)$

$= 1 \, , \, x \neq n\pi \, , \, x \neq \dfrac{\pi}{2} + n\pi \, , \, n \in I$

Example 2

Simplify the trigonometric expression $\cos x \tan x$.

Solution

$\cos x \tan x$

$= (\cos x)\left(\dfrac{\sin x}{\cos x}\right)$

$= \sin x \, , \, x \neq \dfrac{\pi}{2} + n\pi \, , \, n \in I$

Example 3

Simplify $\sec x \csc x \sin(2x)$.

Solution

$\sec x \csc x \sin(2x)$

$= \left(\dfrac{1}{\cos x}\right)\left(\dfrac{1}{\sin x}\right)(2 \sin x \cos x)$

$= 2 \, , \, x \neq n\pi \, , \, x \neq \dfrac{\pi}{2} + n\pi \, , \, n \in I$

To prove an identity, one must use other identities and algebraic means to show that the left side is equal to the right side of an equation.

Example 4

Prove the following identity:

$$2\left(1+\frac{1-\cos^2 x}{\cos^2 x}\right) = 2\sec^2 x$$

Solution

LS   RS

$$2\left(1+\frac{1-\cos^2 x}{\cos^2 x}\right)$$ $$2\sec^2 x$$

$$2\left(1+\frac{\sin^2 x}{\cos^2 x}\right)$$

$$2\left(1+\tan^2 x\right)$$

$$2\sec^2 x$$

$$\text{LS} = \text{RS}$$

Example 5

Prove the following identity:

$$\frac{\tan x + \cot x}{2}\sin 2x = 1$$

Solution

LS   RS

$$\frac{\tan x + \cot x}{2}\sin 2x$$ $$1$$

$$\frac{\dfrac{\sin x}{\cos x}+\dfrac{\cos x}{\sin x}}{2}2\sin x\cos x$$

$$\frac{\sin^2 x + \cos^2 x}{2\sin x\cos x}\left(2\sin x\cos x\right)$$

$$\sin^2 x + \cos^2 x$$

$$1$$

$$\text{LS} = \text{RS}$$

Example 6

Prove that $\sin(x+\pi) = -\sin x$.

Solution

LS   RS

$$\sin(x+\pi)$$ $$-\sin x$$

$$\sin x\cos\pi + \sin\pi\cos x$$

$$\sin x(-1)+(0)\cos x$$

$$-\sin x$$

$$\text{LS} = \text{RS}$$

PRACTICE EXERCISE

1. Simplify the following expressions.

   a) $\cos^2 x - \sin^2 x - \cos(2x)$

   b) $(\sin x + \cos x)^2 - \sin(2x)$

2. Prove the following identities.

   a) $\cos\left(\dfrac{\pi}{2} + x\right) = -\sin x$

b) $\dfrac{\sin^2 x \cos x + \cos^3 x - \cos x \tan^2 x}{2 \sin x} = \dfrac{1 - \tan^2 x}{2 \tan x}$

c) $\dfrac{1 + \sin x}{\cos x} = \dfrac{\cos x}{1 - \sin x}$

d) $\dfrac{1}{1 + \sin x} + \dfrac{1}{1 - \sin x} = 2 \sec^2 x$

REVIEW SUMMARY

In this unit, you have learned how to . . .

- factor expressions containing a sum or difference of cubes using the following equations:

$$a^3 + b^3 = (a+b)(a^2 - ab + b^2)$$
$$a^3 - b^3 = (a-b)(a^2 + ab + b^2)$$

- factor expressions containing rational exponents.

- factor expressions that do not contain perfect squares as a difference of squares such as:

$$x^2 - a = (x + \sqrt{a})(x - \sqrt{a})$$

- rationalize numerators and denominators of expressions that contain radicals

- describe and graph the transformations of functions including reflections, stretches, and translations in terms of

$$y = f(x) \rightarrow y = af(b(x-c)) + d$$

- combine operations using the four basic operations

$$f(x) + g(x)$$
$$f(x) - g(x)$$
$$f(x)g(x)$$
$$\frac{f(x)}{g(x)}$$

- find the composite function of 2 functions

$$f(g(x))$$
$$f(f(x))$$

- use interval notation

- solve quadratic inequalities

- solve rational inequalities

- solve absolute value inequalities

- use trigonometric identities to simplify expressions

PRACTICE TEST

1. Factor the following expressions.

a) $8x^3 + 1$

b) $(x+1)^{\frac{3}{2}} + 5(x+1)^{\frac{1}{2}} + 6(x+1)^{-\frac{1}{2}}$

2. Rationalize the denominator in the following expression.

$$\frac{x-6}{\sqrt{x^2 - x - 25} + \sqrt{5}}$$

3. Given $g(x) = x^2 - x$ and $h(x) = 5x - 1$, solve each of the following functions.

a) $f(x) = g(x)h(x)$

b) $f(x) = g(h(x))$

4. Complete the following chart for the transformations of $y = f(x)$. Put "n/a" if an answer is not possible.

New Functions	Reflection about	Vertical Stretch Factor about x-axis	Horizontal Stretch Factor About y-axis	Vertical Translation	Horizontal Translation
$y = -5f(3x) + 2$					
$y = 2f(-3x + 12)$					
$y = f^{-1}(x) - 6$					
	x-axis	$\frac{1}{3}$	2	Up 1	Left 5

5. For the function $y = -3\sin(4x - \pi) + 6$, determine each of the following characteristics.

a) Amplitude _____

b) Period _____

c) Phase Shift _____

d) Vertical Displacement _____

6. Solve each of the following inequalities and express the answer using interval notation.

    a) $x^2 - 9x - 22 > 0$ **b)** $2x^2 - 5x - 1 \le 0$

    c) $\dfrac{x-5}{x+2} < 0$ **d)** $\dfrac{x^2-1}{x+5} \ge 0$

e) $|x-4|>5$

7. Show that $\csc(2x)+\csc(2x)=\csc x \sec x$.

LIMITS

When you are finished this unit, you should be able to. . .

- explain what a limit is
- explain how a limit can be approximated by examining values near the limit
- evaluate left- and right-hand limits graphically and algebraically
- explain the difference between continuous and discontinuous functions
- simplify functions by factoring and rationalizing in order to evaluate limits
- determine when a limit is undefined
- use limits to determine the slope of a tangent to a curve at a given point

Lesson	Page	Completed on
1. Introduction to Limits	70	
2. Limits for Rational Expressions	78	
3. Using Limits to Find Slopes of Tangents	85	
Review Summary	92	
Practice Test	93	
Answers and Solutions	at the back of the book	

PREREQUISITE SKILLS AND KNOWLEDGE

Prior to beginning this unit, you should be able to. . .

- factor polynomial expressions
- rationalize expressions containing radicals
- simplify rational expressions
- describe slope as an instantaneous rate of change
- explain what a tangent to a curve is
- explain what an asymptote is

Lesson 1 INTRODUCTION TO LIMITS

Consider the geometric sequence

$$\frac{1}{2}, \frac{1}{4}, \frac{1}{8}, \frac{1}{16}, \dots$$

This sequence can be represented by

$$t_n = \left(\frac{1}{2}\right)^n \text{ or } t_n = \frac{1}{2^n}$$

This sequence is infinite. The value of each term gets smaller and smaller as n approaches infinity. Actually, the value of the term keeps getting closer to zero as n approaches infinity but never reaches zero.

We say that the limit is zero.

The limit, 0, is a value that the terms approach but never reach.

Notation $\lim\limits_{n \to \infty}\left(\frac{1}{2^n}\right) = 0$

$\left(\begin{array}{l}\text{Note:} \quad n \to \infty \text{ is read as: } n \text{ approaches infinity}\\ \qquad\qquad n \to 6 \text{ would be read as: } n \text{ approaches 6}\end{array}\right)$

Given $f(x) = x^2 - x - 6$, find $f(4)$.

Since

$$f(4) = 4^2 - 4 - 6$$
$$= 6$$

$$\lim\limits_{x \to 4}\left(x^2 - x - 6\right)$$
$$= 6$$

Here, the limit is the same as $f(4)$. However, this will not always be true.

The limit is how a function behaves near the point being considered, not the actual value of the function at that point.

To determine a limit, we must consider a left and a right limit. In our example, we can consider what happens to the value of the function as x approaches 4 from the left and from the right.

To do this, we look at a table of values as x approaches 4 from the left and right.

The limit is . . ., not near the actual value.

or

The limit is . . ., the limit is not the actual value.

From the left:

x	$f(x)$
3.5	2.75
3.9	5.31
3.99	5.93
3.999	5.99

Notation for this is

$$\lim_{x \to 4^-} \left(x^2 - x - 6\right)$$
$$= 6$$

According to the table, as $x \to 4$ from the left, $f(x)$ approaches 6.

Now, from the right:

x	$f(x)$
4.5	9.75
4.1	6.71
4.01	6.07
4.001	6.007

The notation for this is

$$\lim_{x \to 4^+} \left(x^2 - x - 6\right)$$
$$= 6$$

According to the table, as $x \to 4$ from the right, $f(x)$ approaches 6.

The limit is the same in both cases.

* A limit only exists if the left and right limits both exist and are equal.

$$\lim_{x \to a^-} f(x) = \lim_{x \to a^+} f(x)$$

In the case above, we can write that since

$$\lim_{x \to 4^-} \left(x^2 - x - 6\right) = 6,$$

and

$$\lim_{x \to 4+} \left(x^2 - x - 6\right) = 6,$$

we can conclude that

$$\lim_{x \to 4} \left(x^2 - x - 6\right)$$

exists and is equal to 6.

NOTES

A function, $y = f(x)$, is continuous at a point $x = a$ if:

1. The function has a value (exists) for $x = a$. $f(a)$ exists

2. The limit as $x \to a$ exists.

   $\lim\limits_{x \to a}\left[f(x) \right]$ exists

3. The quantities in (1) and (2) are equal.

LIMITS OF CONTINUOUS FUNCTIONS

Many limits can be found by substituting the value that x is approaching into the function.

This will be true for all continuous functions or functions that are continuous in the region where the limit is to be calculated.

A continuous function is one whose graph has no breaks.

A function, $y = f(x)$, is continuous at a point $x = a$ if:

1. The function has a value (exists) for $x = a$. $f(a)$ exists

2. The limit as $x \to a$ exists. $\lim\limits_{x \to a}\left[f(x) \right]$ exists

3. The quantities in (1) and (2) are equal.

Example 1

Evaluate the following limit.

$$\lim_{x \to 3}\left[2x^2 - 4x \right]$$

Solution

Since the function is continuous,

$$\lim_{x \to 3}\left[2x^2 - 4x \right]$$

$$= 2(3)^2 - 4(3)$$

$$= 30$$

Example 2

Evaluate the following limit.

$$\lim_{x \to 20}\left[2x^2 - 10x \right]$$

Solution

$$\lim_{x \to 20}\left[2x^2 - 10x \right]$$

$$= 2(20)^2 - 10(20)$$

$$= 600$$

PIECEWISE FUNCTIONS

Some functions are defined by different rules in different parts of their domain. These are called piecewise functions. Because of the different rules, there is an opportunity for the function to be discontinuous at certain points.

Example 1

Given $f(x) = \begin{cases} x^2 - 2x + 1 & \text{if } x < 1 \\ 3 - x & \text{if } x \geq 1 \end{cases}$

find $\lim\limits_{x \to 1}\left[f(x)\right]$

Solution

Step 1

First, sketch a graph.

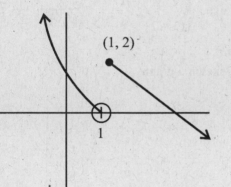

Step 2

Find the limit from the left

$\lim\limits_{x \to 1^-}\left[f(x)\right] = 0$

This can be seen on the graph, or it can be calculated by substituting 1 for x in

$x^2 - 2x + 1$

$= (1)^2 - 2(1) + 1$

$= 0$

Step 3

Find the limit from the right

$\lim\limits_{x \to 1^+}\left[f(x)\right] = 2$

This can seen on the graph, or it can be calculated by substituting 1 for x in

$3-x$

$=3-(1)$

$=2$

$$\lim_{x \to 1^-} f(x) \neq \lim_{x \to 1^+} f(x)$$

Thus, the $\lim_{x \to 1} \left[f(x) \right]$ does not exist since the left and right limits are not equal. The graph is discontinuous at $x=1$.

Example 2

Given $f(x) = \begin{cases} -x^3 & \text{if } x < -1 \\ (x+2)^2 & \text{if } x > -1 \end{cases}$, find $\lim_{x \to -1} \left[f(x) \right]$

Solution

Again, sketch a graph.

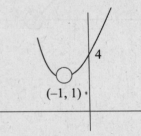

$$\lim_{x \to -1^-} \left[f(x) \right] = 1 \text{ and } \lim_{x \to -1^+} \left[f(x) \right] = 1$$

Thus, $\lim_{x \to -1} \left[f(x) \right] = 1$ since the left and right limits are equal.

Both left and right limits can be calculated by substituting -1 for x in $-x^3$ and $(x+2)^2$.

This graph is discontinuous at $x = -1$ because $f(-1)$ does not exist. This function does not have a value at $x = -1$. However, a limit does exist as x approaches -1.

Example 3

For the function

$$f(x) = \begin{cases} 2x & \text{if } x > 1 \\ x & \text{if } x \le 1 \end{cases}$$

sketch the graph of the function and evaluate each of the following limits.

a) $\lim\limits_{x \to 1^{-}} f(x)$

b) $\lim\limits_{x \to 1^{+}} f(x)$

c) $\lim\limits_{x \to 1} f(x)$

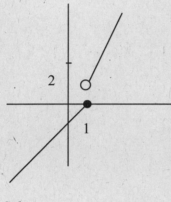

Solution

a)

$$\lim_{x \to 1^{-}} f(x)$$
$$= 0$$

b)

$$\lim_{x \to 1^{+}} f(x)$$
$$= 2$$

c)

$\lim\limits_{x \to 1} f(x)$ does not exist because $\lim\limits_{x \to 1^{-}} f(x) \ne \lim\limits_{x \to 1^{+}} f(x)$

PRACTICE EXERCISE

Evaluate the limits for the following continuous functions.

a) $\lim\limits_{x \to 2} 2x^2 - x$

b) $\lim\limits_{x \to 10} x^2 - 10x$

2. Use the graph of $y = f(x)$ to answer the questions that follow.

$y = f(x)$

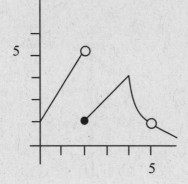

a) Evaluate each of the following limits.

   i. $\lim\limits_{x \to 1} f(x)$

   ii. $\lim\limits_{x \to 2^-} f(x)$

   iii. $\lim\limits_{x \to 2^+} f(x)$

   iv. $\lim\limits_{x \to 2} f(x)$

b) State two values of x for which the function is discontinuous.

3.   Sketch the following function and evaluate the limits that follow.

$$f(x) = \begin{cases} 2x+4 & \text{if } x < -1 \\ x^2 & \text{if } -1 \le x < 2 \\ -x+6 & \text{if } x > 2 \end{cases}$$

a) $\displaystyle\lim_{x \to -1^+} f(x)$

b) $\displaystyle\lim_{x \to -1^-} f(x)$

c) $\displaystyle\lim_{x \to -1} f(x)$

d) $\displaystyle\lim_{x \to 2^-} f(x)$

e) $\displaystyle\lim_{x \to 2^+} f(x)$

f) $\displaystyle\lim_{x \to 2} f(x)$

Lesson 2 *LIMITS FOR RATIONAL EXPRESSIONS*

Consider the following limit.

$$\lim_{x \to 3}\left(\frac{x-3}{x+3}\right)$$

$$=\left(\frac{3-3}{3+3}\right)$$

$$=\frac{0}{6}$$

$$=0$$

Here, the numerator approaches 0 and the denominator approaches 6. In cases where the numerator approaches 0 and the denominator approaches a non-zero value, the limit is 0.

Example 1

Evaluate the following limit.

$$\lim_{x \to -5}\left(\frac{x+5}{x+7}\right)$$

Solution

$$\lim_{x \to -5}\left(\frac{x+5}{x+7}\right)$$

$$=\left(\frac{-5+5}{-5+7}\right)$$

$$=\frac{0}{2}$$

$$=0$$

Now, consider this case where the *denominator* approaches zero.

$$\lim_{x \to 3}\frac{x^2-9}{x-3}$$

If we were to substitute at this point, the expression would be undefined. Instead, we must first simplify the expression so as to remove the term that is causing the denominator to become zero.

We can factor and simplify:

$$\lim_{x \to 3}\frac{x^2-9}{x-3}$$

$$=\lim_{x \to 3}\frac{(x-3)(x+3)}{x-3}$$

$$=\lim_{x \to 3}x+3=6$$

Note that the function is undefined at $x=3$. The graph of the function is discontinuous at $x=3$, but the limit still exists.

Here, the value of the function $f(x) = \dfrac{x^2 - 9}{x - 3}$ approaches 6 as x approaches 3.

This can be shown graphically.

Graph $f(x) = \dfrac{x^2 - 9}{x - 3}$.

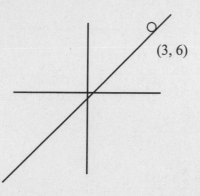

$(3, 6)$

The graph is discontinuous at $x = 3$.

Example 2

Evaluate the following limit.

$$\lim_{x \to -4} \frac{x^2 + 6x + 8}{x^2 + 7x + 12}$$

Solution

$$\lim_{x \to -4} \frac{(x + 4)(x + 2)}{(x + 3)(x + 4)}$$

$$= \lim_{x \to -4} \frac{x + 2}{x + 3}$$

$$= \frac{-4 + 2}{-4 + 3}$$

$$= \frac{-2}{-1}$$

$$= 2$$

In some cases, the calculation to find the limit is more complex.

Example 3

Evaluate the following limit.

$$\lim_{x \to 2}\left(\frac{x - \sqrt{3x - 2}}{x^2 - 4} \right)$$

Solution

Here, you must rationalize the numerator.

$$\lim_{x \to 2}\left(\frac{x - \sqrt{3x - 2}}{x^2 - 4} \right)$$

$$= \lim_{x \to 2} \frac{\left(x - \sqrt{3x - 2} \right)\left(x + \sqrt{3x - 2} \right)}{\left(x^2 - 4 \right)\left(x + \sqrt{3x - 2} \right)}$$

$$= \lim_{x \to 2} \frac{x^2 - 3x + 2}{\left(x^2 - 4 \right)\left(x + \sqrt{3x - 2} \right)}$$

$$= \lim_{x \to 2} \frac{(x - 2)(x - 1)}{(x - 2)(x + 2)\left(x + \sqrt{3x - 2} \right)}$$

$$= \lim_{x \to 2} \frac{(x - 1)}{(x + 2)\left(x + \sqrt{3x - 2} \right)}$$

At this point, 2 can be substituted in for *x* without making the function undefined.

$$= \frac{(2 - 1)}{(2 + 2)\left(2 + \sqrt{3(2) - 2} \right)}$$

$$= \frac{1}{(4)(2 + 2)}$$

$$= \frac{1}{(4)(4)}$$

$$= \frac{1}{16}$$

Example 4

Evaluate the following limit.

$$\lim_{x \to 3} \frac{x - \sqrt{x+6}}{x-3}$$

Solution

$$\lim_{x \to 3} \frac{x - \sqrt{x+6}}{x-3} \frac{\left(x + \sqrt{x+6}\right)}{\left(x + \sqrt{x+6}\right)}$$

$$\lim_{x \to 3} \frac{x^2 - x - 6}{(x-3)\left(x + \sqrt{x+6}\right)}$$

$$\lim_{x \to 3} \frac{(x-3)(x+2)}{(x-3)\left(x + \sqrt{x+6}\right)}$$

$$\lim_{x \to 3} \frac{x+2}{x + \sqrt{x+6}}$$

We can now substitute

$$\lim_{x \to 3} \frac{x+2}{x + \sqrt{x+6}}$$
$$= \frac{3+2}{3 + \sqrt{3+6}}$$
$$= \frac{5}{6}$$

In some cases, the denominator cannot be simplified in a way that allows substitution.

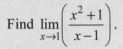

NOTES

Asymptotes will be examined in detail in a later chapter on curve sketching.

Example 5

Find $\lim\limits_{x \to 1}\left(\dfrac{x^2+1}{x-1}\right)$.

Solution

One way to see this limit is to check the graph. Here, the graph will have a vertical asymptote at $x = 1$.

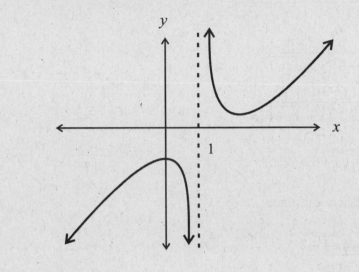

Here we can see that

$$\lim_{x \to 1^+}\left(\frac{x^2+1}{x-1}\right) = +\infty$$

and

$$\lim_{x \to 1^-}\left(\frac{x^2+1}{x-1}\right) = -\infty$$

Another way to verify this limit is to use a table of values in order to see what happens to the values of $f(x)$ as $x \to 1^+$

and $x \to 1^-$.

From the left

x	$f(x)$
.99	−198.01
.999	−1 998.01
.999 9	−19 998

From the right

x	$f(x)$
1.01	202. 01
1.001	2 002.001
1.000 1	20 002

$\lim\limits_{x \to 1} f(x)$ does not exist since the left and right limits are not equal

PRACTICE EXERCISE

1. Evaluate the following limits.

a) $\lim_{x \to 0} \dfrac{x^2 + x}{x}$

b) $\lim_{x \to 3} \dfrac{x^2 - 9}{2x^2 - x - 15}$

c) $\lim_{x \to 5} \dfrac{\sqrt{x-1} - 2}{x - 5}$

d) $\lim_{x \to 2} \dfrac{x^2 + 2x - 8}{x^3 - 8}$

e) $\lim_{x \to -3} \dfrac{\frac{1}{3} + \frac{1}{x}}{3 + x}$

2. Explain why the following limit does not exist.

$$\lim_{x \to 2} \frac{x^2 + 3x + 2}{x^2 - 4}$$

Lesson 3 *USING LIMITS TO FIND SLOPES OF TANGENTS*

Now that a basic understanding of limits has been established, we will summarize some of the basic properties of limits.

PROPERTIES OF LIMITS

1. $\lim\limits_{x \to a} cf(x) = c \lim\limits_{x \to a} f(x)$, where c is a constant.

2. $\lim\limits_{x \to a} \left[f(x) + g(x) \right] = \lim\limits_{x \to a} f(x) + \lim\limits_{x \to a} g(x)$

3. $\lim\limits_{x \to a} \left[f(x) g(x) \right] = \lim\limits_{x \to a} f(x) \lim\limits_{x \to a} g(x)$

4. $\lim\limits_{x \to a} \left[\dfrac{f(x)}{g(x)} \right] = \dfrac{\lim\limits_{x \to a} f(x)}{\lim\limits_{x \to a} g(x)}$

It should be noted that some of the properties above have already been used in our examples.

SECANT LINES

Consider the curve $f(x) = x^2$, with points $P(1, 1)$ and $Q(2, 4)$.

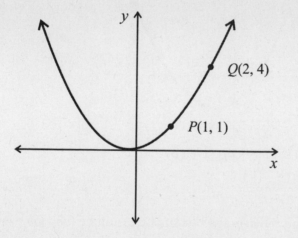

A straight line through points P and Q is called a secant line. A secant line is a line that intersects a curve in at least two points.

The slope, m, of a secant line is given by

$$m = \frac{y_2 - y_1}{x_2 - x_1}$$

In our example, $m = \dfrac{4-1}{2-1}$

$$m = \dfrac{3}{1}$$

The slope, m, can be shown as:

$$m = \dfrac{y_2 - y_1}{x_2 - x_1}$$

or

$$m = \dfrac{y_2 - y_1}{h}$$

h represents the change in x

Some sources refer to this change in x as Δx, but we will use h to represent the change in x.

Take two general points on a curve.

P is (x_1, y_1) or P is $(x, f(x))$ and

Q is (x_2, y_2) or Q is $(x + h, f(x + h))$

Shown graphically

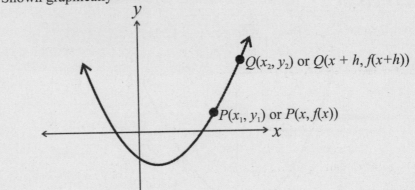

The slope of secant PQ is given by

$$m = \dfrac{f(x+h) - f(x)}{(x+h) - x}$$

and represents the **average rate of change** of the function over that interval.

TANGENT LINES

$Q \to P$ is read as Q approaches P.

As $Q \to P$ in the diagram above, the secant line becomes a tangent line.

As $Q \to P$, $h \to 0$

Thus, the slope of the tangent line at P will be

$$\lim_{x \to 0} \frac{f(x+h) - f(x)}{(x+h) - x}$$

$$= \lim_{h \to 0} \frac{f(x+h) - f(x)}{h}$$

It is important to note that the slope of the tangent at P represents the **instantaneous rate of change** of the function at this point.

Example 1

Given $f(x) = x^2 - x - 6$, find the slope of the tangent line at the point $P(2, -4)$.

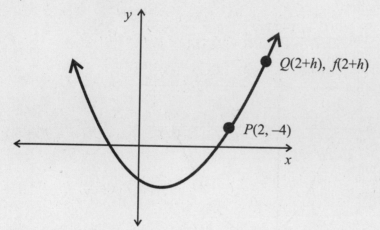

Note: $f(2+h)$ can be found by substituting $(2+h)$ for x in $f(x)$.

Solution

Thus, if $f(2+h) = (2+h)^2 - (2+h) - 6$

then $\lim\limits_{h \to 0} \dfrac{f(x+h) - f(x)}{h}$ becomes

$$\lim_{h \to 0} \frac{f(2+h) - f(2)}{h}$$

$$\lim_{h \to 0} \frac{(2+h)^2 - (2+h) - 6 - (-4)}{h}$$

$$\lim_{h \to 0} \frac{4 + 4h + h^2 - 2 - h - 6 + 4}{h}$$

NOTES

$$\lim_{h \to 0} \frac{3h + h^2}{h}$$

since the h cancels at this point, we can substitute the 0 into the function

$$\lim_{h \to 0} 3 + h$$

$$= 3 + (0)$$

$$= 3$$

The slope of the tangent line at point $P\,(2, -4)$ is 3.

Example 2

Find the slope of the tangent to the function $f(x) = x^2 - x - 12$,

where $x = 4$.

Solution

$$m = \lim_{h \to 0} \left[\frac{f(x+h) - f(x)}{h} \right]$$

$$m = \lim_{h \to 0} \frac{(x+h)^2 - (x+h) - 12 - \left(x^2 - x - 12\right)}{h}$$

$$= \lim_{h \to 0} \frac{4^2 + 2(4)h + h^2 - 4 - h - 12 - 4^2 + 4 + 12}{h}$$

$$= \lim_{h \to 0} \frac{8h + h^2 - h}{h}$$

$$= \lim_{h \to 0} 8 - 1 + h$$

$$= 7$$

Example 3

Find the slope of the tangent line at the point where $x = 4$ on the curve

$f(x) = \dfrac{1}{x}$.

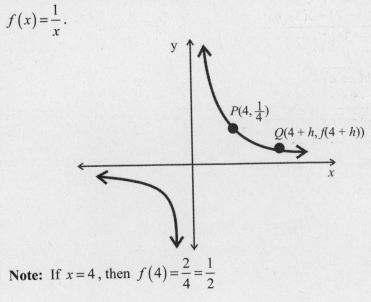

Note: If $x = 4$, then $f(4) = \dfrac{2}{4} = \dfrac{1}{2}$

Solution

The slope of the tangent line is

$$\lim_{h \to 0} \frac{f(x+h) - f(4)}{(4+h) - 4}$$

$$\lim_{h \to 0} \frac{\dfrac{1}{4+h} - \dfrac{1}{4}}{(4+h) - 4}$$

$$\lim_{h \to 0} \frac{4 - (4+h)}{4h(4+h)}$$

$$\lim_{h \to 0} \frac{-1}{4(4+h)}$$

$$= -\frac{1}{16}$$

Example 4

Find the slope of the tangent to $f(x) = \dfrac{x-5}{x}$ at the point where $x = 3$.

Solution

$$m = \lim_{h \to 0} \frac{\dfrac{x+h-5}{x+h} - \dfrac{x-5}{x}}{h}$$

$$= \lim_{h \to 0} \frac{\dfrac{3+h-5}{3+h} - \dfrac{3-5}{3}}{h}$$

$$= \lim_{h \to 0} \frac{\dfrac{h-2}{3+h} - \dfrac{-2}{3}}{h}$$

$$= \lim_{h \to 0} \frac{3(h-2) + 2(3+h)}{3h(3+h)}$$

$$= \lim_{h \to 0} \frac{5h}{3h(3+h)}$$

$$= \lim_{h \to 0} \frac{5}{3(3+h)}$$

$$= \frac{5}{9}$$

PRACTICE EXERCISE

1. Find the slope of the tangent to the function $f(x) = x^2 + 4$ at each of the following points.

   a) $x = 5$ **b)** $x = -3$

2. Find the slope of the tangent to the function $f(x) = 3x - 4$ at each of the following points.

   a) $x = 2$ **b)** $x = 5$

c) What do you notice? Why is this?

3. Find the slope of the tangent to the function $f(x) = x^3 - 3$ at $x = 4$.

4. Find the slope of the tangent to the function $f(x) = \dfrac{x+1}{x-2}$ at $x = 5$.

REVIEW SUMMARY

Now that you have completed this chapter, you should be able to . . .

- explain what a limit is

- explain how a limit can be approximated by examining values near the limit

- evaluate left and right-hand limits graphically and algebraically

$$\lim_{x \to a^+} \text{ and } \lim_{x \to a^-}$$

- explain the difference between continuous and discontinuous functions

- simplify functions by factoring and rationalizing in order to evaluate limits

- determine when a limit is undefined

$$\lim_{x \to a^+} \neq \lim_{x \to a^-}$$

- use limits to determine the slope of a tangent to a curve at a given point

$$m = \lim_{h \to 0} \frac{f(x+h) - f(x)}{h}$$

- Recognize that $\dfrac{f(x + h) - f(x)}{h}$ is the slope of a **secant line** of a function, $y = f(x)$, through the points $(x, f(x))$ and $(x+h, f(x+h))$ on the function $(x+h, f(x+h))$. This slope represents the **average rate of change** of the function over the **interval** that begins at x and ends at $x + h$.

- Recognize that $\displaystyle \lim_{h \to 0} \left[\frac{f(x + h) - f(x)}{h} \right]$ is the slope of a **tangent line** of a function, $y = f(x)$, at the point $(x, f(x))$. This slope represents the **instantaneous rate of change** of the function at a specific point.

PRACTICE TEST

1. For the following function, determine the following limits.

$$f(x) \begin{cases} x^2 & \text{if} \quad x < 1 \\ x+1 & \text{if} \quad 1 \le x < 3 \\ -x+7 & \text{if} \quad x \ge 3 \end{cases}$$

a) $\lim\limits_{x \to 1^+} f(x)$

b) $\lim\limits_{x \to 1^-} f(x)$

c) $\lim\limits_{x \to 1} f(x)$

d) $\lim\limits_{x \to 3^+} f(x)$

e) $\lim\limits_{x \to 3^-} f(x)$

f) $\lim\limits_{x \to 3} f(x)$

g) For what value(s) of x is the function discontinuous?

2. Evaluate the following limits.

a) $\lim\limits_{x \to 9} x^2 - 3x - 5$

b) $\lim\limits_{x \to 7} \dfrac{x^2 - 49}{x - 7}$

c) $\lim_{x \to -1} \dfrac{x^2 - 1}{x^3 + 1}$

d) $\lim_{x \to 9} \dfrac{\sqrt{x - 5} - 2}{9 - x}$

3. For the function $f(x) = x^2 - 5$, determine the slope of the tangent when

   a) $x = 4$

   b) $x = 1$

4. For the function $f(x) = \dfrac{1}{2x}$, determine the slope of the function when $x = 7$.

DERIVATIVES AND DERIVATIVE THEOREMS

When you are finished this unit, you should be able to. . .

- describe the connection between limits and derivatives
- find the derivative of a function by using first principles
- find the derivative of a function by using the power rule
- find the derivative of a function by using the sum and the difference rules
- find the derivative of more complex functions by using the product, the quotient, and the chain rules
- use implicit differentiation in situations where one variable is difficult to isolate
- find 2nd, 3rd, and higher derivatives of algebraic functions
- use the derivative of a function to find the slope and equation of a tangent to that function

PREREQUISITE SKILLS AND KNOWLEDGE

Prior to beginning this unit, you should be able to. . .

- explain what a limit is and how to simplify it
- explain factor complex expressions, including those containing rational exponent and binomial factors
- explain the equation of a line given a point and the slope of the line

Lesson 1 DERIVATIVES USING FIRST PRINCIPLES

You have learned how to calculate the instantaneous rate of change of a function using the limit

$$\lim_{h \to 0} \frac{f(x+h) - f(x)}{h}$$

Here, we are going to further explore the significance of this limit. The function that it produces is so important to our study of the calculus that it has been given its own name: The Derivative.

Later in this chapter, we will develop other methods of finding derivatives. For now, we will continue to use this limit. Using this limit to find the derivative of a function is referred to as finding the derivative using *first principles*. The act of finding a derivative is called **differentiating**.

Because of the somewhat complex origins of the calculus, there are several different notations used to represent derivatives. We will be working with a variety of notations that are in common use in the mathematics community.

All of the following notations are used to represent the derivative of a function.

$$f'(x), \; y', \; \frac{dy}{dx}, \; \text{and} \; \frac{d}{dx}\big(f(x)\big)$$

Example 1

Find the derivative of the following function by using first principles. Use the derivative to find the slope of the tangent at the point (4, 8) and then write the equation of this tangent.

$f(x) = 2x^2 - 6x$

Solution

$$f'(x) = \lim_{h \to 0} \frac{f(x+h) - f(x)}{h}$$

$$= \lim_{h \to 0} \frac{2(x+h)^2 - 6(x+h) - \left(2x^2 - 6x\right)}{h}$$

$$= \lim_{h \to 0} \frac{2\left(x^2 + 2hx + h^2\right) - (6x + 6h) - 2x^2 + 6x}{h}$$

$$= \lim_{h \to 0} \frac{2x^2 + 4xh + 2h^2 - 6x - 6h - 2x^2 + 6x}{h}$$

$$= \lim_{h \to 0} \frac{4hx + 2h^2 - 6h}{h}$$

$$= \lim_{h \to 0} \frac{h(4x + 2h - 6)}{h}$$

$$= \lim_{h \to 0} 4x + 2h - 6$$

$$= 4x - 6$$

So, we can say that the derivative of $f(x) = 2x^2 - 6x$ is

$f'(x) = 4x - 6$.

The slope (m) of the tangent at the point (4, 8) can be found by substituting 4 into the derivative.

$f'(4) = 4(4) - 6$

$\quad\quad = 10$

Using this slope, we can find the equation of the tangent.

$$m = \frac{y_2 - y_1}{x_2 - x_1}$$

$$10 = \frac{y - 8}{x - 4}$$

$$10x - 40 = y - 8$$

$$10x - y = 32$$

Each of the following equations may be used as a starting point for writing the equation of a line.

$$m = \frac{y_2 - y_1}{x_2 - x_1} \quad \text{or}$$

$$(x_2 - x_1)m = (y_2 - y_1) \quad \text{or}$$

$$y = mx + b$$

Example 2

Find the derivative of the following function by using first principles. Use the derivative to find the slope of the tangent at the point $\left(2, \dfrac{1}{4}\right)$, and then write the equation of this tangent.

$$y = \frac{1}{x^2}$$

Solution

$$\frac{dy}{dx} = \lim_{h \to 0} \frac{f(x+h) - f(x)}{h}$$

$$= \lim_{h \to 0} \frac{\dfrac{1}{(x+h)^2} - \dfrac{1}{x^2}}{h}$$

$$= \lim_{h \to 0} \frac{\dfrac{x^2 - (x+h)^2}{x^2(x+h)^2}}{h}$$

$$= \lim_{h \to 0} \frac{x^2 - (x+h)^2}{x^2(x+h)^2 \, h}$$

$$= \lim_{l \to 0} \frac{x^2 - x^2 - 2xh - h^2}{x^2(x+h)^2 \, h}$$

$$= \lim_{h \to 0} \frac{-2xh - h^2}{x^2(x+h)^2 \, h}$$

$$= \lim_{h \to 0} \frac{h(-2x - h)}{x^2(x+h)^2 \, h}$$

$$= \lim_{h \to 0} \frac{-2x - h}{x^2(x+h)^2}$$

$$= \frac{-2x}{x^2(x^2)}$$

$$= -\frac{2}{x^3}$$

Simplify and divide through by h to get to the next step.

The slope at $\left(2, \dfrac{1}{4}\right)$ is $-\dfrac{2}{2^3}$ or $-\dfrac{1}{4}$.

$$-\frac{1}{4} = \frac{y - \dfrac{1}{4}}{x - 2}$$

$$4y - 1 = 2 - x$$

$$x + 4y = 3$$

Example 3

Is the function $f(x) = x^{\frac{2}{3}}$ **differentiable** at all points within its domain?

Solution

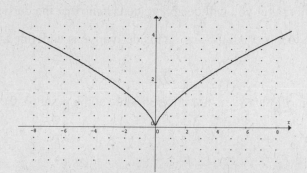

The domain of this function is the set of real numbers.

The function exists at the point (0, 0). However, does the derivative of the function exist at this point?

This question can be answered in two ways.

First, look at the behavior of secant slopes with one point at (0, 0).

The slope of the secant line through the points (0, 0) and (1, 1) would be 1.

The slope of the secant line through the points (0, 0) and $\left(0.1, \ 0.1^{\frac{2}{3}} \right)$

would be approximately equal to 2.15.

The slope of the secant line through the points (0, 0) and $\left(0.01, \ 0.01^{\frac{2}{3}} \right)$

would be approximately equal to 4.64.

The slope of the secant line through the points (0, 0) and $\left(0.001, \ 0.001^{\frac{2}{3}} \right)$

would be approximately equal to 10.

The slopes of these secant lines through the point (0, 0) and another point that is to the **right** of (0, 0) are approaching $+\infty$.

The same process would show that the slopes of secant lines through the point (0, 0) and a point that is to the left of (0, 0) are approaching $-\infty$.

Since these two limits are not equal, a limiting value of secant slopes, as x approaches a value of 0 does not exist and the function does not have a derivative value when $x = 0$.

This can be verified by evaluating the derivative of this function at $x = 0$.

In an upcoming unit you will be able to determine that the derivative of $x^{\frac{2}{3}}$ with respect to x is equal to $\dfrac{2}{3x^{\frac{1}{3}}}$. This derivative is undefined when $x = 0$.

The function $f(x) = x^{\frac{2}{3}}$ is not differentiable at the point $(0, 0)$.

PRACTICE EXERCISE

1. Use first principles to find the derivative of each of the following functions.

   a) $f(x) = 4x^2 - 7$

   b) $y = 2x^3 - 6x$

   c) $y = \dfrac{1}{x}$

   d) $f(x) = \sqrt{3x + 1}$

2. Use first principles to find the derivative of each of the following functions. Use the derivative to find the slope of the tangent at the specified point, and then write the equation for each tangent.

a) $y = 5x^2 - x$ at $(1, 4)$

b) $f(x) = (x+3)^2$ at $(2, 25)$

c) $f(x) = \dfrac{1}{x^2 - 2}$ at $\left(2, \dfrac{1}{2}\right)$

d) $f(x) = \dfrac{x+2}{x^2}$ at $\left(3, \dfrac{5}{9}\right)$

e) $y = \sqrt{5x - 7}$ at $\left(2, \sqrt{3}\right)$

f) $y = \dfrac{3x}{\sqrt{x}}$ at $\left(2, 3\sqrt{2}\right)$

Lesson 2   THE POWER RULE

From first principles, we can derive a rule that allows us to find the derivative of a power function of the form $f(x) = x^n$ more quickly and efficiently.

$$f'(x) = \lim_{h \to 0} \frac{f(x+h) - f(x)}{h}$$

$$= \lim_{h \to 0} \frac{(x+h)^n - x^n}{h}$$

$$= \lim_{h \to 0} \frac{\left(x^n + {}_nC_1 x^{n-1} h + {}_nC_2 x^{n-2} h^2 + \ldots + {}_nC_{n-1} x h^{n-1} + h^n\right) - x^n}{h}$$

$$= \lim_{h \to 0} \frac{{}_nC_1 x^{n-1} h + {}_nC_2 x^{n-2} h^2 + \ldots + {}_nC_{n-1} x h^{n-1} + h^n}{h}$$

$$= \lim_{h \to 0} {}_nC_1 x^{n-1} + {}_nC_2 x^{n-2} h^1 + \ldots + {}_nC_{n-1} x h^{n-2} + h^{n-1}$$

We are using the binomial theorem to expand $(x+h)^n$.

Now, since each term except the first contains h as a factor, we have

$$= {}_nC_1 x^{n-1}$$

$$= nx^{n-1}$$

This result is called the power rule,

where $f(x) = x^n$

$$f'(x) = nx^{n-1}$$

or, using alternate notation

$$\frac{d}{dx}\left(x^n\right) = nx^{n-1}$$

Example 1

Using the power rule, differentiate the following function.

$$f(x) = x^3$$

Solution

$$f'(x) = 3\left(x^{3-1}\right)$$

$$= 3x^2$$

Example 2

Use the power rule to find the derivative of the following function.

$y = 3x^4$

Solution

$$\frac{dy}{dx} = 4\left(3x^{4-1}\right)$$
$$= 12x^3$$

Example 3

Use the power rule to find the derivative of the following function.

$f(x) = 12x^5$

Solution

$$f'(x) = 60x^4$$

DERIVATIVES OF EXPRESSIONS CONTAINING SUMS AND DIFFERENCES

Such expressions often contain constant terms, so it is important to understand how to differentiate a constant.

Consider the function

$y = c$

where c is a constant.

Since there are no variables, when we use first principles to find the derivative, we get

$$\frac{dy}{dx} = \lim_{h \to 0} \frac{f(x+h) - f(x)}{h}$$
$$= \lim_{h \to 0} \frac{c - c}{h}$$
$$= \lim_{h \to 0} \frac{0}{h}$$
$$= \lim_{h \to 0} 0$$
$$= 0$$

So, we can see that the derivative of a constant function is always zero. This makes sense when we consider that the derivative represents the rate of change (slope) of a function at a given value of x, and since the graph of a constant function is a horizontal line, its slope will always be zero.

NOTES

Consider this graph of $y = 5$.

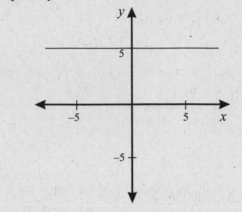

The rate of change of this line is always the same: zero.

THE SUM AND THE DIFFERENCE RULES

For two functions $f(x)$ and $g(x)$, the following rules are always true.

The Sum Rule: The derivative of the sum is equal to the sum of the derivatives.

$$\frac{d}{dx}\big(f(x) + g(x)\big) = \frac{d}{dx}\big(f(x)\big) + \frac{d}{dx}\big(g(x)\big)$$

The Difference Rule: The derivative of the difference is equal to the difference of the derivatives.

$$\frac{d}{dx}\big(f(x) - g(x)\big) = \frac{d}{dx}\big(f(x)\big) - \frac{d}{dx}\big(g(x)\big)$$

Example 4

Find the derivative of the following function.

$f(x) = 3x^4 - 2x^2 + 6$

Solution

$$f'(x) = 4\big(3x^{4-1}\big) - 2\big(x^{2-1}\big) + 0$$
$$= 12x^3 - 4x$$

Example 5

Find the derivative of the following function.

$y = \dfrac{4}{x^2} + 3x$

Solution

First, rewrite the question as

$y = 4x^{-2} + 3x$

Now,

$$\frac{dy}{dx} = -2\left(4x^{-2-1}\right) + 3$$

$$= -8x^{-3} + 3$$

As it is standard practice to leave answers in the same form as the question, finish by writing

$$\frac{dy}{dx} = -\frac{8}{x^3} + 3$$

Example 6

Find the derivative of the following function.

$$f(x) = 3\sqrt{x} - \sqrt[3]{x}$$

Solution

First, write

$$f(x) = 3x^{\frac{1}{2}} - x^{\frac{1}{3}}$$

Now,

$$f'(x) = \frac{1}{2}\left(3x^{\frac{1}{2}-1}\right) - \frac{1}{3}x^{\frac{1}{3}-1}$$

$$= \frac{3}{2\sqrt{x}} - \frac{1}{3\sqrt[3]{x^2}}$$

Example 7

Find the derivative of the following function.

$$y = \frac{2x+3}{\sqrt{x}}$$

Solution

First, write

$$\frac{2x}{\sqrt{x}} + \frac{3}{\sqrt{x}}$$

$$y = 2x^{\frac{1}{2}} + 3x^{\frac{-1}{2}}$$

Now,

$$\frac{dy}{dx} =$$

$$= \frac{1}{\sqrt{x}} - \frac{3}{2\sqrt{x^3}}$$

Now that we can find the slope of the tangent lines at particular points, we can answer a variety of questions regarding functions and their slopes.

Example 8

At what point on the curve $y = x^2 - 3x$ is the slope of the tangent 5?

Solution

First, find the derivative of the function

$$\frac{d_y}{d_x} = 2x - 3$$

Since the derivative is a general expression for slope, set it equal to the desired slope and solve the resulting equation to give the required value of x.

$$2x - 3 = 5$$
$$2x = 8$$
$$x = 4$$

The function has a slope of 5 when $x = 4$. We must also find the y-coordinate of the point. To do this, substitute into the original function.

$$y = x^2 - 3x$$
$$y = (4)^2 - 3(4)$$
$$y = 4$$

The point on the curve where the slope of the tangent is equal to 5 is $(4, 4)$

Example 9

At what point is the tangent to the curve $f(x) = 4x^2 - x + 5$ parallel to the line $7x - y = 20$? (Hint: parallel lines have equal slopes.)

Solution

First, find the slope of $7x - y = 20$.

Arranging the equation into the form $y = mx + b$, we get

$$y = 7x - 20$$

slope = 7

Next, find the derivative of the function $f(x) = 4x^2 - x + 5$

$$f'(x) = 8x - 1$$

and set the function equal to 7.

$$8x - 1 = 7$$
$$x = 1$$

The point where the tangent to the curve $f(x) = 4x^2 - x + 5$ is parallel to the line $7x - y = 20$ is $(1, 8)$.

PRACTICE EXERCISE

1. Use the power rule to find the derivatives of the following functions.

   a) $f(x) = 6x^3$

   b) $y = \sqrt{x}$

   c) $f(x) = \dfrac{1}{x^4}$

   d) $y = 5\sqrt[3]{x^4}$

2. Use the sum and the difference rules to find the derivatives of the following functions.

   a) $f(x) = 5x^3 - 2x$

   b) $y = 4x^2 + x - 5$

   c) $y = 2\sqrt{x} - \dfrac{1}{2}$

   d) $f(t) = \dfrac{4}{t} - \dfrac{1}{t^2}$

e) $y = \dfrac{x^3 - x^2 - x}{x}$

f) $f(x) = \dfrac{x^2 - 2\sqrt{x}}{\sqrt{x}}$

3. Find the derivative of each of the following functions and write the equation of the tangent line at the given point.

a) $y = 7x^2$; $(2, 28)$

b) $f(x) = x - \dfrac{4}{x}$; $(2, 0)$

4. a) At which point does the curve $y = 3x^2 - 4x$ have a tangent with a slope of 2?

b) At which points does the curve $y = x^3 - 3x^2 - 24x$ have horizontal tangent lines?

Lesson 3 **THE PRODUCT RULE**

When working with a function that is a product of two other functions, the derivative is found by applying the following Product Rule.

Given that

$$f(x) = g(x)h(x)$$

$$f'(x) = g(x)h'(x) + h(x)g'(x)$$

Liebniz Notation

$$f(x) = g(x)h(x)$$

$$\frac{d}{dx}f(x) =$$

$$g(x)\frac{d}{dx}h(x) + h(x)\frac{d}{dx}g(x)$$

When using this rule, it is helpful to initially identify the two functions that form the product. Then, find the derivative of each of these functions, and substitute into the product rule.

Example 1

Use the product rule to find the derivative of the following function.

$$f(x) = x^3\left(x^2 + 2x\right)$$

Solution

Identify $g(x)$ and $h(x)$ and find their derivatives.

$$g(x) = x^3$$

$$g'(x) = 3x^2$$

$$h(x) = x^2 + 2x$$

$$h'(x) = 2x + 2$$

Substitute into product rule.

$$f'(x) = g(x)h'(x) + h(x)g'(x)$$

$$f'(x) = x^3(2x + 2) + \left(x^2 + 2x\right)\left(3x^2\right)$$

$$f'(x) = 2x^4 + 2x^3 + 3x^4 + 6x^3$$

$$f'(x) = 5x^4 + 8x^3$$

Example 2

Use the product rule to find the derivative of the following function.

$$y = \sqrt{x}\left(5x^4\right)$$

Solution

First, identify the product's functions and find their derivatives.

$$g(x) = \sqrt{x} = x^{\frac{1}{2}}$$

$$g'(x) = \frac{1}{2}x^{-\frac{1}{2}}$$

$$h(x) = 5x^4$$

$$h'(x) = 20x^3$$

This question could also be done by first expanding the function and then using the power rule. We use the product rule here as it is the topic of this lesson, not out of any preference.

Substitute into product rule and simplify.

$$\frac{dy}{dx} = g(x)h'(x) + h(x)g'(x)$$

$$\frac{dy}{dx} = x^{\frac{1}{2}}\left(20x^3\right) + 5x^4\left(\frac{1}{2}x^{-\frac{1}{2}}\right)$$

$$\frac{dy}{dx} = \frac{1}{2}x^{-\frac{1}{2}}\left[2x\left(20x^3\right) + 5x^4\right]$$

$$\frac{dy}{dx} = \frac{1}{2}x^{-\frac{1}{2}}\left[40x^4 + 5x^4\right]$$

$$\frac{dy}{dx} = \frac{45x^4}{2\sqrt{x}}$$

Example 3

Use the product rule to find the derivative of the following function.

$$f(x) = \left(x^2 - 7x\right)\left(x^3 + 2x - 8\right)$$

Solution

$$g(x) = x^2 - 7x$$
$$g'(x) = 2x - 7$$
$$h(x) = x^3 + 2x - 8$$
$$h'(x) = 3x^2 + 2$$

$$f'(x) = \left(x^2 - 7x\right)\left(3x^2 + 2\right) + \left(x^3 + 2x - 8\right)(2x - 7)$$
$$f'(x) = 3x^4 - 21x^3 + 2x^2 - 14x + 2x^4 - 16x - 7x^3 - 14x + 56$$
$$f'(x) = 5x^4 - 28x^3 + 6x^2 - 44x + 56$$

PRACTICE EXERCISE

1. Find the derivative of each of the following functions using the product rule.

a) $y = (x^3)(15x^4)$

b) $f(x) = (5x^7)\left(\dfrac{6}{x}\right)$

c) $y = \left(5\sqrt{x^3}\right)(9x^4)$

d) $f(x) = (7 - x^2)(\sqrt{x})$

e) $y = (5x^3 - x)\left(\dfrac{1}{2\sqrt{x}}\right)$

f) $f(x) = (3x^2 - x + 18)(2x^3 - x)$

Lesson 4   THE QUOTIENT RULE

When you are given a function that is expressed as a quotient of two other functions, you can use the quotient rule to find the derivative of this composite function.

Quotient Rule:

$$f(x) = \frac{g(x)}{h(x)}$$

$$f'(x) = \frac{h(x)g'(x) - g(x)h'(x)}{(h(x))^2}$$

As with the product rule, it is helpful to first identify the functions (in this case, $g(x)$ and $h(x)$ and find their derivatives. Then, substitute appropriately using the quotient rule.

Example 1

Use the quotient rule to find the derivative of the function.

$$f(x) = \frac{13x^3}{5x - 1}$$

Solution

$$g(x) = 13x^3$$
$$g'(x) = 39x^2$$
$$h(x) = 5x - 1$$
$$h'(x) = 5$$
$$f'(x) = \frac{h(x)g'(x) - g(x)h'(x)}{(h(x))^2}$$
$$f'(x) = \frac{(5x - 1)(39x^2) - (13x^3)(5)}{(5x - 1)^2}$$
$$f'(x) = \frac{195x^3 - 39x^2 - 65x^3}{(5x - 1)^2}$$
$$f'(x) = \frac{130x^3 - 39x^2}{(5x - 1)^2}$$

It is not necessary to expand the denominator in this case, as it will not cancel any numerator terms to simplify the final form. This form most clearly shows the terms present in the completed derivative.

Example 2

Using the quotient rule, complete the differentiation of the function.

$$y = \frac{7x^2 - 3x}{2x^5}$$

Solution

$$g(x) = 7x^2 - 3x$$

$$g'(x) = 14x - 3$$

$$h(x) = 2x^5$$

$$h'(x) = 10x^4$$

$$y' =$$

$$\frac{dy}{dx} = \frac{h(x)g'(x) - g(x)h'(x)}{(h(x))^2}$$

$$\frac{dy}{dx} = \frac{2x^5(14x - 3) - (7x^2 - 3x)(10x^4)}{(2x^5)^2}$$

$$\frac{dy}{dx} = \frac{28x^6 - 6x^5 - 70x^6 + 30x^5}{4x^{10}}$$

$$\frac{dy}{dx} = \frac{-42x^6 + 24x^5}{4x^{10}}$$

$$\frac{dy}{dx} = \frac{2x^5(-21x + 12)}{2x^5(2x^5)}$$

$$\frac{dy}{dx} = \frac{-3(7x - 4)}{2x^5}$$

In this case, the denominator was used to simplify the equation. Squaring the denominator allowed for cancellation/simplification as indicated in the solution above.

Example 3

Find the derivative of the function.

$$f(x) = \frac{7\sqrt{x}}{x^2 - 4x}$$

Solution

$$g(x) = 7\sqrt{x} = 7x^{\frac{1}{2}}$$

$$g'(x) = \frac{7}{2}x^{-\frac{1}{2}}$$

$$h(x) = x^2 - 4x$$

$$h'(x) = 2x - 4$$

$$f'(x) = \frac{h(x)g'(x) - g(x)h'(x)}{(h(x))^2}$$

$$f'(x) = \frac{(x^2 - 4x)\left(\frac{7}{2}x^{-\frac{1}{2}}\right) - 7x^{\frac{1}{2}}(2x - 4)}{(x^2 - 4x)^2}$$

$$f'(x) = \frac{\frac{7}{2}x^{-\frac{1}{2}}\left[(x^2 - 4x) - 2x(2x - 4)\right]}{(x^2 - 4x)^2}$$

$$f'(x) = \frac{7x^2\left(x^2 - 4x - 4x^2 + 8x\right)}{2x^{\frac{1}{2}}(x^2 - 4x)^2}$$

$$f'(x) = \frac{7(-3x^2 + 4x)}{2\sqrt{x}(x^2 - 4x)^2}$$

Important note: All "quotient rule" derivatives can also be done as a "product rule" if you move the denominator up to be multiplied by the numerator. To do this, you must change the sign of the exponent on the denominator.

Example 4

$$f(x) = \frac{2x^3}{(x - 5)}$$

$$= 2x^3(x - 5)^{-1} \quad \text{Now, use the product rule to complete.}$$

PRACTICE EXERCISE

1. Find the derivative of each of the following functions by using the quotient rule.

a) $y = \dfrac{1+x}{3x^2}$

b) $f(x) = \dfrac{5x^2 - 1}{2x + 4}$

c) $y = \dfrac{\sqrt[3]{x^2}}{2\sqrt{x}}$

2. Find the derivative of each of the following functions by using the product and the quotient rules.

a) $y = \dfrac{\left(x^4\right)(2x-1)}{4x^3}$

b) $f(x) = \dfrac{3x^3 - 12x}{(x+3)(2x-7)}$

Lesson 5   THE CHAIN RULE

The Chain Rule is useful in differentiating composite functions; that is, a function composed of simpler functions (often a polynomial function raised to some power).

This can be shown as $f(x) = g(h(x))$, where $f(x)$ is the function we are trying to find the derivative of and $g(h(x))$ is the form of the simpler functions.

The derivative of this composite function is found using the Chain Rule, which states that $f'(x) = g'[h(x)][h'(x)]$

Example 1

Use the Chain Rule to find the derivative of the function.

$f(x) = (x^2 - 2)^4$

Solution

requested derivative = derivative of the outer function × derivative of the inner function

Let $g(x) = x^4$ *and* $h(x) = x^2 - 2$

$f(x) = g[h(x)]$

$f'(x) = g'[h(x)][h'(x)]$

$f'(x) = 4(x^2 - 2)^3 (2x)$

$\quad = 8x(x^2 - 2)^3$

Another approach for this problem involves the use of Liebniz notation.

Let $y = u^4$, where $u = x^2 - 2$. Thus, $\dfrac{dy}{du} = 4u^3$ and $\dfrac{du}{dx} = 2x$

$y = (x^2 - 2)^4$

$y = u^4$

$\dfrac{dy}{dx} = \dfrac{dy}{du}\dfrac{du}{dx}$

$\dfrac{dy}{dx} = \left(\dfrac{dy}{du}\right)\left(\dfrac{du}{dx}\right)$

$\dfrac{dy}{dx} = (4u^3)(2x)$

$\dfrac{dy}{dx} = 4(x^2 - 2)^3 (2x)$

$\dfrac{dy}{dx} = 8x(x^2 - 2)^3$

The Chain Rule can also be shown in Liebniz notation. In Liebniz notation, we can write the original composite equation as $y = g(u)$, where $u = h(x)$ and

$$\frac{dy}{dx} = \frac{dy}{du}\frac{du}{dx}$$

Example 2

Use the Chain Rule to find the derivative of the function.

$$f(x) = \sqrt{3x^4 - x}$$

Solution

Rewrite the function as $f(x) = \left(3x^4 - x\right)^{\frac{1}{2}}$

$$f'(x) = \frac{1}{2}\left(3x^4 - x\right)^{-\frac{1}{2}}\left(12x^3 - 1\right)$$

$$f'(x) = \frac{12x^3 - 1}{2\sqrt{3x^4 - x}}$$

When questions require the use of the Product or Quotient Rule in addition to the Chain Rule, in most cases, the Chain Rule will be secondary (incorporated into the differentiation steps of the Product or Quotient Rule). Examples to illustrate this concept follow.

Example 3

Differentiate

$$f(x) = 3x^2\left(2 - x^2\right)^3$$

Solution

(It makes sense to approach this as a product rule question initially, and then use the Chain Rule when required.)

$$g(x) = 3x^2$$
$$g'(x) = 6x$$
$$h(x) = \left(2 - x^2\right)^3$$
$$h'(x) = 3\left(2 - x^2\right)^2 (-2x)$$
$$h'(x) = -6x\left(2 - x^2\right)^2$$

Notice that the Chain Rule was used to differentiate $h(x)$.

$$f'(x) = 3x^2(-6x)\left(2 - x^2\right)^2 + \left(2 - x^2\right)^3 (6x)$$

$$f'(x) = -18x^3(2 - x^2)^2 + 6x\left(2 - x^2\right)^3$$

$$f'(x) = 6x\left(2 - x^2\right)^2\left[-3x^2 + \left(2 - x^2\right)\right]$$

$$f'(x) = 6x\left(2 - x^2\right)^2\left(-4x^2 + 2\right)$$

Example 4

Differentiate

$$y = \frac{5x^4}{\sqrt{7x-3}}$$

Solution

(Set the question up as a Quotient Rule, and then use the Chain Rule when differentiating the denominator term.)

$$g(x) = 5x^4$$

$$g'(x) = 20x^3$$

$$h(x) = \sqrt{7x-3}$$

$$h(x) = (7x-3)^{\frac{1}{2}}$$

$$h'(x) = \frac{1}{2}(7x-3)^{-\frac{1}{2}}(7)$$

$$\frac{dy}{dx} = \frac{(7x-3)^{\frac{1}{2}}(20x^3) - (5x^4)\left(\frac{1}{2}(7x-3)^{-\frac{1}{2}}(7)\right)}{7x-3}$$

$$\frac{dy}{dx} = \frac{\frac{5}{2}x^3(7x-3)^{-\frac{1}{2}}\left[8(7x-3)-7x\right]}{7x-3}$$

$$\frac{dy}{dx} = \frac{5x^3(56x-24-7x)}{2(7x-3)^{\frac{3}{2}}}$$

$$\frac{dy}{dx} = \frac{5x^3(49x-24)}{2\sqrt{(7x-3)^3}}$$

PRACTICE EXERCISE

1. Differentiate the following problems.

a) $f(x) = (5x^3 - x)^9$

b) $y = \sqrt{x^2 - 2x}$

c) $f(x) = x^3(3x-1)^2$

d) $y = \dfrac{\sqrt{5x}}{2x^2 - 3}$

e) $f(x) = \sqrt{2x\sqrt{x+3}}$

PRACTICE QUIZ

1. Use first principles to find the derivative of the function $f(x) = 6x^2 - x$.

2. Differentiate the following functions.

a) $y = 8x^4 - 6x^3 + x - 7$

b) $f(x) = \sqrt{x}\left(x^2 - 6\right)$

c) $y = \dfrac{3x^3}{x-3}$

d) $f(x) = \left(x^3 + 4\right)^6$

e) $f(x) = \dfrac{x\sqrt{x-1}}{x+2}$

f) $y = x^2\left(3x^2 - 7\right)^4$

3. Find the derivative and use it to determine the slope of the function $f(x) = \dfrac{1}{x^3}$ at the point $\left(2, \dfrac{1}{2}\right)$.

Then, write the equation of this tangent.

Lesson 6 IMPLICIT DIFFERENTIATION

So far, we have been differentiating expressions of the form $y = f(x)$, where y is written explicitly in terms of x. It is not always convenient or possible to isolate the y, and in these cases, we must differentiate with respect to x without first isolating y. This is called implicit differentiation.

Consider the equation $2y = y^2 + 3x^3$.

Isolating y is not an option here, so we will implicitly differentiate both sides of the equation with respect to x. We still consider y to be a function of x, so it is necessary to differentiate y as a function using the chain rule (see below).

$$2y = y^2 + 3x^3$$
$$\frac{d}{dx}(2y) = \frac{d}{dx}\left(y^2 + 3x^3\right)$$
$$2\frac{dy}{dx} = 2y\frac{dy}{dx} + 9x^2$$

Notice that we represent the derivative of y as $\frac{dy}{dx}$. The derivative of x is equal to 1; therefore, it is not necessary to write it as $\frac{dx}{dx}$. Instead, we continue to write it the way that we have all along. Continuing to solve the equation above, we isolate $\frac{dy}{dx}$ next.

$$2\frac{dy}{dx} - 2y\frac{dy}{dx} = 9x^2$$
$$\frac{dy}{dx}(2 - 2y) = 9x^2$$
$$\frac{dy}{dx} = \frac{9x^2}{2 - 2y}$$

The final expression for the derivative contains both x and y, which distinguishes it from other derivatives. This means that both values would be needed in order to find data, such as the slope at a given point.

NOTES

Another way of differentiating this equation (had the question not specifically asked for the implicit method) would be by isolating y and then differentiating.

$$y^2 = 15 - x^2$$
$$(2y)y' = -2x$$
$$y' = \frac{-2x}{2y}$$

Example 1

Differentiate implicitly the relation below with respect to x.

$$x^2 + y^2 = 15$$

Solution

$$\frac{d}{dx}\left(x^2 + y^2\right) = \frac{d}{dx}(15)$$
$$2x + 2y\frac{dy}{dx} = 0$$
$$2y\frac{dy}{dx} = -2x$$
$$\frac{dy}{dx} = \frac{-2x}{2y}$$
$$\frac{dy}{dx} = \frac{-x}{y}$$

Additionally, since it is easy to isolate y in the original expression, it is appropriate to now substitute y into the derivative. Isolating y gives us $y = \pm\sqrt{15 - x^2}$.

$$\frac{dy}{dx} = \frac{-x}{y}$$
$$\frac{dy}{dx} = \frac{-x}{\pm\sqrt{15 - x^2}}$$

Two derivative values exist because the original relation, $x^2 + y^2 = 15$, consists of two functions, $y = +\sqrt{15 - x^2}$ and $y = -\sqrt{15 - x^2}$.

The results above can be verified by differentiating each of these functions.

$$y = +\sqrt{15 - x^2} \qquad\qquad y = -\sqrt{15 - x^2}$$
$$y = \left(15 - x^2\right)^{\frac{1}{2}} \qquad\qquad y = -\left(15 - x^2\right)^{\frac{1}{2}}$$
$$\frac{dy}{dx} = \frac{1}{2}\left(15 - x^2\right)^{-\frac{1}{2}}(-2x) \qquad \frac{dy}{dx} = -\frac{1}{2}\left(15 - x^2\right)^{-\frac{1}{2}}(-2x)$$
$$\frac{dy}{dx} = \frac{-x}{\sqrt{15 - x^2}} \qquad\qquad \frac{dy}{dx} = \frac{x}{\sqrt{15 - x^2}}$$

Example 2

Differentiate implicitly the function below.

$3xy - 2y^2 = 5x$

Solution

(Notice that the term $3xy$ requires the Product Rule.)

$$3x\frac{dy}{dx} + y(3) - 4y\frac{dy}{dx} = 5$$

$$3x\frac{dy}{dx} - 4y\frac{dy}{dx} = 5 - 3y$$

$$\frac{dy}{dx}(3x - 4y) = 5 - 3y$$

$$\frac{dy}{dx} = \frac{5 - 3y}{3x - 4y}$$

Example 3

Differentiate the function given to find the slope at point $(1, 6)$.

$2xy - 15 = -3x^2$

Solution

$$2x\frac{dy}{dx} + y(2) - (0) = -6x$$

$$\frac{dy}{dx} = \frac{-6x - 2y}{2x}$$

To find the slope, substitute in for x and y.

$$\frac{dy}{dx} = \frac{-6(1) - 2(6)}{2(1)}$$

$$slope = \frac{dy}{dx} = -9$$

PRACTICE EXERCISE

1. For each of the following equations, find the derivative with respect to x.

   a) $4x^2 + 4y^2 = 20$

   b) $4xy^2 + 2y = 3x$

   c) $3y - \dfrac{y^4}{x^2} = 2y$

2. For each of the following equations, find the slope of the tangent at the point indicated.

   a) $4x^3 - y^2 = y + 2$ at point $(2, 5)$

   b) $7xy = 21$ at point $\left(6, \dfrac{1}{2}\right)$

3. Write the equation of the line tangent to the curve at the point indicated.

$3x - y^2 + 6y = x^2 - x$ at point $(5, 1)$

Lesson 7 HIGHER DERIVATIVES

The first time that a function is differentiated, the result is called the first derivative. If this derivative is differentiated again, the result is called the second derivative. This process can be repeated as long as it continues to be possible to differentiate. These derivatives (beyond the first derivative) are known as higher derivatives.

The most common notations for the higher derivatives are

In prime notation, the number of tics indicates the derivative. One tic means first derivative, 2 tics mean second derivative etc.

Second derivative: $f''(x)$ or y'' or $\dfrac{d^2 y}{dx^2}$ or $\dfrac{d^2}{dx^2} f(x)$

Third derivative: $f'''(x)$ or y''' or $\dfrac{d^3 y}{dx^3}$ or $\dfrac{d^3}{dx^3} f(x)$

Recall that the first derivative represents the instantaneous rate of change of a function. That is, the slope of the tangent to the function at a point. The second derivative represents the rate at which the slope of the tangents to the function are changing as we move through the domain of the function.

It is important to fully simplify the first derivative before differentiating again (to find the second derivative). This reduces the number of rules and procedures required as well as it keeps the differentiation manageable.

Example 1

Find the second derivative of the function below.

$f(x) = x^3 - 2x^2 + 5x - 7$

Solution
(Find the first derivative, simplify, and differentiate again.)

$f'(x) = 3x^2 - 4x + 5$
$f''(x) = 6x - 4$

Notice the change in degree from cubic in $f(x)$ to quadratic in $f'(x)$ and finally to linear in $f''(x)$. This pattern of reduction in degree is always true with polynomial functions, but the pattern becomes more complex with rational functions.

Example 2

Find the second derivative of the function given.

$$y = \frac{2x^2}{3x-1}$$

Solution

(Start by finding the first derivative by using the Quotient Rule.)

$$\frac{dy}{dx} = \frac{(3x-1)(4x) - 2x^2(3)}{(3x-1)^2}$$

$$\frac{dy}{dx} = \frac{12x^2 - 4x - 6x^2}{(3x-1)^2}$$

$$\frac{dy}{dx} = \frac{6x^2 - 4x}{(3x-1)^2}$$

Now differentiate again using both the Quotient and the Chain Rules.

$$\frac{d^2y}{dx^2} = \frac{(3x-1)^2(12x-4) - \left(6x^2 - 4x\right)(2)(3x-1)(3)}{(3x-1)^4}$$

$$\frac{d^2y}{dx^2} = \frac{2(3x-1)\left[2(3x-1)^2 - 3\left(6x^2 - 4x\right)\right]}{(3x-1)^4}$$

$$\frac{d^2y}{dx^2} = \frac{2\left[18x^2 - 12x + 2 - 18x^2 + 12x\right]}{(3x-1)^3}$$

$$\frac{d^2x}{dx^2} = \frac{4}{(3x-1)^3}$$

NOTES

Example 3

Find the second derivative of the function given.

$$f(x) = \frac{\sqrt{x}}{x+3}$$

Solution

Find the first derivative using the Quotient Rule; then differentiate again

$$f'(x) = \frac{(x+3)\left(\frac{1}{2}x^{-\frac{1}{2}}\right) - \left(x^{\frac{1}{2}}\right)(1)}{(x+3)^2}$$

Extract a common factor

$$f'(x) = \frac{\frac{1}{2}x^{-\frac{1}{2}}(x+3-2x)}{(x+3)^2}$$

$$f'(x) = \frac{3-x}{2\sqrt{x}(x+3)^2}$$

$$f''(x) = \frac{2\sqrt{x}(x+3)^2(-1) - (3-x)\left[\left(2x^{\frac{1}{2}}\right)(2)(x+3) + (x+3)^2\left(x^{-\frac{1}{2}}\right)\right]}{\left[2\sqrt{x}(x+3)^2\right]^2}$$

Extract a common factor

$$f''(x) = \frac{-x^{-\frac{1}{2}}(x+3)\left[2x(x+3) + 4x(3-x) + (x+3)(3-x)\right]}{4x(x+3)^4}$$

$$f''(x) = \frac{-\left(2x^2 + 6x + 12x - 4x^2 + 3x - x^2 + 9 - 3x\right)}{4x^{\frac{3}{2}}(x+3)^3}$$

$$f''(x) = \frac{-\left(-3x^2 + 18x + 9\right)}{4x^{\frac{3}{2}}(x+3)^3}$$

$$f''(x) = \frac{3\left(x^2 - 6x - 3\right)}{4x^{\frac{3}{2}}(x+3)^3}$$

When you are asked to evaluate the second derivative for a given x value, you must first find the second derivative and then substitute the value of x into the second derivative.

Example 4

For the function $f(x) = 12x^4 - 3x^2$, find $f''(-2)$.

Solution

First find $f'(x)$

$f'(x) = 48x^3 - 6x$

and then find $f''(x)$

$f''(x) = 144x^2 - 6$

and then substitute

$f''(-2) = 144(-2)^2 - 6$
$f''(-2) = 570$

PRACTICE EXERCISE

1. Find the second derivative of each of the following functions.

    a) $f(x) = 3x^3 - 9x^2 + 16x - 5$

    b) $f(x) = 10x$

    c) $y = \dfrac{4x}{x-7}$

    d) $y = \left(3x^2 - 5\right)^3$

2. For each of the following functions, find $f''(-1)$.

    a) $f(x) = 7x^3 - 2x$

    b) $f(x) = \dfrac{5x+1}{x^2}$

REVIEW SUMMARY

Now that you have completed this chapter, you should be able to take the derivative of a variety of different functions using the following methods.

- First principles: $f'(x) = \lim\limits_{h \to 0} \dfrac{f(x+h) - f(x)}{h}$

- Power Rule: If $f(x) = x^n$, then $f'(x) = nx^{n-1}$

- Sum and difference rules: $\dfrac{d}{dx}(f(x) + d(x)) = \dfrac{d}{dx}(f(x)) + \dfrac{d}{dx}(g(x))$

  $\dfrac{d}{dx}(f(x) - d(x)) = \dfrac{d}{dx}(f(x)) - \dfrac{d}{dx}(g(x))$

- Product Rule: $f'(g(x)h(x)) = g(x)h'(x) + h(x)g'(x)$

- Quotient Rule: $f'\left(\dfrac{g(x)}{h(x)}\right) = \dfrac{h(x)g'(x) - g(x)h'(x)}{(h(x))^2}$

- Chain Rule: $\dfrac{d}{dx}f(g(x)) = f'(g(x))g'(x)$

- You should be able to differentiate functions in which y is difficult to isolate by using implicit differentiation.

- You should be able to find 2nd and higher derivatives of functions and apply the concepts of these higher derivatives to situations involving velocity and acceleration.

PRACTICE TEST

1. Use first principles to find the derivative of the following function.

$$f(x) = \frac{-5}{\sqrt{x}}$$

2. Identify which rule(s) you should use to differentiate each function, and then use it (them) to find each derivative.

a) $y = 16x^7 - x$ 　　　　　　　　　　　**b)** $f(x) = \frac{-6}{x^3}$

c) $y = 6x\sqrt{x}$ 　　　　　　　　　　　　**d)** $f(x) = \frac{2x}{5 - x}$

e) $f(x) = \sqrt{x^2 - 7}$

f) $y = (x-3)^2 (4x+1)$

3. Find the slope and equation of the tangent of $y = \dfrac{6x^2}{x+1}$ at the point $(1, 3)$.

4. At what point is the slope of the tangent to the function $f(x) = \dfrac{4}{x^2}$ equal to -1?

5. Use implicit differentiation to find $\dfrac{dy}{dx}$ given the following function.

$$3xy = 2x_1^2 - 6y^3$$

6. Find the first and second derivative of each of the following equations.

a) $y = 2x^4 - 3x^2 + 1$

b) $f(x) = \dfrac{2}{\sqrt{x}}$

7. The following function represents the displacement (s) in metres of a particle as a function of time (t) in seconds.

$$s = t^3 - 6t^2 - 8 \qquad\qquad \text{Recall } v = \frac{ds}{dt} \text{ and } a = \frac{dv}{dt}$$

a) Find the velocity and acceleration functions with respect to t.

b) Determine the acceleration after 35 seconds.

NOTES

DERIVATIVES OF TRIGONOMETRIC, LOGARITHMIC, AND EXPONENTIAL FUNCTIONS

When you are finished this unit, you should be able to. . .

- evaluate limits of trigonometric expressions that can be simplified to the form
  $\lim\limits_{\theta \to 0} \dfrac{\sin \theta}{\theta}$ and $\lim\limits_{\theta \to 0} \dfrac{\cos \theta - 1}{\theta}$
- find the derivatives of trigonometric functions involving sine, cosine, tangent, secant, cosecant, and cotangent
- find derivatives of logarithmic functions with any base
- find derivatives of exponential functions
- find derivatives of complex functions that combine trigonometric and logarithmic functions

PREREQUISITE SKILLS AND KNOWLEDGE

Prior to beginning this unit, you should be able to. . .

- apply the Power, Product, Chain, and Quotient Rules to find derivatives
- find exact values of trigonometric functions
- use trigonometric identities to simplify trigonometric expressions
- apply the laws of logarithms

Lesson 1 LIMITS OF TRIGONOMETRIC FUNCTIONS

In order to understand the derivatives that the trigonometric functions will produce, we must first understand how to evaluate two important trigonometric limits.

The first one is $\lim\limits_{\theta \to 0} \dfrac{\sin \theta}{\theta}$

In order to evaluate this limit, we need to use something called the Sandwich Theorem. This theorem involves first evaluating something that we know to be smaller and then evaluating something that we know to be larger. We then make a conclusion about the value of the limit in between these small and large values.

Consider the following diagram, which represents one-quarter of the unit circle.

Recall that the unit circle is defined by $x^2 + y^2 = 1$.

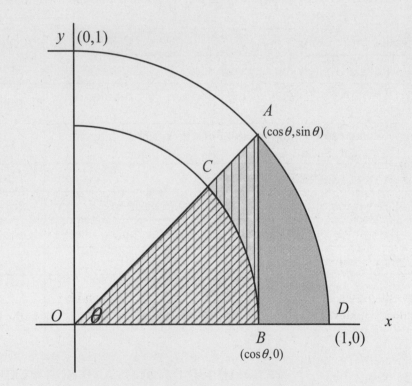

In the diagram above, the radius of the smaller sector is $\cos \theta$ and the radius of the larger sector is 1, and $0 \le \theta \le \dfrac{\pi}{2}$.

On the diagram, you can see that the size of the area of the triangle OAB is between the areas of the two sectors OCB and OAD.

Area of sector OCB	$\leq$	Area of Triangle OAB	$\leq$	Area of sector OAD
$\frac{1}{2}(radius)^2\,\theta$	$\leq$	$\frac{1}{2}(base)(height)$	$\leq$	$\frac{1}{2}(radius)^2\,\theta$
$\frac{1}{2}\left(\cos^2\theta\right)\theta$	$\leq$	$\frac{1}{2}\cos\theta\sin\theta$	$\leq$	$\frac{1}{2}(1)^2\,\theta$

- divide by $\dfrac{1}{2}$

$$\left(\cos^2\theta\right)\theta \quad \leq \quad \cos\theta\sin\theta \quad \leq \quad \theta$$

- divide by $\theta\cos\theta$

$$\cos\theta \quad \leq \quad \frac{\sin\theta}{\theta} \quad \leq \quad \frac{1}{\cos\theta}$$

In order to evaluate our limit, we now need to look at what happens as $\theta \to 0$.

$$\lim_{\theta\to 0}\ \cos\theta \leq \frac{\sin\theta}{\theta} \leq \frac{1}{\cos\theta}$$

$$\lim_{\theta\to 0}\cos\theta \leq \lim_{\theta\to 0}\frac{\sin\theta}{\theta} \leq \lim_{\theta\to 0}\frac{1}{\cos\theta}$$

$$(1) \leq \lim_{\theta\to 0}\frac{\sin\theta}{\theta} \leq (1)$$

As we approach this limit from the left and from the right, it approaches the value of 1. We can conclude:

$$\lim_{\theta\to 0}\frac{\sin\theta}{\theta} = 1$$

This result allows us to evaluate trigonometric limits that can be manipulated mathematically into this form.

Example 1

Evaluate the following limit.

$$\lim_{x \to 0} \frac{\sin(2x)}{x}$$

Solution

Multiply top and bottom by 2:

$$= \lim_{x \to 0} \frac{\sin(2x)(2)}{x(2)}$$

Separate into 2 limits:

$$= \lim_{x \to 0} 2 \lim_{x \to 0} \frac{\sin 2x}{2x}$$

$$= (2)(1)$$

$$= 2$$

Example 2

Evaluate the following limit.

$$\lim_{\theta \to 0} \frac{\sin(3\theta)}{4\theta}$$

Solution

Multiply top and bottom by 3:

$$= \lim_{\theta \to 0} \frac{\sin(3\theta)(3)}{4\theta(3)}$$

Separate into 2 limits:

$$= \lim_{\theta \to 0} \frac{3}{4} \lim_{\theta \to 0} \frac{\sin 3\theta}{3\theta}$$

$$= \frac{3}{4}(1)$$

$$= \frac{3}{4}$$

Example 3

Evaluate the following limit.

$$\lim_{x \to 0} \frac{\sin^2(2x)}{x}$$

Solution

$$= \lim_{x \to 0} \frac{\sin(2x)\sin(2x)}{x}$$

Multiply top and bottom by $4x$:

$$= \lim_{x \to 0} \frac{\sin(2x)\sin(2x)(4x)}{x(4x)}$$

Separate into 3 limits:

$$= \lim_{x \to 0} \frac{\sin(2x)}{2x} \lim_{x \to 0} \frac{\sin(2x)}{2x} \lim_{x \to 0} 4x$$

$$= (1)(1)(4(0))$$

$$= 0$$

We can now develop the second important trigonometric limit. This limit is:

$$\lim_{\theta \to 0} \frac{\cos\theta - 1}{\theta}$$

To evaluate it, we must first multiply top and bottom by the conjugate of the numerator:

$$\lim_{\theta \to 0} \frac{\cos\theta - 1}{\theta}$$

$$\lim_{\theta \to 0} \frac{\cos\theta - 1}{\theta} \frac{(\cos\theta + 1)}{(\cos\theta + 1)}$$

$$= \lim_{\theta \to 0} \frac{\cos^2\theta - 1}{\theta(\cos\theta - 1)}$$

Substitute using the Pythagorean identity:

$$= \lim_{\theta \to 0} \frac{-\sin^2\theta}{\theta(\cos\theta - 1)}$$

Separate into 2 limits:

$$= -\lim_{\theta \to 0} \frac{\sin\theta}{\theta} \lim_{\theta \to 0} \frac{\sin\theta}{\cos\theta + 1}$$

$$= -(1)\left(\frac{\sin(0)}{\cos(0) + 1} \right)$$

$$= -\left(\frac{0}{2} \right)$$

$$= 0$$

The Pythagorean identity:

$$\sin^2 x + \cos^2 x = 1$$

$$\sin^2 x = 1 - \cos^2 x$$

So, we now know our second limit:

$$\lim_{\theta \to 0} \frac{\cos \theta - 1}{\theta} = 0$$

Example 4

Evaluate the following limit.

$$\lim_{x \to 0} \frac{2\cos x - 2}{5x}$$

Solution

$$= \lim_{x \to 0} \frac{2(\cos x - 1)}{5x}$$

Separate into 2 limits:

$$= \lim_{x \to 0} \frac{2}{5} \lim_{x \to 0} \frac{\cos x - 1}{x}$$

$$= \left(\frac{2}{5}\right)(0)$$

$$= 0$$

Example 5

Evaluate the following limit.

$$\lim_{x \to 0} \frac{x\cos(2x) - x}{8x}$$

Solution

$$= \lim_{x \to 0} \frac{x(\cos(2x) - 1)}{4(2x)}$$

Separate into 2 limits:

$$= \lim_{x - 0} \frac{x}{4} \lim_{x \to 0} \frac{\cos 2x - 1}{2x}$$

$$= (0)(0)$$

$$= 0$$

PRACTICE EXERCISE

1. Evaluate the following limits.

a) $\lim\limits_{x\to 0} \dfrac{\sin(4x)}{4x}$

b) $\lim\limits_{x\to 0} \dfrac{2-2\cos x}{x}$

c) $\lim\limits_{\theta\to 0} \dfrac{\sin(4\theta)}{\sin(3\theta)}$

d) $\lim\limits_{x\to 0} \dfrac{\sin(3x)}{3x^2+x}$

e) $\lim\limits_{\theta\to 0} \dfrac{1-\cos(2\theta)}{\theta}$

f) $\lim\limits_{x\to 0} \dfrac{5\tan x-5\sin x}{x\cos x}$

Lesson 2 DERIVATIVES OF TRIGONOMETRIC FUNCTIONS
Part 1: Sine and Cosine

NOTES

First Principles:

$$f'(x) = \lim_{h \to 0} \frac{f(x+h) - f(x)}{h}$$

When taking the derivatives of trigonometric functions, the Power, Product, Quotient, and Chain Rules are all used in the same way that they are used with polynomial functions. The only additional information that is required is the actual derivative of the individual trigonometry functions.

In this lesson, we will look at the derivatives of the sine and cosine functions. To do this, we need to use trigonometric limits and first principles.

Consider the function $f(x) = \sin x$.

To find the derivative, we apply first principles and get:

$$f'(x) = \lim_{h \to 0} \frac{\sin(x+h) - \sin(x)}{h}$$

We then use the sum identity to expand the limit:

Sum Identity:

$\sin(A+B) =$

$\sin A \cos B + \cos A \sin B$

$$f'(x) = \lim_{x \to 0} \frac{\sin x \cos h + \cos x \sin h - \sin x}{h}$$

$$f'(x) = \lim_{x \to 0} \frac{\sin x \cos h - \sin x + \cos x \sin h}{h}$$

$$f'(x) = \lim_{x \to 0} \sin x \left(\frac{\cos h - 1}{h} \right) + \lim_{x \to 0} \cos x \left(\frac{\sin h}{h} \right)$$

$$f'(x) = \sin x \lim_{x \to 0} \left(\frac{\cos h - 1}{h} \right) + \cos x \lim_{x \to 0} \left(\frac{\sin h}{h} \right)$$

From the limits that we developed in the last lesson, we know that

$$\lim_{x \to 0} \left(\frac{\cos h - 1}{h} \right) = 0 \text{ and } \lim_{x \to 0} \left(\frac{\sin h}{h} \right) = 1$$

and so,

$$f'(x) = \sin x (0) + \cos x (1)$$

$$f'(x) = \cos x$$

Our first trigonometric derivative is:

$$\frac{d}{dx}(\sin x) = \cos x$$

The Chain Rule states that $\frac{d}{dx}(\sin u) = \cos u \times \frac{du}{dx}$.

Complementary Angle Identities:

$$\cos x = \sin\left(\frac{\pi}{2} - x \right)$$

and

$$\sin x = \cos\left(\frac{\pi}{2} - x \right)$$

To find the derivative of the function $f(x) = \cos x$, we can use a complementary angle identity in combination with the derivative of $f(x) = \sin x$.

$$y = \cos x$$

$$y = \sin\left(\frac{\pi}{2} - x\right)$$

We now differentiate using the Chain Rule:

$$\frac{dy}{dx} = \cos\left(\frac{\pi}{2} - x\right)(-1)$$

$$\frac{dy}{dx} = -\cos\left(\frac{\pi}{2} - x\right)$$

$$\frac{dy}{dx} = -\sin x$$

This is the second trigonometric derivative:

$$\frac{d}{dx}(\cos x) = -\sin x$$

The Chain Rule states that $\dfrac{d}{dx}(\cos u) = \sin u \times \dfrac{du}{dx}$.

Example 1

Find the derivative of the function $y = 3\sin x$.

Solution

$$\frac{dy}{dx} = 3\cos x$$

The chain rule for the derivative of a sine and cosine function is:

$$\frac{d}{dx}(\sin u) = (\cos u)\left(\frac{du}{dx}\right)$$

$$\frac{d}{dx}(\cos u) = (-\sin u)\left(\frac{du}{dx}\right)$$

Example 2

Differentiate $y = -2\sin(5x)$.

Solution
Using the Chain Rule:
Let $u = 5x$

$$\frac{d}{dx}(-2\sin u) = (-2\cos u)\left(\frac{du}{dx}\right)$$

$$\frac{dy}{dx} = -2\cos(5x)(5)$$

$$\frac{dy}{dx} = -10\cos(5x)$$

You are now able to find the slopes of tangents to curves defined by trigonometric functions at given values of x.

Example 3

Differentiate $f(x) = 4\sin x$ and use the derivative to find the slope of the tangent to the function when $x = \dfrac{\pi}{6}$.

Solution

$f'(x) = 4\cos x$

Slope at $\dfrac{\pi}{6}$ is found by substituting into the derivative

$$f'\left(\frac{\pi}{6}\right) = -4\cos\left(\frac{\pi}{6}\right)$$

$$= -4\left(\frac{\sqrt{3}}{2}\right)$$

$$= -2\sqrt{3}$$

Example 4

Find the derivative of $f(x) = \sin x \cos x$ and find the slope of the tangent at $x = \dfrac{\pi}{3}$.

Solution

Using the Product Rule:

$g(x) = \sin x$

$g'(x) = \cos x$

$h(x) = \cos x$

$h'(x) = -\sin x$

$f'(x) = \sin x(-\sin x) + \cos x(\cos x)$

$f'(x) = -\sin^2 x + \cos^2 x$

Slope at $x = \dfrac{\pi}{3}$:

$$f'\left(\frac{\pi}{3}\right) = -\sin^2\frac{\pi}{3} + \cos^2\frac{\pi}{3}$$

$$f'\left(\frac{\pi}{3}\right) = -\left(\frac{\sqrt{3}}{2}\right)^2 + \left(\frac{1}{2}\right)^2$$

$$= -\frac{1}{2}$$

Example 5

Differentiate the function $f(x) = \dfrac{\sin(3x)}{\cos(x^2)}$.

Solution

Using the Quotient Rule:

$g(x) = \sin(3x)$

$g'(x) = \cos(3x)(3)$

$g'(x) = 3\cos(3x)$

$h(x) = \cos(x^2)$

$h'(x) = \sin(x^2)(2x)$

$h'(x) = 2x\sin(x^2)$

$f'(x) = \dfrac{\cos(x^2)(3\cos(3x)) - \sin(3x)\left[-2x(\sin x^2)\right]}{\cos^2(x^2)}$

$f'(x) = \dfrac{3\cos(x^2)\cos(3x) + 2x\sin(3x)(\sin(x^2))}{\cos^2(x^2)}$

Example 6

Differentiate the function $f(x) = 4\sin^2(x^2 + 2)$.

Solution

In order to correctly use the Chain Rule, it is helpful to first rewrite the function as:

$f(x) = 4\left(\sin(x^2 + 2)\right)^2$

Using the Chain Rule, we find:

$f'(x) = 2(4)\left(\sin(x^2 + 2)\right)\left(\cos(x^2 + 2)\right)(2x)$

$f'(x) = 16x\sin(x^2 + 2)\cos(x^2 + 2)$

Using the sine double angle identity, this can be simplified further:

$f'(x) = 8x\left(2\sin(x^2 + 2)\cos(x^2 + 2)\right)$

$f'(x) = 8x\sin(2(x^2 + 2))$

Example 7

Differentiate $f(x) = 3x^2 \cos^2(2x)$ using the Product and Chain Rules.

Solution

$$g(x) = 3x^2$$

$$g'(x) = 6x$$

$$h(x) = \left(\cos(2x)\right)^2$$

$$h'(x) = 2\cos(2x)\left(-\sin(2x)\right)(2)$$

$$h'(x) = -4\left(\cos(2x)\sin(2x)\right)$$

$$h'(x) = -2\sin(4x)$$

Now, substitute into the Product Rule:

$$f'(x) = 3x^2\left(-2\sin 4x\right) + \cos^2(2x)(6x)$$

$$f'(x) = -6x^2\sin(4x) + 6x\cos^2(2x)$$

Sine Double Angle
Identity:
$$\sin 2A = 2\sin A \cos A$$

PRACTICE EXERCISE

1. Differentiate each of the following trigonometric functions.

   a) $y = 4\cos x$

   b) $f(x) = 3\sin(5x^2)$

   c) $y = \dfrac{\sin^2 x}{\cos(2x)}$

   d) $f(x) = -2\cos^3(7x)$

   e) $y = x\sin x$

2. Find the slope of the tangent to the function $y = \cos^2(2x)$ at the point $x = \dfrac{\pi}{2}$.

Lesson 3 DERIVATIVES OF TRIGONOMETRIC FUNCTIONS
Part 2: Tangent, Cotangent, Secant, and Cosecant

The derivative of $f(x) = \tan x$ can be found by first rewriting the function in terms of sine and cosine.

$f(x) = \tan x$

$f(x) = \dfrac{\sin x}{\cos x}$, $x \neq \dfrac{\pi}{2} + n\pi, n \in I$

Now, using the Quotient Rule:

$g(x) = \sin x$

$g'(x) = \cos x$

$h(x) = \cos x$

$h'(x) = -\sin x$

$f'(x) = \dfrac{\cos x(\cos x) - \sin x(-\sin x)}{\cos^2(x)}$

$f'(x) = \dfrac{\cos^2 x + \sin^2 x}{\cos^2 x}$

Pythagorean Identity:

$\sin^2 A + \cos^2 A = 1$

Using the Pythagorean Identity:

$f'(x) = \dfrac{1}{\cos^2 x}$

$f'(x) = \sec^2 x$

$\dfrac{d}{dx}(\tan x) = \sec^2 x$, $x \neq \dfrac{\pi}{2} + n\pi$

$\dfrac{d}{dx}(\tan u) = \left(\sec^2 u\right)\left(\dfrac{du}{dx}\right)$

Similarly, we can find the derivative of cotangent:

$$y = \cot x$$

$$y = \frac{\cos x}{\sin x}, \ x \neq n\pi, n \in I$$

Pythagorean Identity:

$$\sin^2 A + \cos^2 A = 1$$

Pythagorean Identity:

$$\sin^2 A + \cos^2 A = 1$$

$$g(x) = \cos x$$

$$g'(x) = -\sin x$$

$$h(x) = \sin x$$

$$h'(x) = \cos x$$

$$y' = \frac{-\sin x \sin x - \cos x \cos x}{\sin^2 x}$$

$$y' = \frac{-\sin^2 x - \cos^2 x}{\sin^2 x}$$

$$y' = \frac{-1}{\sin^2 x}$$

$$y' = -\csc^2 x, x \neq n\pi, n \in I$$

$$\frac{d}{dx}(\cot x) = -\csc^2 x$$

$$\frac{d}{dx}(\cot u) = \left(-\csc^2 u\right)\left(\frac{du}{dx}\right)$$

The derivative of the secant and cosecant functions can also be found by first rewriting the functions in terms of sine and cosine.

$$f(x) = \sec x$$

$$f(x) = \frac{1}{\cos x}, \ x \neq \frac{\pi}{2} + n\pi, n \in I$$

$$f(x) = (\cos x)^{-1}$$

$$f'(x) = -(\cos x)^{-2}(-\sin x)$$

$$f'(x) = \frac{\sin x}{\cos^2 x}$$

$$f'(x) = \frac{\sin x}{\cos x \cos x}$$

$$f'(x) = \tan x \sec x, x \neq \frac{\pi}{2} + n\pi, n \in I$$

NOTES

For the cosecant function:

$$y = \csc x$$

$$y = \frac{1}{\sin x}, \quad x \neq n\pi, \ n \in I$$

$$y = (\sin x)^{-1}$$

$$y' = -1(\sin x)^{-2}(\cos x)$$

$$y' = \frac{-\cos x}{\sin^2 x}$$

$$y' = -\cot x \csc x, \quad x \neq n\pi, \ n \in I$$

The derivatives of all six of the trigonometric functions are listed below:

$$\frac{d}{dx}(\sin x) = \cos x \qquad\qquad \frac{d}{dx}(\csc x) = -\cot x \csc x$$

$$\frac{d}{dx}(\cos x) = -\sin x \qquad\qquad \frac{d}{dx}(\sec x) = \tan x \sec x$$

$$\frac{d}{dx}(\tan x) = \sec^2 x \qquad\qquad \frac{d}{dx}(\cot x) = -\csc^2 x$$

These derivatives, expressed using the chain rule, are:

$$\frac{d}{dx}(\sin u) = (\cos x)\left(\frac{du}{dx}\right) \qquad \frac{d}{dx}(\csc u) = (-\cot u)(\csc u)\left(\frac{du}{dx}\right)$$

$$\frac{d}{dx}(\cos u) = (-\sin u)\left(\frac{du}{dx}\right) \qquad \frac{d}{dx}(\sec u) = (\tan u)(\sec u)\left(\frac{du}{dx}\right)$$

$$\frac{d}{dx}(\tan u) = (\sec^2 u)\left(\frac{du}{dx}\right) \qquad \frac{d}{dx}(\cot u) = (-\csc^2 u)\left(\frac{du}{dx}\right)$$

Example 1

Find the derivative of the function $y = 2\sec(3x)$.

Solution

$$y' = 2\tan(3x)\sec(3x)3$$

$$y' = 6\tan(3x)\sec(3x)$$

156

Example 2

Find the derivative of $f(x) = \sin(2x)\tan x$.

Solution

Use the Product Rule and the Chain Rule:

$$g(x) = \sin(2x)$$

$$g'(x) = \cos(2x)(2)$$

$$g'(x) = 2\cos(2x)$$

$$h(x) = \tan x$$

$$h'(x) = \sec^2 x$$

$$f'(x) = \sin(2x)\left(\sec^2 x\right) + \tan x\left(2\cos(2x)\right)$$

$$f'(x) = \sin(2x)\sec^2 x + 2\tan x\cos(2x)$$

Example 3

Find the derivative of the following function:

$$f(x) = \frac{\cot(5x)}{\csc^2(4x)}$$

Solution

Use the Quotient Rule and the Chain Rule:

$$g(x) = \cot(5x)$$

$$g'(x) = -\csc^2(5x)(5)$$

$$g'x = -5\csc^2(5x)$$

$$h(x) = \csc^2(4x)$$

$$h'(x) = 2\left(\csc(4x)\right)\left(-\cot(4x)\csc(4x)\right)(4)$$

$$h'(x) = -8\csc^2(4x)\cot(4x)$$

$$f'(x) = \frac{\csc^2(4x)\left(-5\csc^2(5x)\right) - \cot(5x)\left(-8\csc^2(4x)\cot(4x)\right)}{\csc^2(4x)}$$

$$f'(x) = \frac{-5\csc^2(4x)\csc^2(5x) + 8\cot(5x)\left(\csc^2(4x)\cot(4x)\right)}{\csc^2(4x)}$$

PRACTICE EXERCISE

1. Differentiate the following functions.

   a) $f(x) = 2\cot(2x)$

   b) $y = \sin x \sec(2x)$

   c) $f(x) = \dfrac{\tan(5x-4)}{\cos x^3}$

   d) $y = \csc^3(3x^2)$

PRACTICE QUIZ

1. Evaluate the following limits.

a) $\displaystyle\lim_{x\to 0}\frac{\sin^2(4x)}{2x^2}$

b) $\displaystyle\lim_{x\to 0}\frac{\cos x - 1}{3x}$

2. Differentiate the following trigonometric functions.

a) $y = 4\sin^2 x$

b) $f(x) = \tan^3(5x)$

c) $y = x\cos(4x)$

d) $f(x) = \dfrac{\sec x}{\tan x}$

e) $y = \csc^3\left(x^2 - 1\right)$

f) $y \sin x = 3x - \cos y$

3. Find the slope of the tangent to the function $y = 4\tan^2 x$ at the point $x = \dfrac{\pi}{4}$.

Lesson 4 DERIVATIVES OF FUNCTIONS WITH NATURAL LOGARITHMS

A logarithmic function is the inverse of an exponential function. It is written as:

$$y = \log_b x \text{ where } x > 0, \ x \in \mathbb{R}, \ b > 0, \text{ and } b \neq 1$$

Until now, the logarithmic functions that you have seen have had rational bases. The most common of these bases has been base 10. You will now be introduced to a very important logarithm that has an irrational base: e.

The symbol e represents an irrational number that is defined by either one of the following limits:

$$\lim_{n \to 0} (1 + n)^{\frac{1}{n}} \quad \text{or} \quad \lim_{n \to \infty} \left(1 + \frac{1}{n}\right)^{n}$$

The value of either of these limits is 2.171 828 1....

Because of the importance of the base e logarithm, it is given its own name and a unique notation. Instead of writing it as $y = \log_e x$ as we do with any other base, this logarithm is written as $y = \ln x$. This logarithm is called the *natural logarithm*.

Natural logarithm:
$y = \ln x$

Although the natural logarithm looks different from other logarithms, it behaves in the same way; that is to say that all of the laws of logarithms apply to the natural logarithm.

Now that we have defined the natural logarithm, we will determine what its derivative is. For this, go back to first principles.

The derivative of the function $f(x) = \ln x$

$$f'(x) = \lim_{h \to 0} \frac{\ln(x+h) - \ln x}{h}$$

Using the laws of logarithms:

$$f'(x) = \lim_{h \to 0} \frac{\ln\left(\dfrac{x+h}{x}\right)}{h}$$

$$f'(x) = \lim_{h \to 0} \frac{\ln\left(1 + \dfrac{h}{x}\right)}{h}$$

$$f'(x) = \lim_{h \to 0} \frac{1}{h} \ln\left(1 + \frac{h}{x}\right)$$

Multiply the top and bottom by x:

$$f'(x) = \lim_{h \to 0} \left(\frac{x}{h}\right)\left(\frac{1}{x}\right)\ln\left(1 + \frac{h}{x}\right)$$

$$f'(x) = \frac{1}{x}\lim_{h \to 0} \frac{x}{h}\ln\left(1 + \frac{h}{x}\right)$$

Using the laws of logarithms:

$$f'(x) = \frac{1}{x}\lim_{h \to 0} \ln\left(1 + \frac{h}{x}\right)^{\frac{x}{h}}$$

Now, let $n = \dfrac{h}{x}$

as $h \to 0$, $n \to 0$

So, our derivative can be expressed as

$$f'(x) = \frac{1}{x}\lim_{n \to 0} \ln(1 + n)^{\frac{1}{n}}$$

From the definition at the start of the lesson, we know that

$$\lim_{n \to 0} \ln(1 + n)^{\frac{1}{n}} = e$$

So, we can make the substitution:

$$f'(x) = \frac{1}{x}\ln e$$

Since $\ln e = 1$, we are left with:

$$f'(x) = \frac{1}{x}$$

The chain Rule states that

$$\frac{d}{dx}(\ln x) = \frac{1}{x}$$

$$\frac{d}{dx}(\ln u) = \left(\frac{1}{u}\right)\left(\frac{du}{dx}\right)$$

This result will allow us to find the derivative of logarithmic functions and will help us in the future when we are finding derivatives of exponential functions.

As with all function types, we now need to use this new basic derivative in combination with the Power, Product, Quotient, and Chain rules.

Example 1

Find the derivative of $y = 2\ln x$.

Solution

$$\frac{dy}{dx} = 2\left(\frac{1}{x}\right)$$

$$\frac{dy}{dx} = \frac{2}{x}$$

Example 2

Differentiate $f(x) = 4\ln x$.

Solution

$$f'(x) = 4\left(\frac{1}{x}\right)$$

$$f'(x) = \left(\frac{4}{x}\right)$$

Example 3

Differentiate $y = 4x\ln x$.

Solution

Use the Product Rule:

$$g(x) = 4x$$

$$g'(x) = 4$$

$$h(x) = \ln x$$

$$h'(x) = \frac{1}{x}$$

$$\frac{dy}{dx} = 4x\left(\frac{1}{x}\right) + \ln x(4)$$

$$\frac{dy}{dx} = 4 + 4\ln x$$

Example 4

Differentiate $f(x) = \ln\left(x^2 - x\right)$ using the Chain Rule:

Solution

$$f'(x) = \left(\frac{1}{x^2 - x}\right)(2x - 1)$$

$$f'(x) = \frac{2x - 1}{x^2 - x}$$

Example 5

Differentiate $3y = \ln(xy)$ with respect to x.

Solution

It is necessary to use implicit differentiation and the Product Rule:

$$3\frac{dy}{dx} = \frac{1}{xy}\left(x\frac{dy}{dx} + y(1)\right)$$

$$3\frac{dy}{dx} = \frac{1}{y}\frac{dy}{dx} + \frac{1}{x}$$

$$3\frac{dy}{dx} - \frac{1}{y}\frac{dy}{dx} = \frac{1}{x}$$

$$\frac{dy}{dx}\left(3 - \frac{1}{y}\right) = \frac{1}{x}$$

$$\frac{dy}{dx} = \frac{1}{x\left(3 - \frac{1}{y}\right)}$$

$$\frac{dy}{dx} = \frac{1}{x\left(\frac{3y-1}{y}\right)}$$

$$\frac{dy}{dx} = \frac{y}{3xy - x}$$

PRACTICE EXERCISE

Differentiate each of the following functions.

1. $y = \ln x^2$

2. $f(x) = 3x^2 \ln(x+1)$

3. $y = \dfrac{\ln x}{x^3}$

4. $y = \ln(3x^2 - 1)$

5. $xy = \ln y$

Lesson 5 *DERIVATIVES OF EXPONENTIAL AND LOGARITHMIC FUNCTIONS*

NOTES

Now that you have learned about derivatives of logarithmic functions containing $\ln x$, you can now use this new understanding to find derivatives of exponential functions and logarithmic functions with bases other than e.

Recall than an exponential function is written in the form

$y = b^x$, where $b > 0$, $b \neq 1$ and $b \in \mathbb{R}$

To find the derivative of this function, first take the natural logarithm of both sides

$\ln y = \ln b^x$

Using the laws of logarithms, move the x out of the exponent.

$\ln y = x \ln b$

Now differentiate implicitly by using the method learned in the last lesson.

$\dfrac{1}{y}\dfrac{dy}{dx} = \ln b$

Isolating $\dfrac{dy}{dx}$ leaves

$\dfrac{dy}{dx} = y \ln b$

Since we know from the original question that $y = b^x$, we can substitute as follows

$\dfrac{dy}{dx} = b^x \ln b$

The Chain Rule states that

$\dfrac{d}{dx}\left(b^x\right) = \left(b^x\right)\left(\ln b\right)$

$\dfrac{d}{dx}\left(b^u\right) = \left(b^u\right)\left(\ln b\right)\left(\dfrac{du}{dx}\right)$

Example 1

Find the derivative of $y = 6^x$.

Solution

Using the form explained above, we get

$\dfrac{dy}{dx} = 6^x \ln 6$

Some questions require the Product Rule.

Example 2

Differentiate the function $y = 5x \times 2^x$.

Solution

$g(x) = 5x$

$g'(x) = 5$

$h(x) = 2^x$

$h'(x) = 2^x \ln x$

$$\frac{dy}{dx} = 5x\left(2^x \ln 2\right) + 2^x(5)$$

Factor out the 5 and 2^x

$$\frac{dy}{dx} = 5\left(2^x\right)(x \ln 2 + 1)$$

Example 3

Differentiate $f(x) = \dfrac{3x^2}{4^x}$.

Solution

$g(x) = 3x^2$

$g'(x) = 6x$

$h(x) = 4^x$

$h'(x) = 4^x \ln 4$

$$f'(x) = \frac{4^x(6x) - 3x^2\left(4^x \ln 4\right)}{\left(4^x\right)^2}$$

$$f'(x) = \frac{3x4^x(2 - x \ln 4)}{\left(4^x\right)^2}$$

$$f'(x) = \frac{3x(2 - x \ln 4)}{4^x}$$

It is important to note that since b is a constant, $\ln b$ is also a constant, and it must be treated this way when differentiating.

$\log(MN) = \log M + \log N$

It is important to remember that **ln3** is a constant.

Example 4

Differentiate $y = 2\left(3^{6x^2-x}\right)$.

Solution

Usin the chain rule:

$$\frac{dy}{dx} = 2\left(3^{6x^2-x}\right)(\ln 3)(12x-1)$$

THE SPECIAL CASE OF THE FUNCTION $y = e^x$

Method 1

The derivative of this function is a special case of the derivative of the general exponential function, $y = b^x$.

Another strategy for finding the derivative of $y = e^x$ involves taking the natural logarithm of each side:

$\ln y = \ln e^x$

$\ln y = x \ln e$

Differentiate:

$\frac{1}{y}\frac{dy}{dx} = \ln e$

$\frac{dy}{dx} = y \ln e$

Substitute:

$\frac{dy}{dx} = e^x \ln e$

Since $\ln e = 1$,

$\frac{dy}{dx} = e^x$

Method 2

$$\frac{d}{dx}\left(b^x\right) = \left(b^x\right)\left(\ln b\right)$$

Replacing b with e:

$$\frac{d}{dx}\left(e^x\right) = \left(e^x\right)\left(\ln e\right)$$

Since $\ln e = 1$

$$\frac{d}{dx}\left(e^x\right) = e^x$$

The result is that we can see that e^x is its own derivative! If the exponent of the original function contains an expression more complex than x, we must use the Chain Rule when differentiating.

The Chain Rule states that $\dfrac{d}{dx}\left(e^u\right) = e^4 \times \dfrac{d}{dx}$

Example 5

Differentiate the function $y = e^{2x}$.

Solution

$$y' = e^{2x}\left(2\right)$$

Notice the use of the Chain Rule to differentiate $2x$ in order to obtain the 2 in brackets.

Example 6

Differentiate the function $y = e^{6x^3 - 7x}$

Solution

$$y' = e^{6x^3 - 7x}\left(18x^2 - 7\right)$$

Notice that $18x^2 - 7$ is the derivative of the exponent, $6x^3 - 7x$

Example 7

Find the derivative of the function $y = 5\left(2^{4x^3 - x^2}\right)$.

Solution

Method 1:

$\ln y = \ln 5 \ln 2^{4x^3 - x^2}$

$\ln y = \ln 5 + \left(4x^3 - x^2\right)\ln 2$

$\ln y = \ln 5 + 4x^3 \ln 2 - x^2 \ln 2$

Differentiate:

$\dfrac{1}{y}\dfrac{dy}{dx} = 0 + 12x^2 \ln 2 - 2x \ln 2$

$\dfrac{dy}{dx} = y\left(12x^2 \ln 2 - 2x \ln 2\right)$

$\dfrac{dy}{dx} = 5\left(2^{4x^3 - x^2}\right)(2x \ln 2)(6x - 1)$

Method 2:

Since $\dfrac{d}{dx}\left(b^u\right) = \left(b^u\right)(\ln b)\left(\dfrac{du}{dx}\right)$

$\dfrac{d}{dx}\left[5\left(2^{4x^3 - x^2}\right)\right] = 5\left(2^{4x^3 - x^2}\right)(\ln 2)\left(12x^2 - 2x\right)$

$= 5\left(2^{4x^3 - x^2}\right)(\ln 2)(2x)(6x - 1)$

FINDING DERIVATIVES OF LOGARITHMIC FUNCTIONS WITH BASES OTHER THAN e

A logarithm with any base that is written in the form $y = \log_b x$ can be rewritten in exponential form as $b^y = x$ and differentiated using the procedure outlined above for exponential functions.

$b^y = x$

$\ln b^y = \ln x$

$y \ln b = \ln x$

Differentiate:

$\ln b \dfrac{dy}{dx} = \dfrac{1}{x}$

$\dfrac{dy}{dx} = \dfrac{1}{x \ln b}$

$x\left(\log_b x\right) = \dfrac{1}{x \ln b}$

$\dfrac{d}{dx}\left(\log_b u\right) = \left(\dfrac{1}{u \ln b}\right)\left(\dfrac{du}{dx}\right)$

170

Example 8

Differentiate $y = \log_2(2x - 7)$.

Solution

Method 1:

$$2^y = 2x - 7$$

$$\ln 2^y = \ln(2x - 7)$$

$$y\ln 2 = \ln(2x - 7)$$

$$\ln 2 \frac{dy}{dx} = \frac{1}{2x - 7}(2)$$

$$\frac{dy}{dx} = \frac{2}{(2x - 7)\ln 2}$$

Method 2:

Since $\dfrac{d}{dx}(\log_b u) = \left(\dfrac{1}{u\ln b}\right)\left(\dfrac{du}{dx}\right)$,

$$\frac{dy}{dx} = \left(\frac{1}{(2x - 7)(\ln 2)}\right)(2)$$

$$= \frac{2}{(2x - 7)(\ln 2)}$$

Now that the rules for differentiating trigonometric, logarithmic, and exponential functions are understood, as well as the Power, Product, Quotient, and Chain rules, you can differentiate questions that contain various combinations of these rules and procedures.

Example 9

Differentiate $f(x) = 2x\ln(\sin x)$.

Solution

Use both Product and Chain rules:

$$g(x) = 2x$$

$$g'(x) = 2$$

$$h(x) = \ln(\sin x)$$

$$h'(x) = \frac{1}{\sin x}\cos x$$

$$h'(x) = \cot x$$

$$f'(x) = 2x\cot x + \ln(\sin x)(2)$$

$$f'(x) = 2(x\cot x + \ln(\sin x))$$

We use the identity:
$$\cot x = \frac{\cos x}{\sin x}$$

PRACTICE EXERCISE

1. Differentiate the following exponential functions.

   a) $y = 2^x$

   b) $y = 4\left(5^{x^2}\right)$

   c) $y = 7^{x^3 - x}$

2. Find the derivatives of the following logarithmic functions.

   a) $y = \log_7 x$

   b) $y = 2\log_3(x - 6)$

3. Using the methods used in this chapter combined with the rules for differentiating, differentiate the following complex functions.

a) $f(x) = 2^{\sin x}$

b) $y = 4x^2 \ln x$

c) $f(x) = 2^x x^2$

d) $y = x \ln \cos(2x)^2$

REVIEW SUMMARY

In this unit, you have learned how to . . .

- evaluate limits of trigonometric functions using

$$\lim_{\theta \to 0} \frac{\sin \theta}{\theta} = 1 \quad \text{and} \quad \lim_{\theta \to 0} \frac{\cos \theta - 1}{\theta} = 0$$

- differentiate trigonometric functions applying the following derivatives:

$$\frac{d}{dx}(\sin x) = \cos x \qquad\qquad \frac{d}{dx}(\csc x) = -\cot x \csc x$$

$$\frac{d}{dx}(\cos x) = -\sin x \qquad\qquad \frac{d}{dx}(\sec x) = \tan x \sec x$$

$$\frac{d}{dx}(\tan x) = \sec^2 x \qquad\qquad \frac{d}{dx}(\cot x) = -\csc^2 x$$

- differentiate functions containing natural logarithms using

$$\frac{d}{dx}(\ln x) = \frac{1}{x}$$

- differentiate logarithmic functions with any base by using exponential functions and natural logarithms

$$\frac{d}{dx}(\log_b x) = \frac{1}{x \ln b}$$

- differentiate exponential functions using

$$\frac{d}{dx}\left(b^x\right) = \left(b^x\right)(\ln b)$$

- differentiate exponential functions involving base e using

$$\frac{d}{dx}\left(e^x\right) = e^x$$

- differentiate complex functions that combine trigonometric, logarithmic, and exponential functions

$$\frac{d}{dx}(\sin u) = (\cos x)\left(\frac{du}{dx}\right) \qquad \frac{d}{dx}(\cos u) = (-\sin u)\left(\frac{du}{dx}\right) \qquad \frac{d}{dx}(\tan u) = \left(\sec^2 u\right)\left(\frac{du}{dx}\right)$$

$$\frac{d}{dx}(\csc u) = (-\cot u)(\csc u)\left(\frac{du}{dx}\right) \qquad \frac{d}{dx}(\sec u) = (\tan u)(\sec u)\left(\frac{du}{dx}\right) \qquad \frac{d}{dx}(\cot u) = \left(-\csc^2 u\right)\left(\frac{du}{dx}\right)$$

$$\frac{d}{dx}(\ln u) = \left(\frac{1}{u}\right)\left(\frac{du}{dx}\right) \qquad\qquad \frac{d}{d_x}(\log_b u) = \left(\frac{1}{u \ln b}\right)\left(\frac{du}{dx}\right)$$

$$\frac{d}{dx}\left(e^u\right) = \left(e^u\right)\left(\frac{du}{dx}\right) \qquad\qquad \frac{d}{dx}\left(b^u\right) = \left(b^u\right)(\ln b)\left(\frac{du}{dx}\right)$$

PRACTICE TEST

1. Evaluate the following limit.

$$\lim_{x \to 0} \frac{5\sin 5x}{2x}$$

2. Differentiate the following trigonometric functions.

   a) $y = \csc x$

   b) $y = \sin(3x)\cos x^2$

   c) $y = 2\tan^2(2x - 5)$

   d) $f(x) = 4x^3 \sec(7x)$

3. Find the slope of the tangent to the curve $f(x) = 3\cos^2(2x)$, when $x = \dfrac{\pi}{3}$.

4. Differentiate the following logarithmic and exponential functions.

a) $f(x) = 5\ln 3x$

b) $y = 5^{2x^2}(4x)$

c) $y = \log_2(3x - 9)$

d) $y = 2^{xy}$

5. Find the derivative of the following functions.

a) $f(x) = \sin^2\left(\ln(2x)\right)$

b) $y = 5^{x\sin x}$

NOTES

EXTREME VALUES AND CURVE SKETCHING

When you are finished this unit, you should be able to . . .

- determine x and y intercepts
- determine what type of symmetry a function has
- determine the intervals of increase and decrease for a function
- find the maximum and minimum values of a function
- determine the concavity intervals and inflections points of a function
- relate the graph of a function to the graph of its derivatives
- find the equations of vertical, horizontal, and oblique asymptotes
- solve problems involving extreme

PREREQUISITE SKILLS AND KNOWLEDGE

Prior to beginning this unit, you should be able to. . .

- use interval notation
- solve quadratic equations
- solve inequalities
- divide polynomials by monomials or binomials
- determine first and second derivatives
- evaluate limits

Lesson 1 **INTERCEPTS AND ZEROS**

Throughout this unit, we will be looking at various descriptive elements of functions that enable us to get a good visual understanding of a function.

You should be very familiar with the intercepts or zeros of a function; however, we will re-examine them first.

Y-INTERCEPT

The y-intercept of a function refers to the point where the graph of a function intersects the y-axis. By definition, this occurs when $x = 0$, producing a point of the form $(0, y)$.

To find a y-intercept, we substitute 0 into the function in place of x and evaluate y.

Example 1

Find the y-intercept of the function $y = 4x^2 - 2x - 5$.

Solution
Substitute 0 for x:

$$y = 4(0)^2 - 2(0) - 5$$
$$= -5$$

The y-intercept $= -5$

Using this y-intercept, a point on the graph of the function is $(0, -5)$.

Example 2

Find the y-intercept of the function $y = \dfrac{3x^2 - 1}{5x + 7}$.

Solution
Substitute 0 for x:

$$y = \frac{3(0)^2 - 1}{5(0) + 7}$$
$$= -\frac{1}{7}$$

The y-intercept $= -\dfrac{1}{7}$

X-INTERCEPTS

The *x*-intercepts of a graph correspond to the zeros of the function. Unlike the *y*-intercept, a function can have more than one *x*-intercept. A polynomial function of degree *n* can have up to *n x*-intercepts.

To find the *x*-intercepts, we substitute 0 in for *y*.

Example 1

Find the *x*-intercepts for the function $y = x^2 - 2x - 15$.

Solution

$0 = x^2 - 2x - 15$

$\quad = (x - 5)(x + 3)$

$x = 5, \ x = -3$

The *x*-intercepts are at 5 and -3.

Example 2

Find the *x*-intercepts for the function $y = 2x^2 + 5x - 1$.

Solution

$0 = 2x^2 + 5x - 1$

Since the function does not factor, use the quadratic formula.

$x = \dfrac{-b \pm \sqrt{b^2 - 4ac}}{2a}$

$\quad = \dfrac{-5 \pm \sqrt{(-5)^2 - 4(2)(-1)}}{2(2)}$

$\quad = \dfrac{-5 \pm \sqrt{33}}{4}$

The *x*-intercepts are at $\dfrac{-5 + \sqrt{33}}{4}$ and $\dfrac{-5 - \sqrt{33}}{4}$.

The quadratic formula

$x = \dfrac{-b \pm \sqrt{b^2 - 4ac}}{2a}$

can be used to find the roots of quadratic equations in the form $ax^2 + bx + c = 0$.

Example 3

Find the *x* and *y*-intercepts for the function $y = 2x^2 - 11x + 5$.

Solution

y-intercept

$y = 2(0)^2 - 11(0) + 5$

$\quad = 5$

x-intercepts

$$0 = 2x^2 - 11x + 5$$

$$0 = (2x - 1)(x - 5)$$

$$x = \frac{1}{2} \text{ and } x = 5$$

There is a y-intercept at 5, and x-intercepts at $\frac{1}{2}$ and 5.

Example 4

Find the x and y-intercepts for the function $y = 2\cos x$, where $-\pi \le x \le \pi$.

Solution

y-intercept

$$y = 2\cos(0)$$

$$y = 2(1)$$

$$y = 2$$

x-intercepts

$$0 = 2\cos x$$

$$0 = \cos x$$

$$x = \frac{\pi}{2} \text{ and } x = -\frac{\pi}{2}$$

Example 5

Find the x and y-intercepts for the function $y = 2\cos x - 1$, where $0 \le x \le 2\pi$.

Solution

y-intercept

$$y = 2\cos(0) - 1$$

$$y = 1$$

x-intercept

$$0 = 2\cos x - 1$$

$$\frac{1}{2} = \cos x$$

$$x = \frac{\pi}{3}, x = \frac{5\pi}{3}$$

There is a y-intercept at 1, and x-intercepts at $\frac{\pi}{3}$ and $\frac{5\pi}{3}$.

PRACTICE EXERCISE

1. Find the x- and y-intercepts of the following functions.

   a) $y = 2x - 6$

   b) $y = x^2 - x$

   c) $y = 3x^2 + 10x - 8$

   d) $y = 3\sin x$, where $0 \le x \le \pi$

   e) $y = \dfrac{4x^2 - x}{3x - 7}$

   f) $y = 2x^2 - 3x - 7$

Lesson 2 *SYMMETRY OF FUNCTIONS*

When sketching graphs of functions, it is very useful to know about a curve's symmetry. For example, if a curve is symmetric about the *y*-axis, you really only need to find the various aspects of the graph for the interval $(0, \infty)$ or even $(-\infty, 0)$, since the rest of the graph will be a reflection in the *y*-axis.

In the graph of $f(x) = x^4 - 18x^2 - 19$,

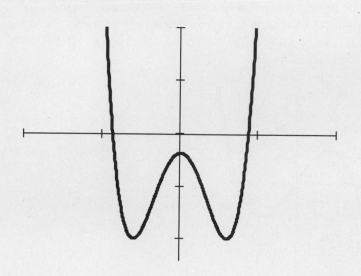

all of the features of the graph that are to the left of the *y*-axis are duplicated in the reflection on the right. Functions that are symmetric about the *y*-axis are called even functions.

To determine whether or not a function, $y = f(x)$, is even, you must find $y = f(-x)$. If $f(x) = f(-x)$, then the function is even.

Example 1

Determine if the function $f(x) = 2x^2 - 5$ is even.

Solution

Find $f(-x)$:

$$f(-x) = 2(-x)^2 - 5$$
$$= 2x^2 - 5$$

Since this is equal to the original function, $f(x) = 2x^2 - 5$, the function is even and has symmetry about the *y*-axis.

Example 2

Is the function $f(x) = x^3 - 2x + 4$ symmetric about the y-axis?

Solution

Find $f(-x)$:

$$f(-x) = (-x)^3 - 2(-x) + 4$$
$$= -x^3 + 2x + 4$$

Since $f(-x) \neq f(x)$, the function is not symmetric about the y-axis.

The other type of symmetry that you should know about is symmetry about the origin. If a function has symmetry about the origin, the graph of the function can be rotated 180° about the origin and it will still look identical to the original graph.

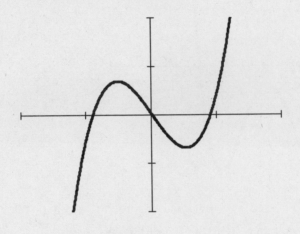

Symmetry about the origin can be seen in the graph $y = x^3 - 20x$ above.

Functions with this type of symmetry are called odd functions. To determine if a function is odd, you must find both $f(-x)$ and $-f(x)$. If $f(-x) = -f(x)$, then the function is odd.

Example 3

Is the function $f(x) = x^4 - 2x$ odd?

Solution

First, find $f(-x)$ and $-f(x)$:

$$f(-x) = (-x)^4 - 2(-x)$$
$$= x^4 + 2x$$
$$-f(x) = -\left[x^4 - 2x\right]$$
$$= -x^4 + 2x$$

Since $f(-x) \neq -f(x)$, this function is *not* odd and does *not* have symmetry about the origin.

Example 4

Is the following function odd?

$$f(x) = \cos(x) - \sin(x)$$

Solution

Find $f(-x)$:

$$f(-x) = \cos(-x) - \sin(-x)$$
$$= \cos(x) - \sin(-x)$$

Find $-f(x)$:

$$-f(x) = -\cos(x) + \sin(x)$$

Since $f(-x) \neq -f(x)$, the function is not odd.

Using identities,
$\cos(x) = \cos(-x)$

Example 5

Determine if the function $f(x) = \dfrac{1}{2}x^5$ is even, odd, or neither.

Solution

Find $f(-x)$:

$$f(-x) = \frac{1}{2}(-x)^5$$
$$= -\frac{1}{2}x^5$$

Find $-f(x)$:

$$-f(x) = -\left[\frac{1}{2}x^5\right]$$
$$= -\frac{1}{2}x^5$$

Since $f(x) \neq f(-x)$, the function is not even and, therefore, is not symmetric about the y-axis. However, since $f(-x) = -f(x)$, the function is odd and, therefore, is symmetric about the origin.

EXTREME VALUES AND CURVE SKETCHING—Lesson 2

PRACTICE EXERCISE

1. Determine whether or not the following functions are even.

   a) $y = 4x^2 - 3$

   b) $f(x) = 2x^3 + 3x - 1$

   c) $y = 4x^4 + 2x^2 - 1$

   d) $y = 2\cos x + 3$

2. Determine whether or not the following functions are odd.

   a) $y = 3x^3$

   b) $y = 4x^2 - x$

CASTLE ROCK RESEARCH   188   Copyright Protected

c) $f(x) = 2x^3 - 5x$

d) $y = \dfrac{1}{2}\sin(2x)$

3. Determine what type of symmetry if any, each of the following functions has.

a) $y = 3x^2 - 5$

b) $y = 2x^3 - 7x$

c) $y = x^3 - x^2$

d) $y = 4\sin x \cos x$

Lesson 3 INTERVALS OF INCREASE AND DECREASE AND MAXIMUM AND MINIMUM VALUES

NOTES

Maximum and minimum values refer to y-values.

A local maximum occurs at a point on a function if the value of the function at that point is larger than the values of the function at all points in the near vicinity of that point.

A local minimum occurs at a point on a function if the value of the function at that point is smaller than the values of the function at all points in the near vicinity of that point.

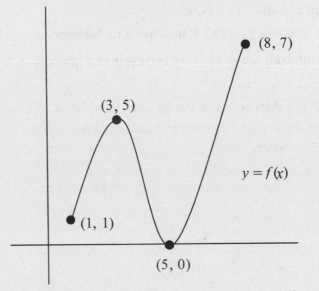

The intervals refer to x-values.

The graph of $f(x)$ is increasing on the intervals (1, 3) and (5, 8) and decreasing on (3, 5). Since $f(x)$ is neither increasing nor decreasing when $x = 3$ and when $x = 5$, 3, and 5 are critical numbers and therefore, are potential maximum or minimum points.

Since $f(x)$ is increasing before $x = 3$ and decreasing after 3, we conclude that a local maximum of 5 occurs at $x = 3$.

Since $f(x)$ is decreasing before $x = 5$ and increasing after $x = 5$, we conclude that a local minimum of 0 occurs at $x = 5$.

Since the function's greatest value is 7 and occurs at the point (8, 7), an absolute maximum of 7 occurs at $x = 8$. Since the function's least value is 0, an absolute minimum of 0 occurs at $x = 5$.

The range value of 7 is both a local maximum and an absolute maximum of this function.

The range value of 0 is both a local minimum and an absolute minimum of this function.

The range value of 1 is a local minimum but not an absolute minimum of this function.

The endpoints of a function must be considered when dealing with a restricted domain.

The derivative of a function represents the instantaneous rate of change of that function.

The sign of the derivative of a function indicates whether the function is increasing, decreasing, or neither, as follows.

When $f'(x) > 0$ in an interval, $y = f(x)$ is increasing in that interval.

When $f'(x) < 0$ in an interval, $y = f(x)$ is decreasing in that interval.

When $f'(x) = 0$ or $f'(x)$ does not exist, the function is neither increasing nor decreasing and *may* have a local extreme (maximum or minimum) value at that point. Any x where $f'(x) = 0$ or $f'(x)$ does not exist is called a critical number. We can combine this information to allow us to find a function's intervals of increase and decrease and local extrema.

Example 1

Find the intervals of increase and decrease and the local maximum and minimum values for $f(x) = x^3 - 3x^2 - 24x + 2$.

Solution

First, find the derivative:

$f'(x) = 3x^2 - 6x - 24$

Next, find critical numbers. Since there are no values of x for which the derivative does not exist, we only need to find values for which $f'(x) = 0$.

$0 = 3x^2 - 6x - 24$

$0 = 3(x - 4)(x + 2)$

$x = 4$ and $x = -2$

These are the critical numbers and may be local extrema. We now need to check the intervals of increase and decrease to see if they are local extrema.

Since the critical numbers $x = 4$ and $x = -2$ are the only places where the function can change from increasing to decreasing, we need to check the intervals before and after these critical numbers.

NOTES

This is illustrated on the number line:

interval 1	–2	interval 2	4	interval 3
(–?, –2)		(–2, 4)		(4, ?)

When checking the intervals using the derivative, we are only interested in seeing if the derivative is positive or negative. The actual value is not significant.

To test, we can choose any x value in the interval. It is most convenient to choose numbers that make calculations easy.

For the interval $(-\infty, -2)$, choose $x = -3$.

$$f'(-3) = 3\big((-3) - 4\big)\big((-3) + 2\big)$$

Consider only the sign,

$$f'(-3) = +(-)(-)$$
$$= +$$

So, the function is increasing on $(-\infty, -2)$.

For the interval $(-2, 4)$, choose $x = 0$.

$$f'(0) = 3\big((0) - 4\big)\big((0) + 2\big)$$
$$= (+)(-)(+)$$
$$= -$$

So, the function is decreasing on $(-2, 4)$.

For the interval $(4, \infty)$, choose $x = 5$.

$$f'(5) = 3\big((5) - 4\big)\big((5) + 2\big)$$
$$= (+)(+)(+)$$
$$= +$$

So, the function is increasing on $(4, \infty)$.

On the number line:

increasing	–2	decreasing	4	increasing
+		?		+

Since the function is increasing before $x = -2$ and decreasing after, we know that a local maximum exists at $x = -2$. The value of this maximum can be found by substituting this value into the original function:

$$f(-2) = (-2)^3 - 3(-2)^2 - 24(-2) + 2$$
$$= -8 - 12 + 48 + 2$$
$$= 30$$

Since the function is decreasing before $x = 4$ and increasing after, we know that a local minimum exists at $x = 4$. We can now find the value of this local minimum through substitution:

$$f(4) = (4)^3 - 3(4)^2 - 24(4) + 2$$
$$= 64 - 48 - 96 + 2$$
$$= -78$$

To summarize:

The function is increasing on $(-\infty, -2) \cup (4, \infty)$ and decreasing on $(-2, 4)$.

The local maximum value at $x = -2$ is 30.

The local minimum value at $x = 4$ is -78.

A summary of steps to find intervals of increase and decrease and maximum and minimum values of a function, $f(x)$, are as follows.

1. Differentiate the function.

2. Find critical values where $f'(x) = 0$ or $f'(x)$ is undefined.

3. Select values in all intervals before and after the critical values to see where the function is increasing or decreasing.

4. Where intervals of increase or decrease indicate extrema, substitute the critical numbers back into the original function to find the extreme value (maximum or minimum).

Example 2

Find the intervals of increase and decrease, and local extrema for the function $f(x) = 2x^3 + \dfrac{x^2}{2} - 2x + 7$.

Solution

$$f'(x) = 6x^2 + x - 2$$
$$0 = 6x^2 + x - 2$$
$$0 = (3x + 2)(2x - 1)$$

The function is defined for all $x \in \mathbb{R}$.

The critical values are $x = -\dfrac{2}{3}$ and $x = \dfrac{1}{2}$.

Number line:

$$\left(-\infty, \frac{1}{2}\right) \quad -\frac{2}{3} \quad\quad \left(-\frac{2}{3}, \frac{1}{2}\right) \quad \frac{1}{2} \quad \left(\frac{1}{2}, \infty\right)$$

NOTES

Since we are only concerned with the sign of the derivative, it is probably most efficient to substitute into the factored form of the derivative.

Select values in each interval to test.

Test values: $-1, 0, 1$

$$f'(-1) = (3(-1)+2)(2(-1)-1)$$
$$= (-)(-)$$
$$= +$$
$$f'(0) = (3(0)+2)(2(0)-1)$$
$$= (+)(-)$$
$$= -$$
$$f'(1) = (3(1)+2)(2(1)-1)$$
$$= (+)(+)$$
$$= +$$

On the number line:

| increasing + | $-\frac{2}{3}$ | decreasing ? | $\frac{1}{2}$ | increasing + |

The function is increasing on $\left(-\infty, -\frac{2}{3}\right) \cup \left(\frac{1}{2}, \infty\right)$.

The function is decreasing on $\left(-\frac{2}{3}, \frac{1}{2}\right)$.

Calculate the local maximum value at $-\frac{2}{3}$:

$$f\left(-\frac{2}{3}\right) = 2\left(-\frac{2}{3}\right)^3 + \frac{\left(-\frac{2}{3}\right)^2}{2} - 2\left(-\frac{2}{3}\right) + 7$$
$$= \frac{215}{27}$$

Calculate the local minimum values at $\frac{1}{2}$:

$$f\left(\frac{1}{2}\right) = 2\left(\frac{1}{2}\right)^3 + \frac{\left(\frac{1}{2}\right)^2}{2} - 2\left(\frac{1}{2}\right) + 7$$
$$= \frac{51}{8}$$

The same procedure can be used to find local extrema on a trigonometric function.

Example 3

Find intervals of increase and decrease, and local extrema for the function:

$f(x) = \sin^2(x)$ where $0 < x \le 2\pi$.

Solution

$$f'(x) = 2\sin(x)\cos(x)$$
$$0 = 2\sin(x)\cos(x)$$

Critical numbers are: $x = \pi, 2\pi$ and $x = \dfrac{\pi}{2}, \dfrac{3\pi}{2}$

On the number line:

$$\left(0, \frac{\pi}{2}\right) \quad \frac{\pi}{2} \quad \left(\frac{\pi}{2}, \pi\right) \quad \pi \quad \left(\pi, \frac{3\pi}{2}\right) \quad \frac{3\pi}{2} \quad \left(\frac{3\pi}{2}, 2\pi\right) \quad 2\pi$$

Test values: $\dfrac{\pi}{4}, \dfrac{3\pi}{4}, \dfrac{5\pi}{4}, \dfrac{7\pi}{4}$

$f'\left(\dfrac{\pi}{4}\right)$ is positive

$f'\left(\dfrac{3\pi}{4}\right)$ is negative

$f'\left(\dfrac{5\pi}{4}\right)$ is positive

$f'\left(\dfrac{7\pi}{4}\right)$ is negative

On the number line:

$$+ \quad \frac{\pi}{2} \quad ? \quad \pi \quad + \quad \frac{3\pi}{2} \quad ? \quad 2\pi$$

local max at $\dfrac{\pi}{2}$: $\quad f\left(\dfrac{\pi}{2}\right) = \sin^2\left(\dfrac{\pi}{2}\right)$

$$= 1$$

local min at π: $\quad f(\pi) = \sin^2(\pi)$

$$= 0$$

local max at $\dfrac{3\pi}{2}$: $\quad f\left(\dfrac{3\pi}{2}\right) = \sin^2\left(\dfrac{3\pi}{2}\right)$

$$= 1$$

local min at 2π: $\quad f(2\pi) = \sin^2(2\pi)$

$$= 0$$

The function is increasing at $\left(0, \dfrac{\pi}{2}\right) \cup \left(\pi, \dfrac{3\pi}{2}\right)$ and

the function is decreasing at $\left(\dfrac{\pi}{2}, \pi\right) \cup \left(\dfrac{3\pi}{2}, 2\pi\right)$.

Example 4

A local maximum or minimum can exist at a domain value for which the first derivative is undefined.

If the sign of the first derivative changes from *positive to negative* across the undefined domain value, and the original function does exist at this domain value, the original function will have a local maximum at this domain value. The sign change indicates that the original function was increasing before and decreasing after the domain value.

If the sign of the first derivative changes from *negative to positive* across the undefined domain value, and the original function does exist at this domain value, the original function will have a local minimum at this domain value. The sign change indicates that the original function was decreasing before and increasing after the domain value.

Study the function $y = x^{\frac{2}{3}}$.

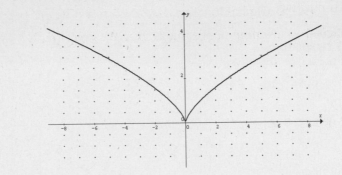

This function obviously has a local minimum at the point $(0,0)$.

Study the first derivative of this function.

$$f(x) = x^{\frac{2}{3}}$$

$$f'(x) = \frac{2}{3}x^{-\frac{1}{3}}$$

$$f'(x) = \frac{2}{3\sqrt[3]{x}}$$

$f'(0)$ is not defined. However, the original function is defined at $x = 0$

$f'(x) < 0$ in the interval $(-\infty, 0)$. This indicates that the original function is decreasing in this interval.

$f'(x) > 0$ in the interval $(0, \infty)$. This indicates that the original function is increasing in this interval.

$$y = f'(x) = \frac{2}{3\sqrt[3]{x}}$$

Since the sign of the first derivative changed from *negative to positive* across $x = 0$, and the original function does exist at $x = 0$, the original function reached a local minimum value of 0 at the point $(0,0)$

PRACTICE EXERCISE

1. For each of the following functions, state the intervals of increase and decrease, and determine the local maximum and minimum values.

a) $y = 2x^2 - 16x + 39$

b) $f(x) = \dfrac{2}{x-3}$

c) $f(x) = 3\sin(x) + 2$, where $0 \le x \le 2\pi$

d) $y = 2\cos^2(2x)$, where $0 < x < \dfrac{3\pi}{4}$

Lesson 4 CONCAVITY AND POINTS OF INFLECTION

In the same way that the first derivative tells us about a function increasing or decreasing, the second derivative tells us about the derivative of the function increasing or decreasing, which then tells us about the change in a function's *rate* of increase or decrease. This change is identified as concavity.

$(2, \infty)$ A function is concave upward in an interval if its rate of change (first derivative) is increasing in that interval. We can also think of this in terms of the slopes of the tangents as we move along the function. Examine the diagrams below.

        concave down   concave up

If the slopes of the tangents to a curve are decreasing, the rate of change is decreasing, and the function is concave down. If the slopes of the tangents are increasing, the rate of change is increasing, and the function is concave up.

In terms of derivatives:

If $f''(x) > 0$ in an interval, then a function is concave up in that interval and its first derivative is increasing in that interval.

If $f''(x) < 0$ in an interval, then a function is concave down in that interval and its first derivative is decreasing in that interval.

Inflection point:

If $f''(c) = 0$ or $f''(c)$ is undefined, an inflection point *may* exist at $x = c$. This is a point where concavity changes from up to down or vice versa.

In order to confirm the existence of an inflection point at $x = c$, we must use the second derivative to check the concavity of the intervals before and after $x = c$. The function must exist at $x = c$ and the sign of the second derivative must change before and after $x = c$.

Example 1

Find the concavity intervals and inflection point(s) for the function
$y = x^3 + 2x^2 - 3x + 1$.

Solution

Step 1

First, find the second derivative:

$y' = 3x^2 + 4x - 3$

$y'' = 6x + 4$

Step 2

Set the second derivative equal to zero and solve for the potential inflection point:

$0 = 6x + 4$

$x = -\dfrac{2}{3}$

An inflection point *may* exist when $x = -\dfrac{2}{3}$. To confirm this, see if the concavity changes at this point.

Check interval	$-\dfrac{2}{3}$	Check interval
$\left(-\infty, -\dfrac{2}{3}\right)$		$\left(-\dfrac{2}{3}, \infty\right)$

Step 3

For the interval $\left(-\infty, -\dfrac{2}{3}\right)$, -1 would make a good test value.

$f''(-1) = 6(-1) + 4$

$\qquad = -2 \qquad$ *negative*

So, the function is concave downward on the interval $\left(-\infty, -\dfrac{2}{3}\right)$.

Step 4

For the interval $\left(-\dfrac{2}{3}, \infty\right)$, 0 is a good test value.

$f''(0) = 6(0) + 4$

$\qquad = 4 \qquad$ *positive*

So, the function is concave upward on the interval $\left(-\dfrac{2}{3}, \infty\right)$.

On the number line:

Concave $-\dfrac{2}{3}$ Concave
downward   upward

Step 5

Since the concavity changes at $x = -\dfrac{2}{3}$, we know that there is an

inflection point at this value. We must now find the y-coordinate of the inflection point.

$$f\left(-\frac{2}{3}\right) = \left(-\frac{2}{3}\right)^3 + 2\left(-\frac{2}{3}\right)^2 - 3\left(-\frac{2}{3}\right) + 1$$

$$= \frac{-8}{27} + \frac{8}{9} + \frac{6}{3} + 1$$

$$= \frac{-8}{27} + \frac{8}{9} + 3$$

$$= \frac{-8 + 24 + 81}{27}$$

$$= \frac{97}{27}$$

Point of inflection is $\left(-\dfrac{2}{3}, \dfrac{97}{27}\right)$

Example 2

Find the concavity intervals and any points of inflection for the function

$f(x) = \dfrac{1}{4}x^4 - x^3 - 2x + 5$.

Solution

$f'(x) = x^3 - 3x^2 - 2$

$f''(x) = 3x^2 - 6x$

Set $f''(x) = 0$ to find potential inflection points:

$0 = 3x^2 - 6x$

$0 = 3x(x - 2)$

$x = 0$ and $x = 2$

NOTES

Intervals:

$(-\infty, 0)$ 0 $(0, 2)$ 2 $(2, \infty)$

Test values: $-1, 1, 3$

$f''(-1) = 3(-1)^2 - 6(-1)$
$\qquad = 3 + 6$
$\qquad = 9 \quad positive$

$f''(1) = 3(1)^2 - 6(1)$
$\qquad = 3 - 6$
$\qquad = -3 \quad negative$

$f''(3) = 3(3)^2 - 6(3)$
$\qquad = 27 - 18$
$\qquad = 9 \quad positive$

On the number line:

Concave   0   Concave   2   Concave
up   down   up

The function is concave up on the intervals $(-\infty, 0) \cup (2, \infty)$ and it is concave down on the interval $(0, 2)$.

Therefore, inflection points exist at $x = 0$ and $x = 2$.

Find y-values:

$f(0) = \dfrac{1}{4}(0)^4 - (0)^3 - 2(0) + 5$
$\qquad = 5$

$f(2) = \dfrac{1}{4}(2)^4 - (2)^3 - 2(2) + 5$
$\qquad = 4 - 8 - 4 + 5$
$\qquad = -3$

Inflection points are $(0, 5)$ and $(2, -3)$.

Example 3

Find the concavity intervals and any points of inflection for the function $y = x - \cos x$ on the interval $(0, 2\pi)$.

Solution

First, find the second derivative:

$y' = 1 + \sin x$

$y'' = \cos x$

Set $f''(x) = 0$:

$0 = \cos x$

$x = \dfrac{\pi}{2}, \; x = \dfrac{3\pi}{2}$

On the number line:

$$\left(0, \frac{\pi}{2}\right) \quad \frac{3\pi}{2} \quad\quad \left(\frac{\pi}{2}, \frac{3\pi}{2}\right) \quad \frac{3\pi}{2} \quad \left(\frac{3\pi}{2}, 2\pi\right)$$

Test values: $\dfrac{\pi}{3}, \; \pi, \; \dfrac{5\pi}{3}$

$f''\left(\dfrac{\pi}{3}\right) = \cos\left(\dfrac{\pi}{3}\right)$

$\qquad = \dfrac{1}{2} \quad positive$

$f''(\pi) = \cos(\pi)$

$\qquad = -1 \quad negative$

$f''\left(\dfrac{5\pi}{3}\right) = \cos\left(\dfrac{5\pi}{3}\right)$

$\qquad = \dfrac{1}{2} \quad positive$

On the number line:

$$\begin{array}{ccccc} \text{Concave} & \dfrac{3\pi}{2} & \text{Concave} & \dfrac{3\pi}{2} & \text{Concave} \\ \text{up} & & \text{down} & & \text{up} \end{array}$$

Concave up $\left(0, \dfrac{\pi}{2}\right) \cup \left(\dfrac{3\pi}{2}, 2\pi\right)$

Concave down $\left(\dfrac{\pi}{2}, \dfrac{3\pi}{2}\right)$

y-values of inflection points:

$$f\left(\frac{\pi}{2}\right) = \left(\frac{\pi}{2}\right) - \cos\left(\frac{\pi}{2}\right)$$

$$= \frac{\pi}{2}$$

$$f\left(\frac{3\pi}{2}\right) = \left(\frac{3\pi}{2}\right) - \cos\left(\frac{3\pi}{2}\right)$$

$$= \frac{3\pi}{2}$$

Inflection points: $\left(\frac{\pi}{2}, \frac{\pi}{2}\right)$ and $\left(\frac{3\pi}{2}, \frac{3\pi}{2}\right)$

Example 4

A point of inflection can exist at a domain value for which the second derivative is undefined. If the sign of the second derivative changes across the undefined domain value, and the original function does exist at this domain value, the original function will have a point of inflection at that domain value.

Study the function $f(x) = \sqrt[3]{x}$

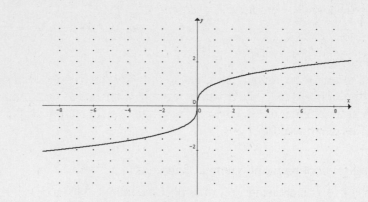

This function obviously has a point of inflection at $(0, 0)$.

Study the second derivative of this function.

$$f(x) = x^{\frac{1}{3}}$$

$$f'(x) = \frac{1}{3}x^{-\frac{2}{3}}$$

$$f''(x) = -\frac{2}{9}x^{-\frac{5}{3}}$$

$$f''(x) = \frac{-2}{9\sqrt[3]{x^5}}$$

$f''(0)$ is not defined. However, the original function is defined at $x = 0$.

$f''(x) > 0$ in the interval $(-\infty, 0)$. This indicates that the original function is concave up in that interval.

$f''(x) < 0$ in the interval $(0, \infty)$. This indicates that the original function is concave down in that interval.

Since the function $f(x) = \sqrt[3]{x}$ exists at $x = 0$ and the sign of the second derivative does change across $x = 0$, a point of inflection exists at $x = 0$. Since $f(0) = \sqrt[3]{0} = 0$, the point of inflection is (0, 0).

GRAPHS

Using the information you have learned so far about the connections between the first and second derivatives and the elements of the graph of the original function, you can connect the graph of a function with the graphs of its derivative functions.

In general, for continuous polynomial functions:

when $f(x)$ is increasing, $f'(x)$ is positive (above the x-axis)

when $f(x)$ is decreasing, $f'(x)$ is negative (below the x-axis)

when $f'(x)$ is increasing, $f''(x)$ is positive

when $f'(x)$ is decreasing, $f''(x)$ is negative

when $f(x)$ has a local maximum or minimum, $f'(x)$ has a zero

when $f(x)$ has an inflection point, $f''(x)$ has a zero

when $f(x)$ is concave up, $f''(x)$ is positive

when $f(x)$ is concave down, $f''(x)$ is negative

SKETCHING GRAPHS OF FUNCTIONS

Combining the concepts covered so far in this chapter, it is now possible for you to create fairly accurate sketches of many functions.

Example 1

Using first and second derivatives, sketch the graph of the given function by examining intervals of increase/decrease, local extrema, intervals of concavity, inflection points, and intercepts.

$$f(x) = 2x^2 - 9x - 5$$

Solution

$$f'(x) = 4x - 9$$

$$0 = 4x - 9$$

$$x = \frac{9}{4}$$

Since $x = \frac{9}{4}$ is a critical number, there is a potential local maximum or minimum there. This can be determined by finding the intervals of increase and decrease.

Test values: $x = 0$ and $x = 3$

$$f'(0) = 4(0) - 9$$

$$f'(0) = negative$$

$$f'(3) = 4(3) - 9$$

$$f'(3) = positive$$

Since the function is decreasing on the interval $\left(-\infty, \frac{9}{4}\right)$ and increasing on the interval $\left(\frac{9}{4}, \infty\right)$, there is a local minimum at $\left(\frac{9}{4}, f\left(\frac{9}{4}\right)\right)$, which is $\left(\frac{9}{4}, -\frac{121}{8}\right)$.

This minimum point is a key point on the graph of this function, and should be one of the first points graphed. We know that the function is decreasing over the entire interval before this and increasing after. We can check the concavity to confirm this, and then use the intercepts to give a more accurate sketch.

$$f''(x) = 4$$

Since the second derivative is constant and positive, we know that the function is always concave up. This confirms what we found using the first derivative. This also tells us that there are no inflection points.

y-intercept: x-intercepts:

$f(0) = -5$

$$0 = 2x^2 - 9x - 5$$
$$0 = (2x+1)(x-5)$$
$$x = 5 \quad x = -\frac{1}{2}$$

There is one y-intercept at $(0, -5)$ and two x-intercepts at $(5, 0)$ and $\left(-\frac{1}{2}, 0\right)$.

These points should be added to the sketch and connected, along with the local minimum, with a smooth curve as follows:

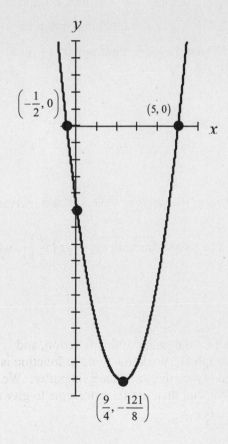

$\left(-\frac{1}{2}, 0\right)$ $(5, 0)$

$\left(\frac{9}{4}, -\frac{121}{8}\right)$

Example 2

Using first and second derivatives, sketch the graph of the given function by examining intervals of increase/decrease, local extrema, intervals of concavity, inflection points, and the y-intercept.

$$f(x) = 2x^3 - 3x^2 - 72x + 24$$

Solution

$$f'(x) = 6x^2 - 6x - 72$$
$$0 = 6(x-4)(x+3)$$

$$x = 4 \quad x = -3$$

Since -3 and 4 are critical numbers, we will check the test values:
$$x = -5 \quad x = 0 \quad x = 5$$

$$f'(-5) = positive$$
$$f'(0) = negative$$
$$f'(5) = positive$$

The function is increasing on the intervals $(-\infty, -3) \cup (4, \infty)$ and is decreasing on the interval $(-3, 4)$. There is a local maximum at $(-3, f(-3))$, which is $(-3, 159)$, and a local minimum at $(4, f(4))$, which is $(4, -184)$.

These points should be graphed and labelled.

$$f''(x) = 12x - 6$$
$$0 = 12x - 6$$
$$x = \frac{1}{2}$$

Concavity test values:
$$x = 0 \text{ and } x = 1$$
$$f''(0) = negative$$
$$f''(1) = positive$$

The function is concave down on $\left(-\infty, \dfrac{1}{2}\right)$ and concave up on $\left(\dfrac{1}{2}, \infty\right)$

and therefore, has an inflection point at $\left(\dfrac{1}{2}, f\left(\dfrac{1}{2}\right)\right)$, which is

$\left(\dfrac{1}{2}, -12.5\right)$. Graph and label this inflection point.

y-intercept:

$f(0) = 24$

The y-intercept is at $(0, 24)$.

Using all of these points and intervals together, we get the following graph:

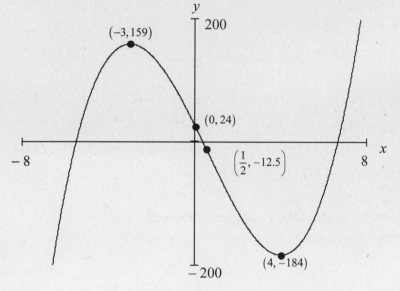

Example 3

Given the graph of the **derivative function**, $y = f'(x)$, below, sketch the original function, f.

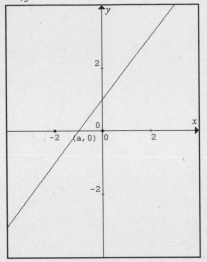

Solution

The derivative function, f', shown is a linear function with a zero at $x = a$. The original function, f, must be quadratic.

Values of $f'(x)$ in the interval $(-\infty, a)$ are negative, indicating that the function f was decreasing.

Values of $f'(x)$ in the interval (a, ∞) are positive, indicating that the function f was increasing.

Function f is a parabola, with a minimum value occurring when $x = a$. There is not enough information to determine what the value of the minimum is.

The original function, f, could be any one of an infinite number of quadratic functions

with a minimum occurring at $x = a$. The graph below shows the derivative function, f', along with a number of possible functions, f.

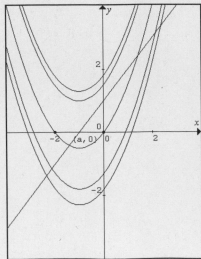

PRACTICE EXERCISE

5. Use the following diagram to fill in the blanks below.

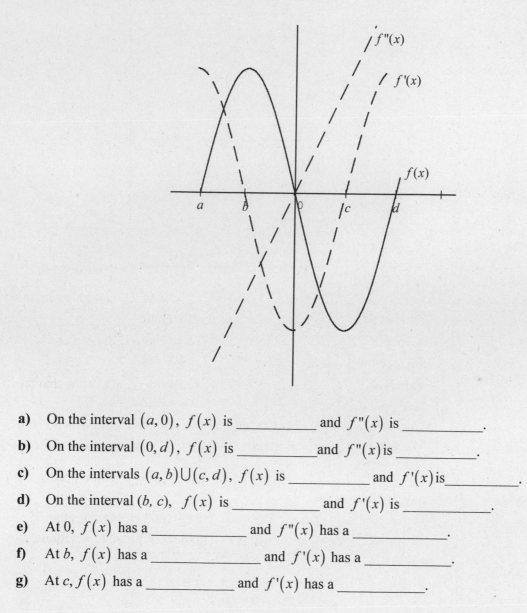

a) On the interval $(a, 0)$, $f(x)$ is _____ and $f''(x)$ is _____.

b) On the interval $(0, d)$, $f(x)$ is _____ and $f''(x)$ is _____.

c) On the intervals $(a, b) \cup (c, d)$, $f(x)$ is _____ and $f'(x)$ is _____.

d) On the interval (b, c), $f(x)$ is _____ and $f'(x)$ is _____.

e) At 0, $f(x)$ has a _____ and $f''(x)$ has a _____.

f) At b, $f(x)$ has a _____ and $f'(x)$ has a _____.

g) At c, $f(x)$ has a _____ and $f'(x)$ has a _____.

2. Find the concavity intervals and inflection points for each of the following functions.

a) $f(x) = x^2 - 8x$

b) $f(x) = 5x^3 - 5x^2 + 8$

c) $f(x) = \dfrac{x^2 - 1}{x}$

d) $f(x) = 5\cos(2x) - x$, where $0 < x < \pi$

3. Using the x values of a, b, c, d, and 0 shown on the following graph, state the interval(s) over which each statement below is true.

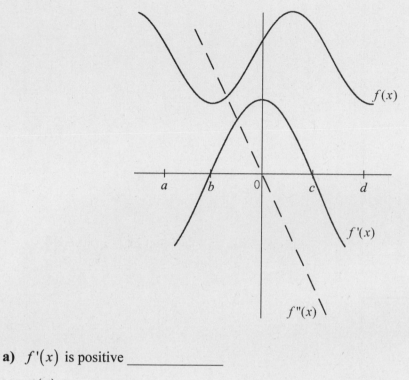

a) $f'(x)$ is positive _____

b) $f(x)$ is concave down _____

c) $f''(x)$ is positive _____

d) $f(x)$ is decreasing _____

4. Using first and second derivatives, sketch the graph of the given function by examining intervals of increase/decrease, local extrema, intervals of concavity, inflection points, and y-intercept.

$$f(x) = 4x^3 - 3x^2 - 36x + 12$$

5. For each derivative function, f', draw a possible sketch of function f.

a)

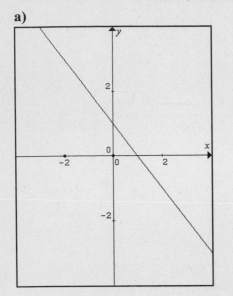

b)

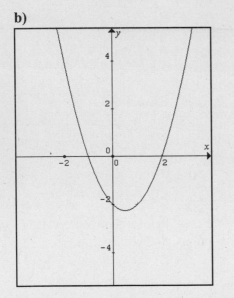

Lesson 5 OPTIMIZATION PROBLEMS

It is often desirable to find conditions that allow us to maximize or minimize a particular quantity. For example, we may want to maximize the area or volume that can be constructed with a particular quantity of material that we have. Or if a set area is required, we may wish to minimize the required materials and hence, the cost.

Since derivatives allow us to locate and calculate maximum and minimum values of a function, we can use calculus to find the optimum values for the type of problem outlined above.

Example 1

Two numbers have a difference of 3. What is the minimum product that these two numbers can have?

Solution

Step 1

First, write an expression for the quantity you are trying to minimize or maximize.

In this case, it is the product of two numbers.

Let x be one of the numbers and let y be the other number.

So, the expression for the product is: $P = xy$

Step 2

Next, use the other information that you know to express the product in terms of only one variable. Since the two numbers can have a difference of 3, we can say

$x - y = 3$

   or

$y = x - 3$

When we substitute this into $P = xy$, we get $P = x(x - 3)$

We now have a function whose minimum value we want to know. We can now take the derivative of this function and set it equal to zero to find a point that potentially is a maximum or a minimum for that function:

$$P = x^2 - 3x$$

$$\frac{dP}{dx} = 2x - 3$$

$$0 = 2x - 3$$

$$\frac{3}{2} = x$$

NOTES

Using test values, we can confirm that this value will produce a minimum.

On the number line:

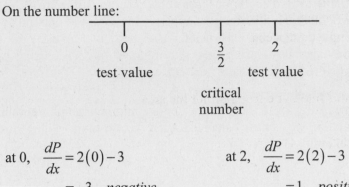

at 0, $\dfrac{dP}{dx} = 2(0) - 3$

$= -3$ *negative*

at 2, $\dfrac{dP}{dx} = 2(2) - 3$

$= 1$ *positive*

Since the function is decreasing before $x = \dfrac{3}{2}$ and increasing after $x = \dfrac{3}{2}$, we have confirmed that a local minimum value exists at that point.

Since the question asks for the minimum product, we must calculate this value:

$P = x(x - 3)$

$= \dfrac{3}{2}\left(\dfrac{3}{2} - 3\right)$

$= \dfrac{-9}{4}$

The minimum product of two numbers with a difference of 3 is $-\dfrac{9}{4}$.

Example 2

A family wants to create a fenced pen for their pet rabbits. The pen is to be built against their house with 3 sides of fence and the house forming a rectangular pen. If they have 24 metres of fencing, what is the maximum area that they can fence off for the rabbits?

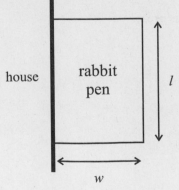

Solution

Let l be the length of the pen and w be the width.

The area of the pen is: $A = lw$

The total length of fence is

$24 = l + 2w$

$l = 24 - 2w$

Substitute this into our expression for the area:

$A = lw$

$\quad = (24 - 2w)w$

$\quad = 24w - 2w^2$

$\dfrac{dA}{dw} = 24 - 4w$

$\quad 0 = 24 - 4w$

$\quad 6 = w$

Check where the function is increasing or decreasing around the critical number:

At $w = 0$,

$\dfrac{dA}{dw} = 24 - 4(0)$

$\quad = 24 \quad positive$

At $w = 7$

$\dfrac{dA}{dw} = 24 - 4(7)$

$\quad = -4 \quad negative$

Since the function is increasing before $w = 6$ and decreasing after $w = 6$, there is a maximum area when $w = 6$ metres.

Substitute to find this area:

$A = (2u - 2x)x$

$\quad = (24 - 2(6))(6)$

$\quad = 72 \text{ m}^2$

Example 3

A box with a square base and an open top must have a volume of $108\,000\text{ cm}^3$. Find the dimensions of the box that minimize the material required to make the box.

Solution

Let *SA* be the surface area of the box.
Let *s* be the side length of the base
and *h* be the height of the box.

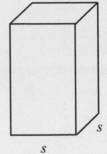

SA = area of the base + 4 × area of the sides

$SA = s^2 + 4hs$

Using the expression for volume, eliminate the variable *h*.

$$V = s^2 h$$

$$108\,000 = s^2 h$$

$$\frac{108\,000}{s^2} = h$$

Substituting, we get:

$$SA = s^2 + 4\left(\frac{108\,000}{s^2}\right)s$$

$$= s^2 + \frac{432\,000}{s}$$

$$= s^2 + 432\,000 s^{-1}$$

$$\frac{d(SA)}{ds} = 2s - \frac{432\,000}{s^2}$$

To find the minimum, set the derivative equal to zero.

$$0 = 2s - \frac{432\,000}{s^2}$$

$$\frac{432\,000}{s^2} = 2s$$

$$432\,000 = 2s^3$$

$$\sqrt[3]{\frac{432\,000}{2}} = s$$

$$60 = s$$

Check where the function is increasing or decreasing around the critical number:

when $s = 1$,

$$\frac{d(SA)}{ds} = 2(1) - \frac{432\,000}{1^2}$$
$$= 2 - 432\,000$$
$$= negative$$

when $s = 100$,

$$\frac{d(SA)}{ds} = 2(100) - \frac{432\,000}{100^2}$$
$$= 200 - 43.2$$
$$= positive$$

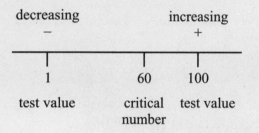

Since the derivative is negative before and positive after $s = 60$, there is a local minimum when $s = 60$. When $s = 60$:

$$h = \frac{108\,000}{60^2}$$
$$= 5$$

So, the dimensions are: side lengths of 60 cm and a height of 30 cm.

PRACTICE EXERCISE

1. Find 2 positive numbers whose product is 100 and whose sum is a minimum.

2. Find the dimensions of a rectangle whose area is 8 000 cm^2 and whose perimeter is as small as possible.

3. Find the maximum area of a triangle inscribed in a semicircle of diameter 40 cm. Use the diagram below to help you.

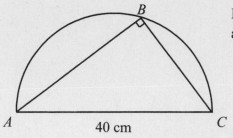

Recall that an angle inscribed in a semicircle is always a right angle.

4. A farmer wishes to build a fence around a rectangular pasture and divide it into 2 rectangular areas as shown in the diagram below:

The farmer has 600 m of fencing. Find the maximum *total* area that he can fence.

5. A piece of wire 20 cm long is to be cut into two pieces. One piece will be bent into a square and the other will be bent into an equilateral triangle. How should the wire be cut to enclose a minimum total area?

PRACTICE QUIZ

1. Determine what symmetry, if any, the following function has.

$$f(x) = \frac{4x^4 - 1}{x^2}$$

2. Determine the intervals of increase and decrease, as well as any maximum and minimum values for the following functions.

a) $f(x) = x^2 - 4x + 1$ 　　　　　　　　　　　**b)** $y = \dfrac{x^2 + 1}{x}$

3. Determine the concavity intervals and inflection points for the following functions.

   a) $y = x^3 + 2x^2 - x + 4$ **b)** $f(x) = 2\sin x$, where $0 < x < 2\pi$

4. A manufacturer wants to make a can that will hold 355 mL of soup. What should the dimensions of the can be so that the cost required (materials) to make the can is a minimum?
Recall that 355 mL = 355 cm³.

Lesson 6   *VERTICAL ASYMPTOTES*

A vertical asymptote is a vertical line that a function approaches, but never reaches.

Vertical asymptotes *can* occur whenever a function is undefined. However, the existence of the asymptote must be confirmed by closely examining the function's behaviour at values approaching the undefined value.

For this, we use left- and right-hand limits.

A function, $y = f(x)$, has a vertical asymptote at $x = c$ if $f(c)$ is undefined and:

$$\lim_{x \to c^+} \left[f(x) \right] = \infty$$

or

$$\lim_{x \to c^-} \left[f(x) \right] = \infty$$

or

$$\lim_{x \to c^+} \left[f(x) \right] = -\infty$$

or

$$\lim_{x \to c^-} \left[f(x) \right] = -\infty$$

Example 1

Find any vertical asymptotes for the function

$y = \dfrac{3}{x-2}$, and describe the function's behaviour near the asymptotes.

Use this information to sketch the function near the asymptotes.

Solution

The function is undefined when the denominator is equal to zero.

$x - 2 = 0$

$x = 2$

To confirm the existence of an asymptote, evaluate the limits.

$$\lim_{x \to 2^+} \frac{3}{x-2} \quad \text{and} \quad \lim_{x \to 2^-} \frac{3}{x-2}$$

Since functions become very large or very small near asymptotes, it is not necessary to calculate actual values. Instead, we are interested only in whether the values are very small positive numbers, very small negative numbers, or approaching $\pm \infty$.

NOTES

$$\lim_{x \to 2^+} \frac{3}{x-2}$$

As x approaches 2 from the right, it continues to be larger than 2, but gets very close to 2. So, $x - 2$ becomes very small, but stays positive.

For example, if $x = 2.01$, $y = \dfrac{3}{2.01-2} = \dfrac{3}{0.01} = +300$

$$\lim_{x \to 2^+} \frac{3}{x-2} = +\infty$$

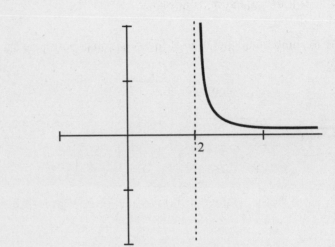

To see what is happening from the left, let $x = 1.99$.

$$y = \frac{3}{1.99-2} = \frac{3}{-0.01} = -300$$

$$\lim_{x \to 2^-} \frac{3}{x-2} = -\infty$$

On the graph, we have:

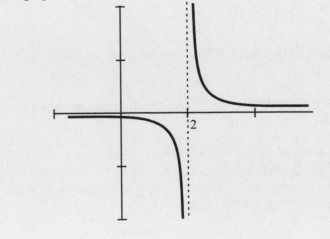

Example 2

Determine any asymptotes of the following function and sketch the function at those asymptotes.

$$f(x) = \frac{4}{x^2 - x - 12}$$

Solution

The function is undefined when the denominator is equal to zero.

$$x^2 - x - 12 = 0$$

$$(x-4)(x+3) = 0$$

$x = 4$ and $x = -3$ are potential asymptotes

Let $x = 4.01$ to study the behaviour of this function as x approaches 4 from the right.

$$y = \frac{4}{(4.01-4)(4.01+3)} \doteq 57.06$$

$$\lim_{x \to 4^+} \left(\frac{4}{x^2 - x - 12} \right) = +\infty$$

Let $x = 3.99$ to study the behaviour of this function as x approaches 4 from the left.

$$y = \frac{4}{(3.99-4)(3.99+3)} \doteq -57.22$$

$$\lim_{x \to 4^-} \left(\frac{4}{x^2 - x - 12} \right) = -\infty$$

Let $x = -2.99$ to study the behaviour of this function as x approaches -3 from the right.

$$y = \frac{4}{(-2.99-4)(-2.99+3)} \doteq -57.22$$

$$\lim_{x \to -3^+} \left(\frac{4}{x^2 - x - 12} \right) = -\infty$$

Let $x = -3.01$ to study the behavior of this function as x approaches -3 from the left.

$$y = \frac{4}{(-3.01-4)(-3.01+3)} \doteq +57.06$$

$$\lim_{x \to -3^-} \left(\frac{4}{x^2 - x - 12} \right) = +\infty$$

NOTES

Sketch the function in the vicinity of its vertical asymptotes:

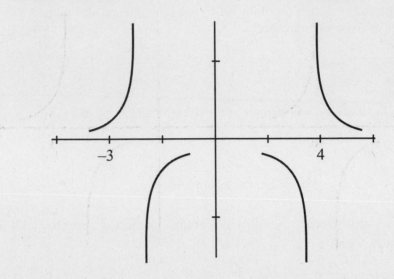

We are only considering the graph near the asymptotes and are therefore, not adding other details.

Example 3

Find any vertical asymptotes for the following function and sketch the function near these asymptotes.

$$f(x) = \frac{x+2}{x^2 + 3x - 18}$$

Solution

Make the denominator equal to zero:

$$x^2 + 3x - 18 = 0$$

$$(x-3)(x+6) = 0$$

$$x = 3 \text{ and } x = -6$$

By using appropriate test values before and after 3 and −6 we find that:

$$\lim_{x \to 3^+} \frac{(x+2)}{(x-3)(x+6)} = +\infty$$

$$\lim_{x \to 3^-} \frac{(x+2)}{(x-3)(x+6)} = -\infty$$

$$\lim_{x \to -6^+} \frac{(x+2)}{(x-3)(x+6)} = +\infty$$

$$\lim_{x \to -6^-} \frac{(x+2)}{(x-3)(x+6)} = -\infty$$

Sketch the function in the vicinity of its vertical asymptotes:

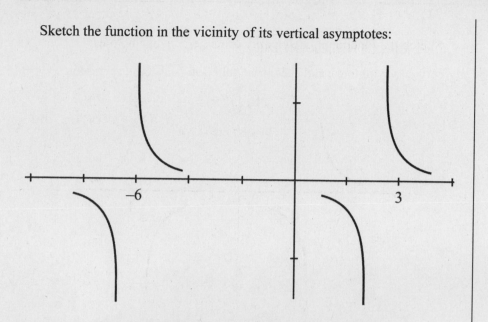

The presence of a no permissible value does not always indicate the presence of a vertical asymptote for a function.

Example 4

Determine the behavior of the function $y = \dfrac{x^2 - 9}{x - 3}$ in the vicinity of its no permissible value.

Solution

$y = \dfrac{x^2 - 9}{x - 3}$, $x \neq 3$ simplifies to $y = \dfrac{(x+3)(x-3)}{x-3} = x+3$, $x \neq 3$.

$\displaystyle\lim_{x \to 3}\left(\dfrac{x^2 - 9}{x - 3}\right) = \lim_{x \to 3}(x+3) = 6$

This function has a point of discontinuity at $(3\,,6)$. A vertical asymptote does not exist.

PRACTICE EXERCISE

1. Determine the location of any vertical asymptotes, and sketch the function near these asymptotes.

   a) $f(x) = \dfrac{1}{x+1}$

   b) $f(x) = \dfrac{2}{x^2 + 2x - 3}$

   c) $f(x) = \sec x$ on interval $(0, 2\pi)$

   d) $y = \dfrac{x+5}{x+4}$

Lesson 7 HORIZONTAL ASYMPTOTES

In our study of vertical asymptotes, the limits involved were those in which *x* was approaching a particular finite value, and the function, or *y*-value, approached positive or negative infinity.

Our study of horizontal asymptotes has us examining what happens to the function as *x* approaches positive or negative infinity. If the function approaches a finite value, *l*, there is said to be a horizontal asymptote at $y = l$.

Horizontal asymptotes behave differently than vertical asymptotes. As illustrated below, the function can exist at $y = l$. In other words, the graph of the function can cross the horizontal asymptote.

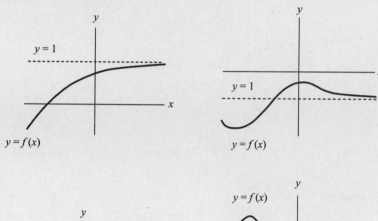

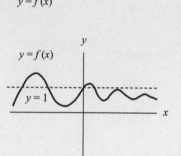

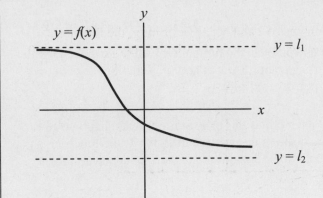

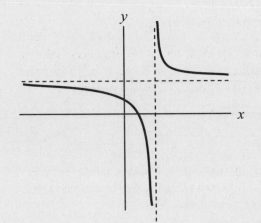

Many functions have both vertical and horizontal asymptotes:

Example 1

Find the horizontal asymptotes for the function $f(x) = \dfrac{5}{x}$.

Solution

Since horizontal asymptotes are found by examining what happens as x approaches positive or negative infinity, evaluate

$\lim\limits_{x \to \infty} \dfrac{5}{x}$ and $\lim\limits_{x \to -\infty} \dfrac{5}{x}$

With simple functions like this one, simply consider what happens numerically as x becomes larger:

$\dfrac{5}{10} = 0.5$, $\dfrac{5}{1\,000} = 0.05$, $\dfrac{5}{1\,000\,000} = 0.000\,005$, etc.

As x gets larger, $\dfrac{5}{x}$ gets closer and closer to 0. As $x \to +\infty$, $y \to 0$.

$\lim\limits_{x \to +\infty} \dfrac{5}{x} = 0$

The same is also true as x approaches $-\infty$. As $x \to -\infty$, $y \to 0$.

$\lim\limits_{x \to -\infty} \dfrac{5}{x} = 0$

232

So, as x approaches both positive and negative infinity, the function approaches zero. Therefore, there exists a horizontal asymptote at $y = 0$.

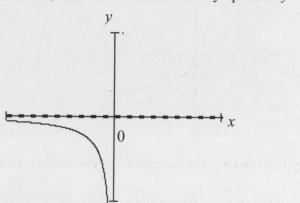

When dealing with more complex rational functions, it is necessary to employ more structured algebraic procedures. First, use the results from the above example. For any integer a and any positive integer n:

$$\lim_{x \to \infty} \frac{a}{x^n} = 0 \text{ and } \lim_{x \to -\infty} \frac{a}{x^n} = 0$$

The following procedure requires that we first divide each term by the highest power of x in the denominator, and then break the expression into separate limits and evaluate each separately.

Example 2

Evaluate the following limit and state the equation of any horizontal asymptotes.

$$\lim_{x \to \infty} \frac{2x^2 + x - 5}{7x^2 - 2x + 4}$$

Solution

$$= \lim_{x \to \infty} \frac{\dfrac{2x^2 + x - 5}{x^2}}{\dfrac{7x^2 - 2x + 4}{x^2}}$$

Since we are considering large values of x, we can assume that $x \neq 0$.

Hint: divide all terms by the largest power of x, then take $\lim_{x \to \infty}$

$$= \lim_{x \to \infty} \frac{\dfrac{2x^2}{x^2} + \dfrac{x}{x^2} - \dfrac{5}{x^2}}{\dfrac{7x^2}{x^2} - \dfrac{2x}{x^2} + \dfrac{4}{x^2}}$$

$$= \lim_{x \to \infty} \frac{2 + \dfrac{1}{x} - \dfrac{5}{x^2}}{7 - \dfrac{2}{x} + \dfrac{4}{x^2}}$$

$$= \frac{\displaystyle\lim_{x \to \infty} \left(2 + \dfrac{1}{x} - \dfrac{5}{x^2}\right)}{\displaystyle\lim_{x \to \infty} \left(7 - \dfrac{2}{x} + \dfrac{4}{x^2}\right)}$$

$$= \frac{\displaystyle\lim_{x \to \infty} 2 + \lim_{x \to \infty} \dfrac{1}{x} - \lim_{x \to \infty} \dfrac{5}{x^2}}{\displaystyle\lim_{x \to \infty} 7 - \lim_{x \to \infty} \dfrac{2}{x} + \lim_{x \to \infty} \dfrac{4}{x^2}}$$

$$= \frac{2 + 0 - 0}{7 - 0 + 0}$$

$$= \frac{2}{7}$$

Therefore, the function $y = \dfrac{2x^2 + x - 5}{7x^2 - 2x + 4}$ has a horizontal asymptote

at $y = \dfrac{2}{7}$.

```
Plot1  Plot2  Plot3
\Y1■■2X^2+X-5)/(
7X^2-2X+4)
\Y2=
\Y3=
\Y4=
\Y5=
\Y6=
```

Example 3

Evaluate the following limit and give the equation of any horizontal asymptotes.

$$\lim_{x\to\infty} \frac{5x^2 - 2x + 1}{3x + 1}$$

Solution

$$= \lim_{x\to\infty} \frac{\dfrac{5x^2}{x^2} - \dfrac{2x}{x^2} + \dfrac{1}{x^2}}{\dfrac{3x}{x^2} + \dfrac{1}{x^2}}$$

$$= \lim_{x\to\infty} \frac{5 - \dfrac{2}{x} + \dfrac{1}{x^2}}{\dfrac{3}{x} + \dfrac{1}{x^2}}$$

$$= \frac{5 - 0 + 0}{0 + 0}$$

$$= \frac{5}{0}, \text{ which is undefined. } \therefore \text{No horizontal asymptote.}$$

Since the function $y = \dfrac{5x^2 - 2x + 1}{3x + 1}$ approaches infinity when x

approaches infinity, there is no horizontal asymptote.

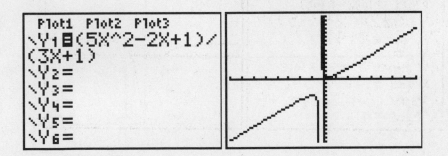

Example 4

Evaluate the following limit and give the equations of any horizontal asymptotes.

$$\lim_{x\to\infty} \frac{-3x^3 - 2x^2 + 1}{6x^3 - x^2 + 6}$$

Although it does sometimes become apparent what the equations of the asymptotes will be, it is important to understand and show the process using limits.

NOTES

Solution

$$= \lim_{x \to \infty} \frac{\dfrac{-3x^3}{x^3} - \dfrac{2x^2}{x^3} + \dfrac{1}{x^3}}{\dfrac{6x^3}{x^3} - \dfrac{x^2}{x^3} + \dfrac{6}{x^3}}$$

$$= \lim_{x \to \infty} \frac{-3 - \dfrac{2}{x} + \dfrac{1}{x^3}}{6 - \dfrac{1}{x} + \dfrac{6}{x^3}}$$

$$= \frac{\displaystyle\lim_{x \to \infty}(-3) - \lim_{x \to \infty}\dfrac{2}{x} + \lim_{x \to \infty}\dfrac{1}{x^3}}{\displaystyle\lim_{x \to \infty} 6 - \lim_{x \to \infty}\dfrac{1}{x} + \lim_{x \to \infty}\dfrac{6}{x^3}}$$

$$= \frac{-3 - 0 + 0}{6 - 0 + 0}$$

$$= -\frac{1}{2}$$

Therefore, the function $y = \dfrac{-3x^3 - 2x^2 + 1}{6x^3 - x^2 + 6}$ has a horizontal asymptote

at $y = -\dfrac{1}{2}$.

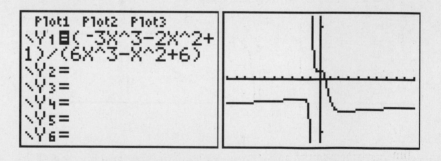

Now that you have examined the vertical and horizontal asymptotes, you can answer questions that ask for the equations of both.

Example 5

Find the equations of the vertical and horizontal asymptotes for the following function and use them to draw a rough sketch of the function.

$$f(x) = \frac{x^2 + x - 7}{3x^2 - 3}$$

Solution

Step 1

First, find the vertical asymptotes.

Identify no permissible values and verify that the function approaches $+\infty$ or $-\infty$ in the near vicinity

of these values.

$$3x^2 - 3 = 0$$

$$3(x+1)(x-1) = 0$$

$$x = \pm 1$$

$$\lim_{x \to 1^+} \frac{x^2 + x - 7}{3(x+1)(x-1)} = -\infty$$

$$\lim_{x \to 1^-} \frac{x^2 + x - 7}{3(x+1)(x-1)} = \infty$$

$$\lim_{x \to -1^+} \frac{x^2 + x - 7}{3(x+1)(x-1)} = \infty$$

NOTES

$$\lim_{x \to -1^-} \frac{x^2 + x - 7}{3(x+1)(x-1)} = -\infty$$

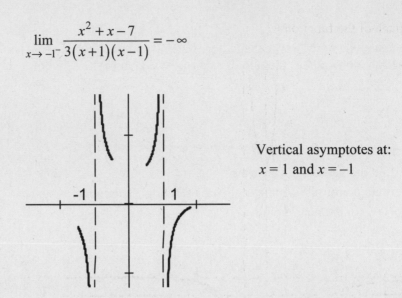

Vertical asymptotes at:
$x = 1$ and $x = -1$

Step 2

Next, find the equations of the horizontal asymptotes.

As x approaches ∞:

$$\lim_{x \to \infty} \frac{x^2 + x - 7}{3x^2 - 3}$$

$$= \lim_{x \to \infty} \frac{\dfrac{x^2}{x^2} + \dfrac{x}{x^2} - \dfrac{7}{x^2}}{\dfrac{3x^2}{x^2} - \dfrac{3}{x^2}}$$

$$= \lim_{x \to \infty} \frac{1 + \dfrac{1}{x} - \dfrac{7}{x^2}}{3 - \dfrac{3}{x^2}}$$

$$= \frac{\lim_{x \to \infty} 1 + \lim_{x \to \infty} \dfrac{1}{x} - \lim_{x \to \infty} \dfrac{7}{x^2}}{\lim_{x \to \infty} 3 - \lim_{x \to \infty} \dfrac{3}{x^2}}$$

$$= \frac{1 + 0 - 0}{3 - 0}$$

$$= \frac{1}{3}$$

Therefore, there is a horizontal asymptote at $y = \dfrac{1}{3}$.

A sketch of the function is:

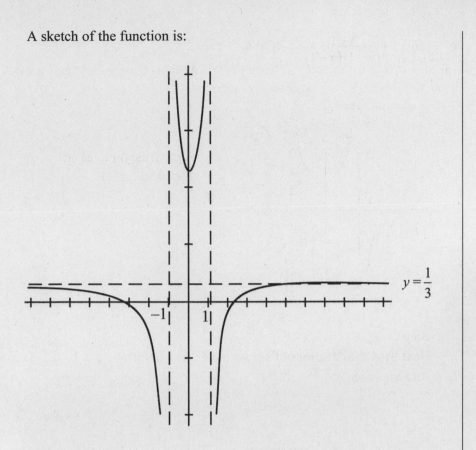

$y = \dfrac{1}{3}$

You can find the x- and y-intercepts, as discussed in lesson 1 of this chapter, to give added detail to this sketch.

This function also illustrates, as mentioned earlier, that the graph of a function can cross a horizontal asymptote.

In this case, $f(6) = \dfrac{1}{3}$.

PRACTICE EXERCISE

1. Determine the equations of the horizontal asymptotes for each of the following functions, if they exist, by evaluating the $\lim\limits_{x \to \pm\infty} f(x)$.

a) $f(x) = \dfrac{x^2}{x^3 - 4}$

b) $f(x) = \dfrac{2x^2 - x}{4x^2 - 3}$

c) $f(x) = \dfrac{-5x^3 - 4x^2}{3x^2 + x}$

d) $f(x) = \dfrac{-4x^3 + 2x^2 - 1}{6x^3 - x + 5}$

2. Find the equations of the vertical and horizontal asymptotes for each of the following functions and draw a rough sketch of each graph.

a) $f(x) = \dfrac{2x+1}{x-3}$

b) $f(x) = \dfrac{-4x^2 - x}{x^2 - 2x - 15}$

NOTES

Lesson 8   OBLIQUE ASYMPTOTES

You are now familiar with vertical and horizontal asymptotes. The third type of linear asymptote is called an oblique asymptote. The asymptote is defined by the equation $y = mx + b$, where $m \neq 0$.

As with other asymptotes, the graph of the function approaches the oblique line. In other words, the distance between the function and the oblique asymptotes approaches 0.

In general, a function $y = f(x)$ has an oblique asymptote at $y = mx + b$:

$$\lim_{x \to \infty} \left[f(x) - (mx + b) \right] = 0$$

or

$$\lim_{x \to -\infty} \left[f(x) - (mx + b) \right] = 0$$

In terms of the graph, we see:

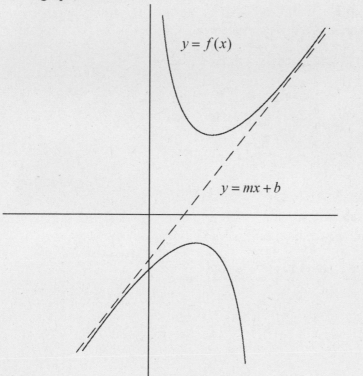

As with horizontal asymptotes, we use division to determine the equation of the asymptote.

Rational functions have oblique asymptotes when the degree of the numerator exceeds that of the denominator by 1.

If you are familiar with synthetic division, you may wish to use that method of dividing polynomials.

Example 1

Find the equation of the oblique asymptote for the function

$$f(x) = \frac{3x^2 - 2x + 1}{x + 2}.$$

Solution

Step 1

Use long division or synthetic division of polynomials to divide the numerator by the denominator.

$$
\begin{array}{r}
3x - 8 \\
x+2 \overline{\smash{\big)}\, 3x^2 - 2x + 1} \\
\underline{3x^2 + 6x} \\
-8x + 1 \\
\underline{-8x - 16} \\
17
\end{array}
$$

$$
\begin{array}{c|rrr}
x+2 & 3 & -2 & 1 \\
    &   & 6 & -16 \\
\hline
    & 3 & -8 & 17
\end{array}
$$

Step 2

Express as a division statement.

$$f(x) = \frac{3x^2 - 2x + 1}{x + 2} = 3x - 8 + \frac{17}{x + 2}$$

so

$$f(x) = 3x - 8 + \frac{17}{x + 2}$$

$$f(x) - (3x - 8) = +\frac{17}{x + 2}$$

Step 3

Evaluate the limit.

Finding the limit as x goes to infinity, we have

$$\lim_{x \to \infty} \left[f(x) - (3x - 8) \right] = \lim_{x \to \infty} \left[\frac{17}{x + 2} \right]$$

If we can show that the right side is equal to zero, we will have shown that there is an oblique asymptote at $y = 3x - 8$.

$$\lim_{x \to \infty} \left[f(x) - (3x - 8) \right] = \lim_{x \to \infty} \frac{\dfrac{17}{x}}{\dfrac{x}{x} + \dfrac{2}{x}}$$

$$= \lim_{x \to \infty} \frac{\dfrac{17}{x}}{1 + \dfrac{2}{x}}$$

$$= \frac{\displaystyle\lim_{x \to \infty} \frac{17}{x}}{\displaystyle\lim_{x \to \infty} 1 + \lim_{x \to \infty} \frac{2}{x}}$$

$$= \frac{0}{1 + 0}$$

$$= 0$$

The limit, as x approaches negative infinity, will produce the same result.

Step 4

State the equation of the asymptote.

Since we have shown that the distance between $f(x)$ and the line $y = 3x - 8$ approaches 0, as x approaches infinity, we have established that there is an oblique asymptote at $y = 3x - 8$.

NOTES

Combine this with the graphing skills you learned in the lesson on graphing vertical asymptotes. You can sketch the graph as follows:

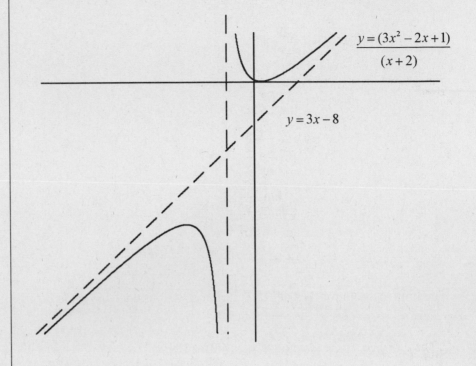

$$y = \frac{(3x^2 - 2x + 1)}{(x + 2)}$$

$$y = 3x - 8$$

Example 2

Determine the equation of the oblique asymptote of the function

$$f(x) = \frac{2x^2 + 5x - 1}{x + 2}.$$

Solution

$$
\begin{array}{r}
2x + 1 \\
x + 2 \overline{\smash{\big)}\ 2x^2 + 5x - 1} \\
\underline{2x^2 + 4x} \\
x - 1 \\
\underline{x + 2} \\
-3
\end{array}
$$

So,

$$\frac{2x^2 + 5x - 1}{x + 2} = 2x + 1 - \frac{3}{x + 2}$$

$$f(x) - (2x + 1) = \frac{-3}{x + 2}$$

$$\lim_{x \to \infty}\left[f(x) - (2x + 1)\right] = \lim_{x \to \infty}\frac{-3}{x + 2}$$

$$= \lim_{x \to \infty}\frac{\dfrac{-3}{x}}{\dfrac{x}{x} + \dfrac{2}{x}}$$

$$= \frac{\displaystyle\lim_{x \to \infty}\frac{-3}{x}}{\displaystyle\lim_{x \to \infty}1 + \lim_{x \to \infty}\frac{2}{x}}$$

$$= \frac{0}{1 + 0}$$

$$= 0$$

$\therefore$ The equation of the asymptote is $y = 2x + 1$.

Example 3

Find the equation of the asymptote for the function

$$f(x) = \frac{4x^3 - 2x^2 + 3x + 5}{x^2 - x}.$$

Solution

$$
\begin{array}{r}
4x + 2 \\
x^2 - x \overline{\smash{\big)}\, 4x^3 - 2x^2 + 3x + 5} \\
\underline{4x^3 - 4x^2} \\
2x^2 + 3x \\
\underline{2x^2 - 2x} \\
5x + 5
\end{array}
$$

So,

$$\frac{4x^3 - 2x^2 + 3x + 5}{x^2 - x} = 4x + 2 + \frac{5x + 5}{x^2 - x}$$

$$f(x) - (4x + 2) = \frac{5x + 5}{x^2 - x}$$

$$\lim_{x \to \infty}\left[f(x) - (4x + 2) \right] = \lim_{x \to \infty} \frac{5x + 5}{x^2 - x}$$

$$= \lim_{x \to \infty} \frac{\dfrac{5x}{x^2} + \dfrac{5}{x^2}}{\dfrac{x^2}{x^2} - \dfrac{x}{x^2}}$$

$$= \frac{\lim_{x \to \infty} \dfrac{5}{x} + \lim_{x \to \infty} \dfrac{5}{x^2}}{\lim_{x \to \infty} 1 - \lim_{x \to \infty} \dfrac{x}{x^2}}$$

$$= \frac{0 + 0}{1 - 0}$$

$$= 0$$

$\therefore$ The equation of the asymptote is $y = 4x + 2$.

The next example demonstrates techniques that can be used to sketch a graph of a function without the aid of a graphing calculator.

Example 4

Sketch the function $f(x) = \dfrac{2x}{x^2 + 4}$, using information about:

Domain and range
Intercepts
Asymptotes
Intervals of increase and decrease
Local maximum and minimum values
Intervals of concavity
Points of inflection

Solution

Domain: The function $f(x) = \dfrac{2x}{x^2 + 4}$ is defined for all real numbers.

Range: The range will be identified at the end of this solution.

Vertical asymptotes: Since this function is defined for all real number values of x, there are no vertical asymptotes.

248

Horizontal asymptotes:

$$\lim_{x \to \pm\infty} \left(\frac{2x}{x^2+4} \right) = 0 \quad \text{Thus, } y = 0 \text{ is a horizontal asymptote.}$$

First derivative information:

$$f(x) = \frac{2x}{x^2+4}$$

Using the quotient rule:

$$f'(x) = \frac{\left(x^2+4\right)(2) - (2x)(2x)}{\left(x^2+4\right)^2}$$

$$f'(x) = \frac{2\left(4-x^2\right)}{\left(x^2+4\right)^2}$$

Critical values occur when either the numerator or denominator of the first derivative equal zero. The numerator is zero when $x = 2$ or -2. The denominator can never be zero.

The critical values are the endpoints of the 3 intervals to be tested.

These intervals are: $(-\infty, -2)$, $(-2, 2)$, and $(2, \infty)$

Using test values, we find that:

$f'(x) < 0$ for $(-\infty, -2)$ The original function must be decreasing in this interval.

$f'(x) > 0$ for $(-2, 2)$ The original function must be increasing in this interval.

$f'(x) < 0$ for $(2, \infty)$ The original function must be decreasing in this interval.

Since the sign of the first derivative changed from negative to positive at $x = -2$,

the original function reached a local minimum at $x = -2$.

Since $f(-2) = -\dfrac{1}{2}$, a local minimum occurs at the point $\left(-2, -\dfrac{1}{2} \right)$.

Since the sign of the first derivative changed from positive to negative at $x = 2$, the original function reached a local maximum at $x = 2$.

Since $f(2) = \dfrac{1}{2}$, a local maximum occurs at the point $\left(2, \dfrac{1}{2} \right)$.

Second derivative information:

$$f'(x) = \frac{2(4-x^2)}{(x^2+4)^2}$$

Using the quotient rule:

$$f'(x) = \frac{2(4-x^2)}{(x^2+4)^2}$$

$$f''(x) = \frac{(x^2+4)^2(-4x) - 2(4-x^2)(2)(x^2+4)(2x)}{(x^2+4)^4}$$

$$f''(x) = \frac{(4x)(x^2-12)}{(x^2+4)^3}$$

To identify critical values, observe that the numerator is zero when $x = 0$ or $x = \pm\sqrt{12}$.

The denominator will never be zero.

The intervals to test are:

$(-\infty, -\sqrt{12})$, $(-\sqrt{12}, 0)$, $(0, \sqrt{12})$ and $(\sqrt{12}, +\infty)$.

$f''(x) < 0$ for $(-\infty, -\sqrt{12})$ The original function is concave down in this interval.

$f''(x) > 0$ for $(-\sqrt{12}, 0)$ The original function is concave up in this interval.

$f''(x) < 0$ for $(0, \sqrt{12})$ The original function is concave down in this interval.

$f''(x) > 0$ for $(\sqrt{12}, +\infty)$ The original function is concave up in this interval.

Since the sign of the second derivative changes at all 3 critical values and the original function is defined at these values, the original function has points of inflection at these values.

Since $f(0) = 0$, $f(-\sqrt{12}) = -\frac{\sqrt{12}}{8}$, and $f(\sqrt{12}) = \frac{\sqrt{12}}{8}$, points of inflection occur at $(0, 0)$, $\left(-\sqrt{12}, -\frac{\sqrt{12}}{8}\right)$, and $\left(\sqrt{12}, \frac{\sqrt{12}}{8}\right)$.

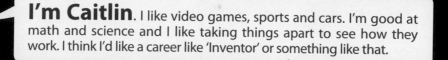

I'm Caitlin. I like video games, sports and cars. I'm good at math and science and I like taking things apart to see how they work. I think I'd like a career like 'Inventor' or something like that.

As an engineer, I know a lot about design. I'm now leading a group of engineers designing **high-performance** snowmobiles!

I gained more than technical knowledge in my engineering education—I'm now running **my own** oil and gas **company!**

I'm creating new ways to integrate computers into everyday devices, like televisions, cars, and home security systems.

I've discovered a **new material** that will help your cell phone or laptop charge up in minutes instead of hours!

DESIGN CREATE INVENT THINK DREAM = ENGINEER

The next generation of engineers will change the world in ways we can only begin to imagine, and the U of A Faculty of Engineering wants you to be a part of it!

A U of A Engineering degree is your key to a career with unlimited possibilities—if you're a creative problem solver looking for a rewarding profession

that can impact the world around you, **ENGINEERING IS THE CHOICE FOR YOU.**

To learn more about engineering, visit:
www.engineering.ualberta.ca

FACULTY OF
ENGINEERING
UNIVERSITY OF ALBERTA

DESIGN
CREATE
INVENT
THINK
DREAM

ENGINEER

tan²

I'M ANDREA

I'm an environmental engineer! I can't remember when I decided this was what I wanted to do. I'm an environmentalist and wanted to go into engineering to have a positive impact on the environment.

When I studied engineering at the University of Alberta I was in the Co-op program, which means I gained

VALUABLE PAID WORK EXPERIENCE

while going to school. I worked in the Yukon as an inspector for a highway project, then worked at two abandoned mines that were being cleaned up. We rebuilt a shore line on a lake and decontaminated soil around the mines. In the winter, I worked as the environmental inspector and helped move all of the equipment once the ice roads were opened.

THIS IS TOTALLY THE KIND OF WORK I WANTED TO DO!

I'm really happy with my degree. I feel confident, well educated, and prepared for anything!

The next generation of engineers will change the world in ways we can only begin to imagine, and the U of A Faculty of Engineering wants you to be a part of it!

The things you use every day—the iPod you listen to, the cell phone you text with, even the systems that provide you with clean drinking water—have all been designed and built by engineers. Things you will use in the future—eco-friendly energy sources, innovative medical technology and revolutionary social media networks—will be the products of tomorrow's creative engineers. You could be one of them!

To learn more about engineering, please visit:
www.engineering.ualberta.ca

FACULTY OF
ENGINEERING
UNIVERSITY OF ALBERTA

DESIGN
CREATE
INVENT
THINK
DREAM
ENGINEER

ab^{r-1}

cos^2

I'M MICHAEL

I run my own company and design and sell apps for a living! The U of A is where I first felt I was coming into my own. Studying computer engineering, I just watched myself constantly grow. I learned that I could take on new challenges and do new things. Everyone says, 'Engineering is really hard,' and, 'You'll be gone in a year.' But the truth is that you just

START GROWING AND GROWING!

Eventually, I got this feeling that any time I walked toward a new challenge, I knew it might be tough to get through but whatever was on the other side would be awesome.

So today, when I see a problem that looks really thorny, something maybe you'd rather avoid, I look at it and say

'THIS IS GONNA BE AWESOME!'

I started my first company a few months after graduating because I really wanted to run my own business. It was hard, but I've gotten better at that, too. I've started a few more companies and I like working with students who want to start their own companies too, so they can be as successful as possible!

Engineers are just like artists—they're creative. For me, that means building apps and building companies—and helping other people along the way.

The next generation of engineers will change the world in ways we can only begin to imagine, and the U of A Faculty of Engineering wants you to be a part of it!

The things you use every day—the iPod you listen to, the cell phone you text with, even the systems that provide you with clean drinking water—have all been designed and built by engineers. Things you will use in the future—eco-friendly energy sources, innovative

medical technology and revolutionary social media networks—will be the products of tomorrow's creative engineers. You could be one of them!

To learn more about engineering, please visit:

www.engineering.ualberta.ca

FACULTY OF
ENGINEERING
UNIVERSITY OF ALBERTA

By sketching the graph, we can now identify the range of the function as $-\dfrac{1}{2} \le y \le \dfrac{1}{2}$.

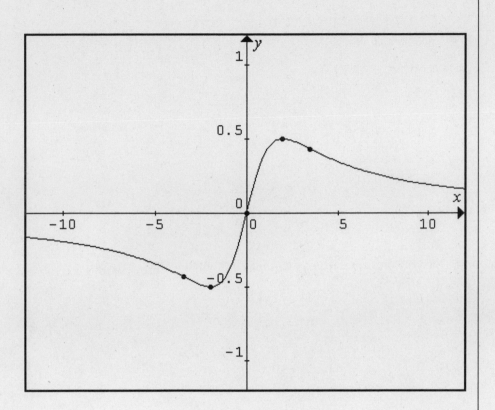

PRACTICE EXERCISE

1. Which of the following functions will have an oblique asymptote?

   a) $f(x) = \dfrac{3x^2 - x}{x + 7}$

   b) $f(x) = \dfrac{-5x + 2}{x - 3}$

   c) $f(x) = \dfrac{3x^2 + 4}{x}$

   d) $f(x) = \dfrac{3x^3 - x^2}{x^2 + 5}$

   e) $f(x) = \dfrac{6x^3 + 2x^2 + 3x + 1}{-7x^3 + x}$

   f) $f(x) = \dfrac{4x^4 + 6}{2x^2 - 1}$

2. Find the equation of the oblique asymptotes for each of the following functions.

   a) $f(x) = \dfrac{2x^2 + 3}{x}$

   b) $f(x) = \dfrac{3x^2 - 7x}{x - 2}$

   c) $f(x) = \dfrac{6x^3 - 5x}{x^2 + 1}$

   d) $f(x) = \dfrac{-4x^3 + 2x^2 + x - 4}{x^2 - 2x}$

REVIEW SUMMARY

In this unit, you have learned how to. . .

- determine x- and y-intercepts by substituting zero in for each in turn

- determine what type of symmetry a function has by applying the rules:
  - when $f(x) = f(-x)$, the function is even and symmetric about the y-axis
  - when $-f(x) = f(-x)$, the function is odd and symmetric about the origin

- determine the intervals of increase and decrease for a function using the critical values of the first derivative

- find the maximum and minimum values of a function

- determine the concavity intervals and inflections points of a function using the second derivative of a function

- describe how the graph of a function relates to the graph of its derivatives

- find the equations of vertical, horizontal, and oblique asymptotes by evaluating left- and right-hand limits and limits at infinity

- solve optimization problems using the principles of maximum and minimum values

PRACTICE TEST

1. Use the following graph to answer the questions below.

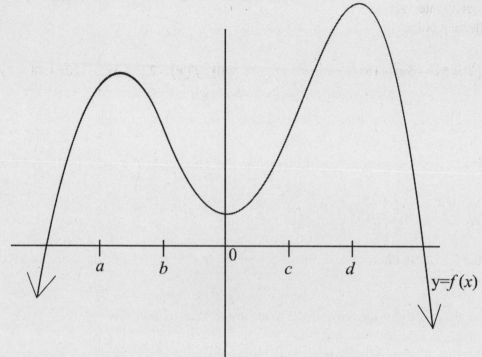

The function graphed above is a degree 4 polynomial function. Using $\pm\infty$, a, b, and 0, state the interval(s) or x-values when each of the following situations is true.

a) $f(x)$ is increasing _____

b) $f'(x)$ is negative _____

c) $f''(x)$ is positive _____

d) $f'(x) = 0$ _____

2. For the following functions, determine
  a) the intervals of increase and decrease
  b) any local maximum and minimum values
  c) the concavity intervals
  d) any inflection points

  i) $f(x) = 5x^3 - 5x^2 - 15$

  ii) $f(x) = 2x^3 + 3x^2 - 120x + 48$

3. For the function $f(x) = \dfrac{x+2}{x^2-9}$,

a) determine the x- and y-intercepts

b) determine the equation of any vertical asymptotes and the left- and right-hand limits as the function approaches the asymptote

c) determine the equation of any horizontal asymptotes

d) determine the intervals of increase/decrease and any maximum or minimum values

e) determine the intervals of concavity and any points of inflection

f) use the information from parts (a), (b), (c), (d) and (e) above to sketch a graph of the function

4. For the function $f(x) = \dfrac{x^2 + 4x + 4}{x + 1}$,

   a)   determine the x- and y-intercepts

   b)   determine the equation of any vertical asymptotes and the left- and right-hand limits, as the function approaches the asymptote

   c)   determine the equation of the oblique asymptote

   d)   determine the intervals of increase/decrease and any maximum or minimum values

   e)   determine the intervals of concavity and any points of inflection

   f)   use the information from parts (a), (b), (c), (d) and (e) above to sketch a graph of the function

5. A new square-bottomed juice box needs to be designed to hold 1 litre of juice. What should the dimensions of the box be so that it has a minimum surface area. Recall that $1L = 1\ 000\ cm^3$.

6. What is the maximum possible area of an isosceles triangle whose equal sides each measure 10 cm?

7. Using first and second derivatives, sketch the graph of the given function by examining intervals of increase/decrease, local extrema, intervals of concavity, inflection points, and the y-intercept.

$$f(x) = -x^3 + 4x^2 + 3x + 5$$

APPLICATIONS OF DERIVATIVES

When you are finished this unit, you should be able to. . .

- find and use the velocity function, given a displacement function
- find and use the acceleration function, given a displacement function
- determine unknown rates in problems involving volumes and areas
- determine unknown rates in problems involving triangles
- determine and use the marginal cost function
- determine and use the marginal revenue function
- use the profit function to determine the level of production that will yield maximum profit
- determine growth and decay functions and use them to determine instantaneous rates of growth and decay
- use Newton's Method to approximate roots of equations

PREREQUISITE SKILLS AND KNOWLEDGE

Prior to beginning this unit, you should be able to. . .

- differentiate polynomial and rational functions
- differentiate trigonometric functions
- differentiate exponential functions
- calculate areas and volumes of geometric shapes
- determine trigonometric ratios
- use the law of sines and law of cosines
- use the Pythagorean Theorem
- use the idea of exponential growth and decay to solve related problems

Lesson 1   *DISTANCE, VELOCITY, AND ACCELERATION*

It is important to have a clear understanding of what a derivative represents. For any function, $f(x)$, the derivative $f'(x)$ represents the rate of change of that function for any value of x in its domain.

If the function is expressing displacement, s, as a function of time, t, the derivative of this function represents the rate at which the displacement is changing with respect to time, which is also known as velocity.
Similarly, the rate at which the velocity is changing, with respect to time, is called acceleration.

$$\text{displacement} = s$$

$$\text{velocity} = v = \frac{ds}{dt}$$

$$\text{acceleration} = a = \frac{dv}{dt} = \frac{d^2 s}{dt^2}$$

The sign of the velocity indicates whether the displacement is increasing or decreasing at that instant in time.
If $\bar{v} > 0$, then $\bar{s}$ is increasing at that instant.
If $\bar{v} < 0$, then $\bar{s}$ is decreasing at that instant.

The sign of the acceleration indicates whether the velocity is increasing or decreasing at that instant in time.
If $\bar{a} > 0$, then $\bar{v}$ is increasing at that instant.
If $\bar{a} < 0$, then $\bar{v}$ is decreasing at that instant.

Throughout this chapter, we will use Leibniz notation as it lends itself very well to the discussion of rates.
Recall that when using Leibniz notation, the first derivative is represented as $\frac{dy}{dx}$.

The following function represents the displacement, with respect to time, of an object that has been thrown off a 250 m cliff in a downward direction at a velocity of 9 m/s.

$$s = -4.9t^2 - 9t + 250$$

For questions involving falling objects, we assume the ground has a displacement of zero, and that all points above the ground have a positive displacement.

NOTES

Its velocity can, therefore, be represented by the first derivative of this function:

$$v = \frac{ds}{dt} = -9.8t - 9$$

If we take the derivative again, we get the acceleration function:

$$a = \frac{dv}{dt} = -9.8$$

Since gravity is the force that produces a constant acceleration toward Earth, the acceleration is a constant that does not change with respect to time.

The sign of $\bar{a}$ indicates what $\bar{v}$ is doing. Since $\bar{a} < 0$ for the duration of this problem, the velocity of this object must be decreasing at all times. The velocitiy function can be used to illustrate this point.

$$v(0) = -9.8(0) - 9 = -9$$

$$v(1) = -9.8(1) - 9 = -18.8$$

Example 1

The function $s = -4.9t^2 - 12t + 180$ represents the displacement of a particular falling object with respect to time in seconds.
Answer the following questions about this object's fall.

a) How long does it take the object to fall to the ground?
b) What is the object's velocity just before impact and what is its maximum speed?
c) How long does it take the object to reach a downward speed of 20 m/s?
d) What is the velocity of the object when $t = 3$ s?
e) What is the maximum acceleration?

Solution

a) Sketch the situation:

Quadratic formula:

$$x = \frac{-b \pm \sqrt{b^2 - 4ac}}{2a}$$

When the object hits the ground, displacement is 0 m, so substitute 0 in for s and solve for t.

$s = -4.9t^2 - 12t + 180$

$0 = -4.9t^2 - 12t + 180$

Use the quadratic formula to solve for t:

$$t = \frac{-(-12s) \pm \sqrt{(-12s)^2 - 4(-4.9)(180)}}{2(-4.9)}$$

$t \approx 4.96s$

It will take 4.96 s for the object to fall to the ground.

The work is shown using rounded values; however, all calculations are made without rounding. Rounding should only take place at the last step.

b) Find the velocity function:

$v = \dfrac{ds}{dt} = -9.8t - 12$

Substitute the time it takes the object to reach the ground, since the maximum speed occurs just as the object hits the ground.

$v = -9.8(4.96s) - 12$

$v = -60.6\,\text{m/s}$

The velocity is –60.6 m/s.

The negative sign attached to the velocity indicates the downward direction of the velocity.

The object reaches a maximum speed (not velocity) of 60.6 m/s just before impact.

Since this problem deals with a restricted domain, $0 \le t \le \dfrac{12 - \sqrt{3672}}{-9.8}$,

the endpoints of the velocity function must be considered.

$v(0) = -12$ m/s and $v\left(\dfrac{12 - \sqrt{3672}}{-9.8}\right) \doteq -60.6$ m/s.

Studying the graph of the velocity-time function in its restricted domain enables us to see that the velocity of –60.0 m/s is an absolute minimum value.

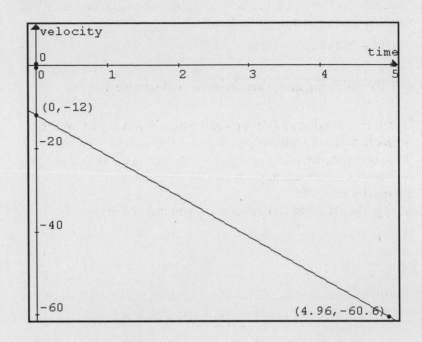

c) Substitute the velocity of –20 m/s into the velocity function.
$$-20 = -9.8t - 12$$
$$t = 0.82\text{s}$$
It will take 0.82 s to reach a velocity of –20 m/s.

d) At $t = 3$ s, the velocity is found by substituting 3 in for t.
$$v = -9.8(3\text{s}) - 12$$
$$v = -41.4\text{m/s}$$

e) Find the acceleration function.
$$a = \frac{dv}{dt} = -9.8\text{m/s}^2$$

This is a constant function. The acceleration does not change and, therefore, has a maximum of –9.8 m/s^2.

Example 2

On a distant, yet-to-be-discovered planet, the acceleration due to gravity is less than it is on Earth. On this planet, a particular falling object's displacement, as a function of time, is:

$$s = -3.2t^2 + 2.5t + 70$$

Answer the following questions about this falling object.

a) Sketch the situation and determine the time that it would take the object to reach the ground.

b) What is the object's
   i) velocity at 1.5 seconds?
   ii) maximum speed?

c) What is the acceleration due to gravity on this planet?

Solution

a)

Cliff $s = 70$ m

$s = -3.2t^2 + 2.5t + 70$

$s = 0$ m   Ground

$$0 = -3.2t^2 + 2.5t + 70$$

$$t = \frac{-(2.5) \pm \sqrt{(2.5)^2 - 4(-3.2)(70)}}{2(-3.2)}$$

$$t = 5.08$$

b) i) $s = -3.2t^2 + 2.5t + 70$

$$v = \frac{ds}{dt}$$

$$= -6.4t + 2.5$$

at $t = 1.5$

$$v = -6.4(1.5s) + 2.5$$

$$= -7.1 \text{ m/s}$$

ii) $v = -6.4(5.08s) + 2.5 \ = -30.0 \text{ m/s}$

The object reaches a maximum speed of 30.0 m/s just before impact.

c) $a = \dfrac{dv}{dt} = -6.4 \text{ m/s}^2$

PRACTICE EXERCISE

1. A bullet is fired straight up in the air at a speed of 900 m/s. The equation relating its height as a function of time is $h = -4.9t^2 + 900t + 2.4$.

   a) How long does it take the bullet to hit the ground?

   b) What are the maximum and minimum values of the velocity of the bullet?

   c) What is the velocity of the bullet after 60 seconds?
   Which direction is the bullet traveling?

2. On the moon, an object is dropped straight down into a crater 150 m deep. The height of the object from the bottom of the crater, as it falls, is given by $h = -0.8t^2 + 150$.

a) What is the falling object's maximum speed?

b) What is the acceleration due to gravity on the moon?

3. On three different planets, the following functions express the height of an object that is thrown downward and is falling 200 m.

Neptune: $h = -5.88t^2 - 8t + 200$

Mars: $h = -1.85t^2 - 8t + 200$

Venus: $h = -4.45t^2 - 8t + 200$

a) What is the acceleration due to gravity on each planet?

b) What is the maximum speed of the falling object on Venus?

c) How much faster is the maximum speed of the falling object on Neptune than the velocity on Mars?

Lesson 2   RATES OF CHANGE INVOLVING AREA AND VOLUME

Calculus is all about dynamic situations, and the topic of related rates is an excellent illustration of how we can use derivatives to discover information about some dynamic relationships in geometry.

Consider a spherical balloon that is being inflated with air. Because we are inflating the balloon, there are a number of dynamic or changing quantities involved. These include the balloon's volume, surface area, and radius.

Consider in particular the radius and volume. We know that these quantities are related through the formula for the volume of a sphere:

$$V = \frac{4}{3}\pi r^3 \ .$$

However, since the balloon is being inflated, these quantities of volume and radius are changing, and this change is happening with the passage of time. Therefore we have rates of change, which is where derivatives are involved.

In order to change this volume formula to make it describe a dynamic situation, we must differentiate it implicitly with respect to time.
The introduction of time necessitates the introduction of a new variable into the process of differentiation.

Each variable or changing quantity, must be differentiated with respect to time (*t*), yielding:

$$\frac{dV}{dt} = \frac{4}{3}\pi \left(3r^2 \frac{dr}{dt} \right)$$

$$\frac{dV}{dt} = 4\pi r^2 \frac{dr}{dt}$$

It is important to recall that π is a constant and not a variable.

When inflating a balloon by mechanical means, it is easy to measure the rate at which the volume is increasing, but less easy to measure the rate at which the radius increases. This method allows us to use rates that we can easily measure, or obtain information about, in order to calculate rates that are harder to measure directly.

In general, the procedure to follow for this type of problem is:
- Sketch and label a diagram.
- Identify, assign, and define variables and rates.
- Relate known and desired quantities using established mathematical relationships (formulas).
- Use substitution to minimize the number of variables in the relation to the number that are needed.
- Substitute only fixed, unchanging values into the formula.
- Differentiate with respect to time.
- Substitute changing values and rates into the differentiated expression.
- Solve for the desired rate.

Example 1

Consider the inflating balloon. If the volume is increasing at a rate of 125 cm³/s, calculate the rate at which the radius is increasing when the radius measures 10 cm.

Solution

Sketch and define.

V = volume

r = radius = 10 cm

$$\frac{dV}{dt} = 125 \text{ cm}^3/\text{s}$$

$$\frac{dr}{dt} = ?$$

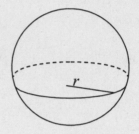

For the purposes of this question, assume that the balloon is a perfect sphere.

Relate and differentiate:

$$V = \frac{4}{3}\pi r^3$$

$$\frac{dV}{dt} = 4\pi r^2 \frac{dr}{dt}$$

We cannot substitute $r = 10$ cm until *after* we differentiate because r is a changing quantity.

Substitute:

$$125 = 4\pi\left(10\text{cm}\right)^2 \frac{dr}{dt}$$

The desired quantity can be isolated before or after substitution.

$$\frac{dr}{dt} = \frac{125 \text{ cm}^3/\text{s}}{400\pi\text{ cm}^2}$$

$$= \frac{5}{16\pi} \text{ cm/s}$$

This should be left as an exact value unless a decimal approximation is specifically requested or required.

The radius of the balloon is increasing at a rate of $\dfrac{5}{16\pi}$ cm/s at the instant in time that $r = 10$ cm.

Example 2

A cube is shrinking and maintaining its shape. If the side length of the cube is decreasing at a rate of 2 cm/s, at what rate is the surface area decreasing when the side length is 25 cm?

Solution

SA = Surface area

s = side length = 25 cm

$\dfrac{d\,SA}{dt} = ?$

$\dfrac{ds}{dt} = -2$ cm/s

Note that $\dfrac{ds}{dt}$ is negative. This is because the side length is decreasing.

$SA = 6s^2$

$\dfrac{d(SA)}{dt} = 12s\dfrac{ds}{dt}$

$\dfrac{d(SA)}{dt} = 12(25\,\text{cm})(-2\ \text{cm/s})$

$\qquad\qquad = -600\ \text{cm}^2/\text{s}$

The negative, again, indicates a decreasing quantity.

When the side length is 25 cm, the surface area is decreasing at a rate of 600 cm^2/s.

Example 3

The radius of a spherical balloon is decreasing at a rate of 3.5 cm/s. At what rate is the surface area of the balloon decreasing when the radius is 14 cm?

Solution

SA = Surface area

r = radius = 14 cm

$\dfrac{d\,SA}{dt} = ?$

$\dfrac{dr}{dt} = -3.5$ cm/s

$SA = 4\pi r^2$

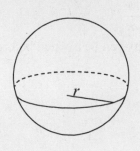

$$\frac{d(SA)}{dt} = 8\pi r \frac{dr}{dt}$$
$$= 8\pi(14\,\text{cm})(-3.5\,\text{cm/s})$$
$$= -392\pi$$

When the radius is 14 cm, the surface area is decreasing at a rate of $392\pi\,\text{cm}^2/\text{s}$.

Example 4

A circle's area is changing at a rate of $-22\,\text{cm}^2/\text{s}$. At what rate is the radius of the circle changing when the circumference of the circle is 120 cm?

Solution

The change in circumference is not the rate that we are given, nor is it the rate that we want to find. The information about the circumference is useful only in that it allows us to find the radius at the point of time that we are interested in.

A = area
r = radius
circumference $= 2\pi r$

$$120\,\text{cm} = 2\pi r$$
$$r = \frac{60\,\text{cm}}{\pi}$$

$$\frac{dA}{dt} = -22\ \text{cm}^2/\text{s}$$

$$\frac{dr}{dt} = ?$$

$$A = \pi r^2$$

$$\frac{dA}{dt} = \pi 2r \frac{dr}{dt}$$

$$-22\ \text{cm}^2/\text{s} = 2\pi\left(\frac{60\ \text{cm}}{\pi}\right)\frac{dr}{dt}$$

$$-22\ \text{cm}^2/\text{s} = 120\ \text{cm}\frac{dr}{dt}$$

$$\frac{dr}{dt} = -\frac{22\,\text{cm}^2/\text{s}}{120\ \text{cm}}$$

$$= -\frac{11}{60}\ \text{cm/s}$$

When the circumference of the circle is 120 cm, the radius is changing at a rate of $-\frac{11}{60}$ cm/s.

Example 5

A water tank has the shape of an upright cylinder. The cylinder is filling at a rate of 1.5 m³/minute. If the tank has a radius of 2 m, at what rate is the water level increasing when the water is 3.2 m deep?

Solution

V = volume

r = radius = 2 m (constant)

h = height of water = 3.2 m

$$\frac{dV}{dt} = 1.5 \text{ m}^3/\text{s}$$

$$\frac{dh}{dt} = ?$$

$$V = \pi r^2 h$$

We can substitute the value of the radius because it is not changing:

$$V = \pi (2\text{m})^2 h$$

$$V = 4\,\text{m}^2 \pi h$$

$$\frac{dV}{dt} = 4\,\text{m}^2 \pi \frac{dh}{dt}$$

$$1.5 \text{ m}^3/\text{min} = 4\,\text{m}^2 \pi \frac{dh}{dt}$$

$$\frac{dh}{dt} = \frac{1.5\,\text{m}^3/\text{min}}{4\pi\,\text{m}^2}$$

$$\frac{dh}{dt} = \frac{15\,\text{m}^3/\text{min}}{40\pi\,\text{m}^2}$$

$$= \frac{3\,\text{m}^3/\text{min}}{8\pi\,\text{m}^2}$$

The height is changing at a rate of $\frac{3}{8\pi}$ m/min.

Example 6

Water is draining out of a cone-shaped tank at a rate of 2.5 m^3/min.
The tank has a height of 8 m and a diameter, at the top, of 5 m.
At what rate is the water level dropping when the depth of water is 2.8 m?

Solution

V = volume

R = radius

h = height = 2.8 m (at the moment of interest)

$$\frac{dV}{dt} = -2.5 \text{ m}^3/\text{min}$$

$$\frac{dr}{dt} = \text{not given}$$

$$\frac{dh}{dt} = ?$$

$$V = \frac{1}{3}\pi r^2 h$$

$r = 2.5$

$h = 8$

Since the radius at the moment of interest is not given or requested information, we can use information in the question to eliminate this variable.

The ratio of height and radius of the water in the tank will remain constant throughout the fill and is given by:

$$\frac{r}{h} = \frac{2.5\,\text{m}}{8\,\text{m}}$$

$$\frac{r}{h} = \frac{5}{16}$$

$$r = \frac{5}{16}h$$

Substitute into the formula:

$$V = \frac{1}{3}\pi \left(\frac{5}{16}h\right)^2 h$$

$$V = \frac{25\pi}{768}h^3$$

$$\frac{dV}{dt} = \frac{25\pi}{256}h^2 \frac{dh}{dt}$$

$$-2.5 = \frac{25\pi}{256}(2.8)^2 \frac{dh}{dt}$$

$$\frac{-2.5(256)}{(2.8)^2 25\pi} = \frac{dh}{dt}$$

$$\frac{dh}{dt} = \frac{-160}{49\pi}$$

The water level is decreasing at a rate of $\dfrac{160}{49\pi}$ m/min.

PRACTICE EXERCISE

1. For each of the following problems, find the desired rate.

   a) $V = s^3$

   $\dfrac{ds}{dt} = 3$ m/s

   Find $\dfrac{dV}{dt}$ when $s = 10$ m.

   b) $A = \pi r^2$

   $\dfrac{dA}{dt} = -1.2$ m^2/s

   Find $\dfrac{dr}{dt}$ when $A = 15$ m^2.

2. The area of a square is increasing at a rate of 20 cm^2/s. At what rate is the side length increasing when the side length is 200 cm?

3. The volume of a melting spherical ball of snow is decreasing at a rate of 40 cm^3/s. If it is assumed that the ball of snow is melting uniformly, at what rate is the radius decreasing when the radius of the ball is 3.5 cm?

4. A landscaping company is pouring rock chips into a conical pile with a constant ratio of 2:5 between the radius and height. The volume of the rock chips is increasing at a rate of 1.8 m^3/min. At what rate is the height increasing when the radius is 3 m?

5. The volume of an expanding cube is increasing at a rate of 6 m^3/s. At what rate is the length of the side of the cube increasing when the surface area of the cube is 40 m^2?

Lesson 3   RATES OF CHANGE INVOLVING TRIANGLES

As with the other types of related rates questions, one of the first steps in the question is determining how the variables relate to one another. Because we will be working with triangles, the relationships will be defined by any of the following methods:

- similar triangle ratios
- Pythagorean Theorem
- right-angle trigonometry ratios:

$$\sin \theta = \frac{opposite}{hypoteneuse}$$

$$\cos \theta = \frac{adjacent}{hypoteneuse}$$

$$\tan \theta = \frac{opposite}{adjacent}$$

Law of Sines

$$\frac{\sin A}{a} = \frac{\sin B}{b} = \frac{\sin C}{c}$$

Law of Cosines

$$a^2 = b^2 + c^2 - 2bc \cos A$$

Example 1

A 15 foot ladder is leaning against a building. The base of the ladder begins sliding away from the wall at a rate of 2.5 ft/s.

a) At what rate is the ladder sliding down the wall when the top of the ladder is 3 feet from the floor?

b) At what rate is the angle formed by the ladder and the floor decreasing when the base of the ladder is 10 ft from the wall? (Round your answer to 2 decimal places).

Solution

Let *x* represent the changing distance from the base of the ladder to the wall. Let *y* represent the changing distance from the top of the ladder to the floor, along the wall. Let θ be the angle formed by the floor and the ladder.

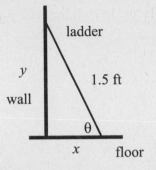

a) Using the Pythagorean Theorem:

$$c^2 = a^2 + b^2$$

$$15\,\text{ft}^2 = x^2 + y^2$$

$$225\,\text{ft}^2 = x^2 + y^2$$

$$0 = 2x\frac{dx}{dt} + 2y\frac{dy}{dt}$$

The ladder is sliding away from the wall at a rate of 2.5 ft/s, so,

$$\frac{dx}{dt} = 2.5\,\text{ft/s}$$

When *y* = 3 ft,

$$x = \sqrt{225\,\text{ft}^2 - (3\text{ft})^2}$$

$$= \sqrt{216}\,\text{ft}^2$$

$$= 6\sqrt{6}\text{ft}$$

Substitute for $\frac{dx}{dt}$, *x,* and *y*:

$$0 = 2x\frac{dx}{dt} + 2y\frac{dy}{dt}$$

$$0 = 2\left(6\sqrt{6}\text{ft}\right)(2.5\,\text{ft/s}) + 2(3\,\text{ft})\frac{dy}{dt}$$

$$\frac{dy}{dt} = -5\sqrt{6}$$

When the top of the ladder is 3 feet from the floor, the ladder is sliding down the wall at a rate of $5\sqrt{6}$ ft/s.

b) Using trigonometric ratios:

$$\cos\theta = \frac{x}{15\,\text{ft}}$$

$$-(\sin\theta)\frac{d\theta}{dt} = \frac{1}{15\,\text{ft}}\frac{dx}{dt}$$

When the base of the ladder is 10 ft from the wall:

$$\cos\theta = \frac{10\,\text{ft}}{15\,\text{ft}}$$

$$\theta = \cos^{-1}\left(\frac{10}{15}\right)$$

$$\approx 0.841$$

Substitute for θ and $\dfrac{dx}{dt}$:

$$-(\sin\theta)\frac{d\theta}{dt} = \frac{1}{15}\frac{dx}{dt}$$

$$-(\sin(0.841))\frac{d\theta}{dt} = \frac{1}{15}(2.5)$$

$$\frac{d\theta}{dt} = \frac{-2.5}{15\sin(0.841)}$$

$$\approx -0.22$$

The angle is decreasing at a rate of 0.22 rad/s when the base of the ladder is 10 ft from the wall.

This problem can be solved in another way, without determining the value of the angle θ.

At the instant that $x = 10$ m, $y = \sqrt{15^2 - 10^2} = \sqrt{125} = 5\sqrt{5}$ m

and $\sin\theta = \dfrac{5\sqrt{5}}{15} = \dfrac{\sqrt{5}}{3}$.

Rearranging our derivative equation:

$$-(\sin\theta)\frac{d_\theta}{d_t} = \frac{1}{15}\frac{d_x}{d_t}$$

$$\frac{d_\theta}{d_t} = -\frac{\dfrac{d_x}{d_t}}{15\sin\theta}$$

Substituting values:

$$\frac{d_\theta}{d_t} = -\frac{2.5}{15\left(\dfrac{\sqrt{5}}{3}\right)} \doteq -0.22 \text{ rad/s}$$

Example 2

A streetlight is 6 m tall. A person who is 2 m tall is walking away from the light at a rate of 1.5 m/s. How fast is the tip of the shadow cast by the person moving away from the base of the light post?

Solution

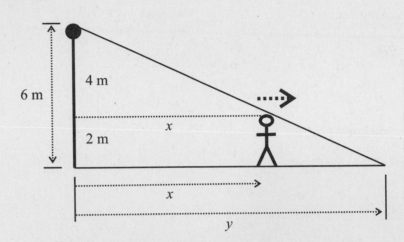

Let x be the distance that the person is from the light post.
Let y be the distance the shadow is from the light post.
By similar triangles:

$$\frac{x}{4\,\mathrm{m}} = \frac{y}{6\,\mathrm{m}}$$

$$\left(\frac{1}{4}\right)\frac{dx}{dt} = \left(\frac{1}{6}\right)\frac{dy}{dt}$$

$$\left(\frac{6\,\mathrm{m}}{4\,\mathrm{m}}\right)\left(\frac{dx}{dt}\right) = \frac{dy}{dt}$$

$$\frac{dy}{dt} = \frac{3}{2}(1.5\,\mathrm{m/s})$$
$$= \frac{9}{4}\,\mathrm{m/s}$$
$$= 2.25\,\mathrm{m/s}$$

The shadow is moving at a speed of 2.25 m/s away from the light post.

Example 3

At 1:00 P.M., a van is 140 km due north of a car. The van is travelling due west at 60 km/h and the car is heading north at 50 km/h. At what rate is the distance between them changing at 3:00 P.M.?

Solution

At 1:00 P.M.

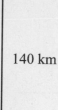

Van

140 km

Car

At 3:00 P.M.

Van ———— 120 km

x

z ... y | 40 km

Car

100 km

$$z = \sqrt{(120\,\text{km})^2 + (40\,\text{km})^2}$$
$$= \sqrt{1\,600\,\text{km}^2}$$
$$= 40\sqrt{10}\,\text{km}$$

Let x be the horizontal distance between the vehicles.
Let y be the vertical distance between the vehicles.
Let z be the shortest distance between the vehicles.

$$\frac{dx}{dt} = 60\,\text{km/h}, \qquad \frac{dy}{dt} = -50\,\text{km/h}, \qquad \frac{dz}{dt} = ?$$

Using the Pythagorean Theorem:

$$x^2 + y^2 = z^2$$

$$2x\frac{dx}{dt} + 2y\frac{dy}{dt} = 2z\frac{dz}{dt}$$

Substitute

$$2(120\,\text{km})(60\,\text{km/h}) + 2(40\,\text{km})(-50\,\text{km/h}) = 2\left(40\sqrt{10}\,\text{km}\right)\frac{dz}{dt}$$

$$\frac{dz}{dt} = \frac{(120\,\text{km})(60\,\text{km/h}) + (40\,\text{km})(-50\,\text{km/h})}{\left(40\sqrt{10}\,\text{km}\right)}$$

$$= \frac{130}{\sqrt{10}}\,\text{km/h}$$

The distance between the car and van is increasing at a rate of $\dfrac{130}{\sqrt{10}}$ km/h.

Example 4

A triangle has 2 sides of length 15 cm and 17 cm. The angle between these sides is increasing at a rate of $\dfrac{\pi}{24}$ rads/s. At what rate is the length of the third side increasing when the opposite angle measures $\dfrac{\pi}{3}$ rads?

Solution

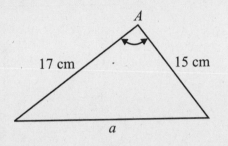

Using the Law of Cosines:

$a^2 = b^2 + c^2 - 2bc \cos A$

When $A = \dfrac{\pi}{3}$,

$a = \sqrt{(17\,\text{cm})^2 + (15\,\text{cm})^2 - 2(17\,\text{cm})(15\,\text{cm})\cos\left(\dfrac{\pi}{3}\right)}$

$ = \sqrt{289 + 225 - 510\left(\dfrac{1}{2}\right)}$

$ = \sqrt{259}\,\text{cm}$

$\dfrac{dA}{dt} = \dfrac{\pi}{24}$ rad/s

$\dfrac{da}{dt} = ?$

$$a^2 = b^2 + c^2 - 2bc\cos A$$

$$a^2 = (17\,\text{cm})^2 + (15\,\text{cm})^2 - 2(17\,\text{cm})(15\,\text{cm})\cos A$$

$$2a\frac{da}{dt} = 0 + 0 + 510\sin A\frac{dA}{dt}$$

$$2\left(\sqrt{259}\,\text{cm}\right)\frac{da}{dt} = 510\sin\left(\frac{\pi}{3}\right)\left(\frac{\pi}{24}\right)$$

$$\frac{da}{dt} = \frac{\dfrac{85\pi}{4}\left(\dfrac{\sqrt{3}}{2}\right)}{2\sqrt{259}}$$

$$= \frac{85\pi\sqrt{3}}{16\sqrt{259}}$$

$$\approx 1.8 \text{ cm/s}$$

The side is increasing at a rate of 1.8 cm/s.

PRACTICE EXERCISE

1. A man and a woman walk away from the same location at the same time. The man travels east at a rate of 2 m/s. The woman travels south at a rate of 1.8 m/s. At what rate is the distance between them increasing 5 minutes later?

2. A spotlight set on the ground is shining on a wall 20 m away. A person 1.7 m tall walks away from the light toward the wall at a rate of 1.4 m/s. At what rate is the shadow cast on the wall decreasing in height when the person is 14 m from the light?

3. A child is flying a kite. When her arm is outstretched, her hand is 1.6 m off the ground. The kite is at a constant altitude of 16.6 m. The wind is blowing the kite horizontally at a rate of 4 m/s.
At what rate is the length of string increasing when there is 30 m of string between the child's hand and the kite?

4. The length of the hypotenuse of a right triangle is constant at 64 cm. The vertical leg of the triangle is decreasing at a rate of 5 cm/s. At what rate is the angle opposite the vertical side changing when the horizontal side is 40 cm long?

5. A triangle's altitude is increasing at a rate of 3 cm/min and the triangle's area is increasing at a rate of 9 cm^2/min. At what rate is the base changing when the altitude is 20 cm and the area is 300 cm^2?

6. Two sides of a triangle have fixed lengths of 20 cm and 24 cm. The third side is increasing at a rate of 3.5 cm/s. When the third side is 15 cm in length, what is the rate of change for the angle between the fixed sides?

PRACTICE QUIZ

1. The height in metres from the ground of a falling object after t seconds is found to be $h = -4.9t^2 + 5t + 85$.

   a) How long will it take the falling object to reach the ground?

   b) What is the maximum speed of the falling object?

   c) What is the velocity of the object after 2.5 s?

   d) What is the acceleration of the falling object?

2. Find the unknown rate.
   $V = \dfrac{4}{3}\pi r^3$; $\dfrac{dV}{dt} = -6 \text{ m}^3/\text{s}$, when $r = 5 \text{ m}$, $\dfrac{dr}{dt} = ?$

3. A drop of water creates a circular ripple that moves outward at a rate of 20 cm/s. At what rate is the circumference of the circle increasing when the area of the circle is 10 000 cm^2?

4. As the sun rises, the shadow cast by a 15 m tree is decreasing at a rate of 55 cm/h. At what rate is the angle of elevation from the shadow to the sun increasing when the shadow is 15 m in length?

Lesson 4   APPLICATIONS IN ECONOMICS

Consider the function $C(x)$, where C is the total cost for a business or company to produce x items. Increasing the number of items produced has a corresponding increase in cost, ΔC. This means that the average rate at which the cost changes is given by:

$$\Delta C = C(x + \Delta x) - c(x)$$

$$\frac{\Delta C}{\Delta x} = \frac{C(x_1 + \Delta x) - C(x_1)}{\Delta x}$$

We can recognize this expression from first principles:

$$\lim_{\Delta x \to 0} \frac{C(x_1 + \Delta x) - C(x_1)}{\Delta x} = \frac{dC}{dx}$$

This case, in which $\Delta x \to 0$, is called the marginal cost (the rate at which cost is changing with respect to production).

Hence, marginal cost $= \dfrac{dC}{dx}$.

In other words, the derivative of the cost function is the marginal cost function.

Example 1

The following equation is the cost function for the production of x items:

$$C(x) = 5\,000 + 3x + 0.02x^2$$

Find the marginal cost function, and determine the marginal cost when there are 600 items being produced.

Solution

$$C'(x) = 3 + 0.04x$$

$$C'(600) = 3 + 0.04(600)$$
$$= 3 + 24$$
$$= \$27 \text{ per item}$$

Example 2

The cost function for the production of x items for a particular company is:

$C(x) = 8\,000 + 6x + 0.015x^2$

How many items are being produced if the marginal cost is \$21.78?

Solution

$C'(x) = 6 + 0.03x$

$21.78 = 6 + 0.03x$

$15.78 = 0.03x$

$526 = x$

When the marginal cost is \$21.78, 526 items are being produced.

Some of the other important functions in economics include the *demand* or *price* function, $p(x)$, and the revenue function, $R(x) = xp(x)$.

The derivative of the revenue function, $R'(x)$, represents the rate of change of revenue with respect to the number of items sold, x. This function is called the marginal revenue function.

By definition, Profit = Revenue − Cost.
So, it makes sense that

$P(x) = R(x) - C(x)$

and

$P'(x) = R'(x) - C'(x)$

Using what we know about extreme values, we know that $P(x)$ can have a maximum value when $P'(x) = 0$.

It follows then, when $P'(x) = 0$:

$P'(x) = R'(x) - C'(x)$

$0 = R'(x) - C'(x)$

$C'(x) = R'(x)$

We can conclude that if the profit is a maximum, the marginal cost and marginal revenue are equal.

Since companies are interested in maximizing profit; this is a very useful application.

Example 3

A company determines that its demand function for selling x widgets is

$p(x) = 10 - 0.02x.$

a) Determine the revenue function $R(x)$.

b) Determine the marginal revenue function $R'(x)$.

c) Determine the marginal revenue when 1 800 items are sold.

d) How many items must be sold to have marginal revenue of -46?

Solution

a) $R(x) = xp(x)$

$R(x) = x(10 - 0.02x)$

$\quad = 10x - 0.02x^2$

b) $R'(x) = 10 - 0.04x$

c) $R'(1\ 800) = 10 - 0.04(1\ 800)$

$\quad = 10 - 72$

$\quad = -62$

This means that the rate at which the revenue is changing is $-\$62$/item when 1 800 items are sold.

d) $-46 = 10 - 0.04x$

$\dfrac{-56}{-0.04} = x$

$1\ 400 = x$

1 400 items must be produced

Example 4

A company produces x batches of its product and has determined that its demand function is

$$p(x) = 5.5 - 0.012x$$

and its cost function is

$$C(x) = 90 + 1.5x - 0.02x^2 + 0.000\,3x^3.$$

Determine the number of batches that the company must produce in order to maximize its profit.

Solution

For maximum profit, $C'(x) = R'(x)$. We need to:

• determine the revenue function, $R(x)$

• determine $C'(x)$ and $R'(x)$

• set $C'(x) = R'(x)$ and solve the resulting equation

$$R(x) = xp(x)$$
$$= x(5.5 - 0.012x)$$
$$R(x) = 5.5x - 0.012x^2$$

$$C'(x) = 1.5 - 0.04x + 0.000\,9x^2$$

$$R'(x) = 5.5 - 0.024x$$

$$C'(x) = R'(x)$$
$$1.5 - 0.04x + 0.000\,9x^2 = 5.5 - 0.024x$$
$$0.000\,9x^2 - 0.016x - 4 = 0$$
$$x = \frac{-(-0.016) \pm \sqrt{(-0.016)^2 - 4(0.000\,9)(-4)}}{2(0.000\,9)}$$
$$\approx 76.146$$

The company should produce 76 batches in order to maximize profit.

PRACTICE EXERCISE

1. A cost function, for cost in dollars, is represented as $C(x) = 3\,000 + 4.2x + 0.01x^2$.

   a) What is the marginal cost function?

   b) Determine the marginal cost when production is at 1 000 units.

   c) How many units need to be produced to give a marginal cost of $40?

2. A demand function is $p(x) = 6 - 0.008x$.

   a) What is the revenue function?

   b) What is the marginal revenue function?

   c) Determine the marginal revenue when 650 items are produced.

3. Using the demand function from question 2, and the cost function
$C(x) = 55 + 1.9x - 0.009x^2 + 0.000\,08x^3$,

   a) What is the profit function?

   b) How many items need to be produced in order to maximize profit?

Lesson 5 *APPLICATIONS IN BIOLOGICAL SCIENCES*

EXPONENTIAL GROWTH AND DECAY

The function that describes continuous exponential growth or decay

is $f(t) = Ae^{kt}$. It will be derived in an upcoming unit.

This function models exponential growth or decay as a function of time where:

* $f(t)$ is the amount of the growing or decaying substance after a time t

* t is the time in hours, minutes, seconds, or years, etc.

* A is the initial amount of the substance $(f(0) = A)$

* e is the base of the natural logarithm

* k is a constant; when $k > 0$, $f(t)$ is a growth function and when $k < 0$,

    $f(t)$ is a decay function

Many functions that are growing or decaying exponentially are discrete, but can be modelled with this continuous function.

Because the growth and decay functions are exponential, the rate of growth and decay is changing. We can use derivatives to determine these rates at any particular time.

Example 1

The number of bacteria in a particular culture after t hours is known to be

$$f(t) = 1\,000e^{\left(\frac{1}{2}\ln 4\right)t}.$$

a) What is the rate of bacterial growth after t hours?

b) What is the rate of bacterial growth after 5 hours?

Solution

a) $f(t) = 1\,000e^{\left(\frac{1}{2}\ln 4\right)t}$

$f'(t) = 1\,000\left(\frac{1}{2}\ln 4\right)e^{\left(\frac{1}{2}\ln 4\right)t}$

$= 500\ln 4e^{\left(\frac{1}{2}\ln 4\right)t}$

b) $f'(t) = 500\ln 4e^{\left(\frac{1}{2}\ln 4\right)t}$

$f'(5) = 500\ln 4e^{\left(\frac{1}{2}\ln 4\right)5}$

$\approx 22\,180.71$

The answer to this type of question is more meaningful as a decimal approximation than as an exact value.

After 5 hours, the bacteria is growing at a rate of 22 181 bacteria/hour.

NOTES

Example 2

The mass of a radioactive substance, in grams, after t days is known to be $f(t) = 100e^{\left(-\frac{\ln 2}{125}\right)t}$.

a) What is the rate of radioactive decay after t days?
b) What is the rate of radioactive decay after 100 days?

Solution

a) $f(t) = 100e^{\left(-\frac{\ln 2}{125}\right)t}$

$f'(t) = 100e^{\left(-\frac{\ln 2}{125}\right)t}\left(-\frac{\ln 2}{125}\right)$

$= -\frac{4\ln 2}{5}e^{\left(-\frac{\ln 2}{125}\right)t}$

b) $f'(100) = -\frac{4\ln 2}{5}e^{\left(-\frac{\ln 2}{125}\right)100}$

$f'(100) \approx -0.318$

The mass is decreasing at a rate of 0.318 g/day.

Example 3

The number of bacteria in a particular culture after t hours is known to be $f(t) = 3\,000e^{\left(\frac{1}{4}\ln 5\right)t}$.

How long will it take for the growth rate to be 10 000 bacteria/hour?

Solution

$f'(t) = 3000e^{\left(\frac{1}{4}\ln 5\right)t}\left(\frac{1}{4}\ln 5\right)$

$= 750\ln 5e^{\left(\frac{1}{4}\ln 5\right)t}$

Substitute 10 000 in for $f'(t)$:

$10\,000 = 750\ln 5e^{\left(\frac{1}{4}\ln 5\right)t}$

$\frac{10\,000}{750\ln 5} = e^{\left(\frac{1}{4}\ln 5\right)t}$

Take the natural log of both sides:

$$\ln\left(\frac{10\ 000}{750\ln 5}\right) = \ln\left(e^{\left(\frac{1}{4}\ln 5\right)t}\right)$$

$$\ln\left(\frac{10\ 000}{750\ln 5}\right) = \left(\frac{1}{4}\ln 5\right)t$$

$$t = \frac{\ln\left(\frac{10\ 000}{750\ln 5}\right)}{\frac{1}{4}\ln 5} \approx 5.25$$

It will take 5.25 hours for the growth rate to be 10 000 bacteria/hour.

Example 4

A bacteria culture has an initial count of 500 bacteria. After 4 hours, there are 2 000 bacteria present.

a) Find the function that gives the number of bacteria as a function of time.

b) Find the function that gives the growth rate as a function of time.

c) Find the growth rate of the bacteria after 6 hours.

d) How long will it take for the growth rate to reach 11 000 bacteria/hour?

Solution

a) Using $f(t) = Ae^{kt}$ we can substitute in the given information and solve for k:

$f(t) = 2\ 000$ when $t = 4$.

$A = 500$

So, $2\ 000 = 500e^{k4}$

Solving for k:

$$\frac{2\ 000}{500} = e^{k4}$$

$$4 = e^{k4}$$

$$\ln(4) = \ln\left(e^{k4}\right)$$

$$\ln(4) = 4k$$

$$k = \frac{\ln(4)}{4}$$

Use the value for k to rewrite the function:

$$f(t) = 500e^{\left(\frac{\ln(4)}{4}\right)t}$$

b) Find $f'(t)$

$$f'(t) = 500e^{\left(\frac{\ln(4)}{4}\right)t}\frac{\ln(4)}{4}$$

$$= 125\ln(4)e^{\left(\frac{\ln(4)}{4}\right)t}$$

c) Solve for $f'(t)$ at $t = 6$ hours:

$$f'(6) = 125\ln(4)e^{\left(\frac{\ln(4)}{4}\right)6}$$

$$\approx 1\,386.29$$

d) Solve for t when $f'(t) = 11\,000$

$$11\,000 = 125\ln(4)e^{\left(\frac{\ln(4)}{4}\right)t}$$

$$\frac{11\,000}{125\ln(4)} = e^{\left(\frac{\ln(4)}{4}\right)t}$$

$$\ln\left(\frac{11\,000}{125\ln(4)}\right) = \ln\left(e^{\left(\frac{\ln(4)}{4}\right)t}\right)$$

$$\ln\left(\frac{11\,000}{125\ln(4)}\right) = \left(\frac{\ln(4)}{4}\right)t$$

$$t = \frac{\ln\left(\dfrac{11\,000}{125\ln(4)}\right)}{\dfrac{\ln(4)}{4}} \approx 11.98$$

It will take 11.98 hours for the growth rate to reach 11 000 bacteria/hour.

PRACTICE EXERCISE

1. Which of the following functions is a growth function and which is a decay function?

   a) $f(t) = 40e^{\frac{-\ln 3}{7}t}$ **b)** $f(t) = 1\,000e^{\left(\frac{1}{4}\ln 2\right)t}$

2. The mass, in grams, of a radioactive substance remaining after t days is given by $f(t) = 35e^{\frac{-\ln 3}{40}t}$.

   a) Find the decay rate after t days.

   b) Find the decay rate after 20 days.

3. The number of bacteria after t hours is given by $f(t) = 1\,500e^{\frac{\ln 3}{7}t}$.

   a) Determine the growth rate after 5 hours.

b) Determine the length of time it will take for the growth rate to reach 2 000 bacteria per hour.

4. A sample of a radioactive substance has a mass of 100 g. After 30 days, it has a mass of 25 g.
   a) What is the mass after t days?

   b) What is the decay rate after t days?

   c) How long will it take the decay rate to reach -3 g/day?

Lesson 6 NEWTON'S METHOD

The method referred to in this lesson's title is a method for approximating the root(s) of equations of the form $f(x) = 0$.

Newton's Method is sometimes called the Newton–Raphson Method.

This method involves using a procedure that produces a result. You will then repeat this procedure using this result as an input. Each time the procedure is repeated, the better the approximation is.

In particular, Newton's Method is useful for approximating roots of complicated equations. It is also useful for programming computers and calculators in order for them to calculate approximate roots as required.

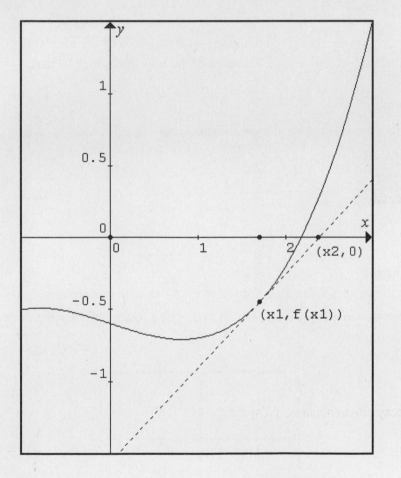

If x_1 is the first approximation of the the zero of the function, $y = f(x)$ above, then the slope of the tangent line through the two points $(x_1, \; f(x_1))$ and $(x_2, \; 0)$ must equal the value of the derivative of the function at $x = x_1$.

$$\frac{f(x_1)-0}{x_1-x_2} = f'(x_1)$$

$$\frac{f(x_1)}{f'(x_1)} = x_1 - x_2$$

$$x_2 = x_1 - \frac{f(x_1)}{f'(x_1)}$$

The value of x_2 can be used in the same way to find the next approximation, x_3.

Generally, each approximation of the zero will be closer to the actual value than the previous one.

By Newton's Method, the approximate root of $f(x)=0$ is

$$x_{n+1} = x_n - \frac{f(x_n)}{f'(x_n)}; \quad n=1,2,3\ldots; \quad f'(x_n) \neq 0,$$

where x_1 is the first approximation and is provided by the user who chooses a reasonable approximation of the root with which to start.

Example 1

Use Newton's Method to approximate a root for $f(x)=x^3-2x-6$.

Solution
Step 1
Find $f'(x)$:

$$f'(x)=3x^2-2$$

Step 2
Choose an approximate value for x_1 to be the first approximation.
Using the graph will allow you to choose a reasonable starting point.
Let $x_1 = 2$

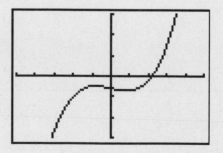

Step 3

Substitute and solve for the 2nd approximation:

$$x_2 = x_1 - \frac{f(x_1)}{f'(x_1)}$$

$$= 2 - \frac{(2)^3 - 2(2) - 6}{3(2)^2 - 2}$$

$$= 2 + \frac{1}{5}$$

$$= \frac{11}{5} \approx 2.2$$

Step 4

Repeat:

$$x_3 = x_2 - \frac{f(x_2)}{f'(x_2)}$$

$$= \frac{11}{5} - \frac{\left(\frac{11}{5}\right)^3 - 2\left(\frac{11}{5}\right) - 6}{3\left(\frac{11}{5}\right)^2 - 2}$$

$$= \frac{11}{5} + \frac{31}{1565}$$

$$\approx 2.18$$

This third approximation is accurate to two decimal places.

Example 2

Use the third approximation of Newton's method to approximate a root of $x^2 - 5x - 7 = 0$. Use $x_1 = 6$.

Solution

$$f(x) = x^2 - 5x - 7$$

$$f'(x) = 2x - 5$$

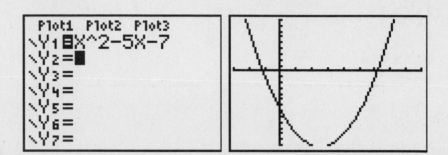

$$x_2 = x_1 - \frac{f(x_1)}{f'(x_1)}$$

$$= 6 - \frac{(6)^2 - 5(6) - 7}{2(6) - 5}$$

$$= 6 - \left(-\frac{1}{7}\right)$$

$$= \frac{43}{7} \approx 6.142\,86$$

$$x_3 = x_2 - \frac{f(x_2)}{f'(x_2)}$$

$$= \frac{43}{7} - \frac{\left(\frac{43}{7}\right)^2 - 5\left(\frac{43}{7}\right) - 7}{2\left(\frac{43}{7}\right) - 5}$$

$$= \frac{43}{7} - (-0.002\,801)$$

$$\doteq 6.140\,06$$

Example 3

Using $x_1 = 2.5$, find the third approximation for the root of $x^2 - 3 = \dfrac{1}{x-2}$.

Solution

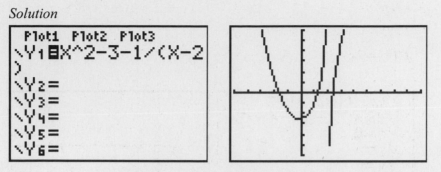

Simplify:

$$f(x) = x^2 - 3 - \frac{1}{x-2} = x^2 - 3 - (x-2)^{-1}$$

$$f'(x) = 2x + (x-2)^{-2} = 2x + \frac{1}{(x-2)^2}$$

$$f(x) = x^3 - 2x^2 - 3x + 5$$

$$f'(x) = 3x^2 - 4x - 3$$

$$x_2 = x_1 - \frac{f(x_1)}{f'(x_1)}$$

$$x_2 = 2.5 - \frac{(2.5)^2 - 3 - \dfrac{1}{2.5-2}}{2(2.5) + \dfrac{1}{(2.5-2)^2}}$$

$$x_2 = 2.5 - \frac{1.25}{9.000\,0}$$

$$x_2 \doteq 2.361$$

$$x_3 = x_2 - \frac{f(x_2)}{f'(x_2)}$$

$$x_3 = 2.361 - \frac{(2.361)^2 - 3 - \dfrac{1}{(2.361-2)}}{2(2.361) + \dfrac{1}{(2.361-2)^2}}$$

$$x_3 = 2.361 - \frac{-0.195\,7}{12.395\,4}$$

$$x_3 \doteq 2.377$$

PRACTICE EXERCISE

Use Newton's method to find the desired approximation of the roots for the following equations.

1. $x^2 - 12 = 0$; $x_1 = 2$; $x_4 = ?$

2. $x^3 - 5x - 5 = 0$; $x_1 = 2$; $x_3 = ?$

3. $\sin x = 0$; $x_1 = 3$; $x_3 = ?$,

   (where x is in radians)

4. $x^2 - 2 = \dfrac{x+4}{x}$; $x_1 = 2$; $x_3 = ?$

5. $4\sin^2 x - 3 = 0$; $x_1 = 1$; $x_3 = ?$
(where x is in radians)

REVIEW SUMMARY

In this unit, you have learned how to . . .

• find and use the velocity function given a displacement function as follows

$$v = \frac{ds}{dt}$$

• find and use the acceleration function given the displacement function as follows

$$a = \frac{dv}{dt} = \frac{d^2v}{dt^2}$$

• determine unknown rates in problems involving volumes and areas by use of the chain rule and implicit differentiation with respect to t.

• determine unknown rates in problems involving triangles by using some or all of:
  – similar triangle ratios
  – Pythagorean Theorem
  – right-angle trigonometry ratios

  $$- \sin\theta = \frac{opposite}{hypoteneuse}$$

  $$- \cos\theta = \frac{adjacent}{hypoteneuse}$$

  $$- \tan\theta = \frac{opposite}{adjacent}$$

  – Law of Sines
  $$\frac{\sin A}{a} = \frac{\sin B}{b} = \frac{\sin C}{c}$$
  – Law of Cosines
  $$a^2 = b^2 + c^2 - 2bc\cos A$$

• determine and use the marginal cost function given the cost function, $C(x)$

• determine and use the marginal revenue function given the price (demand) function, $p(x)$

• use the profit function to determine the level of production that will yield maximum profit by solving
$C'(x) = R'(x)$

• determine growth and decay functions, and use them to determine instantaneous rates of growth and decay

• use Newton's method to approximate roots of equations:

$$x_{n+1} = x_n - \frac{f(x_n)}{f'(x_n)}$$

PRACTICE TEST

1. The height in metres of a falling object as a function of time in seconds is defined by
$h = -4.9t^2 - 6t + 9$.

    a) What is the object's maximum and minimum velocity, and its maximum speed?

    b) How long does it take the object to reach a velocity of −10 m/s?

2. Determine the unknown rate for each of the following questions.

   a) $A = 4\pi r^2$; $r = 12\,\text{m}$; $\dfrac{dr}{dt} = -1.5\,\text{m/s}$; $\dfrac{dA}{dt} = ?$

   b. $A = 2\pi r^2 + 2\pi rh$; $h = 2r$; $r = 3\,\text{cm}$; $\dfrac{dA}{dt} = 50\,\text{cm}^2/\text{s}$; $\dfrac{dr}{dt} = ?$

3. A conical water tank has a height of 7 metres and a diametre of 6 metres. It is draining at a rate of $2\text{m}^3 / \text{min.}$

   At what rate is the water level decreasing when

   a) the water level is 4 m?

b) the radius at the top of the water is 1 m?

4. A train is 100 km due east of a car at 4:00 P.M. The car travels due north at a rate of 60 km/h and the train travels due west at a rate of 70 km/h. At what rate is the distance between them changing at

a) 5:00 P.M. ?

b) 6:30 P.M. ?

5. The cost of producing x items is defined by $C(x) = 400 + 3x + 0.013x^2$. The price (demand) function is $p(x) = 2 + 0.02x$.

a) Determine the marginal cost of producing 100 items.

b) Determine the marginal revenue if 800 items are produced.

c) How many items should be produced to maximize profit?

6. A bacterial culture has grown from 650 to 1 950 bacteria in 2 hours.

a) Determine the number of bacteria as a function of time.

b) What is the growth rate of the bacteria after 10 hours?

7. Use Newton's method to approximate the following functions:

   a) x_3 for $x^3 + 2x - 1 = 0$, where $x_1 = 1$

   b) x_3 for $x^2 - 4x - 5 = 0$, where $x_1 = 3$

NOTES

314

ANTIDERIVATIVES AND AREA

When you are finished this unit, you should be able to. . .

- find the antiderivative of a simple polynomial function
- find the antiderivative of a simple trigonometric function
- find the antiderivative of an exponential function
- use antiderivatives to solve problems with initial conditions
- solve 2nd order differential equations with Hooke's Law as an application
- evaluate a definite integral
- find the signed area under a curve
- find the area between curves
- approximate area using the Rectangular Rule
- approximate area using Reimann Sums
- approximate area using the Trapezoidal Rule

PREREQUISITE SKILLS AND KNOWLEGDE

Prior to beginning this unit, you should be able to. . .
- describe the relationship between displacement, velocity and acceleration using derivatives
- determine derivatives of functions
- use sigma notation
- find points of intersection between two functions
- sketch curves using derivatives
- determine the area of basic geometric figures

Lesson 1   *THE ANTIDERIVATIVE*

You have learned how to take the derivative of a function or equation. By doing so, the derivative or differential equation is obtained. These derivatives can be used to observe rates of change.

For example, we can plot a function on a standard x/y Cartesian coordinate graph, and then, by finding the derivative of the function, we know the slope of that original function at any point. This derivative is the familiar $\dfrac{dy}{dx}$. It enables us to find the instantaneous rate of change of the original function at any value of x.

As well, we can take the derivative of a displacement-time function and obtain the velocity of that object (at any moment in time). If s is the displacement of the object at any time, then t:

$$v = \frac{ds}{dt}$$

The velocity of an object at any time t, gives the instantaneous rate of change of the displacement of the object at that time, t.

Since the velocity-time function is the first derivative of the displacement-time function, the sign of the velocity tells us how the displacement is changing.

If $v > 0$ within some interval of time, then s must be increasing in that interval.

If $v < 0$ within some interval of time, then s must be decreasing in that interval.

Differentiating the velocity-time function yields the acceleration-time function. The acceleration-time function is both the first derivative of the velocity-time function and the second derivative of the displacement-time function.

$$a = \frac{dv}{dt} = \frac{d^2 s}{dt^2}$$

If $a > 0$ within some time interval, then the velocity of the object must be increasing within that interval and the displacement-time function must be concave up within that interval.

If $a < 0$ within some time interval, then the velocity of the object must be decreasing within that interval and the displacement-time function must be concave down within that interval.

In many instances, it is useful to be able to go back a step in the differentiation process and observe a function before it was differentiated. The process of determining the original function when its derivative value is known is called **integration**.

In this unit, the usefulness of the antiderivative will become apparent through example. For now, a concrete look at the mechanics behind the process (of finding the antiderivative) is given.

Consider the following functions and their first derivatives:

$$y_1 = 2x^2 \qquad\qquad y_2 = 2x^2 + 4 \qquad\qquad y_3 = 2x^2 - 6$$

$$\frac{dy_1}{dx} = 4x \qquad\qquad \frac{dy_2}{dx} = 4x \qquad\qquad \frac{dy_3}{dx} = 4x$$

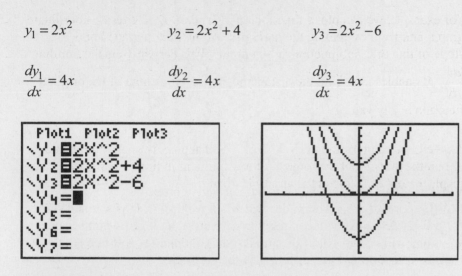

Each of the original functions does contain a common $2x^2$ term but the constant in each case is different. All three of these when graphed, are vertical translations of each other. However, the first derivative of each of these functions is identical. In each instance, the results $2x^2$, $2x^2 + 4$, and $2x^2 - 6$ are **antiderivative** values of $4x$. It should be apparent that $4x$ has an infinite number of antiderivatives, each with a different constant value C attached to the $2x^2$.

If $\dfrac{dy}{dx} = 4x$, then $y = 2x^2 + C$.

A **slopefield** for a differential equation gives a picture of its family of antiderivative functions.

Each segment on the slopefield represents a portion of the tangent line at a particular point on an antiderivative function.

Using the differential equation $\dfrac{dy}{dx} = 4x$:

At a point $(2, 1)$ on one of the antiderivative functions the slope of the tangent line will be equal to $\dfrac{dy}{dx}\Big|_{x=2} = 4(2) = 8$.

At a point $(-1\ 5)$ on one of the antiderivative functions the slope of the tangent line will be equal to $\dfrac{dy}{dx}\Big|_{x=-1} = 4(-1) = -4$.

A slope field for the differential equation $\frac{dy}{dx} = 4x$ is shown below.

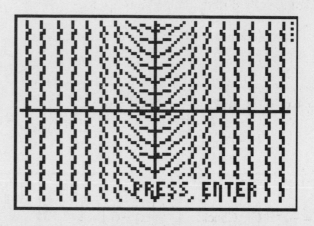

What does this teach us about the antiderivative process?

Most importantly it is a reminder that when we take a step back and solve for the antiderivative value of a given derivative, an infinite number of solutions will occur. All of the antiderivative functions will be vertical translations of each other, differing in the constant C.

DIFFERENTIAL EQUATIONS AND THE INDEFINITE INTEGRAL

A **differential equation** is an equation containing a quotient of differentials. Thus, a differential equation is an equation that contains a derivative or a number of derivatives.

From previous section $\frac{dy}{dx} = 4x$ is a differential equation.

The dx and dy are the differentials. Their quotient yields the derivative of y with respect to x.

We have **solved the differential equation** when we have found all of the functions whose derivative is equal to the differential equation.

Thus, the solution to the differential equation $\frac{dy}{dx} = 4x$ is $y = 2x^2 + C$.

Another symbol that represents the solution of a differential equation is the **indefinite integral.**

$$\int (4x)\, dx = 2x^2 + C$$

The **4x** is the **integrand.** The integrand is the derivative of the function that we are searching for.

The **dx** is the **differential** with the x representing the variable that we are integrating with respect to.

Example 1

Evaluate the following indefinite integrals.

Verify your solution by differentiating your results.

a) $\int (6)\, dx$

Solution

$\int (6)\, dx = 6x + C$ Check: $\dfrac{d}{dx}(6x + C) = 6$

b) $\int (x)\, dx$

Solution

$\int (x)\, dx = \dfrac{1}{2}x^2 + C$ Check: $\dfrac{d}{dx}\left(\dfrac{1}{2}x^2 + C\right) = x$

c) $\int \left(x^2\right) dx$

Solution

$\int \left(x^2\right) dx = \dfrac{1}{3}x^3 + C$ Check: $\dfrac{d}{dx}\left(\dfrac{1}{3}x^3 + C\right) = x^2$

The pattern that you should see developing in the previous example presents a formula for reversing the power rule in the integration process.

In general: $\int \left(x^n\right) dx = \dfrac{x^{n+1}}{(n+1)} + C$

It should be noted that this general statement is true for all real number values of n except -1.

This generalization can be extended for powers with a numerical coefficient of "a".

$\int \left(ax^n\right) dx = a \int \left(x^n\right) dx = a\left[\dfrac{x^{n+1}}{(n+1)}\right] + C \;, \; n \neq -1$

NOTES

Example 2

Evaluate each indefinite integral:

a) $\int \left(x^{10} \right) dx$

Solution

$$\int \left(x^{10} \right) dx = \frac{x^{10+1}}{(10+1)} + C = \frac{1}{11} x^{11} + C$$

b) $\int \left(20x^4 \right) dx$

Solution

$$\int \left(20x^4 \right) dx = 20 \int \left(x^4 \right) dx = 20 \left[\frac{x^{4+1}}{(4+1)} \right] + C = 4x^5 + C$$

c) $\int \left(p^3 \right) dp$

Solution

$$\int \left(p^3 \right) dp = \frac{1}{4} p^4 + C$$

The results for all of the questions in the previous two examples could have been found by solving a differential equation.

Let us study the problem of evaluating $\int \left(x^{10} \right) dx$ again.

Remember that this question is asking us to find the functions that have derivative values of x^{10}.

Written as a differential equation:

$$\frac{dy}{dx} = x^{10}$$

Separate the differentials *dx and dy* by multiplying both sides of the differential equation by *dx*.

$$dy = \left(x^{10} \right) dx$$

Integrate both sides:

$$\int dy = \int \left(x^{10} \right) dx$$

or

$$\int (1) dy = \int \left(x^{10} \right) dx$$

To solve the left side ask yourself what you must take the derivative of with respect to *y*, in order to arrive at 1 as your derivative value.

To solve the right side ask yourself what you must take the derivative of with respect to x, in order to arrive at x^{10} as your derivative value. Don't forget about the constants on both sides.

$$\int (1) dy = \int \left(x^{10} \right) dx$$

$$y + C_1 = \frac{1}{11} x^{11} + C_2$$

Combining the two constants will simply produce another constant.

$$y = \frac{1}{11} x^{11} + C$$

Example 3

Evaluate $\int (\cos x) dx$

Solution

Method 1

Simply recognizing that the derivative of $\sin x$ with respect to x is $\cos x$:

$$\int (\cos x) dx = \sin x + C$$

Method 2

Solve the differential equation $\dfrac{dy}{dx} = \cos x$:

$$\frac{dy}{dx} = \cos x$$

$$dy = (\cos x) dx$$

$$\int (1) dy = \int (\cos x) dx$$

$$y + C_1 = \sin x + C_2$$

$$y = \sin x + C$$

Example 4

Evaluate $\int\left(\sqrt[3]{x}\right)dx$

Solution

$\int\left(\sqrt[3]{x}\right)dx$

$= \int\left(x^{\frac{1}{3}}\right)dx$

$= \dfrac{x^{\frac{1}{3}+1}}{\left(\frac{1}{3}+1\right)} + C$

$= \dfrac{x^{\frac{4}{3}}}{\frac{4}{3}} + C$

$= \dfrac{3}{4}x^{\frac{4}{3}} + C$

Integrating a **sum** or **difference** of functions can be accomplished by integrating the individual functions and adding or subtracting the results.

$$\int\left[f(x)+g(x)\right]dx = \int\left(f(x)\right)dx + \int\left(g(x)\right)dx$$

This **may not** be done with **products** or **quotients** of functions.

Example 5

Evaluate $\int\left(3x^2-10x+11\right)dx$

Solution

$\int\left(3x^2-10x+11\right)dx$

$= \int\left(3x^2\right)dx - \int\left(10x\right)dx + \int\left(11\right)dx$

$= \left[(3)\dfrac{x^{2+1}}{(2+1)} + C_1\right] - \left[(10)\dfrac{x^{1+1}}{(1+1)} + C_2\right] + \left[11x + C_3\right]$

$= x^3 - 5x^2 + 11x + C$

You should now realize that a sound knowledge of the derivatives of functions that have been addressed in previous units will aid you in evaluating indefinite integrals
A list of some important indefinite integrals are provided below.
In each case, you should notice that the derivative of the result is equal to the integrand.

- $\int \left(kf(x) \right) dx = k \int \left(f(x) \right) dx$ (Where k is a constant)
- $\int \left[f(x) + g(x) \right] dx = \int \left[(x) \right] dx + \int \left[g(x) \right] dx$

- $\int (a) dx = ax + C$, where "a" is a constant
- $\int \left(x^n \right) dx = \dfrac{x^{n+1}}{(n+1)} + C$, $n \neq -1$
- $\int \left(ax^n \right) dx = \dfrac{ax^{n+1}}{(n+1)} + C$, $n \neq -1$

- $\int (\cos x) dx = \sin x + C$
- $\int (\sin x) dx = -\cos x + C$
- $\int \left(\sec^2 x \right) dx = \tan x + C$
- $\int (-\csc x \cot x) dx = \csc x + C$
- $\int (\sec x \tan x) dx = \sec x + C$
- $\int \left(-\csc^2 x \right) dx = \cot x + C$

- $\int \left(e^x \right) dx = e^x + C$
- $\int \left(b^x \ln b \right) dx = b^x + C$

- $\int \left(\dfrac{1}{x} \right) dx = \ln |x| + C$
- $\int \left(\dfrac{1}{x \ln b} \right) dx = \log_b \left(|x| \right) + C$

Example 6

Evaluate $\int \left(e^x + x^{\frac{2}{3}} - \frac{1}{x} \right) dx$

Solution

$\int \left(e^x + x^{\frac{2}{3}} - \frac{1}{x} \right) dx$

$= e^x + \frac{3}{5} x^{\frac{5}{3}} - \ln|x| + C$

INTEGRATION BY SUBSTITUTION

Let us attempt to evaluate $\int \left[(2x)^3 \right] dx$

This problem appears to involve nothing more than reversing the power rule. However, one key feature differentiates this problem from previous examples. The base of the power is no longer just x.

Simply reversing the power rule does not work.

$\int \left[(2x)^3 \right] dx \neq \frac{(2x)^{3+1}}{(3+1)} + C$

$\int \left[(2x)^3 \right] dx \neq \frac{(2x)^4}{4} + C$

We can verify this by expanding the power first and then integrating.

$\int \left[(2x)^3 \right] dx$

$= \int \left(8x^3 \right) dx$

$= (8) \frac{x^{3+1}}{(3+1)} + C$

$= 2x^4 + C$

Can we integrate this power without expanding it first? The answer is **yes**. Using the method of substitution, let $u =$ the base of the power.

$u = 2x$

It follows that $\frac{du}{dx} = 2$ or $du = 2dx$ or $dx = \frac{du}{2}$

Replacing $2x$ with u and dx with $\frac{du}{2}$,

$\int \left[(2x)^3 \right] dx$ becomes $\int \left[(u)^3 \right] \left(\frac{du}{2} \right)$

The constant $\dfrac{1}{2}$ can be moved in front of the integral giving

$$\dfrac{1}{2}\int(u)\,du$$

$$\dfrac{1}{2}\int(u)\,du = \dfrac{1}{2}\left[\dfrac{1}{4}u^4 + C_1\right] = \dfrac{1}{8}u^2 + C$$

Note that $\left(\dfrac{1}{2}\right)(C_1)$ simply yields some other constant, C.

Replacing u with its original value of $2x$ gives

$$\int\left[(2x)^3\right]dx = \dfrac{1}{8}(2x)^4 + C$$

We can check this result by differentiating:

$$\dfrac{d}{dx}\left[\dfrac{1}{8}(2x)^4 + C\right] = (4)\left(\dfrac{1}{8}\right)(2x)^3(2) = (2x)^3$$

The method of substitution may seem to be quite cumbersome for this example. However, substitution can simplify some complex problems.

Example 7

Simplify $\displaystyle\int(10x+7)^8\,dx$

Solution

Attempting to expand first and integrate each term would be exhausting.

Let $u = 10x + 7$

$$\dfrac{du}{dx} = 10 \quad \text{or} \quad du = 10dx \quad \text{or} \quad dx = \dfrac{du}{10}$$

$$\int(10x+7)^8\,dx$$

$$= \int(u)^8\left(\dfrac{du}{10}\right)$$

$$= \dfrac{1}{10}\int\left(u^8\right)du$$

$$= \dfrac{1}{10}\left[\dfrac{u^{8+1}}{(8+1)} + C_1\right]$$

$$= \dfrac{1}{90}u^9 + C$$

$$= \dfrac{1}{90}(10x+7)^9 + C$$

Example 8

Evaluate $\int\left[\left(\sqrt{5x^2+8}\right)(20x)\right]dx$

Solution

$$\int\left[\left(\sqrt{5x^2+8}\right)(20x)\right]dx = \int\left[\left(5x^2+8\right)^{\frac{1}{2}}(20x)\right]dx$$

Let $u = 5x^2 + 8$

Thus, $\dfrac{du}{dx} = 10x$ or $du = 10xdx$ or $dx = \dfrac{du}{10x}$

$$\int\left[\left(5x^2+8\right)^{\frac{1}{2}}(20x)\right]dx$$

$$= \int(u)^{\frac{1}{2}}(20x)\left(\frac{du}{10x}\right)$$

$$= 2\int(u)^{\frac{1}{2}}du$$

$$= 2\left[\frac{u^{\frac{1}{2}+1}}{\left(\frac{1}{2}+1\right)} + C_1\right]$$

$$= 2\left[\frac{2}{3}u^{\frac{3}{2}} + C_1\right]$$

$$= \frac{4}{3}u^{\frac{3}{2}} + C$$

$$= \frac{4}{3}\left(5x^2+8\right)^{\frac{3}{2}} + C$$

The method of substitution is not restricted to examples involving powers.

Example 9

Evaluate $\int \sin(10x)\,dx$

Solution

Let $u = 10x$

$$\frac{du}{dx} = 10 \quad \text{or} \quad du = 10dx \quad \text{or} \quad dx = \frac{du}{10}$$

$\int \sin(10x)\,dx$

$= \int \sin(u)\left(\frac{du}{10}\right)$

$= \frac{1}{10}\int \sin(u)\,du$

$= \frac{1}{10}\left(-\cos(u) + C_1\right)$

$= -\frac{1}{10}\cos(10x) + C$

Example 10

Evaluate $\int \left(e^{4x^2}\right)(2x)\,dx$

Solution

Let $u = 4x^2$

$$\frac{du}{dx} = 8x \quad \text{or} \quad du = 8xdx \quad \text{or} \quad dx = \frac{du}{8x}$$

$\int \left(e^{4x^2}\right)(2x)\,dx$

$= \int \left(e^u\right)(2x)\left(\frac{du}{8x}\right)$

$= \frac{1}{4}\int \left(e^u\right)du$

$= \frac{1}{4}\left[e^u + C_1\right]$

$= \frac{1}{4}e^{4x^2} + C$

Example 11

Evaluate $\int \left[\dfrac{1}{(7x)} + \dfrac{1}{(7x)^2} \right] dx$

This problem is solved by applying the rule for integrating the sum of two or more functions. $\int \left[f(x) + g(x) \right] dx = \int \left[(x) \right] dx + \int \left[g(x) \right] dx$

$\int \left(\dfrac{1}{7x} \right) dx + \int \left(\dfrac{1}{(7x)^2} \right) dx = \dfrac{1}{7} \int (x) dx + \int (7x)^{-2} dx$

$\dfrac{1}{7} \int \left(\dfrac{1}{x} \right) dx = \dfrac{1}{7} \ln|x| + C_1$

Using substitution for $\int (7x)^{-2} dx$:

$u = 7x, \ dx = \dfrac{du}{7}$

$\int (7x)^{-2} dx = \int (u)^{-2} \left(\dfrac{du}{7} \right) = \dfrac{1}{7} \int \left(u^{-2} \right) du = \dfrac{1}{7} \left(\dfrac{u^{-1}}{-1} + C_2 \right) = -\dfrac{1}{7}(7x)^{-1} + C_3$

Thus, $\dfrac{1}{7} \int (x) dx + \int (7x)^{-2} dx = \dfrac{1}{7} \ln|x| - \dfrac{1}{7}(7x)^{-1} + C$

Example 12

Evaluate $\int \left(\sin^3 x \right) (\cos x) dx$

Solution

$\int \left(\sin^3 x \right) (\cos x) dx = \int (\sin x)^3 (\cos x) dx$

Let $u = \sin x$. Thus, $\dfrac{du}{dx} = \cos x$ or $dx = \dfrac{du}{\cos x}$

$\int (\sin x)^3 (\cos x) dx$

$= \int \left(u^3 \right) (\cos x) \left(\dfrac{du}{\cos x} \right)$

$= \int \left(u^3 \right) du$

$= \dfrac{u^{3+1}}{(3+1)} + C$

$= \dfrac{1}{4} u^4 + C$

$= \dfrac{1}{4} \sin^4 x + C$

PRACTICE EXERCISE

1. Solve the following differential equations.

   a) $\dfrac{dy}{dx} = -3x^2 - 2x + 1$

   b) $\dfrac{dp}{dz} = \dfrac{3}{z} - \dfrac{3}{z^2} + \dfrac{2}{z^3}$, $z \neq 0$

   c) $\dfrac{dy}{dx} = \sec^2 x$

   d) $\dfrac{du}{dy} = y - \cos y$

2. Evaluate each indefinite integral.

   a) $\int \left(x^5\right) dx$

   b) $\int \left(5^x\right)(\ln 5)\, dx$

   c) $\int \left(\sin^2 x + \cos^2 x\right) dx$

   d) $\int \left(27e^x\right) dx$

3. Use the method of substitution to evaluate each of the following indefinite integrals.

a) $\int (5x-3)^{12}\, dx$

b) $\int \left(\sqrt{4x^2 - 10x} \right) (4x-5)\, dx$

c) $\int \left[\cos^4 (8x) \right] \left[\sin(8x) \right] dx$

d) $\int \left(e^{\ln(4x)} \right) \left(\dfrac{1}{x} \right) dx$

Lesson 2 DIFFERENTIAL EQUATIONS WITH INITIAL CONDITIONS

When the concept of the antiderivative was first introduced, it was made clear that a general constant must be included. Whenever we find the antiderivative and include the constant, we are finding the most general antiderivative. However, it is possible to solve for C if we are given additional information. This information must apply to the original (antiderivative) function, and therefore is called the initial condition.

For example, one of the earlier uses of the differentiation process was to find the rate of change of the displacement of an object (s) with respect to time. This produces the velocity, $\frac{ds}{dt} = v$. If we know the velocity of an object (and it is constant), we can multiply by time to find the displacement (over the time given). However, there may be an initial condition to consider. For example, the object at time zero, may begin at a displacement away from the starting point.

The problem of finding a particular antiderivative function, given its derivative and a point on the function is called an **initial value problem**.

Example 1

Solve for y if $\frac{dy}{dx} = 4x$ and $y = 7$ when $x = 1$.

Solution

Step 1:

The family of antiderivative functions is found by integrating the differential equation.

$$\frac{dy}{dx} = 4x$$

$$y = 2x^2 + C$$

Step 2:

Substitute the point (1, 7) into the equation from step 1

$$y = 2x^2 + C$$
$$7 = 2(1)^2 + C$$
$$C = 5$$

The solution to the initial value problem is $y = 2x^2 + 5$.

Example 2

Consider the following problem:

Mr. Jones stands a short distance behind a black sedan driving directly away from him at a velocity of 50 km/hr. If it is assumed the velocity can be considered constant over the time period, how far is the sedan away from Mr. Jones after 6 minutes?

Solution

We know that velocity is $v = \dfrac{ds}{dt} = 50 \, \text{km/h}$.

The general antiderivative is $s = 50t + C$.

Given this new function and knowing that the time is 6 min, or one-tenth of an hour, then $s = 5 + C$. That is, the sedan has moved 5 km in the 6 min. But, the sedan is more than 5 km away from Mr. Jones. It is then 5 km plus the initial distance C that it started at.

If we are now given more initial condition information such as the fact that Mr. Jones was 10 metres behind the sedan at time zero, we can solve the entire question.

$s = 50t + C$

$s = 50(0.1) + 0.01$

$s = 5.01 \, \text{km}$

After 6 min the sedan is 5.01 km away from Mr. Jones.

GRAPHS

Differential equations with initial conditions are commonly used to solve graphical problems. In the introduction to this unit, we saw how three parabolas (identical except for the vertex) gave identical differential equations

Example 3

The slope at any given point on a function is described as $\dfrac{x}{2}$. The function has a y-intercept of 3. Find the equation of the original function.

Solution

First we must translate the written problem into a differential equation. Then we take the antiderivative and apply the given initial condition.

$$slope = \frac{dy}{dx} = \frac{x}{2}$$

Now find the general antiderivative:

$$y = \frac{x^2}{4} + C$$

Apply the initial condition:
[a given point on the original graph is (0, 3)]

$$3 = \frac{(0)^2}{4} + C$$

$$C = 3$$

Write out the original function:

$$y = \frac{x^2}{4} + 3$$

There are many additional types of differential equations with initial conditions. The displacement/velocity/acceleration and the curve/slope questions are among the most common. A sound knowledge of differentiation and integration is the key to solving all of them.

GRAVITY

Example 4

A person standing on top of a 50 metre tall building throws a ball upward with a velocity of 10 metres per second. If it is assumed that gravity can be considered to be 9.8 m/s^2 downward, what is the displacement-time function that represents the motion of the ball?

Solution

Begin with acceleration: $a = \dfrac{dv}{dt} = -9.8$ m/s^2

Integrate once to determine the family of velocity-time functions:

$a = -9.8$

$v = \int (-9.8)\,dt$

$v = -9.8t + C_1$

The initial velocity of the ball was 10 m/s. $v(0) = 10$

Use the point (0, 10) to solve for C_1.

$10 = -9.8\,(0) + C_1$

$C_1 = 10$

The velocity-time function is $v = -9.8t + 10$

Integrate a second time to find the family of displacement-time functions.

$s = \int (-9.8t + 10)\,dt$

$s = -4.9t^2 + 10t + C_2$

By assigning the top of the building as the reference point for the motion of the ball, its displacement at time zero is zero. $s(0) = 0$

Use the point (0, 0) to solve for C_2.

$0 = 4.9(0)^2 + 10(0) + C_2$

$C_2 = 0$

The displacement-time function is:

$s = -4.9t^2 - 9.8t$

This function will give the ball's displacement with respect to the top of the building.

If we chose to let the ground be our reference point, the object's displacement at time zero would be 50 m.

We would use the point (0, 50) to solve for C_1.

$50 = -4.9(0)^2 - 9.8(0) + C_2$

$C_2 = 50$

The displacement-time function would now be:

$s = -4.9t^2 - 9.8t + 50$

This function will give the ball's displacement with respect to the ground.

SPRINGS / PENDULUMS

One special type of differential equation takes the form

$\dfrac{d^2y}{dx^2} + ky = 0$, where $k > 0$. This can also be expressed as

$f''(x) + kf(x) = 0$ or $y'' + ky = 0$. In each case, k is a constant greater than zero and there is a second order differential equation (as well as the original function) involved. These differential equations and their solutions are applied to problems involving springs, pendulums, or other periodic oscillations.

Since our second-order differential equation involves the original function, we cannot simply find its antiderivative. Rather, we must find a way to express the original function so that taking its derivative twice will produce the given second-order differential equation. We can begin by looking at what we know of the sine and cosine functions:

$$
\begin{array}{ll}
y = \sin 2x & y = \cos 2x \\
y' = \cos 2x & y' = -2\sin 2x \\
y'' = -4\sin 2x & y'' = -4\cos 2x \\
y'' = -(4)\sin 2x & y'' = -(4)\cos 2x \\
y'' = -(4)y & y'' = -(4)y
\end{array}
$$

From this information, we find that $y'' + ky = 0$ which is the form of the second-order, differential in question.

Also note that by the time we have reached the second derivative, the constant in front of the sine or cosine function is the square of the value inside the sine or cosine function.

Using these facts we can state that a solution to $y'' + ky = 0$ will take the general form: $y = A\sin\left(\sqrt{k}x\right) + B\cos\left(\sqrt{k}x\right)$, where $k > 0$, but A or B may be equal to zero.

Example 4

The displacement (s) of a pendulum from the centre is given by the

formula $\dfrac{d^2s}{dt^2} + 9s = 0$.

Also, we are given the initial conditions that at time zero $s = 0$ and $s' = \dfrac{1}{2}$.

Find the original displacement function.

Solution

To solve, use the sample equation $y = A\sin\left(\sqrt{k}x\right) + B\cos\left(\sqrt{k}x\right)$.

For this question we will use $s = y$, $t = x$ and $s'' = \dfrac{d^2s}{dt^2}$.

So, $s = A\sin 3t + B\cos 3t$.

Now apply the initial conditions $t = 0$ and $s = 0$.

$0 = A\sin 0 + B\cos 0$

For this to be true, B must be zero.

$s = A\sin 3t$

$s' = 3A\cos 3t$

Apply the fact that at time zero, this first derivative is one-half.

$\dfrac{1}{2} = 3A\cos 0$

$A = \dfrac{1}{6}$

$s = \dfrac{1}{6}\sin 3t$

HOOKE'S LAW

A direct application of the sample equation we developed for springs, pendulums, etc., is detailed in Hooke's Law. This law basically states that a force is required to stretch a spring beyond its natural position:

$F(s) = ks$, $k > 0$. This force is opposed by Newton's Law of Motion that

states: $F = ma \Rightarrow$, $F = m\dfrac{d^2s}{dt^2}$ an opposing/restoring force.

These are equal, so we can begin to set up the second-order differential:

$ks = -m\dfrac{d^2s}{dt^2}$ Newton's Force is negative because it is opposing.

$\dfrac{d^2s}{dt^2} + \dfrac{k}{m}s = 0$

This problem will have an initial solution of the form

$s = A\sin\left(\sqrt{\dfrac{k}{m}}t\right) + B\cos\left(\sqrt{\dfrac{k}{m}}t\right)$, which can be solved with the given initial

conditions.

CONTINUOUS EXPONENTIAL GROWTH/DECAY

In a continuous exponential growth or decay problem, the rate at which a quantity, y, changes is proportional to the value of the quantity at that instant.

$\dfrac{dy}{dt} = ky$ where k is a constant.

Example 5

An account pays continuous interest at a rate of 5.2%. If the account balance at the end of 8 years is $1 000 then what was the initial balance and what is the equation relating the amount of money, y, in the account and the time, t, elapsed in years?

Solution

$$\frac{dy}{dt} = ky$$

Separating the differentials and integrating:

$$\left(\frac{1}{y}\right)dy = kdx \ \left(\text{where } k = 0.052\right)$$

$$\int\left(\frac{1}{y}\right)dy = \int 0.052dx$$

$$\ln|y| + C_1 = 0.052x + C_2$$

$$\ln|y| = 0.052x + C$$

Converting to exponential form:

$$e^{0.052x + C} = |y|$$

We can remove the absolute value sign since y cannot be negative.

$$y = e^{0.052x + C}$$

$$y = \left(e^C\right)\left(e^{0.052t}\right)$$

Use the point (8 , 1 000) to solve for e^C.

$$1000 = \left(e^C\right)\left(e^{(0.052)(8)}\right)$$

$$e^C = \frac{1000}{e^{0.416}} \doteq 659.68$$

The equation representing this continuous growth is

$$y = 659.68e^{0.052t}$$

PRACTICE EXERCISE

1. Solve the following differential equations using the initial conditions given.

   a) Given that an object accelerates according to the function $a(t) = t + 1$, what are the equations representing velocity and displacement given that initial velocity is 0 and initial displacement is also 0 where $t \geq 0$?

   b) Given $a = 3\sin t$ for $t \geq 0$ find s if $v(0) = 1$ and $s(0) = 1$.

   c) Find the equation of a function y given that $\dfrac{d^2 y}{dx^2} = x - 1$ and knowing that at the origin the rate of change of the function is 1. As well, the original function passed through the point $(1, 2)$.

d) An object has a velocity defined as $v = 2t - 1$ in metres/second for all $t \geq 1$. Find the distance travelled by the object from $t = 3$ to $t = 5$.

e) Solve $y'' + 16y = 0$ given that when $x = \dfrac{\pi}{2}$, $y = 1$, and $y' = 1$.

f) A spring with a mass of 0.5 kg has a natural length of 0.1 m. A force of 10 N is required to stretch it to 0.2 m. If the spring is stretched to 3 times its normal length, held at rest and then released, what is the displacement of the mass at time t?

g) The rate at which a rabbit population grows is proportional to the number of rabbits present at any particular instant. If there are 100 rabbits present now and 900 rabbits present in 2 years then what number of rabbits will be present in 3 years?

PRACTICE QUIZ

1. Evaluate $\int \left(2x^2 - 3\right) dx$.

2. Evaluate $\int \left(2e^{2x} - \sin x\right) dx$.

3. Find the antiderivative of $f'(x) = 3 - \dfrac{3}{x}$ where $x \neq 0$.

4. Solve the following differential equation with the given initial conditions given.

    $\dfrac{ds}{dt} = t^2 - 1$ where $s = 1$ at $t = 0$.

5. Find $F(x)$ given that $F'(x) = x$, and that the point $\left(1, -\frac{1}{2}\right)$ lies on $F(x)$.

6. If $y'' + ky = 0$ and a solution exists at $y = A\sin\left(\sqrt{k}x\right) + B\cos\left(\sqrt{k}x\right)$, solve

$y'' + 100y = 0$ when $y = 0$, when $x = 0$, and when $y' = 2$ when $x = 0$.

7. Evaluate $\int \left(\cos^3 x\right) dx$

Lesson 3   *SIGNED AREA*

In this lesson we are interested in calculating the signed area under a curve (signed area between the curve and the x-axis) between a left and right boundary. These boundaries are often denoted by the variables a and b. Once we observe the areas of a few curves we will discover another application of the antiderivative. From that point, we will look at more complex curves.

We begin with the function $y = x$ which is a linear function passing through the origin. Observe the diagram below.

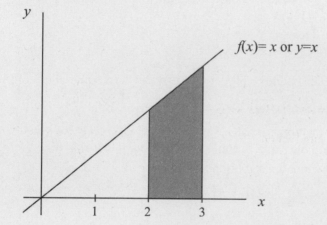

Ignore the shaded region for now and observe the area under the curve $f(x) = x$ between the origin and the line at $x = 2$. We do not need to draw a line upward at the origin since the value of the curve (or function) is zero. We do extend a line upward at $x = 2$. These left- and right-hand boundaries could be labeled as $[a, \ b]$ or $[0, \ 2]$, or in any similar fashion.

What is the area under this function for this region? We note that this is just a triangle with a base equal to two and a height equal to two as well. Use the geometric formula for area of a triangle:

$$A = \frac{bh}{2}$$

$$A = \frac{2^2}{2}$$

$$A = 2$$

Notice that we have evaluated $\frac{x^2}{2}$ at $x = 2$.

We should recognize $\frac{x^2}{2}$ as being an antiderivative of x.

The area under the curve from the origin to $x = 2$ is exactly two units squared. We also noted that this area could have been found using the antiderivative of the function (at this point).

If x were in centimeters, the area would be 2 cm^2.

Example 1

Examine the shaded region for the function $f(x) = x$. Find the signed area of this region using a geometric formula. Find a general formula for finding the signed area of the region if the upper boundary is unknown. Compare this general formula to the function (Hint: look at what we know about antiderivatives).

Solution

Using the diagram again we initially examine the shaded region which is a trapezoid.

Area for a trapezoid is base times the average height.

$$A = (3-2)\left[\frac{f(2)+f(3)}{2}\right]$$

$A = \dfrac{5}{2}$ This is the exact geometric area (units squared are implicit).

Now, if the upper (right) boundary were unknown, let's say x, we would use the same formula only with variables this time.

We know that the left boundary is 2.

$$A(x) = (x-2)\left[\frac{f(2)+f(x)}{2}\right]$$

$$A(x) = \left(\frac{1}{2}\right)(2+x)(x-2)$$

$$A(x) = \frac{x^2}{2} - 2$$

This is the general formula for finding the signed area in the interval $[0, x]$ where the right boundary is unknown. We can see that this is just an antiderivative of the function $f(x) = x$, and it even has a constant (C), which in this case, is -2.

The signed area between the function $f(x) = x$ and the x-axis in the interval with a left boundary of 2 and a right boundary of $x = 3$ is:

$$A(3) = \frac{3^2}{2} - 2 = \frac{9}{2} - \frac{4}{2} = \frac{5}{2}$$

Changing the left boundary would simply change the constant of integration in the antiderivative function. Does this constant really matter when it comes to finding signed area in an interval? The answer is no.

If we were to use the general antiderivative function and we *knew* the left- and right-hand values, we could substitute both values in the function. This would give us two areas. One area (using the left-hand value) would be the area under the curve from some x-value to the left-hand boundary. The other area (using the right-hand value) would give the total area under the curve from that x-value to the right-hand boundary. Then, we simply subtract the two areas to obtain only the signed area between the two boundaries.

The general antiderivative for this problem is $A(x) = \dfrac{x^2}{2} + C$.

The signed area between our function and the x-axis in the interval [2, 3] is simply

$$\left(\frac{1}{2}x^2 + C\right)\Bigg|_2^3$$

$$= A(3) - A(2)$$

$$= \left[\frac{3^2}{2} + C\right] - \left[\frac{2^2}{2} + C\right]$$

$$= \frac{5}{2}$$

The value of C was unimportant since it cancels by subtraction.

This is the key to signed area under a curve. It can be determined that, given a function $y = f(x)$ that is continuous over an interval $[a, b]$, the signed area under that function can be found by using the general antiderivitive $A(x)$. Furthermore, the area of the right-hand region less the area of the left-hand region gives the signed area over the desired interval: $A(b) - A(a)$.

Example 2

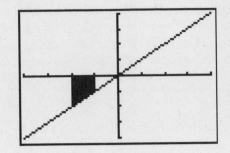

Observe the function $f(x) = x$ in the region shown above.

Determine the resulting signed area between the function and the x-axis in the interval $[-2, -1]$. Determine a formula for finding the signed area

Solution

The area of the trapezoid is: (Notice that the heights are negative)

$$A = \left(-1 - (-2)\right)\left[\frac{f(-1) + f(-2)}{2}\right]$$

$$A = (1)\left[\frac{-1 + (-2)}{2}\right]$$

$$A = -\frac{3}{2}$$

Now calculate the signed area of the trapezoid in the interval $[-2, x]$.

$$A(x) = \left(x - (-2)\right)\left[\frac{f(-2) + f(x)}{2}\right]$$

$$A(x) = (x + 2)\left[\frac{-2 + x}{2}\right]$$

$$A(x) = \frac{x^2 - 4}{2}$$

$$A(x) = \frac{1}{2}x^2 - 2$$

The signed area in the interval $[-2, -1]$ is found by replacing x, the right boundary, with -1.

$$A(-1) = \frac{1}{2}(-1)^2 - 2 = -\frac{3}{2}$$

The other option for finding the signed area in the interval $[-2, -1]$ is to find the general antiderivative $A(x) = \frac{1}{2}x^2 + C$, and then calculate the value of $A(-1) - A(-2)$.

The **change** in the general antiderivative function represents the accumulated signed area under the function $f(x) = x$ in the interval $[-2, -1]$.

$$\left(\frac{1}{2}x^2 + C\right)\Big|_{-2}^{-1}$$

$$= A(-1) - A(-2)$$

$$= \left[\frac{1}{2}(-1)^2 + C\right] - \left[\frac{1}{2}(-2)^2 + C\right]$$

$$= -\frac{3}{2}$$

Notice that the result is negative. Part of the reason is because the area is below the x-axis. The other part will be discussed later.

Example 3

We are given a linear function: $f(x) = x + 1$. Find the signed area under this function in the interval $[1, \ x]$ and create a general formula.

Compare this with the original function.

Determine the signed area between this function an the x-axis in the intervals $[1, 4]$

Solution

We will use the trapezoid formula so we can organize the information that will be substituted in accordingly. The length of the base along the x-axis is from 1 to x or $(x-1)$ units long. The two heights will be $f(1) = 1 + 1 = 2$ and $f(x) = x + 1$.

$$A(x) = (x-1)\left[\frac{2 + (x+1)}{2}\right]$$

$$A(x) = \frac{1}{2}\left(x^2 + 2x - 3\right)$$

$$A(x) = \frac{x^2}{2} + x - \frac{3}{2}$$

This is just an antiderivative of the original function with the constant being $-\frac{3}{2}$.

The signed area in the interval $[1, 4]$ is the value of $A(4)$.

$$A(4) = \frac{4^2}{2} + 4 - \frac{3}{2}$$

$$A(4) = \frac{21}{2}$$

Again we can find the general antiderivative of our function $f(x) = x + 1$ and determine its change over the interval [1, 4].

$$A(x) = \frac{1}{2}x^2 + x + C$$

$$\left(\frac{1}{2}x^2 + x + C\right)\Bigg|_1^4$$

$$= A(4) - A(1)$$

$$= \left(\frac{1}{2}(4)^2 + 4 + C\right) - \left(\frac{1}{2}(1)^2 + 1 + C\right)$$

$$= 8 + 4 + C - \frac{1}{2} - 1 - C$$

$$= \frac{21}{2}$$

PROOFS AND MORE METHODS

At this point we will use the concrete examples given above to exemplify the fact that the signed area under a curve is given by the change in the antiderivative. It is important to remember that the function needs to be continuous over the interval in question. Using a general function shown below, we will present a basic proof.

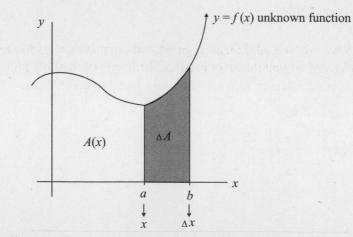

In the diagram above, we see an unknown function that is continuous at all points shown in the interval [a, b]. If we call the area under the curve, from $0 \rightarrow x$, A or more clearly $A(x)$, we can say that moving the right-hand boundary over a distance Δx will create a change in areas, ΔA. The value of 0 was chosen to simplify the process. Any other real number value could have been used.

$$A'(x) = \lim_{\Delta x \to 0} \frac{\Delta A}{\Delta x} \quad \text{or expanded} \quad A'(x) = \lim_{\Delta x \to 0} \frac{A(x + \Delta x) - A(x)}{\Delta x}$$

The ΔA, or new area can be depicted using a trapezoid and calculated using the formula for area of a trapezoid. But this is an approximation because the trapezoid is not exact with the function's shape. However, as we make Δx very small the approximation becomes closer and equality is achieved with the limit as shown.

$$A'(x) = \lim_{\Delta x \to 0} \frac{\Delta A}{\Delta x}$$

$$A'(x) = \lim_{\Delta x \to 0} \frac{\frac{1}{2}(\Delta x)\left[f(x) + f(x + \Delta x)\right]}{\Delta x}$$

$$A'(x) = \frac{f(x) + f(x)}{2}$$

$$A'(x) = f(x)$$

In the second step of this proof we cancel the Δx in the numerator and the denominator and then apply the limit of the change in x to obtain the simplified third step.

If we can find the signed area under a curve and take the derivative of that area function we arrive back at the original function. By the reverse process (which is true) we can take a given function (curve), find its antiderivative, and from this obtain the signed area under that curve. To obtain a numeric answer, we need to know the values of the left and right-hand boundaries.

In Lesson 5 we will see additional proofs that show that the signed area under a curve can be obtained by the antiderivative (or indefinite integral).

Example 4

Find the signed area under the function $y = \cos x$ for the interval $\left[0, \dfrac{\pi}{2}\right]$.

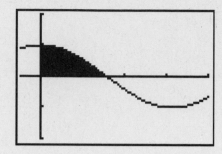

Solution

$f(x) = \cos x$

$A(x) = \int (\cos x)\, dx = \sin x + C$

The signed area is the value of

$$(\sin x + C)\bigg|_{0}^{\frac{\pi}{2}}$$

$$= A\left(\frac{\pi}{2}\right) - A(0)$$

$$= \left[\sin\left(\frac{\pi}{2}\right) + C\right] - \left[\sin(0) + C\right]$$

$$= 1$$

PRACTICE EXERCISE

1. Find the signed area under the curve for each of the following functions over the interval indicated.

a) $f(x) = \dfrac{1}{x}$ $\quad [1,\ 3]$

b) $f(x) = \sin x$ $\quad [0,\ \pi]$

c) $\dfrac{f(x)}{2} = x^2 - 1$ $\quad [2,\ 3]$

d) $f(x) = \dfrac{2\sqrt{x}}{3}$ $\quad [1,\ 4]$

e) $f(x) = x^2 - 4x$ $\quad [0,\ 3]$

f) $f(x) = e^x$ $\quad [0,\ 1]$

Lesson 4 THE DEFINITE INTEGRAL AND THE FUNDAMENTAL THEOREM OF CALCULUS

NOTES

The previous section illustrated a method for determining the signed area between a continuous function $y = f(x)$ and the x-axis in an interval $[a, b]$.

This lesson will introduce a symbol for that signed area.

Riemann Sums

The work done by Georg Friedrich Bernhard Riemann (1826 – 1866) provided a method for determining the signed area between a continuous function and the x-axis in a interval $[a, b]$ by considering the limiting value of the sums of the areas of geometric figures, such as rectangles or trapezoids, that approach the value of the desired signed area as the number of these figures approaches infinity.

For convenience, we let the widths of these geometric figures be equal. However, this is not essential. Eventually as the number of geometric figures approaches infinity, the width of each figure will approach zero, no matter what its initial value was.

Consider the problem of finding the signed area between the function $y = x^2$ and the x-axis in the interval $[0, 4]$.

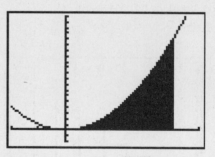

Right Rectangular Approximation Method (RAM)

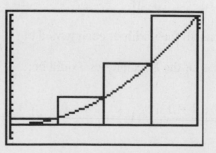

The diagram shows 4 rectangles, each with its upper right corner on the function. The sum of the areas of the 4 rectangles would be an over-approximation of the desired signed area under the function.

The width of each rectangle is the interval width divided by the number of rectangles.

$$\frac{4-0}{4} = 1$$

The length of each rectangle is the value of the function at the right edge x-value of each rectangle.

The length of the first rectangle is $f(1) = 1^2 = 1$

Thus, the area of the first rectangle is $\left(\frac{4-0}{4}\right)\left[f(1)\right] = (1)(1) = 1$

The length of the second rectangle is $f(2) = 2^2 = 4$

The area of the second rectangle is $\left(\frac{4-0}{4}\right)\left[f(2)\right] = (1)(4) = 4$

The total area of all 4 rectangles is:

$$\left(\frac{4-0}{4}\right)\left[f(1)\right] + \left(\frac{4-0}{4}\right)\left[f(2)\right] + \left(\frac{4-0}{4}\right)\left[f(3)\right] + \left(\frac{4-0}{4}\right)\left[f(4)\right]$$

$$= (1)(1) + (1)(4) + (1)(9) + (1)(16)$$

$$= 30$$

Again, this area is larger than the desired area.

How could we create a closer approximation?
The answer to this question is to use more rectangles.

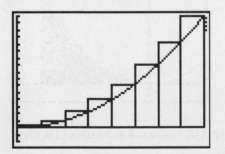

If 8 rectangles are used, the width of each would be $\frac{4-0}{8} = \frac{1}{2}$.

The sum of the areas of the 8 rectangles would be:

$$\left(\frac{4-0}{8}\right)\left[f\left(\frac{1}{2}\right)\right] + \left(\frac{4-0}{8}\right)\left[f(1)\right] + \left(\frac{4-0}{8}\right)\left[f\left(\frac{3}{2}\right)\right] + \dots + \left(\frac{4-0}{8}\right)\left[f(4)\right]$$

$$= \left(\frac{1}{2}\right)\left(\frac{1}{2}\right)^2 + \left(\frac{1}{2}\right)(1)^2 + \left(\frac{1}{2}\right)\left(\frac{3}{2}\right)^2 + \dots + \left(\frac{1}{2}\right)(4)^2$$

$$= 25.5$$

Although this approximation is closer to the area that we seek than the previous one, it is still not the exact value.

Consider the use of n rectangles.

The width of each rectangle would be $\dfrac{4-0}{n}$ or $\dfrac{4}{n}$.

The sum of the areas of the n rectangles is:

$$\left(\frac{4}{n}\right)\left[\left(\frac{4}{n}\right)^2\right] + \left(\frac{4}{n}\right)\left[\left(\frac{8}{n}\right)^2\right] + \left(\frac{4}{n}\right)\left[\left(\frac{16}{n}\right)^2\right] + ... + \left(\frac{4}{n}\right)\left[\left(\frac{4}{n}\right)^2\right]$$

Extracting a common factor:

$$= \left(\frac{4}{n}\right)\left(\frac{4}{n}\right)^2 \left[1^2 + 2^2 + 3^2 + ... + n^2\right]$$

It is known that $1^2 + 2^2 + 3^2 + ... + n^2 = \dfrac{n(n+1)(2n+1)}{6}$

$$\left(\frac{4}{n}\right)\left(\frac{4}{n}\right)^2 \left[1^2 + 2^2 + 3^2 + ... + n^2\right]$$

$$= \left(\frac{4}{n}\right)\left(\frac{4}{n}\right)^2 \left[\frac{n(n+1)(2n+1)}{6}\right]$$

$$= \left(\frac{64}{n^3}\right)\left[\frac{2n^3 + 3n^2 + n}{6}\right]$$

$$= \frac{32\left(2n^3 + 3n^2 + n\right)}{3n^3}$$

$$= \frac{64n^3 + 96n^2 + 32n}{3n^3}$$

This result gives the sum of the areas of n rectangles for this problem. The desired area under the curve is the limiting value of this result as the number of rectangles approaches infinity.

$$\lim_{n\to\infty}\left[\frac{64n^3 + 96n^2 + 32n}{3n^3}\right]$$

$$= \lim_{n\to\infty}\left[\frac{64n^3}{3n^3}\right] + \lim_{n\to\infty}\left[\frac{96n^2}{3n^3}\right] + \lim_{n\to\infty}\left[\frac{32n}{3n^3}\right]$$

$$= \lim_{n\to\infty}\left[\frac{64}{3}\right] + \lim_{n\to\infty}\left[\frac{32}{n}\right] + \lim_{n\to\infty}\left[\frac{32}{3n^2}\right]$$

$$= \frac{64}{3} + 0 + 0$$

$$= \frac{64}{3}$$

The signed area between the function $f(x) = x^2$ and the x-axis in the interval [0, 4] equals $\dfrac{64}{3}$.

Other types of approximations are shown below.

Left Rectangular Approximation Method (LRAM)

This approach will yield under-approximations of the signed area desired. The diagram below shows 8 rectangles, each with the upper-left corner on the function.

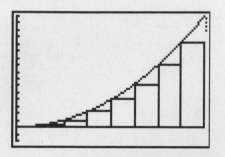

Midpoint Rectangular Approximation Method (MRAM)

The diagram below shows 8 rectangles, each with the midpoint of the top of each rectangle on the function.

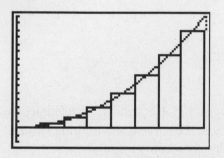

Another method would involve the use of **trapezoids**, where the upper-left and upper-right corners of the trapezoid lie on the function.

It should be apparent that due to the shape of the function in the specified interval, some methods give better approximations of signed area under a function than others when a finite number of figures is used. However, as the number of geometric figures approaches infinity, all methods will yield the same limit.

Remember that values of **signed area** can be negative. A rectangle or trapezoid lying below the x-axis will have a negative length, and thus, a negative area.

THE DEFINITE INTEGRAL

The signed area between a function $y = f(x)$ and the x-axis in an interval $[a, b]$ is equal to the limiting value of the sums of n geometric figures, as n approaches infinity.

Using n rectangles of equal width, the width of each rectangle is $\left(\dfrac{b-a}{n}\right)$.

We can call this width Δx.

Let x_i be the x-value within the ith rectangle representing where the top of the rectangle contacts the function. Thus, the height of the rectangle is equal to $f(x_i)$.

The area of this rectangle is $(f(x_i))(\Delta x)$.

The desired signed area under the curve is the limiting value of the sum of the areas of all n rectangles

as $n \to \infty$.

$$\lim_{n \to \infty} \left[\sum_{i=1}^{n} \left[(f(x_i)(\Delta x)) \right] \right]$$

This limit has a special symbol: $\displaystyle\lim_{n \to \infty} \left[\sum_{i=1}^{n} \left[(f(x_i)(\Delta x)) \right] \right] = \int_{a}^{b} f(x)\,dx$

The symbol $\displaystyle\int_{a}^{b} f(x)\,dx$ is the **definite integral** of the function f from a to b.

The parts of the definite integral are defined below:

$\displaystyle\int$ is the **integration sign**. It symbolizes a limit of sums.

$f(x)$ is the **integrand**.

a is the **lower limit of integration**.

b is the **upper limit of integration**.

dx is the differential, with x indicating the variable with which the integration is with respect to.

What does the value of a definite integral represent?

The value of $\int_a^b f(x)\,dx$ represents the **accumulated signed area** between the function $y = f(x)$ and the x-axis, beginning the accumulation at a and ending at b.

How is a definite integral calculated?

From a previous lesson, there is a connection between the function being integrated and its antiderivative function.

This connection is formalized in the Fundamental Theorem of Calculus.

The Fundamental Theorem of Calculus

If f is a continuous function on the interval $[a, b]$, then

$$\int_a^b f(x)\,dx = A(b) - A(a)$$

where A is any antiderivative of f.

This means that a definite integral represents the **change** in any of its antiderivative functions over the specified interval.

Example 1

a) Evaluate $\int_{-1}^{5} (x+1)\,dx$

Solution

Method 1:

Step 1:

Determine the general antiderivative of the integrand.

$$\int (x+1)\,dx = \frac{1}{2}x^2 + x + C$$

Step 2:

The desired signed area is

$$\left(\frac{1}{2}x^2 + x + C \right)\Big|_{-1}^{5}$$

$$= A(5) - A(-1)$$

$$= \left[\frac{1}{2}(5^2) + 5 + C \right] - \left[\frac{1}{2}(-1)^2 + (-1) + C \right]$$

$$= \left[\frac{35}{2} \right] - \left[-\frac{1}{2} \right]$$

$$= 18$$

NOTES

Method 2:

Most graphing calculators have the capability of calculating and displaying the signed area.

The sequence is shown below using a TI-84 Plus calculator.

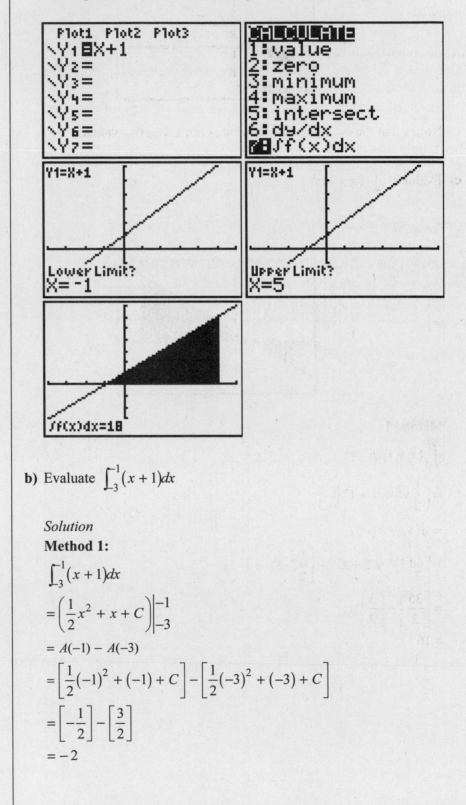

b) Evaluate $\int_{-3}^{-1}(x+1)dx$

Solution

Method 1:

$$\int_{-3}^{-1}(x+1)dx$$

$$=\left(\frac{1}{2}x^2 + x + C\right)\Bigg|_{-3}^{-1}$$

$$= A(-1) - A(-3)$$

$$=\left[\frac{1}{2}(-1)^2 + (-1) + C\right] - \left[\frac{1}{2}(-3)^2 + (-3) + C\right]$$

$$=\left[-\frac{1}{2}\right] - \left[\frac{3}{2}\right]$$

$$= -2$$

Method 2:

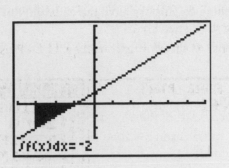

Notice that the accumulated signed area has a negative value.

c) Evaluate $\int_{-3}^{5}(x+1)\,dx$

Solution

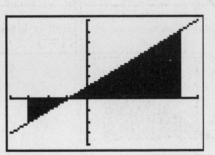

Method 1:

$\int_{-3}^{5}(x+1)\,dx$

$=\left(\dfrac{1}{2}x^2 + x + C\right)\Big|_{-3}^{5}$

$= A(5) - A(-3)$

$= \left[\dfrac{1}{2}(5)^2 + 5 + C\right] - \left[\dfrac{1}{2}(-3)^2 + (-3) + C\right]$

$= \left[\dfrac{35}{2}\right] - \left[\dfrac{3}{2}\right]$

$= 16$

NOTES

It is important to note that this result is the **accumulated signed area** under the function, beginning the accumulation at $x = -3$ and ending at $x = 5$.

In other words, the result of 16 is the sum of the results of parts a and b.
$16 = 18 + (-2)$

$\int_{-3}^{5}(x + 1)\,dx$ did **not** yield the total **area** shown in the diagram.

This is because part of the area is below the x-axis and part is above.

The results of this example show an important property of definite integrals.

The previous example showed that the following was true:

$$\int_{-3}^{-1}(x+1)\,dx + \int_{1}^{5}(x+1)\,dx = \int_{-3}^{5}(x+1)\,dx$$
$$(-2) \quad + \quad 18 \quad = \quad 16$$

In general:

$$\int_{a}^{b} f(x)\,dx + \int_{b}^{c} f(x)\,dx = \int_{a}^{c} f(x)\,dx$$

The next example shows another important property of definite integrals.

Example 2

a) What do you notice about $\int_{-1}^{5}(x + 1)\,dx$ and $\int_{5}^{-1}(x +1)\,dx$?

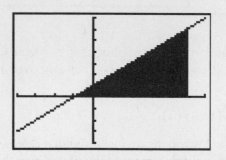

Solution

$$\int_{-1}^{5}(x + 1)\,dx = A(5) - A(-1) = 18$$

$$\int_{5}^{-1}(x + 1)\,dx = A(-1) - A(5) = -18$$

This should be no surprise. Reversing the order of subtraction changes the sign of the difference.

This means that **accumulated signed area** is not only dependent upon where the area lies in relation to the x-axis. It is also dependent upon how the area is accumulated. Areas entirely above the x-axis can have a negative signed area value if the area is accumulated from right to left instead of left to right.

b) What do you notice about $\int_{-3}^{-1}(x+1)\,dx$ and $\int_{-1}^{-3}(x+1)\,dx$?

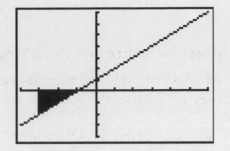

Solution

$$\int_{-3}^{-1}(x+1)\,dx = A(-1) - A(-3) = -2$$

$$\int_{-1}^{-3}(x+1)\,dx = A(-3) - A(-1) = +2$$

Areas entirely below the x-axis can have a positive signed area value if the area is accumulated from right to left instead of left to right.

In general:

$$\int_{a}^{b} f(x)\,dx = -\int_{b}^{a} f(x)\,dx$$

A definite integral represents the **change** in any of its antiderivative functions over the specified interval.

A definite integral involving an integrand that represents acceleration would give the **change** in the object's velocity over the specified time interval.

$$\int_{a}^{b}\big[a(t)\big]\,dt = v(b) - v(a)$$

A definite integral involving an integrand that represents velocity would give the **change** in displacement of the object over the specified time interval.

$$\int_{a}^{b}\big[v(t)\big]\,dt = s(b) - s(a)$$

Example 3

An object is projected upward from the earth's surface with an initial speed of 98 m/s.

a) What is the object's change in velocity in the first 3 s of motion?

Solution

We must first establish a reference point and a direction convention. If we let the point of release (ground level) be the reference point, then the object's displacement is zero at that point.

The reference point can be placed anywhere along the object's line of motion. The direction convention establishes the sign of the velocity. For this problem, the object will have positive velocity when traveling up and negative velocity when traveling down. Note that reversing these velocity sign conventions would have no effect on our final answer.

The following initial information can now be stated:

The initial velocity of the object is $+98 \text{ m/s}^2$.

The acceleration of the object is -9.81 m/s^2 for the **duration** of the problem.

A negative acceleration means that the velocity of the object must be decreasing.

The object in this problem begins with a velocity of $+98 \text{ m/s}$.

On its way up, traveling in the positive direction, its velocity will change to $+60$ m/s at some point, then to $+20$ m/s, and eventually to 0 m/s. It will then begin to fall, traveling in the negative direction. Its velocity will change from 0 m/s to -20 m/s at some point, then to -60 m/s at some point.

Since the velocity is decreasing, the acceleration is negative.

$$a(t) = -9.8 \text{m/s}^2$$

The object's change in velocity is simply the value of the definite integral shown below. Notice that the integrand is the value of the acceleration for the problem.

$$\int_0^3 (-9.8)\, dt$$

The general antiderivative for the integrand is $\int(-9.8)\,dt = -9.8t + C_1$.

If we name this general antiderivative $V(t)$:

$$\int_0^3 (-9.8)\,dt$$

$$= (-9.8t + C)\Big|_0^3$$

$$= V(3) - V(0)$$

$$= \left[-9.8(3) + C_1\right] - \left[-9.8(0) + C_1\right]$$

$$= -29.4 \text{ m/s}$$

The object's change in velocity during the first 3 seconds of motion was –29.4 m/s.

b) Determine the velocity-time function for the motion of this object. Use this function to find the object's change in displacement in the first 12 s of motion and its distance traveled in this time.

Solution

$$V(t) = \int(-9.8)\,dt = -9.8 + C_2$$

Using the initial condition, $V(0) = +9.8$:

$$98 = -9.8(0) + C_2$$

$$C_2 = 98$$

$$V(t) = -9.8t + 98$$

A graph of the velocity-time function is shown below:

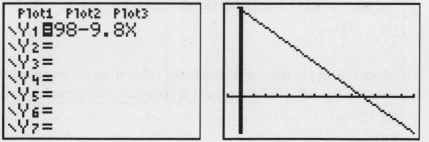

The **change** in displacement in the first 12 s is:

$$\int_0^{12} (-9.8t + 98)\,dt$$

Using $s(t) = -4.9t^2 + 98t + C_3$:

$$\int_0^{12} (-9.8t + 98)\,dt$$

$$= \left(-4.9t^2 + 98t + C_3\right)\Big|_0^{12}$$

$$= s(12) - s(0)$$

$$= \left[-4.9(12)^2 + 98(12) + C_2\right] - \left[-4.9(0)^2 + 98(0) + C_2\right]$$

$$= [470.4] - [0]$$

$$= 470.4 \text{ m}$$

The object's **change** in displacement was 470.4 m in the first 12 s of motion.

The change in displacement and the distance traveled are **not** the same value in this problem. This is because the object changed direction within the time interval. We can calculate the value of C_3 and display the displacement-time function.

Using $s(0) = 0$ (since the object was at the reference point at $t = 0$:

$$s(t) = -4.9t^2 + 98t + C_3$$

$$0 = -4.9(0)^2 + 9.8(0) + C_3$$

$$C_3 = 0$$

$$s(t) = -4.9t^2 + 98t$$

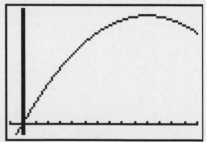

First we must determine when the object changed direction. This occurs at its maximum height where its velocity was momentarily zero.

$$v(t) = -9.8t + 98$$

$$0 = -9.8t + 98$$

$$t = 10 \text{ s}$$

NOTES

The total **distance** traveled during the interval [0, 12] can be found by calculating the changes in displacement during the intervals [0, 10] and [10, 12]. Since distance is a scalar quantity and cannot be negative, we calculate the sum of the absolute value of the definite integrals.

$$\text{Distance traveled} = \left| \int_0^{10} (-9.8t + 98)\, dt \right| + \left| \int_{10}^{12} (-9.8t + 98)\, dt \right|$$

$$\left| \int_0^{10} (-9.8t + 98)\, dt \right| + \left| \int_{10}^{12} (-9.8t + 98)\, dt \right|$$

$$= \left| B(10) - B(0) \right| + \left| B(12) - B(10) \right|$$

$$= \left| \left[-4.9(10)^2 + 98(12) + C_2 \right] - \left[-4.9(0)^2 + 98(0) + C_2 \right] \right|$$

$$+ \left| \left[-4.9(12)^2 + 98(12) + C_2 \right] - \left[-4.9(0)^2 + 98(10) + C_2 \right] \right|$$

$$= \left| 490 \right| + \left| -19.6 \right|$$

$$= 509.6 \text{ m}$$

Functions Defined As Integrals

Example 4

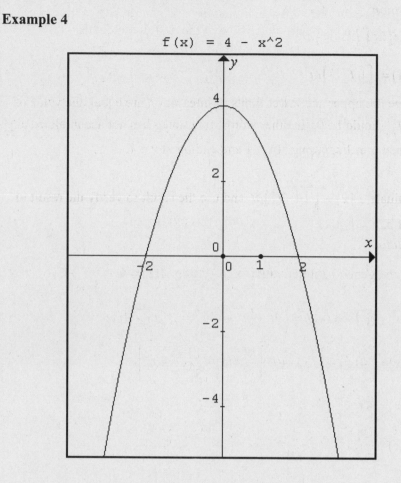

f(x) = 4 - x^2

The graph above shows the function $f(x) = 4 - x^2$.

a) Describe the meaning of function g if $g(x) = \int_1^x \left(4 - t^2\right) dt$.

Solution

First we observe that function f is the integrand of the definite integral (Do not worry about the use of a different variable, t).

Thus, function f is the **derivative function** of function g.

It follows that function g is an **antiderivative** of function f.

The lower an upper limits of integration are 1 and x, respectively.

Function g is a function that accumulates signed area under function f, beginning its accumulation at $x = 1$ and stopping at some value x.

b) Without doing any calculations, what is the value of $g(1)$?

Solution

$$g(x) = \int_1^x \left(4 - t^2\right) dt$$

$$g(1) = \int_1^1 \left[f(t) \right] dt$$

Since the upper and lower limits of integration are equal, the value of $g(1)$ should be 0. In other words, function g has not accumulated any signed area beginning at $x = 1$ and ending at $x = 1$.

c) Evaluate $g(x) = \int_1^x \left(4 - t^2\right) dt$ and use the result to verify the result in part b.

Solution

Let the general antiderivative of $4 - t^2$ be $A(t) = 4t - \dfrac{1}{3}t^3 + C$.

$$g(x) = \int_1^x \left(4 - t^2\right) dt = \left(4t - \frac{1}{3}t^3 + C \right)\Bigg|_1^x = A(x) - A(1)$$

$$g(x) = \left[4(x) - \frac{1}{3}(x)^3 + C \right] - \left[4(1) - \frac{1}{3}(1)^3 + C \right]$$

$$g(x) = 4x - \frac{1}{3}x^3 - 4 + \frac{1}{3}$$

$$g(x) = -\frac{1}{3}x^3 + 4x - \frac{11}{3}$$

We can verify the result of part b by evaluating $g(1)$.

$$g(1) = -\frac{1}{3}(1)^3 + 4(1) - \frac{11}{3}$$

$$g(1) = 0$$

d) Is the value of $g(0)$ a positive or negative result? Verify your answer.

Solution

$$g(x) = \int_1^x \left(4 - t^2\right) dt$$

$$g(0) = \int_1^0 \left(4 - t^2\right) dt$$

This means that signed area is being accumulated under function f, beginning at $x = 1$ and ending at $x = 0$.

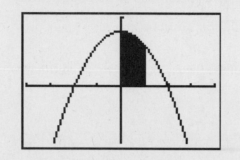

This area lies above the x-axis. However, the signed area is being accumulated from right to left. Thus, the value of $g(0)$ is negative.

We verify this by using $g(x) = -\dfrac{1}{3}x^3 + 4x - \dfrac{11}{3}$.

$$g(0) = -\frac{1}{3}(0)^3 + 4(0) - \frac{11}{3}$$

$$g(0) = -\frac{11}{3}$$

Definite integrals can be used to find total area enclosed between a function and the x-axis.

Example 5

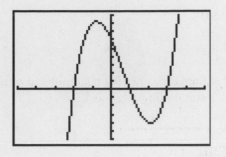

Determine the area enclosed by the function $f(x) = x^3 - 2x^2 - 5x + 6$ and the x-axis in the interval $[-2, 3]$

Solution

The question asks for **area**, not **signed area**.

Step 1:

Determine the zeros of function f in the interval $[-2, 3]$.

$$0 = x^3 - 2x^2 - 5x + 6$$

Since $f(1) = 0$, $(x-1)$ must be a factor of the cubic polynomial.

Using synthetic division:

$$x-1 \begin{array}{|rrrr} 1 & -2 & -5 & 6 \\ & -1 & 1 & 6 \\ \hline 1 & -1 & -6 & 0 \end{array}$$

$$f(x) = (x-1)(x^2 - x - 6)$$

$$f(x) = (x-1)(x+2)(x-3)$$

The zeros of function f are 1, –2, and 3.

Step 2:

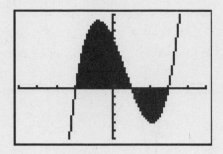

The area can be found by determining the sum of the absolute values of 2 definite integrals.

$$\text{Total area} = \left| \int_{-2}^{1} \left[f(x) \right] dx \right| + \left| \int_{1}^{3} \left[f(x) \right] dx \right|$$

The general antiderivative for function f is

$$A(x) = \frac{1}{4}x^4 - \frac{2}{3}x^3 - \frac{5}{2}x^2 + 6x + C.$$

$$\left| \int_{-2}^{1} \left[f(x) \right] dx \right| + \left| \int_{1}^{3} \left[f(x) \right] dx \right| = \begin{array}{l} = \left| \frac{63}{4} \right| + \left| -\frac{16}{3} \right| \\ = \frac{253}{12} \\ \doteq 21.08 \end{array}$$

$$\left| \left(\frac{1}{4}x^4 - \frac{2}{3}x^3 - \frac{5}{2}x^2 + 6x + C \right) \Big|_{-2}^{1} \right| + \left| \left(\frac{1}{4}x^4 - \frac{2}{3}x^3 - \frac{5}{2}x^2 + 6x + C \right) \Big|_{1}^{3} \right|$$

$$= \left\| \left[\frac{1}{4}(1)^4 - \frac{2}{3}(1)^3 - \frac{5}{2}(1)^2 + 6(1) + C \right] - \left[\frac{1}{4}(-2)^4 - \frac{2}{3}(2)^3 - \frac{5}{2} - (2)^2 + 6(-2) + C \right] \right\| +$$

$$\left\| \left[\frac{1}{4}(3)^4 - \frac{2}{3}(3)^3 - \frac{5}{2}(3)^2 + 6(3) + C \right] - \left[\frac{1}{4}(1)^4 - \frac{2}{3}(1)^3 - \frac{5}{2}(1)^2 + 6(1) + C \right] \right\|$$

$$= \left\| \left[\frac{1}{4}(1)^4 - \frac{2}{3}(1)^3 - \frac{5}{2}(1)^2 + 6(1) + C \right] - \left[\frac{1}{4}(-2)^4 - \frac{2}{3}(-2)^3 - \frac{5}{2}(-2)^2 + 6(-2) + C \right] \right\| +$$

$$\left\| \left[\frac{1}{4}(3)^4 - \frac{2}{3}(3)^3 - \frac{5}{2}(3)^2 + 6(3) + C \right] - \left[\frac{1}{4}(1)^4 - \frac{2}{3}(1)^3 - \frac{5}{2}(1)^2 + 6(1) + C \right] \right\|$$

$$= \left\| \left[\frac{37}{12} \right] - \left[-\frac{38}{3} \right] \right\| + \left\| \left[-\frac{9}{4} \right] - \left[\frac{37}{12} \right] \right\|$$

With the use of technology, this problem can be solved very easily.

The function $f(x) = |x^3 - 2x^2 - 5x + 6|$ is the original function

$f(x) = x^3 - 2x^2 - 5x + 6$ with all points that were originally below the

x-axis now reflected in the x-axis to positions above the x-axis.

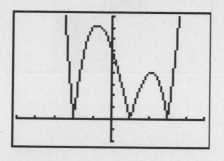

The area desired is

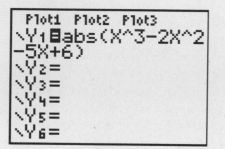

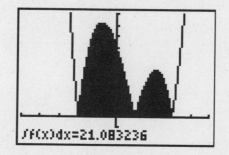

AVERAGE VALUE OF A FUNCTION

Consider the function $f(x) = x + 1$ in the interval [2, 5].

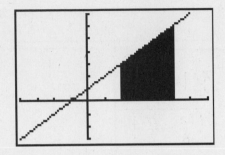

$f(2) = 3$ The value of the function at the left boundary of the interval is 3. This represents the height of the region at its left edge.

$f(5) = 6$ The value of the function at the right boundary of the interval is 6. This represents the height of the region at its right edge.

Since the function is linear, we can see that its **average value** within the interval is 4.5. (The average of 3 and 6)

The average value of the function and its width can be used to find the signed area of the region. We say signed area because parts or even all of a function could be below the x-axis in the interval.

Signed area = (interval width)(average value of function)
In this example, the signed area would equal $(5 - 2)(4.5) = 13.5$ units squared.

This signed area is also the value of $\int_{2}^{5}(x+1)dx$

Any continuous function $y = f(x)$, must have an average value that occurs at least once within a specified interval [a, b].

Rearranging **Signed area = (interval width)(average value of function)**:

Average value of a function $= \dfrac{\text{signed area}}{\text{interval width}}$

Average value of a function $= \dfrac{\int_{a}^{b}\left[f(x)\right]dx}{(b-a)}$

372

Example 6

Determine the average value of the function $f(x) = \sec^2 x$ in the interval $\left[\dfrac{2\pi}{3}, \dfrac{5\pi}{6} \right]$.

Solution

$$\text{Average value} = \frac{\displaystyle\int_{\frac{2\pi}{3}}^{\frac{5\pi}{6}} \left(\sec^2 x \right) dx}{\left(\dfrac{5\pi}{6} - \dfrac{2\pi}{3} \right)}$$

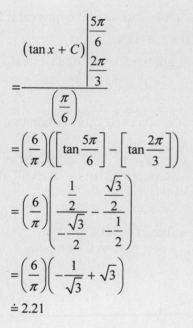

$$= \frac{\left. \left(\tan x + C \right) \right|_{\frac{2\pi}{3}}^{\frac{5\pi}{6}}}{\left(\dfrac{\pi}{6} \right)}$$

$$= \left(\frac{6}{\pi} \right) \left(\left[\tan \frac{5\pi}{6} \right] - \left[\tan \frac{2\pi}{3} \right] \right)$$

$$= \left(\frac{6}{\pi} \right) \left(\frac{\frac{1}{2}}{-\frac{\sqrt{3}}{2}} - \frac{\frac{\sqrt{3}}{2}}{-\frac{1}{2}} \right)$$

$$= \left(\frac{6}{\pi} \right) \left(-\frac{1}{\sqrt{3}} + \sqrt{3} \right)$$

$$\doteq 2.21$$

PRACTICE EXERCISE

1. Approximate the signed area under the function $f(x) = 4 - x^2$ in the interval [0, 4] by using a left rectangular approximation with 4 rectangles.

2. Evaluate each definite integral algebraically. Verify your result with your graphing calculator.

a) $\int_{-4}^{3} (4 - x^2) dx$

b) $\int_{\frac{\pi}{2}}^{\frac{5\pi}{3}} (\sin t + \cos t) dt$

c) $\int_{2}^{3} \left(\frac{1}{x} \right) dx$

d) $\int_{-1}^{3} (e^{2p}) dp$

3.

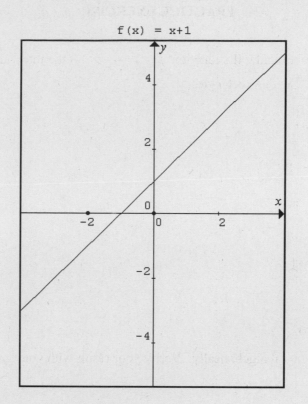

f(x) = x+1

Function p is defined as $p(x) = \int_{-2}^{x} \left[f(t) \right] dt$.

a) Evaluate $p(x)$

b) Determine the value of $p(-2)$, $p(3)$, and $p(-3)$

4. Determine the total area enclosed by the function $f(x) = \sin x$ and the x-axis in the interval $\left[\dfrac{\pi}{6}, \dfrac{4\pi}{3} \right]$.

5. Solve for x if $\displaystyle\int_{2}^{x} (2t - 3)\, dt = 12$.

6. Determine the value of $\int_2^5 \big[f(x) \big] dx$ if $\int_2^4 \big[f(x) \big] dx = 10$ and $\int_4^5 \big[f(x) \big] dx = -17$

7. Determine the value of $\int_2^5 \big[f(x) \big] dx$ if $\int_4^2 \big[f(x) \big] dx = 10$ and $\int_5^4 \big[f(x) \big] dx = -17$

8. Determine the average value of the function $f(x) = 4 - x^2$. Where does the function take on this value?

Lesson 5 *AREA BETWEEN CURVES*

In this lesson, we will expand upon our ability to find the area under a continuous function. Up to this point, our areas have used the x-axis as a foundation (a lower determining edge). We will learn how to find the enclosed area between any two continuous functions within an interval.

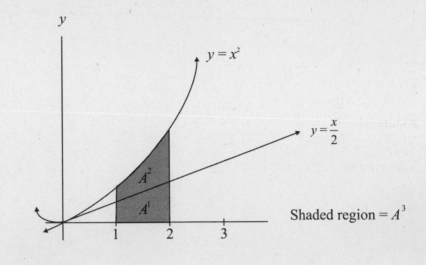

Shaded region = A^3

Example 1

Find the area enclosed by the functions $f(x) = x^2$ and $g(x) = \dfrac{x}{2}$ in the interval $[1, 2]$.

Solution

Method 1

Step 1

Determine the area between function f and the x-axis in the interval $[1, 2]$.

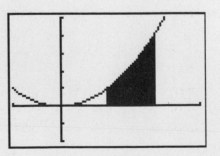

$$\text{Area} = \int_1^2 \left(x^2\right) dx = \left(\frac{1}{3}x^3 + C_1\right)\bigg|_1^2 = \left[\frac{1}{3}(2)^3 + C_1\right] - \left[\frac{1}{3}(1)^3 + C_1\right] = \frac{7}{3}$$

Step 2

Determine the area between function g and the x-axis in the interval $[2, 3]$.

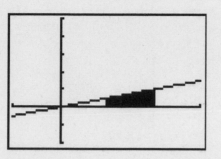

$$\text{Area} = \int_2^3 \left(\frac{x}{2}\right) dx = \left(\frac{1}{4}x^2 + C_2\right)\Big|_1^2 = \left[\frac{1}{4}(2)^2 + C_2\right] - \left[\frac{1}{4}(1)^2 + C_2\right] = \frac{3}{4}$$

Step 3

The area between the 2 functions in the interval $[2, 3]$ is the difference between the 2 areas calculated in the first 2 steps.

$$\text{Enclosed area} = \frac{7}{3} - \frac{3}{4} = \frac{19}{12}$$

Method 2

Step 1

Determine the **difference function** $d(x) = f(x) - g(x)$, where function

f is the **upper function** in the interval and function g is the **lower function**.

$$d(x) = x^2 - \frac{1}{2}x$$

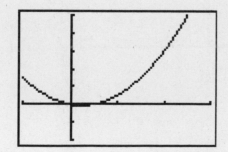

The area between the difference function and the *x*-axis in the interval [1, 2] will equal the area between the 2 original functions in the same interval.

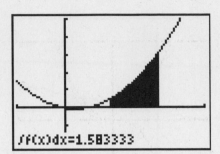

$$\int_1^2 \left(x^2 - \frac{1}{2}x \right) dx$$

$$= \left(\frac{1}{3}x^3 - \frac{1}{4}x^2 + C \right)\Big|_1^2 = \left[\frac{1}{3}(2)^3 - \frac{1}{4}(2)^2 + C \right] - \left[\frac{1}{3}(1)^3 - \frac{1}{4}(1)^2 + C \right] = \frac{19}{12}$$

CURVE INTERSECTIONS

In many cases we are not dealing with a simple case of one curve hovering nicely over a lower curve for the entire interval in question.
Sometimes, the curves intersect and after the intersection point, the curve that was the higher curve initially becomes the lower curve. In order to deal with these possibilities it is useful to graph the two functions over the given interval (at least) and see if we have intersection points.

Knowing where the graphs intersect and how they position themselves before and after these intersection points allows us to continue solving for area between curves questions. Often, these intersection points are part of the question (see next example). Note that we are only interested in intersection points or discontinuity, within the interval in question.

Example 2

Determine the area enclosed by the functions $p(x) = x^2$ and $q(x) = x^3$

in the interval extending from the origin to the x-component of their point of intersection.

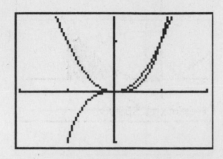

Solution

Step 1

Determine the point(s) of intersection of the two functions.

This occurs when:

$p(x) = q(x)$

$x^2 = x^3$

$0 = x^3 - x^2$

$0 = x^2(x-1)$

$x = 0$ or $x = 1$

Step 2

Observe that function p is the upper function and q is the lower function in the interval $[0, 1]$.

The difference function is $d(x) = p(x) - q(x)$.

The enclosed area is:

$$\int_0^1 \left(x^2 - x^3\right) dx = \left(\frac{1}{3}x^3 - \frac{1}{4}x^4 + C\right)\Bigg|_0^1$$

$$= \left[\frac{1}{3}(1)^3 - \frac{1}{4}(1)^4 + C\right] - \left[\frac{1}{3}(0)^3 - \frac{1}{4}(0)^4 + C\right]$$

$$= \left[\frac{1}{12}\right] - [0]$$

$$= \frac{1}{12}$$

Example 3

Determine the area enclosed by the y-axis and the functions $f(x) = \tan x$ and $g(x) = 2 - x^3$.

Solution

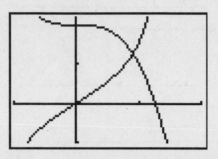

Step 1

Determine the point of intersection of functions f and g (Do not assume that this happens at $x = 1$).

$$f(x) = g(x)$$

$$\tan x = 2 - x^3$$

$$0 = 2 - x^3 - \tan x$$

$$x \doteq 0.902 \quad \text{(Using technology)}$$

Step 2

Enclosed area =

$$\int_0^{0.902} \left(2 - x^3 - \tan x\right) dx$$

$$\doteq 1.16$$

PRACTICE EXERCISE

1. Find the area of the region between the given curves over the indicated interval. If there are intersection points, indicate them.

   a) $f(x) = x^2$ and $g(x) = 1$ in quadrant I

   b) $f(x) = x^2$ and $g(x) = 1$, between both intersection points

   c) $y = -x^2 + 4$ and $y = -2x$ for any area bounded between the curves and the y-axis (as a right-hand boundary) i.e. only areas left of or touching the y-axis

d) $y = x^2 - 4$, above the x-axis and the line $x = 4$

e) $y = \sin x$ and $y = \cos x$ between the y-axis and $\dfrac{\pi}{4}$ radians along the positive x-axis

f) $y = x^3 - 3x^2 + x + 4$, $y = -x^2 + 4x + 4$, and the y-axis, in Cartesian Quadrant I

Lesson 6   *AREA USING NUMERICAL METHODS (REVISITED)*

If we are given a function that is continuous over an interval $a \to b$ and if we can find an indefinite integral (antiderivative), we can find $F(b) - F(a)$. Thus, we can find the accumulated signed area under the curve over the stated interval. Functions exist, however, in which the antiderivative is difficult to find. These functions need a new method for calculating the area under the curve. In this lesson, we will look at a number of numerical methods that can be used.

In Chapter 8, we will learn several stratagems for finding the definite integral. However, even given those new tools there will still be useful applications for numerical methods.

RECTANGULAR RULE

The first numerical method we examine proposes dividing the area under the given function $f(x)$ up into a number of rectangles. These rectangles are of equal length along the x-axis and if there are n such rectangles created between $a \to b$, then each one is of length $\dfrac{b-a}{n}$.

Figure 1

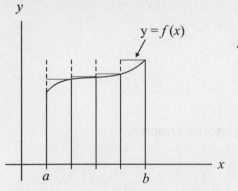

4 rectangles each of length

$\dfrac{b-a}{4}$ along the x-axis

Figure 2

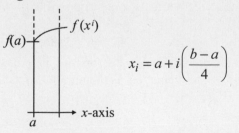

$$x_i = a + i\left(\frac{b-a}{4}\right)$$

The height of each of the rectangles is equal to $f(x)$. This presents a problem since the function has most likely changed in height over the length of the rectangle. Notice in Figure 2 that $f(x)$ at a is not the same as $f(x)$ at the point that has been moved to the right along the x-axis a distance of $\dfrac{b-a}{4}$. We call this point $f(x_i)$ where $x_i = a + i\left(\dfrac{b-a}{n}\right)$ and $n = 4$ (in this specific case).

For our first attempts to solve the area problem using numerical methods we must accept the fact that this is still just an approximation. Be aware that the height $f(x)$ we are using is not exact.

Note: The function drawn in Figure 1 increases right along the x-axis. Because of this fact, the rectangles drawn have a larger $f(x_i)$ farther right.

This means that our approximation using the Rectangular Rule will be larger than the actual value. All of the rectangles drawn in Figure 1 touch the function at the right-most point of the rectangle, but the area of that rectangle is larger than the area under the curve for that interval. If we are given a function that only decreases over the interval $a \rightarrow b$, then our approximation will be smaller than the actual value. If the function both increases and decreases, we cannot make an initial assessment of the approximation.

Each of the areas of the rectangles is added and the result is our numerical approximation. We note this with summation notation:

$$\frac{b-a}{n}\sum_{i=1}^{n} f(x_i) \quad \text{*see Reimann Sum next}$$

Our concern over the discrepancy in height between the start and end-point of the each rectangle would be diminished if used more rectangles and made each rectangle smaller in width. This will make the difference between $f(x_i)$ and $f(x_{i+1})$ smaller, giving a better approximation of the actual height. We know that the number of rectangles is inversely proportional to the width of each one so if we make the number of rectangles as large as possible and make the width as small as possible, a better approximation would be found.

The actual value of the accumulated signed area under the function is the limiting value of the sum of the areas of the rectangles as the number of rectangles approaches infinity.

$$\lim_{n \to \infty} \sum_{i=1}^{n} f(x_i)\Delta x_i$$

For our purposes, we will not evaluate this limit of an infinite sum. This is a partial proof that leads to the Fundamental Theorem of Calculus (see Chapter 8). The whole proof is beyond the scope of this course.

We can now say that an approximation of the definite integral (and the signed area under the curve of $f(x)$ for a given interval $[a, b]$) is given by:

$$\int_a^b f(x)\,dx \approx l\sum_{i=1}^{n} f(x_i), \text{ where } l = \frac{b-a}{n}.$$

Also, we obtain better approximations if n is larger.

Example 1

Determine the signed area under the function $f(x) = x$ in the interval [0, 4].

We choose this simple function because we are able to find the area under this curve graphically. As well, we are able to find its antiderivative.

Solution

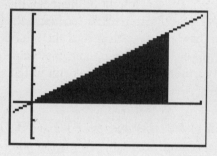

Graphically, the area under the line $y = x$ from in the interval [0, 4] is exactly half of a 4×4 square. So, the area is 8 units squared.

Signed area $= \int_0^4 (x)\,dx = \left.\left(\frac{1}{2}x^2 + C\right)\right|_0^4 = \left[\frac{1}{2}(4)^2\right] - [0] = 8$

Now we will attempt to find the area for 4 rectangles and for a greater number of rectangles by using the Rectangular Rule.

Rectangles: 4   Interval: $[0, 4]$ $\frac{b-a}{n} \Rightarrow \frac{4}{4} = 1$

$x_i = a + i\left(\frac{b-a}{n}\right)$

$\quad = 0 + 1i$

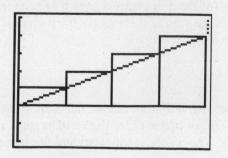

Area approximation:

$$= l\sum_{i=1}^{4} f(x_i) = 1\left[f(x_1) + f(x_2) + f(x_3) + f(x_4) \right]$$

$$= 1 + 2 + 3 + 4$$

$$= 10$$

Rectangles: 40 $\qquad \dfrac{b-a}{n} = \dfrac{4}{40} = \dfrac{1}{10} \qquad x_i = 0 + i\left(\dfrac{1}{10}\right)$

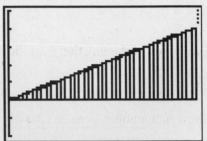

Area approximation:

$$= l\sum_{i=1}^{40} f(x_i)$$

$$= \frac{1}{10}\left(\frac{1}{10} + \frac{2}{10} + \frac{3}{10} + ... + \frac{38}{10} + \frac{39}{10} + \frac{40}{10} \right)$$

$$= 8.2$$

Use a calculator or the summation formula.

This answer is much closer to the actual area. Notice that the function in question only increases over the interval and as noted earlier, this means our approximation(s) will be larger than the actual value.

RIEMANN SUMS

A German mathematician, Bernhard Reimann (1826–1866), is credited with developing a theorem for finding areas under a curve using rectangular areas. This theorem in its simplest form, is the idea proposed by the Rectangular Rule.

$$\frac{b-a}{n}\sum_{i=1}^{n} f(x_i)$$

This is a form of the Rectangular Rule and also the general Reimann Sum. This sum is sometimes denoted by a cursive S, or indicated by name.

Reimann also noticed that the value of $f(x)$ or height of the function, was different at the beginning and the end of the rectangle being used. We noted this concern earlier. Reimann chose to create two additional sums dealing with the same function as his general sum.

Upper Reimann Sum: For this sum, we are using the same summation and interval notation as before, except that for the height we use the maximum value of the function over the sub-interval (rectangle).

$$S_n = \frac{b-a}{n}\left(\sum_{i=1}^{n} M_i\right)$$

M is the maximum value of the function over the interval i.

We can plot a given function on a graph (even if increasing and decreasing) and draw in a number of rectangles of width $\dfrac{b-a}{n}$.

Over each rectangular sub-interval in question, we can see the M_i which is the height of the (tallest) rectangle needed to touch the highest point along the function (over that interval). At the same time, we can also see m_i or the minimum point along the function in that sub-interval.

The height of the rectangle is the tallest rectangle that can be drawn that is completely underneath the function at all points on the interval and that touches the function.

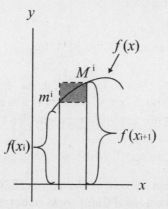

In the diagram we have a section of a function that we want to break-up using the Rectangular Rule. We are only concerned with the one rectangular interval shown and do not need to know if the function is increasing overall, decreasing overall, or both. In the given section, the function rises from a minimum value of m_i, at $f(x_i)$, to a maximum value of M_i at $f(x_{i+1})$. The difference in area of the two rectangles that can be drawn is shown by the shaded region.

Lower Reimann Sum: $s_n = \dfrac{b-a}{n}\left(\displaystyle\sum_{i=1}^{n} m_i\right)$

Since the upper sum deals with an approximation that is larger than the actual area, and the lower sum deals with an approximation that is smaller than the actual area, we can say:

$S_n \leq$ general Reimann sum $\leq S_n$

Notice that the subscript n can be used to find how many rectangles need to be used.

Example 2

We will attempt to find the area under the familiar function $f(x) = x^2$ from the origin to 1 using Reimann sums. Use four rectangular intervals. Graph and solve for the upper and lower sums.

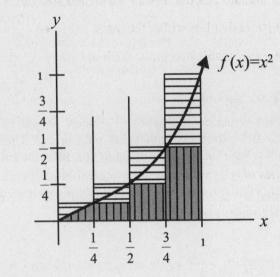

Solution

$$\frac{b-a}{n} = \frac{1-0}{4} = \frac{1}{4}$$

Intervals are at $\frac{1}{4}, \frac{1}{2}, \frac{3}{4}$ and bounded by $0 \rightarrow 1$.

In the diagram, we can see the different heights of the rectangles for the upper and lower sums.

For the upper sums, we have a rectangle of height (M): $\frac{1}{16}, \frac{1}{4}, \frac{9}{16}, 1$.

These values correspond to the values of x squared $\left(\frac{1}{4}, \frac{1}{2}, \frac{3}{4}, 1\right)$.

The areas of each of these rectangles is found by multiplying its height by its length, which is $\frac{1}{4}$ because of the interval length.

$$S_4 = \frac{1}{4}\left(\frac{1}{16} + \frac{1}{4} + \frac{9}{16} + 1\right)$$

$$S_4 = \frac{15}{32}$$

In the diagram, the large rectangles include the areas shaded with vertical lines and the areas shaded with horizontal lines.

For the lower sums, we have only three rectangles, since over the first rectangular area $\left(0 \to \frac{1}{4}\right)$, the function has a value of zero (the origin).

We find the sum of the other three rectangles corresponding to the rectangles in the diagram which have vertical lines.

$$s_4 = \frac{1}{4}\left(0 + \frac{1}{16} + \frac{1}{4} + \frac{9}{16}\right)$$

$$s_4 = \frac{7}{32}$$

We now know that the function has a total signed area under its curve in the interval $[0, 1]$ that lies within the range of $\frac{7}{32} \leftrightarrow \frac{15}{32}$. So this does give us another viable numerical method to use.

TRAPEZOIDAL RULE

The next method for numerical evaluation of area involves then division of the functional area into trapezoids (rather than rectangles). The trapezoids employed have a flat base (the x-axis), two sides of different lengths (the two differing values of $f(x)$ along the sub-interval), and a top side that is slanted. The slanted top side is a closer approximation of the curve than the straight line of a rectangle.

Each trapezoid is of width $\frac{b-a}{n}$ given an interval $[a, b]$ and n trapezoids employed (all in the same manner as the Rectangular Rule). A trapezoid with heights of $f(x_i)$ and $f(x_{i+1})$ has an area given by the formula:

$\frac{b-a}{n}\left(\frac{f(x_i) + f(x_{i+1})}{2}\right)$. That is, the length along the x-axis multiplied by the average height. (In this way, one can think of a rectangle as being a trapezoid with sides of equal height).

To simplify, we can use $y = f(x)$ for trapezoids, where $i = 1 \ldots n$.

We then add up the areas of n trapezoids over the interval $[a, b]$ where $x_i = a + \frac{b-a}{n}(i)$.

$$A = \frac{b-a}{n}\left(\frac{y(a) + y(1)}{2}\right) + \frac{b-a}{n}\left(\frac{y(1) + y(2)}{2}\right) + \ldots + \frac{b-a}{n}\left(\frac{y(n-1) + y(b)}{2}\right)$$

or in another form:

$$A = \frac{b-a}{2n}\left[f(a) + 2f(x_1) + \ldots + 2f(x_{n-1}) + f(b)\right]$$

NOTES

Example 3

Use the Trapezoid Rule to evaluate the area under the curve of the function $f(x) = \dfrac{1}{x}$ over the interval [1, 5] using 8 trapezoids.

Solution

Find the trapezoid length: $\dfrac{b-a}{n} \Rightarrow \dfrac{5-1}{8} = \dfrac{1}{2}$

$a = 1$, $x_1 = 1 + \dfrac{1}{2}$, $x_2 = 1 + 2\left(\dfrac{1}{2}\right)$, ..., $x_8 = 5$, or as follows

1, 1.5, 2, 2.5, 3, 3.5, 4, 4.5, 5

8 trapezoids of length 0.5 starting at 1 and ending at 5 (interval) and since $f(x) = \dfrac{1}{x}$, we can find $f(a) \to f(b)$ and employ our formula.

$$A = \frac{b-a}{2n}\left[f(a) + 2f(x_1) + ... + 2f(x_{n-1}) + f(b)\right]$$

$$A = \frac{1}{2(2)}\left(1 + 2\left(\frac{2}{3}\right) + 2\left(\frac{1}{2}\right) + 2\left(\frac{2}{5}\right) + 2\left(\frac{1}{3}\right) + 2\left(\frac{2}{7}\right) + 2\left(\frac{1}{4}\right) + 2\left(\frac{2}{9}\right) + \frac{1}{5}\right)$$

$$A = \frac{1}{4}\left(\frac{821}{126}\right)$$

$$A = \frac{821}{504}$$

$$A = 1.63$$

Note that the actual value of this signed area is:

$$\int_1^5 \left(\frac{1}{x}\right)dx = \left(\ln|x| + C\right)\Big|_1^5 = \left[\ln 5\right] - \left[\ln 1\right] \doteq 1.61$$

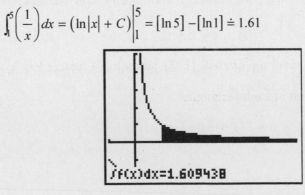

∫f(x)dx=1.609438

PRACTICE EXERCISE

1. a) Use the Rectangular Rule to approximate the area under the curve of $f(x) = \cos x$ for the interval of $\left[0, \dfrac{\pi}{2}\right]$. Use six rectangles.

b) For the function in (a) solve for the area using the antiderivative and then compare answers.

2. Given $f(x) = \dfrac{1}{x}$, over the interval $[1, \ 3]$ and using 4 rectangles

a) Find the width of each rectangle.

b) List the boundaries of each rectangle (sub-interval for each).

c) What would be the height of each rectangle to be used in a Reimann Sum for a lower sum (m) and an upper sum (M)?

3. a) Find the area under the curve $y = 2x^2 + 1$ from 0 to 2 using approximation with the Trapezoid Rule and using 4 trapezoids.

b) Find the area under the curve in (a) using a definite integral and then compare answers.

REVIEW SUMMARY

In this unit, you have learned how to . . .

- find the antiderivative of a simple polynomial function

  when $f(x)=x^n$, $F(x)=\dfrac{x^{n+1}}{n+1}$

- find the antiderivative of a simple trigonometric function

  $f(x)=\sin x \quad F(x)=-\cos x, \quad f(x)=\cos x \quad F(x)=\sin x$

- find the antiderivative of an exponential function

  $f(x)=e^{kx} \quad F(x)=\dfrac{e^{kx}}{k}$

- use substitution to evaluate indefinite integrals

- use antiderivatives to solve problems with initial conditions

- solve 2nd order differential equations with Hooke's Law as an application

- evaluate a definite integral

- find the area under a curve over an interval $[a,\ b]$

- find the area between curves

- approximate area using the Rectangular Rule

- approximate area using Reimann Sums

  $S_n=\dfrac{b-a}{n}\left(\sum_{i=1}^{n} M_i\right)$ and $s_n=\dfrac{b-a}{n}\left(\sum_{i=1}^{n} m_i\right)$

- approximate area using the Trapezoidal Rule

  $\dfrac{b-a}{2n}\left[f(a)+2f(x_1)+...+2f(x_{n-1})+f(b)\right]$

- find the average value of a function

PRACTICE TEST

1. Evaluate each indefinite integral:

   a) $\int \left(-\dfrac{e^{-x}}{2} + 2\cos x \right) dx$

   b) $\int (\sin x - \pi)\, dx$

2. A stone falls from rest off a cliff that is 50 m tall. Using $9.8\,\text{m/s}^2$ for the acceleration due to gravity, calculate to one decimal place the time it takes the stone to reach the ground.

3. A spring hangs with a mass of 0.1 kg in its rest position. The spring and mass are stretched downward 0.02 m by a 1 force, and then released from rest. Use Hooke's Law to find an equation representing the displacement (s) of the mass at any time (t).

4. A triangular area is enclosed under the line $y = 3x + 1$ above the x-axis and bounded on the right by the line $x = 2$.

   a) Where does the function $f(x) = 3x + 1$ touch the x-axis?

   b) Calculate the area of the triangle formed using the geometric area formula.

   c) Use a definite integral to calculate the area under the curve from the intersection point found in (a) to 2 (the line $x = 2$).

5. Find the area bounded by the curves of $f(x) = x+1$ and $g(x) = \dfrac{x}{3}$ on the interval $[0, 3]$ using the following two methods.

a) Use the difference of 2 definite integrals.

b) Use one definite integral involving a difference function.

6. Approximate the area under $f(x) = x^2 + 1$ over the interval $[0, 4]$ using the Rectangular Rule with 4 rectangles. Compare your approximation with the actual area as found by using the antiderivative and show all your work.

7. Approximate the area under $f(x) = x^2 + 1$ over the interval $[0, 4]$ using the Trapezoidal Rule with 8 trapezoids. Compare this answer with the answers from question 6.

8. Approximate the area under $f(x) = \dfrac{1}{2 + \sin^2 x}$ over the interval $[0, \pi]$ and use 4 trapezoids.

9. Evaluate each definite integral:

a) $\int_{-2}^{4} \left(3x^2 + 2x - 1\right) dx$

b) $\int_{0}^{\pi} \left(\cos 10x\right) dx$

10. Given $p(x) = \int_{-1}^{x} \left(3t^2 - 4\right) dt$

a) What is the value of $p(-1)$?

b) What is the value of $p'(-1)$?

c) Evaluate $p(x)$

d) What is the value of $p(5)$?

11. Determine the average value of the function $f(x) = \cos x$ in the interval $\left[\dfrac{\pi}{6}, \dfrac{\pi}{3}\right]$.

12. Function f shown below is the **derivative** function of function g.

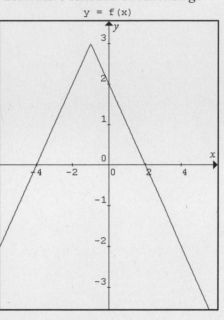

$$g(x) = \int_{-4}^{x} \left[f(t)\right] dt$$

a) Evaluate $g(2)$.

b) Evaluate $g'(2)$.

NOTES

METHODS OF INTEGRATION AND APPLICATIONS

When you are finished this unit, you should be able to. . .

- use the Fundamental Theorem of Calculus
- determine integrals using the method of substitution
- determine integrals using the method of partial fraction
- determine integrals using integration by parts
- determine which integration method to use given a particular type of integral
- determine volumes of revolution

PREREQUISITE SKILLS AND KNOWLEDGE

Prior to beginning this unit, you should be able to. . .

- find the antiderivative of a basic function
- solve a system of equations
- use the formulas for the volume of geometric solids
- use the chain and product rule
- use the equations of parabolas and circles

Lesson 1 FUNDAMENTAL THEOREM OF CALCULUS (REVISITED)

NOTES

We have studied how to differentiate a function (find its derivative) and integrate a function (find its antiderivative).

Integrals can be calculated as limits of sums, a long and arduous process. However, there is a concise method for determining the value of a definite integral. For a continuous function, $y = f(x)$ on an interval $[a, b]$, the accumulated signed area under the curve $f(x)$ from point a to point b can be represented by the definite integral: $\int_a^b f(x)\,dx$.

From our study of accumulated signed area under a curve, we know this is equal to , where $F(x)$ is any antiderivative of . In other words,
$F'(x) = f(x)$.

The Fundamental Theorem of Calculus has two parts.

Part 1
If f is a continuous function on an interval $[a, b]$, then
$$F(x) = \int_a^x f(t)\,dt$$
has a derivative at every point within the interval $[a, b]$, such that
$$\frac{d}{dx}\big[F(x)\big] = \frac{d}{dx}\int_a^x f(t)\,dt = f(x)$$

The first part of the Fundamental Theorem of Calculus states that the definite integral of a continuous function is a differentiable function of its upper limit of integration. It also states that the integrand of the definite integral is the derivative of that differentiable function. In other words, part 1 guarantees that an antiderivative for any continuous function must exist.

Part 2
If f is a continuous function on an interval $[a, b]$ and F is any antiderivative of f, then $\int_a^b f(x)\,dx = F(b) - F(a)$

The second part describes how to evaluate a definite integral.
It states that the definite integral of a continuous function on a interval $[a, b]$ is equal to the change in any of its antiderivatives in that interval.

Example 1

Evaluate $\int_1^3 x^2 dx$

Solution

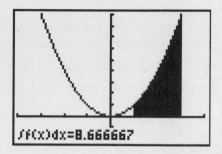

$\int f(x) dx = 8.666667$

This function $f(x) = x^2$ is a parabola with the vertex at the origin. It is continuous at all points; therefore, it is continuous over the interval in question [1, 3]. The most general antiderivative of $f(x)$ is

$F(x) = \dfrac{x^3}{3} + C$. The constant will not be a concern as we will be subtracting the two antiderivatives and therefore, removing it.

$$\int_1^3 x^2 dx$$

$$= \left(\frac{1}{3}x^2 + C \right) \Bigg|_1^3$$

$$= \left[\frac{1}{3}(3)^2 \right] - \left[\frac{1}{3}(1)^2 \right]$$

$$= \frac{26}{3}$$

NOTATION

Notice that another way of denoting $F(b) - F(a)$ is $F(x)\big|_a^b$.

We can now say:

$$\int_a^b x^2 dx = \frac{x^3}{3} \bigg|_a^b = F(b) - F(a), \text{ where } F'(x) = f(x)$$

TABLE AND PROPERTIES

We can create tables of integration showing the integrals (antiderivatives) we have learned. Advanced Calculus texts often have appendices with tables of integrals, beginning with the basics but concentrating on complicated integrals. In lessons 2 to 4 of this chapter, we will learn new techniques for solving more complicated integrals, at which point you can expand or create your own integral tables.

Some known indefinite integrals are:

$$\int 1\,dx = x + C$$

$$\int x\,dx = \frac{x^2}{2} + C$$

$$\int x^n\,dx = \frac{x^{n+1}}{n+1} + C \quad n \neq -1$$

$$\int \cos x\,dx = \sin x + C$$

$$\int \sin x\,dx = -\cos x + C$$

$$\int \sec^2 x\,dx = \tan x + C$$

$$\int \frac{1}{x}\,dx = \ln|x| + C \quad x \neq 0$$

$$\int e^x\,dx = e^x + C$$

$$\int e^{kx}\,dx = \frac{e^{kx}}{k} + C$$

In the above table, we do not list $\int 2\cos x\,dx$ as this is simply

$2\int \cos x\,dx$.

This illustrates the following two properties of integrals.

i) $\int kf(x)\,dx = k\int f(x)\,dx$, where k is a constant

(not to be confused with C)

This can be verified by taking the derivative of each side. The property is illustrated by the fact that

$$\frac{d}{dx}2x = 2$$

$$(2)\frac{d}{dx}x = 2(1) = 2$$

Differentiating and integrating are reverse processes.

ii) $\int [f(x) + g(x)]\,dx = \int f(x)\,dx + \int g(x)\,dx$

This can also be verified by taking the derivative of each side by remembering the commutative property of derivatives, or by the following:

$$\int [\cos x + \cos x]\,dx = \int \cos x\,dx + \int \cos x\,dx$$

$$\int 2\cos x\,dx = 2\int \cos x\,dx$$

PRACTICE EXERCISE

1. Given $\int_a^b f(x)\,dx = F(3) - F(1)$, find a and b.

2. In order to apply the fundamental theorem of calculus, a function must be _____ over the region imposed by the limits of integration.

3. Given $f(x) = \dfrac{1}{x^2}$, and $F'(x) = f(x)$, find $F(x)$.

4. Find $\int \sin x\,dx$.

5. Evaluate $\int_0^\pi \sin x\,dx$.

6. Evaluate $\int_2^3 4\,dx$.

7. Complete the equation: $\int 2\cos x\,dx = \int \cos x\,dx + \int$

Lesson 2   INTEGRATION BY SUBSTITUTION

The method of integration by substitution is a technique through which we express the function in simpler terms by utilizing a new variable, solve the function, and then restore the original variable.

Example 1

Evaluate $\int 2x\left(x^2+1\right)dx$

Solution

There are a number of methods to solve this integral. First, we will use a replacement variable for the more complex of the two functions:

$$u = \left(x^2 + 1\right)$$

$$\frac{du}{dx} = 2x$$

$$du = (2x)\,dx$$

and $dx = \dfrac{du}{2x}$

$$\int \left(x^2 + 1\right)(2x)\,dx$$

$$= \int (u)\,du$$

$$= \frac{u^2}{2} + C$$

$$= \frac{\left(x^2 + 1\right)^2}{2} + C$$

$$= \frac{1}{2}\left(x^2 + 1\right)^2 + C$$

In order to check this result, its derivative should be equal to the original integrand.

$$\frac{d}{dx}\left[\frac{1}{2}\left(x^2 + 1\right)^2\right]$$

$$= (2)\left(\frac{1}{2}\right)\left(x^2 + 1\right)^{2-1}(2x)$$

$$= \left(x^2 + 1\right)(2x)$$

Another approach for this problem involves expanding the integrand and integrating the individual terms of the result.

$$\int (2x)\left(x^2 + 1\right)dx$$

$$= \int \left(2x^3 + 2x\right)dx$$

$$= \int \left(2x^3\right)dx + \int (2x)\,dx$$

$$= 2\int \left(x^3\right)dx + 2\int (x)\,dx$$

$$= 2\left(\frac{1}{4}x^4 + C_1\right) + 2\left(\frac{1}{2}x^2 + C_2\right)$$

$$= \frac{1}{2}x^4 + x^2 + C_3$$

$$= \frac{1}{2}x^4 + x^2 + \frac{1}{2} + C$$

$$= \frac{1}{2}\left(x^4 + 2x^2 + 1\right) + C$$

$$= \frac{1}{2}\left(x^2 + 1\right)^2 + C$$

Notation: The notation for proper substitution in integration is presented here, but the process in practice becomes clear through examples.

The **Chain Rule** for derivatives states that

$$\frac{d}{dx}\Big[F\big(g(x)\big)\Big]dx = \Big[F'\big(g(x)\big)\Big]\Big[g'(x)\Big]$$

Reversing this statement and stating it in terms of integrals:

$$\int \Big[F'\big(g(x)\big)\Big]\Big[g'(x)\Big]dx = F\big(g(x)\big) + C$$

If $g(x)$ is replaced with u, then $u = g(x)$ and $du = g'(x)\,dx$.

The equation $\int \Big[F'\big(g(x)\big)\Big]\Big[g'(x)\Big]dx = F\big(g(x)\big) + C$ can be written as

$$\int F'(u)\,du = \int f(u)\,du = F(u) + C$$

Example 2

Evaluate $\int (x^2 + 6)^8 (2x)\,dx$

Solution

$u = x^2 + 6 = g(x)$

$f(u) = u^8$

$g'(x) = 2x$

$f(g(x)) = (x^2 + 6)^8$

$\int (x^2 + 6)^8 (2x)\,dx$

$= \int f(g(x)) g'(x)\,dx$

$= \int f(u)\,du$

$= \dfrac{1}{9} u^9 + C$

$= \dfrac{1}{9}(x^2 + 6)^9 + C$

Example 3

Find $\int 20x(x+1)^{\frac{1}{2}}\,dx$ by substitution.

Solution

Let $u = (x+1)^{\frac{1}{2}}$, then $u^2 = (x+1)$ and $x = u^2 - 1$ (replace variable later). Now differentiate:

$(2u)\dfrac{du}{dx} = 1$

$(2u)\,du = dx$

Replace into original integral:

$\int 20(u^2 - 1)u(2u)\,du$

$40\int (u^4 - u^2)\,du$

$40\left(\dfrac{u^5}{5} - \dfrac{u^3}{3}\right) + C$

$8u^5 - \dfrac{40u^3}{3} + C$

$8(\sqrt{x+1})^5 - \dfrac{40(\sqrt{x+1})^3}{3} + C$

Example 4

Evaluate $\int \cos x (\sin x + 1) \, dx$.

Solution

Let $u = (\sin x + 1)$

$du = \cos x \, dx$

Manipulate this equation to isolate dx:

$$dx = \frac{du}{\cos x}$$

$$\int u \, du$$

$$\frac{u^2}{2} + C$$

Rewrite original with new variable, integrate, and solve:

$$\frac{(\sin x + 1)^2}{2} + C$$

Substitution can also be used for definite integrals:

If $u = g(x)$, then

$$\int_a^b f(g(x)) g'(x) \, dx = \int_{g(a)}^{g(b)} f(u) \, du$$

Example 5

Evaluate $\int_2^3 e^{2x} \, dx$

Solution

Let $u = 2x$.

Then $\dfrac{du}{dx} = 2$ or $du = 2dx$ or $dx = \dfrac{du}{2}$

Now find the new limits of integration.

When $x = 2$, $u = 2(2) = 4$

When $x = 3$, $u = 2(3) = 6$

$\int_2^3 e^{2x} \, dx$ becomes

$$\frac{1}{2} \int_4^6 e^u \, du$$

$$= \frac{1}{2} \left(e^u + C \right) \Big|_4^6$$

$$= \frac{1}{2} \left(e^6 - e^4 \right)$$

$$\doteq 174.415$$

We can check this result with a graphing calculator.

NOTES

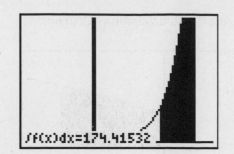

Example 6

Evaluate the following definite integral using substitution. Apply the limits of the integral in the last step (after replacing the original variables).

$$\int_0^3 \left(\sqrt{x+1} \right) dx$$

Solution

$$u = (x+1)^{\frac{1}{2}}$$

$$u^2 = x+1$$

$$2u\frac{du}{dx} = 1$$

$$(2u)\,du = dx$$

The integrand becomes $u(2u)\,du$

Determine the new limits of integration.

When $x = 0$, $u = \sqrt{0+1} = 1$.

When $s = 3$, $u = \sqrt{3+1} = 2$.

$$\int_0^3 \left(\sqrt{x+1} \right) dx$$

$$= \int_1^2 (u)(2u\,du)$$

$$= 2\int_1^2 u^2\,du$$

$$= 2\left(\frac{1}{3}u^3 + C \right)\Big|_1^2$$

$$= 2\left(\left[\frac{1}{3}(2)^3 \right] - \left[\frac{1}{3}(1)^2 \right] \right)$$

$$= 2\left(\frac{8}{3} - \frac{1}{3} \right)$$

$$= \frac{14}{3}$$

412

We can check this result with a graphing calculator.

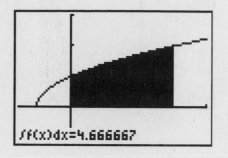

$\int f(x)dx=4.666667$

PRACTICE EXERCISE

1. Evaluate the following indefinite integrals.

   a) $\int \cot x\, dx$

   b) $\int \dfrac{2e^{\sqrt{x}}}{\sqrt{x}}\, dx$

2. Evaluate the following definite integrals using the substitution of variable u.

   a) $\displaystyle\int_{0}^{2}\left[\dfrac{x}{\left(2+x^2\right)^2}\right] dx$

3. Evaluate the integral $\int_3^4 \left(\dfrac{1}{x-1} \right) dx$,

   a) Solve using substitution and evaluate the integral over the substitute variable.

   b) Solve without substitution and compare with the answer from (a).

Lesson 3 INTEGRATION BY PARTIAL FRACTIONS

NOTES

The method of partial fractions as an integration technique, involves breaking down an integrand that contains a quotient of polynomials into simpler fractions. You should review their skills related to adding fractions, dividing polynomials, and working with systems of equations for this lesson.

Consider the integral $\int \frac{A(x)}{B(x)} dx$ where $A(x)$, $B(x)$ are polynomials

(rational functions) in x.

There are two cases for the relationship in degree of the numerator and denominator. Either $A(x)$ is of the same degree or higher than $B(x)$ or the numerator is of lesser degree.

Recall that the degree of a polynomial is equal to the largest exponent of the variable involved.

$A(x) = -2x^2 - 45x^{-6} + 120$

The largest power of variable here is shown by the first term (and is two). The -6 on the second term should not be confused as being larger, nor the constant 120.

Case I: $A(x)$ is of equal or greater degree to $B(x)$

In this case, the first step is to divide the polynomials (numerator divided by denominator). This will produce a quotient polynomial and a remainder. The quotient can then be integrated using any previously learned technique. The remainder (if not zero) will then be a fraction with the degree of the denominator now greater than the numerator. This part is now Case II.

Basically: $\int \frac{A(x)}{B(x)} dx \rightarrow \int Q(x) dx + \int \frac{R(x)}{B(x)} dx$

After we divide $A(x)$ by $B(x)$, there is a quotient $Q(x)$ and a remainder $R(x)$. The remainder could be zero but if not, remember from division of polynomials that that remainder $R(x)$ is still divided by the original divisor $B(x)$. Now the quotient function is no longer a fraction and can be integrated using known methods, leaving us only with the second case to consider, where $R(x)$ is of lesser degree to the denominator.

$R(x)$ can be a constant (i.e., degree zero for x) and in this case, this integral can be solved immediately without proceeding to Case II. The first example illustrates this result.

Example 1

Evaluate the following integral using partial fractions.

$\int \frac{2x^2 - x + 1}{x + 1} dx$

Solution
Divide the polynomials, obtaining:

$\frac{2x^2 - x + 1}{x + 1} = 2x - 3 + \frac{4}{x + 1}$

$\int \frac{2x^2 - x + 1}{x + 1} dx$

$$= \int (2x-3)\,dx + \int \frac{4}{x+1}\,dx$$

$$= x^2 - 3x + C_1 + 4\ln|x+1| + C_2$$

$$= x^2 - 3x + 4\ln|x+1| + C$$

In this case, the remainder was a constant and so did not require additional use of partial fractions. If the remainder is not a constant, then this reverts to Case II.

Case II: $A(x)$ is of lesser degree than $B(x)$.

To begin solving this situation it is helpful to review addition of polynomial fractions. You can then look at the reverse process which is the essential case in partial fractions.

We are given $\dfrac{1}{x+1} + \dfrac{2}{x+2}$ as a starting point. If this were the integrand of

an integral, the solution would be $\ln|x+1| + \ln|x+2| + C$ with the restriction that $x \neq -1$ and -2.

Now add the fractions by finding common denominators, distributing, and adding.

$$\frac{1(x+2)}{(x+1)(x+2)} + \frac{2(x+1)}{(x+1)(x+2)}$$

$$\frac{3x+4}{(x+1)(x+2)}$$

$$\frac{3x+4}{x^2+3x+3}$$

If this fraction were the integrand of an integral, the solution would not be

apparent using previous techniques. The integral of $\dfrac{3x+4}{x^2+3x+3}$ can be

found when partial fractions are employed.

Begin by factoring the denominator. Factoring the denominator gives $(x+1)(x+2)$. We split the function into the sum of two fractions, providing unknown numerators.

$$\frac{3x+4}{x^2+3x+3} = \frac{A}{(x+1)} + \frac{B}{(x+2)}$$

This is just working backward from adding fractions.

To get the final result of $3x+4$, we need to determine values for A and B that make the following statement true.

$$3x+4 = A(x+2) + B(x+1)$$

In this step we want the denominator to be as simple as possible, so if the term of highest degree (in this case, the x^2) has any leading coefficient other than 1 you must factor it out. Recall that one of the rules of integration allows us to bring a constant out in front of the integral.

$$\int 2f(x)\,dx \to 2\int f(x)\,dx$$

This is equal and allowed.

This equation is true only if $A + B = 3$ (for the xs to be true) and also if $2A + B = 4$ (for the constant to be correct).

This gives us a system of two equations with two unknowns.

$A + B = 3$

$2A + 2B = 6$　　　　　Multiply the first system by two:

$2A + 2B = 6$

$2A + B = 4$　　　　　Subtract the second system, solve for B:

$B = 2$

Then, $A = 1$.

Apply this to the fractions:

$$\frac{3x + 4}{x^2 + 3x + 3} = \frac{1}{x+1} + \frac{2}{x+2}$$

The process is complete. We could now integrate the right-hand side.

MORE PARTIAL FRACTIONS

Before proceeding with examples of this system, it is useful to indicate some of the different types of partial fractions one can encounter.
Then a sampling of these will be worked out in the examples and problems presented.

All are for Case II situations. Case I situations are not shown here as they will produce a quotient which is not a fraction and possibly a remainder, which is a Case II example.

Different Types of Partial Fractions

1. The numerator is a constant: This can occur when $A(x)$ is divided by $B(x)$, producing a quotient and a remainder. This remainder may be a constant, still divided by $B(x)$. In this case, the method of partial fractions is not required (but can still be used). It is often possible at this point to solve the integral using known methods.

2. The denominator is a product of linear factors. This case is detailed above in the example of $\dfrac{3x + 4}{x^2 + 3x + 3}$. The denominator was able to be expressed as two linear factors and the numerator was able to be solved using a system of equations.

3. The denominator has a linear term, raised to an exponent of two or higher. In this example, the linear factor is repeated so the set up to solve is slightly different. An example is shown below.

$$\frac{x+1}{(x+3)^2}$$

This can be rewritten as $\dfrac{x+1}{(x+3)^2} = \dfrac{A}{(x+3)} + \dfrac{B}{(x+3)^2}$.

Multiplying for a common denominator gives $x+1 = A(x+3) + B$.

Continue until solved.

The above case can be applied if the denominator term is a higher power than two, using the same method only adding another fraction for each consecutively higher power.

4. The denominator is a function of degree two or higher that can be reduced. See Example 1

Example 1

Evaluate $\displaystyle\int \frac{1}{x^2-25}\,dx$

Solution

This has a constant in the numerator. But this integral is not one we have dealt with, so we choose to employ the method of partial fractions. Note that the denominator is a difference of squares.

$$\frac{1}{x^2-25} \Rightarrow \frac{A}{x+5} + \frac{B}{x-5}$$
$$1 = A(x-5) + B(x+5)$$

Obtain two equations by observing the values for x and 1.
$$A+B=0$$
$$-5A+5B=1$$

Solving gives $A = -\dfrac{1}{10}$, $B = \dfrac{1}{10}$.

Applying this gives $\dfrac{1}{-10(x+5)} + \dfrac{1}{10(x-5)}$

Finally,

$$\int \frac{1}{x^2-25}\,dx = \int \frac{1}{-10(x+5)} + \frac{1}{10(x-5)} = -\frac{1}{10}\ln|x+5| + \frac{1}{10}\ln|x-5| + C$$

5. The denominator has a quadratic factor that cannot be reduced. In this case, we will still create partial fractions but the numerator on the quadratic factor will be $Ax + B$ instead of just a constant.

See the following examples for more detail.

Example 2

Evaluate $\int \dfrac{(x-1)}{(x^2+1)(x+1)} dx$

Solution

$$\frac{(x-1)}{(x^2+1)(x+1)} = \frac{Ax+B}{(x^2+1)} + \frac{C}{(x+1)}$$

$$x-1 = (Ax+B)(x+1) + C(x^2+1)$$

Set up a system:
$$A + C = 0$$
$$A + B = 1$$
$$B + C = -1$$

The system of three equations with three unknowns was set up to compare the number of x^2s, the number of xs, and the constant term. Solving this system produces:
$$A = 1$$
$$B = 0$$
$$C = -1$$

Now, substitute in and complete the integration:

$$\int \left(\frac{1x}{x^2+1} - \frac{1}{x+1} \right) dx$$

$$\frac{\ln\left|x^2+1\right|}{2} - \ln|x+1| + C$$

6. Combinations of the above types of partial fractions (numbered 1 to 5) are in one form or another. More complex partial fractions can be solved by following the patterns presented already.

Example 3

Evaluate $\int \dfrac{x}{x^4 + 3x^2 + 2}\,dx$

Solution

Observe that the denominator can be factored:

$$\frac{x}{\left(x^2+1\right)\left(x^2+2\right)}$$

Now, approach this with the pattern of number 5 above:

$$\frac{Ax+B}{\left(x^2+1\right)} + \frac{Cx+D}{\left(x^2+2\right)}$$

Continue by setting up the systems of equations and solving:

$$\frac{x}{\left(x^2+1\right)\left(x^2+2\right)} \Rightarrow \frac{(Ax+B)\left(x^2+2\right)}{\left(x^2+1\right)} + \frac{(Cx+D)\left(x^2+1\right)}{\left(x^2+2\right)}$$

Distribute numerators

$$Ax^3 + 2Ax + Bx^2 + 2B$$

$$Cx^3 + Cx + Dx^2 + D$$

Set up equations by comparing the left-hand side to the right-hand side. For example, there are $0\ x^3$s on the LHS, so on the RHS we can say that by $A + C = 0$ continuing, we get

$$A + C = 0$$

$$B + D = 0$$

$$2A + C = 1$$

$$2B + D = 0$$

Solving this system gives:

$$C = -1,\ B = 0,\ A = 1,\ D = 0$$

Now, substitute and integrate:

$$\int \left(\frac{1x}{\left(x^2+1\right)} - \frac{1x}{\left(x^2+2\right)} \right) dx$$

$$\frac{\ln\left|x^2+1\right|}{2} - \frac{\ln\left|x^2+2\right|}{2} + C$$

PRACTICE EXERCISE

1. Use the method of partial fractions to solve the following indefinite integrals.

a) $\int \dfrac{x+1}{x^2}\,dx$

b) $\int \dfrac{x^3 - x^2 - 1}{x+1}\,dx$

c) $\int \dfrac{1}{2x^2 - 2}\,dx$

d) $\int \dfrac{x+2}{(x+1)^2}\,dx$

2. Solve the following integrals.

a) $\displaystyle\int_{3}^{4}\left(\frac{-x-1}{x^2-3x+2}\right)dx$

b) $\displaystyle\int_{3}^{4}\left(\frac{2x-4}{2(x-2)^2}\right)dx$

Lesson 4 INTEGRATION BY PARTS

Another useful method for evaluating integrals is the method of integration by parts, a strategy found by examining the Product Rule for derivatives.

Product Rule:

$$\frac{d}{dx}\big(f(x)g(x)\big) = f(x)g'(x) + g(x)f'(x)$$

If we take the antiderivative of the Product Rule, we obtain a new formula.

$$\int \left[\frac{d}{dx}\big[f(x)g(x)\big]\right]dx = \int \big[f(x)g'(x)\big]dx + \int \big[g(x)f'(x)\big]dx$$

$$f(x)g(x) = \int f(x)g'(x)dx + \int g(x)f'(x)dx$$

Rearrange this to obtain:

$$\int f(x)g'(x)dx = f(x)g(x) - \int g(x)f'(x)dx$$

The practical application of this technique becomes clear as we present a number of examples. The key to remembering this technique is that we choose $g'(x)$ to be the more complicated part of the integrand (and we can integrate it with known methods).

If we are given $\int \frac{x}{2}\big(e^{2x}\big)dx$, we can apply integration by parts to solve. It is often helpful to the student to initially write out the separate parts required for the formula, and then to apply them.

$$f(x) = \frac{x}{2}$$

$$f'(x) = \frac{1}{2}$$

$$g'(x) = e^{2x}$$

We chose $g'(x)$ as e^{2x} because it is the more complex function.

$$g(x) = \frac{e^{2x}}{2}$$

$$\int \frac{x}{2}\big(e^{2x}\big)dx = \frac{x}{2}\left(\frac{e^{2x}}{2}\right) - \int \left(\frac{e^{2x}}{2}\right)\left(\frac{1}{2}\right)dx$$

$$= \frac{xe^{2x}}{4} - \frac{e^{2x}}{8} + C$$

Differential Notation: Some texts or questions you may encounter present this method using the following notation:

$$u = f(x), \ v = g(x), \ du = f'(x)dx, \ dv = g'(x)dx$$

$$\int u\,dv = uv - \int v\,du$$

Example 1

Find $\int x \cos x\,dx$ using integration by parts.

Solution

$$f(x) = x$$

$$f'(x) = 1$$

$$g'(x) = \cos x$$

$$g(x) = \sin x$$

$$\int f(x)g'(x)dx = f(x)g(x) - \int g(x)f'(x)dx$$

So using this, we can find the original integral on the right-hand side of the equal sign.

$$= x(\sin x) - \int \sin x (1)\,dx$$

$$= x\sin x + \cos x + C$$

Example 2

Find $\int_0^{\pi} \big((\sin 2x)(x)\big)dx$.

Solution
Rearrange this so that the more complex function is in the spot of $g'(x)$, then apply the formula.

$$\int_0^{\pi} \big((x)(\sin 2x)\big)dx$$

Step 1

Evaluate $\int x\sin(2x)dx$ using integration by parts.

$$f(x) = x \ , \ g'(x) = \sin 2x \ , \ f'(x) = 1 \ , \ g(x) = -\frac{1}{2}\cos 2x$$

$$\int x\sin(2x)dx = (x)\left(-\frac{1}{2}\cos 2x\right) - \int\left(-\frac{1}{2}\cos 2x\right)(1)\,dx$$

$$= -\frac{1}{2}x\cos 2x + \frac{1}{4}\sin 2x + C$$

Step 2

Evaluate the definite integral.

$$\int_0^\pi \left((\sin 2x)(x) \right) dx$$

$$= \left(-\frac{1}{2} x \cos 2x + \frac{1}{4} \sin 2x + C \right) \Bigg|_0^\pi$$

$$= \left[-\frac{1}{2} \pi \cos 2\pi + \frac{1}{4} \sin 2\pi \right] - \left[-\frac{1}{2}(0) \cos 0 + \frac{1}{4} \sin 0 \right]$$

$$= \left[-\frac{1}{2} \pi + 0 \right] - \left[0 + 0 \right]$$

$$= -\frac{1}{2} \pi$$

$$\doteq -1.571$$

We can verify this with a graphing calculator.

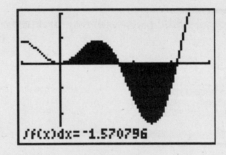

Definite Integral by Parts: When we are given limits of integration (definite integral), we must apply those upper and lower boundaries to the entire right-hand side of the integration by the parts formula.

Up to this point for integration, we have denoted these boundaries after integration with the line following the integrated function, i.e., $F(x) \Big|_a^b$.

This same method can be used for $f(x) g(x)$. Alternately the square bracket can be used (as shown in the example above).

Example 3

Find $\int x \ln x\, dx$ using integration by parts.

Solution

$$\int f(x)g'(x)\,dx = f(x)g(x) - \int g(x)f'(x)\,dx$$

Although $\ln x$ is more complex, we cannot easily find its integral, so we rearrange the formula as.

$$\int \ln x\,(x)\,dx$$

$$f(x) = \ln x$$

$$f'(x) = \frac{1}{x}$$

$$g'(x) = x$$

$$g(x) = \frac{x^2}{2}$$

Then, by the integration by parts formula, our required integral is.

$$\ln x \left(\frac{x^2}{2} \right) - \int \frac{x^2}{2}\left(\frac{1}{x} \right) dx$$

$$= \frac{x^2 \ln x}{2} - \frac{x^2}{4} + C$$

This is fine, or as a single fraction, the answer becomes:

$$= \frac{x^2 (2\ln x - 1)}{4} + C$$

PRACTICE EXERCISE

1. Solve the following integrals by using integration by parts.

   a) $\int (2x+1)e^{-x}dx$

   b) $\int x\cos(3x)\, dx$

   c) $\int x\sec^2 x\, dx$, given that $\int\tan x = -\ln|\cos x|$

d) $\int \dfrac{xe^x}{2}dx$

e) $\int_0^\pi 2x\cos x\,dx$

f) $\int_0^{\frac{\pi}{2}} 2x\cos x\,dx$

PRACTICE QUIZ

1. Evaluate the following definite integral.

$$\int_0^\pi (x + \cos x)\, dx$$

2. Solve the following indefinite integral using substitution.

$$\int 2\tan x\, dx$$

3. Solve the following integral using partial fractions (Hint: look for a difference of squares).

$$\int \frac{(x^2 - 1)}{(x^2 - 1)^2 (x - 1)}\, dx$$

4. Solve the following integral using integration by parts.

$$\int 2x \cos x \, dx$$

5. Evaluate the following definite integral.

$$\int_1^2 \left(\frac{e^x}{1 - e^x} \right) dx$$

6. Determine the following indefinite integral

$$\int \left(4 - x^2 \right) dx \quad - \quad \int \left(x - x^2 \right) dx$$

Lesson 5   *VOLUMES OF REVOLUTION*

In this lesson we will develop an application using integration of the area under a curve and the fundamental theorem of calculus. To begin, we observe the following two points:

1. If we rotate a two-dimensional region about a line, a three-dimensional solid is produced. For example (see Figure 1 and 1.1) if we start with a rectangle and rotate it about the *x*-axis, we obtain a cylindrical disk. The original rectangle has a width which we can denote as Δx and a height, y. The resulting disk has a volume that we can calculate.

   From this point on when we say "rotate about" an axis, this means a full 360° rotation. Any exception will be stated clearly.

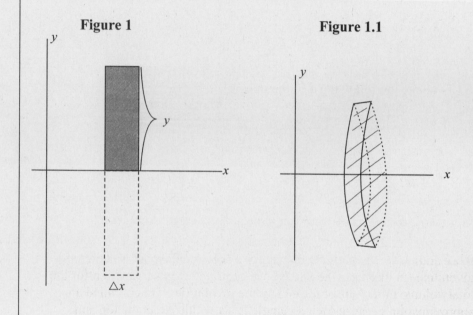

Figure 1   **Figure 1.1**

Recall that the volume of any cylinder is $V = \pi r^2 h$. In this case, the radius is equal to the height of the original rectangle (y). The height of the cylindrical disk is the same as the length (Δx).

Therefore, $V = \pi y^2 \Delta x$.

2. A function can be broken down into small regions denoted by rectangles (or trapezoids). Each of these rectangles can then be rotated about a line, producing a three-dimensional solid. In Figure 2 and 2.1 we see the given function, $f(x)$ rotated out the *x*-axis. Each of the rectangles of width Δx, produces a cylindrical disk. The total resulting solid is called a Volume of Revolution.

Figure 2

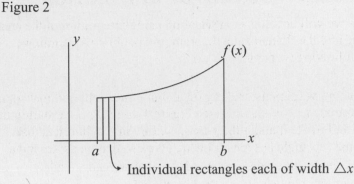

Individual rectangles each of width $\triangle x$

Figure 2.1

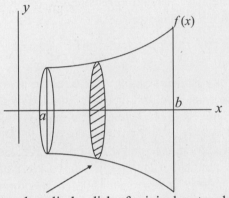

Sample cylinder disk of original rectangle width $\triangle x$

If we add the areas of all the rectangles and rotate them all around the given line (in this case, the *x*-axis), we can find an approximation for the total volume of the object formed by the revolution. This is called an approximation because each rectangle has a width Δx, at the top and bottom. At the height, *y*, this is equal to the function $f(x)$. But unless this is a linear function parallel to the axis of rotation, the height, *y*, at $f(x) + \Delta x$, will be slightly different than at $f(x)$. To make the approximation exact, we need to employ limits and the concept of infinity. This is one of the complex proofs that can be used to explain the Fundamental Theorem of Calculus, which we have not proven yet.

We need to break the interval in question (i.e.,[a, b]) into as many rectangles as possible. If we can create *n* rectangles, each of width Δx, and let $n \to \infty$, then Δx should approach zero or in theory, be insignificantly different than *x*. So, the height at each point *x* along the graph should equal $f(x)$. This will allow us to find the area under the curve (integral or antiderivative). Then by applying the formula for volume of revolution, we can find the volume by integration.

This translates as the definite integral: $\int_a^b \pi \left[f(x) \right]^2 dx$ or $\pi \int_a^b \left[f(x) \right] dx$.

$$V = \int_a^b \pi \left[f(x) \right]^2 dx = \pi \int_a^b \left[f(x) \right] dx$$

This is sometimes illustrated using the formula $V = \pi \left[f(x_i) \right]^2 \Delta x_i$, where the intervals x_i are added and the limit is determined by the following sum:

$$V = \lim_{n \to \infty} \sum_{i=1}^{n} \left[\pi \left[f(x_i) \right]^2 \Delta x_i \right]$$

The right-hand side of the above equation translates to the definite integral we are using, noting that the boundaries are $a \to b$.

Example 1

Consider the equation for a circle of radius 2 centered on the origin. This is $x^2 + y^2 = 4$. If we wished to find the area bounded by this function we would find the area above and below the x-axis separately, and add. We could also multiply by two as the two areas are equal. If we simply used the integral of the function, the answer would be zero because exactly half the function is above the x-axis and half is below. Similarly, if we rotated the function about the x-axis we would obtain a volume of revolution. However, the bottom half of the function would create its own solid at the same time as the top half. So, we need to rotate only the top section $\left(x^2 + y^2 = 4 \text{ for } y \geq 0 \right)$.

Solution

Begin with the equation $x^2 + y^2 = 4$ and note that the interval $a \to b$ is from $-2 \to 2$ (the two end points of the circle centred on the origin and radius $= 2$).

Isolate y^2 or y. (As our formula uses y^2, we will use this):

$$y^2 = 4 - x^2$$
$$\left[f(x) \right]^2 = 4 - x^2$$

Now, use the formula for volume of revolution:

$$V = \int_{-2}^{2} \pi f(x)^2\, dx$$

$$= \pi \int_{-2}^{2} \left(4 - x^2\right) dx$$

$$= \pi \left(4x - \frac{1}{3}x^3 + C\right)\Bigg|_{-2}^{2}$$

$$= \pi \left(\left[4(2) - \frac{1}{3}(2)^3\right] - \left[4(-2) - \frac{1}{3}(-2)^3\right]\right)$$

$$= \pi \left(\left[\frac{16}{3}\right] - \left[-\frac{16}{3}\right]\right)$$

$$= \frac{32\pi}{3}$$

Example 2

Find the volume of revolution of the above function (Example 1) by rotating only the section in Cartesian Quadrant I.

Solution

In this case we will set up the equation as before, but the interval $a \to b$ will be limited to $0 \to 2$. Then to find the whole volume, we must multiply the answer by two. This process of revolving only a smaller section is a useful method of simplifying the calculation process. However, it can only be used if our function is symmetrical.

$$V = \int_{0}^{2} \pi (4 - x^2)^2\, dx$$

$$= \left(4x\pi - \frac{\pi x^3}{3}\right)\Bigg|_{0}^{2}$$

$$= \frac{16\pi}{3}$$

This answer multiplied by two, gives us the same answer as in Example 1.

Example 3

Show how we can prove that the answers in examples 1 and 2 are correct by using the geometric formula for volume of a sphere.

Solution

The volume of a sphere is: $V = \dfrac{4}{3}\pi r^3$

Although you may try to solve by substituting the original formula for radius or some other complex manner, the solution is actually very straightforward. We know that our original conic section rotated, will produce a sphere. The radius of the original circle is two units. Place this information into the formula for volume of a sphere:

$$V = \frac{4}{3}\pi(2)^3$$
$$= \frac{4}{3}8\pi$$
$$= \frac{32\pi}{3}$$

The answer is the same as in both examples above. The geometric formulas for solids can be used to check answers involving revolutions, so long as the solid created is regular (i.e., one we have a formula for).

436

PRACTICE EXERCISE

1. For each of the following functions, we will be rotating the section about the x-axis. Find the volume of the solid created over the given interval.

   a) $f(x) = x^2$ in the interval $[2, 3]$.

   b) Find the interval in radians and apply the interval that corresponds to $\left[0, 45^0\right]$.

   c) $y = 2$ in the interval $[0, 3]$ (Confirm answer through the use of a geometric formula)

   d) $y = (x-1)^2$ in the interval $[0, 1]$.

e) $y = (x-1)^2$ in the interval $[1, 2]$. Then compare with question d.

f) $y = \sqrt{x}$ in the interval $[0, a]$. Then evaluate where $a = 2$.

REVIEW SUMMARY

In this unit, you have learned how to . . .

- apply the Fundamental Theorem of Calculus

$$\int_a^b f(x)\,dx = F(b) - F(a)$$

- determine integrals using the method of substitution

- determine integrals using the method of partial fraction

- determine integrals using integration by parts

$$\int f(x)g'(x)\,dx = f(x)g(x) - \int g(x)f'(x)\,dx$$

- determine which integration method to use given a particular type of integral

- determine volumes of revolution using integrals

$$V = \pi \int_a^b \left[f(x) \right]^2 dx$$

PRACTICE TEST

1. The Fundamental Theorem of Calculus states that:

    $\int_a^b f(x)\,dx =$ _____ , given that _____ is an antiderivative of f.

    Also f is _____ on the interval $(a \rightarrow b)$.

2. Find $\int (6x^2 - \sin x)\,dx$.

3. Find $\int \left[\sqrt{3x^2 - 5}\,(12x) \right] dx$.

440

4. Find $\int\left(3\sin^5 x\cos x\right)dx$.

5. Find $\int 5x\sin x\,dx$.

6. Find $\int x^2 e^x dx$ (Hint: the solution requires two steps).

7. Choose any two of the above indefinite integrals from question 6 and evaluate them over the interval [0, 1], i.e., $\int_0^1$. Indicate what method of integration was used initially.

8. Resolve $\dfrac{x+2}{(x+4)^2}$ into partial fractions. If this were an integral, what conditions would be placed on the values of the variable (limits of integration)?

9. Illustrate the form that the partial fraction decomposition will take for the following functions. Do not set up the system or solve.

a) $\dfrac{2x}{\left(x^2 - x - 1\right)\left(x - 3\right)}$

b) $\dfrac{x^2 - x + 1}{\left(x - 2\right)^3 \left(x^2 + x + 1\right)}$

10. Find the volume of revolution for the following function, revolved about the x-axis:

$y = x^2 - 6x + 9$ in the interval $[3, 5]$. Describe the original function.

NOTES

STUDENT NOTES AND PROBLEMS

**Answers
and
Solutions**

Research Corp

NOTES

PRE-CALCULUS

Lesson 1—Factoring

PRACTICE EXERCISE
Answers and Solutions

1. $= (2x-5y)\left(4x^2+10xy+25y^2\right)$

$8x^3-125y^3$

$= (2x-5y)\left((2x)^2+(2x)(5y)+(5y)^2\right)$

$= (2x-5y)\left(4x^2+10xy+25y^2\right)$

3. $= a^{\frac{1}{2}}(2a+3)(a-1)$

$2a^{\frac{5}{2}}+a^{\frac{3}{2}}-3a^{\frac{1}{2}}$

$= a^{\frac{1}{2}}\left(2a^{\frac{4}{2}}+a^{\frac{2}{2}}-3\right)$

$= a^{\frac{1}{2}}\left(2a^2+a-3\right)$

$= a^{\frac{1}{2}}(2a+3)(a-1)$

5. $= (x+2)^{\frac{3}{2}}(x-1)$

$(x+2)^{\frac{5}{2}}-3(x+2)^{\frac{3}{2}}$

$= (x+2)^{\frac{3}{2}}\left[(x+2)^{\frac{2}{2}}-3\right]$

$= (x+2)^{\frac{3}{2}}\left[(x+2)^1-3\right]$

$= (x+2)^{\frac{3}{2}}(x-1)$

7. $= \dfrac{1}{\sqrt{2x-5}}$

$\dfrac{(2x-5)^{\frac{1}{2}}+4(2x-5)^{\frac{-1}{2}}}{2x-1}$

$= \dfrac{(2x-5)^{\frac{-1}{2}}\left[(2x-5)\frac{2}{2}+4\right]}{2x-1}$

$= \dfrac{(2x-5)^{\frac{-1}{2}}(2x-5+4)}{2x-1}$

$= \dfrac{(2x-5)^{\frac{-1}{2}}(2x-1)}{2x-1}$

$= \dfrac{1}{\sqrt{2x-5}}$

Lesson 2—Rationalizing Numerators and Denominators

PRACTICE EXERCISE
Answers and Solutions

1. a) $= \dfrac{x+2\sqrt{x}}{x^2-4x}$

$\dfrac{1}{x-2\sqrt{x}}\times\dfrac{x+2\sqrt{x}}{x+2\sqrt{x}}$

$= \dfrac{x+2\sqrt{x}}{x^2-4x}$

b) $= \left(\sqrt{x}-\sqrt{5}\right)$

$\dfrac{x-5}{\sqrt{x}+\sqrt{5}}\times\dfrac{\sqrt{x}-\sqrt{5}}{\sqrt{x}-\sqrt{5}}$

$= \dfrac{(x-5)\left(\sqrt{x}-\sqrt{5}\right)}{x-5}$

$= \left(\sqrt{x}-\sqrt{5}\right)$

c) $= -4\left(\sqrt{2-x}-\sqrt{2}\right)$

$\dfrac{4x}{\sqrt{2-x}+\sqrt{2}}$

$= \dfrac{4x}{\sqrt{2-x}+\sqrt{2}}\times\dfrac{\sqrt{2-x}-\sqrt{2}}{\sqrt{2-x}-\sqrt{2}}$

$= \dfrac{4x\sqrt{2-x}-\sqrt{2}}{2-x-2}$

$= -4\left(\sqrt{2-x}-\sqrt{2}\right)$

(Beside 7.) $\left(x-\sqrt{20}\right)\left(x+\sqrt{20}\right)$

$= \left(x-2\sqrt{5}\right)\left(x+2\sqrt{5}\right)$

Lesson 3—Operations with Functions and Composition of Functions

---

PRACTICE EXERCISE
Answers and Solutions

1. a)

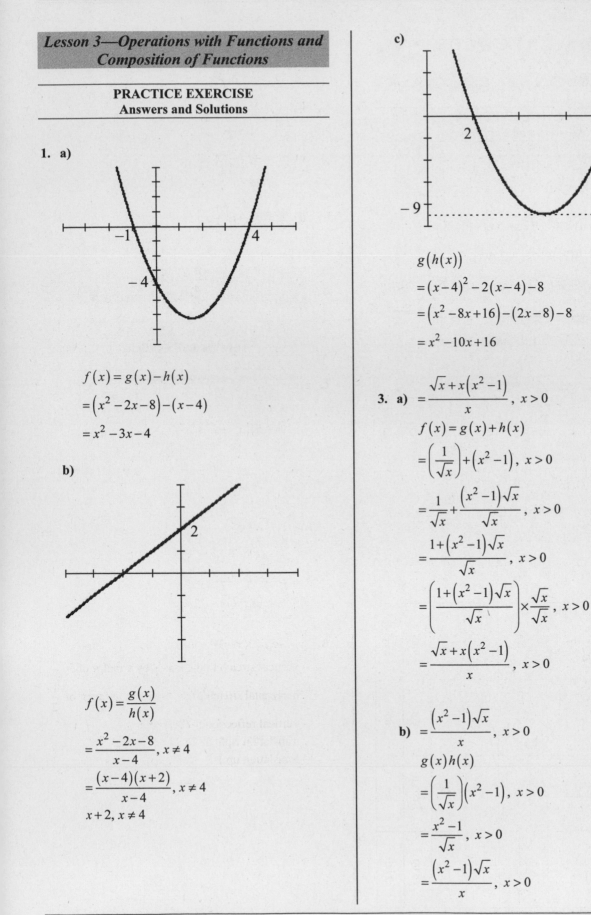

$$f(x) = g(x) - h(x)$$
$$= \left(x^2 - 2x - 8\right) - \left(x - 4\right)$$
$$= x^2 - 3x - 4$$

b)

$$f(x) = \frac{g(x)}{h(x)}$$

$$= \frac{x^2 - 2x - 8}{x - 4}, x \neq 4$$

$$= \frac{(x-4)(x+2)}{x-4}, x \neq 4$$

$$x + 2, x \neq 4$$

c)

$$g(h(x))$$
$$= (x-4)^2 - 2(x-4) - 8$$
$$= \left(x^2 - 8x + 16\right) - (2x - 8) - 8$$
$$= x^2 - 10x + 16$$

3. a) $= \dfrac{\sqrt{x} + x\left(x^2 - 1\right)}{x}, \; x > 0$

$$f(x) = g(x) + h(x)$$

$$= \left(\frac{1}{\sqrt{x}}\right) + \left(x^2 - 1\right), \; x > 0$$

$$= \frac{1}{\sqrt{x}} + \frac{\left(x^2 - 1\right)\sqrt{x}}{\sqrt{x}}, \; x > 0$$

$$= \frac{1 + \left(x^2 - 1\right)\sqrt{x}}{\sqrt{x}}, \; x > 0$$

$$= \left(\frac{1 + \left(x^2 - 1\right)\sqrt{x}}{\sqrt{x}}\right) \times \frac{\sqrt{x}}{\sqrt{x}}, \; x > 0$$

$$= \frac{\sqrt{x} + x\left(x^2 - 1\right)}{x}, \; x > 0$$

b) $= \dfrac{\left(x^2 - 1\right)\sqrt{x}}{x}, \; x > 0$

$$g(x) h(x)$$

$$= \left(\frac{1}{\sqrt{x}}\right)\left(x^2 - 1\right), \; x > 0$$

$$= \frac{x^2 - 1}{\sqrt{x}}, \; x > 0$$

$$= \frac{\left(x^2 - 1\right)\sqrt{x}}{x}, \; x > 0$$

---

c) $= \dfrac{1-x}{x}$, $x > 0$

$h\big(g(x)\big)$

$= \big(g(x)\big)^2 - 1$

$= \left(\dfrac{1}{\sqrt{x}}\right)^2 - 1$, $x > 0$

$= \dfrac{1}{x} - 1$, $x > 0$

$= \dfrac{1-x}{x}$, $x > 0$

Lesson 4—Transformations of Functions

PRACTICE EXERCISE
Answers and Solutions

1.

	Equation of Transformation	Line that the Graph is Reflected In	Vertical Stretch Factor about the x-axis	Horizontal Stretch Factor about the y-axis	Vertical Translation	Horizontal Translation
a)	$y = -5f(2x) + 1$	x-axis	5	$\frac{1}{2}$	1 up	n/a
b)	$y = f(3x - 6)$	n/a	1	$\frac{1}{3}$	n/a	2 right
c)	$y = -f(-x) - 2$	x-axis, y-axis	1	1	2 down	n/a
d)	$y = f^{-1}(x) - 7$	$y = x$	1	1	7 down	n/a
e)	$y = -7f\left(-\frac{1}{3}x - 3\right) + 8$	x-axis, y-axis	7	3	8 up	9 left

3. a) $y = f\left(-\dfrac{1}{2}x\right)$

b) $y = f^{-1}(x)$

c) $y = -f\left(\dfrac{1}{2}(x+4)\right) - 1$

d) $y = -1.5f\left(\dfrac{1}{2}x\right)$

e) $y = \dfrac{1}{2}f\left(2\left(x - \dfrac{\pi}{4}\right)\right) - \dfrac{1}{2}$

Practice Quiz

Answers and Solutions

1. a) $(x-5)\left(x^2 + 5x + 25\right)$

b) $= \dfrac{x^2 - 14x + 52}{(x-7)^{\frac{1}{2}}}$

$(x-7)^{-\frac{1}{2}}\left((x-7)^2 + 3\right)$

$= \dfrac{x^2 - 14x + 52}{(x-7)^{\frac{1}{2}}}$

3. $y = -5f(2(x-3)) + 1$

– vertical stretch in the x-axis by a factor of 5

– horizontal stretch in the y-axis by a factor of $\dfrac{1}{2}$

– vertical reflection in the x-axis
– translation right 3
– translation up 1

Lesson 5—Interval Notation

PRACTICE EXERCISE
Answers and Solutions

1. a) $(-5, 8)$

b) $[2, \infty)$

c) $(-\infty, 1) \cup [10, \infty)$

d) $(-\infty, -1) \cup [0, 10]$

e) $(-\infty, 7] \cup (12, 15]$

f) $(-\infty, 0) \cup (0, \infty)$

2. a) $[-3, \infty)$

b) $(-\infty, 0] \cup (5, \infty)$

c) $(-\infty, -9) \cup (-9, \infty)$

Lesson 6—Quadratic Inequalities

PRACTICE EXERCISE
Answers and Solutions

1. a) $(-3, 5)$

$x^2 - 2x - 15 = 0$

$(x - 5)(x + 3) = 0$

$x = 5 \quad x = 3$

Test values: $x = -4, 0, 6$
Check:

$(-4)^2 - 2(-4) - 15 = 9$

$\qquad 9 \not< 0$

$(0)^2 - 2(0) - 15 = -15$

$\quad -15 < 0$

$(6)^2 - 2(6) - 15 = 9$

$\quad\; 9 \not< 0$

$= (-3, 5)$

b) $(-\infty, -7] \cup \left[\dfrac{1}{2}, \infty\right)$

$2x^2 + 13x - 7 = 0$

$(2x - 1)(x + 7) = 0$

$x = \dfrac{1}{2} \quad x = -7$

Test values: $x = -8, 0, 1$
Check:

$2(-8)^2 + 13(-8) - 7 = 17$

$\qquad\qquad 17 \geq 0$

$(0)^2 + 13(0) - 7 = -7$

$\qquad\qquad -7 \not\geq 0$

$2(1) + 13(1) - 7 = 8$

$\qquad\qquad 8 \geq 0$

$= (-\infty, -7] \cup \left[\dfrac{1}{2}, \infty\right)$

c) $[-3, 3]$

$x^2 - 9 = 0$

$x = \pm 3$

Test values: $x = -4, 0, 4$
Check:

$(-4) - 9 = 7$

$\quad 7 \not\leq 0$

$(0)^2 - 9 = -9$

$\quad -9 \leq 0$

$(4)^2 - 9 = 7$

$\quad 7 \not\leq 0$

$= [-3, 3]$

d) $\left(-\infty, -\sqrt{6}\right) \cup \left(\sqrt{6}, \infty\right)$

$x^2 - 6 = 0$

$x = \pm\sqrt{6}$

Test values: $x = -3, 0, 3$

Check

$$(-3)^2 - 6 = 3$$

$$3 > 0$$

$$(0) - 6 = -6$$

$$-6 \ngtr 0$$

$$(3)^2 - 6 = 3$$

$$3 > 0$$

$$= \left(-\infty, -\sqrt{6}\,\right) \cup \left(\sqrt{6}, \infty\right)$$

e) $(-\infty, -2] \cup [5, \infty]$

$$-x^2 + 3x + 10 = 0$$

$$-(x - 5)(x + 2) = 0$$

$$x = 5 \quad x = -2$$

Test values: $x = -3, 0, 6$

Check:

$$-(-3)^2 + 3(-3) + 10 = -8$$

$$-8 \le 0$$

$$-(0)^2 + (0) + 10 = 10$$

$$10 \nleq 0$$

$$-(6)^2 + 3(6) + 10 = -8$$

$$-8 \le 0$$

$$= (-\infty, -2] \cup [5, \infty]$$

f) $\left(-\infty, -2 - \sqrt{11}\,\right] \cup \left[-2 + \sqrt{11}, \infty\right)$

$$x^2 + 4x - 7 = 0$$

$$x = \frac{-4 \pm \sqrt{(4)^2 - 4(1)(-7)}}{2(1)}$$

$$x = -2 \pm \sqrt{11}$$

Test values: $x = -6, 0, 2$

Check:

$$(-6)^2 + 4(-6) - 7 = 5$$

$$5 \ge 0$$

$$(0)^2 + 4(0) - 7 = -7$$

$$-7 \ngeq 0$$

$$(2)^2 + 4(2) - 7 = 5$$

$$5 \ge 0$$

$$= \left(-\infty, -2 - \sqrt{11}\,\right] \cup \left[-2 + \sqrt{11}, \infty\right)$$

Lesson 7—Rational Inequalities

PRACTICE EXERCISE
Answers and Solutions

1. a) $(0, 2)$

Undefined value
$x = 0$
Solve equality

$$\frac{x - 2}{x} = 0$$

$$x = 2$$

Test values $x = -1, 1, 3$

Check

$$\frac{-1 - 2}{-1} = 3$$

$$3 \nless 0$$

$$\frac{1 - 2}{1} = -1$$

$$-1 < 0$$

$$\frac{3 - 2}{3} = \frac{1}{3}$$

$$\frac{1}{3} \nless 0$$

$$= (0, 2)$$

b) $(-\infty, -5) \cup (0, \infty)$

Undefined values
$x + 5 = 0$

$$x = -5$$

Solve equality

$$\frac{x}{x + 5} = 0$$

$$x = 0$$

Test values $x = -6, -1, 1$

Check

$$\frac{-6}{-6+5} = 6$$

$$6 > 0$$

$$\frac{-1}{-1+5} = \frac{-1}{4}$$

$$\frac{-1}{4} \not> 0$$

$$\frac{1}{1+5} = \frac{1}{6}$$

$$\frac{1}{6} > 0$$

$$= (-\infty, -5) \cup (0, \infty)$$

c) $(-\infty, 3)$

Undefined values

$$x - 3 = 0$$

$$x = 3$$

Solve equality

$$\frac{x^2}{x-3} = 0$$

$$x = 0$$

Test values $x = -1, 1, 4$

Check

$$\frac{(-1)^2}{(-1)-3} = \frac{-1}{4}$$

$$\frac{-1}{4} \leq 0$$

$$\frac{1^2}{1-3} = \frac{-1}{2}$$

$$\frac{-1}{2} \leq 0$$

$$\frac{(4)^2}{4-3} = 16$$

$$16 \not\leq 0$$

$$= (-\infty, 3)$$

d) $[-2, -1) \cup [3, \infty)$

Undefined values

$$x + 1 = 0$$

$$x = -1$$

Solve equality

$$\frac{x^2 - x - 6}{x+1} = 0$$

$$x^2 - x - 6 = 0$$

$$(x-3)(x+2) = 0$$

$$x = 3 \quad x = -2$$

Test values $x = -3, \dfrac{-3}{2}, 0, 4$

Check

$$\frac{(-3)^2 - (-3) - 6}{-3+1} = -3$$

$$-3 \not\geq 0$$

$$\frac{\left(-\dfrac{3}{2}\right)^2 - \left(-\dfrac{3}{2}\right) - 6}{-\dfrac{3}{2}+1} = \frac{-9}{2}$$

$$\frac{9}{2} \geq 0$$

$$\frac{(0)^2 - (0) - 6}{0+1} = -6$$

$$-6 \not\geq 0$$

$$\frac{(4)^2 - (4) - 6}{4+1} = \frac{6}{5}$$

$$\frac{6}{5} \geq 0$$

$$= (-2, -1) \cup (3, \infty)$$

e) $(-\infty, \infty)$

Undefined values

$$x^2 + 4 = 0$$

$$x = \sqrt{-4}$$

No real solution, so no undefined values.

Solve equality

$$\frac{3}{x^2 + 4} = 0$$

No solution

Test value $x = 0$

$$\frac{3}{0^2 + 4} = \frac{3}{4}$$

$$\frac{3}{4} > 0$$

So all values of x satisfy the inequality:

$$(-\infty, \infty)$$

f) $\left(\dfrac{1-\sqrt{21}}{2},0\right)\cup\left(\dfrac{1+\sqrt{21}}{2},\infty\right)$

Undefined values

$x^2-x-5=0$

$x=\dfrac{-(-1)\pm\sqrt{(-1)-4(1)(-5)}}{2(1)}$

$=\dfrac{1\pm\sqrt{21}}{2}$

Solve the equality

$\dfrac{x}{x^2-x-5}=0$

$\qquad x=0$

Test values $x=-2,-1,1,3$

Check

$\dfrac{-2}{(-2)^2-(-2)-5}=-2$

$\qquad\qquad -2\not> 0$

$\dfrac{-1}{(-1)^2-(-1)-5}=\dfrac{1}{3}$

$\qquad\qquad \dfrac{1}{3}>0$

$\dfrac{1}{(1)-(1)-5}=\dfrac{-1}{5}$

$\qquad\qquad \dfrac{-1}{5}\not> 0$

$\dfrac{3}{3^2-3-5}=3$

$\qquad\qquad 3>0$

$=\left(\dfrac{1-\sqrt{21}}{2},0\right)\cup\left(\dfrac{1+\sqrt{21}}{2},\infty\right)$

Lesson 8—Absolute Value Inequalities

PRACTICE EXERCISE
Answers and Solutions

1. a) $(-6,4)$

Case 1	Case 2
$x+1<5$	$-(x+1)<5$
$x<4$	$x+1>-5$
$=(-6,4)$	$x>-6$

b) $(-\infty,-8)\cup(4,\infty)$

Case 1	Case 2
$x+2>6$	$-(x+2)>6$
$x>4$	$x+2<-6$
$=(-\infty,-8)\cup(4,\infty)$	$x<-8$

c) $[1,\,7]$

Case 1	Case 2
$(x-4)-3\le 0$	$-(x-4)-3\le 0$
$x-4\le 3$	$x-4\ge -3$
$x\le 7$	$x\ge 1$
$=[1,\,7]$	

d) $\left(-\dfrac{4}{5},\dfrac{8}{5}\right)$

Case 1	Case 2
	$-(5x-2)<6$
$5x-2<6$	$5x-2>-6$
$x<\dfrac{8}{5}$	$5x>-4$
$=\left(-\dfrac{4}{5},\dfrac{8}{5}\right)$	$x>\dfrac{-4}{5}$
	$5x-2>-6$

e) $(-\infty,0)\cup(0,\infty)$

Case 1	Case 2
$\dfrac{x-5}{x}\ge 0$	$-\left(\dfrac{x-5}{x}\right)\ge 0$
$x-5\ge 0$	$\dfrac{x-5}{x}\le 0$
$x\ge 5$	$x-5\le 0$
	$x\le 5$

Undefined values: $x=0$

$=(-\infty,0)\cup(0,\infty)$

Lesson 9—Using Trigonometric Identities

PRACTICE EXERCISE
Answers and Solutions

1. a) $= 0$

$$\cos^2 x - \sin^2 x - \cos(2x)$$
$$= \cos^2 x - \left(1 - \cos^2 x\right) - \left(2\cos^2 x - 1\right)$$
$$= \cos^2 x - 1 + \cos^2 x - 2\cos^2 x + 1$$
$$= 0$$

b) $= 1$

$$\left(\sin x + \cos x\right)^2 - \sin(2x)$$
$$= \sin^2 x + 2\sin x\cos x + \cos^2 x - 2\sin x\cos x$$
$$= \sin^2 x + \cos^2 x$$
$$= 1$$

Practice Test

Answers and Solutions

1. a) $(2x+1)\left(4x^2 - 2x + 1\right)$

b) $\dfrac{(x+3)(x+4)}{(x+1)^{\frac{1}{2}}}$

$$(x+1)^{\frac{3}{2}} + 5(x+1)^{\frac{1}{2}} + 6(x+1)^{-\frac{1}{2}}$$
$$= (x+1)^{-\frac{1}{2}}\left((x+1)^2 + 5(x+1) + 6\right)$$
$$= (x+1)^{-\frac{1}{2}}\left((x+1)+2\right)\left((x+1)+3\right)$$
$$= \dfrac{(x+3)(x+4)}{(x+1)^{\frac{1}{2}}}$$

3. a) $= 5x^3 - 6x^2 + x$

$$f(x) = \left(x^2 - x\right)(5x - 1)$$
$$= 5x^3 - x^2 - 5x^2 + x$$
$$= 5x^3 - 6x^2 + x$$

b) $= 25x^2 - 15x + 2$

$$f(x) = (5x-1)^2 - (5x-1)$$
$$= 25x^2 - 15x + 2$$

5. a) Amplitude: 3

b) Period: $\dfrac{\pi}{2}$

c) Phase Shift: right $\dfrac{\pi}{4}$

d) Vertical Displacement: 6

7. $\csc(2x) + \csc(2x) = \csc x \sec x$

LS	RS
$\csc(2x) + \csc(2x)$	$\csc x \sec x$
$2\csc(2x)$	
$\dfrac{2}{\sin(2x)}$	
$\dfrac{2}{2\sin x\cos x}$	
$\dfrac{1}{\sin x\cos x}$	
$\csc x\sec x$	
LS = RS	

LIMITS

Lesson 1—Introduction to Limits

PRACTICE EXERCISE
Answers and Solutions

1. **a)** 6

$$\lim_{x \to 2} 2(x)^2 - x$$
$$= 2(2)^2 - 2$$
$$= 6$$

b) 0

$$\lim_{x \to 10} x^2 - 10x$$
$$= 10^2 - 10(10)$$
$$= 0$$

3.

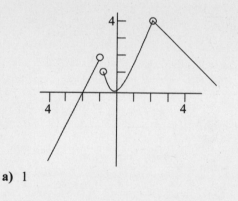

a) 1

b) 2

c) Does not exist

d) 4

e) 4

f) 4

Lesson 2—Limits for Rational Expressions

PRACTICE EXERCISE
Answers and Solutions

1. **a)** 1

$$\lim_{x \to 0} \frac{x(x+1)}{x}$$
$$= \lim_{x \to 0} x + 1$$
$$= (0) + 1$$
$$= 1$$

b) $\frac{6}{11}$

$$\lim_{x \to 3} \frac{(x+3)(x-3)}{(2x+5)(x-3)}$$
$$= \lim_{x \to 3} \frac{x+3}{2x+5}$$
$$= \frac{(3)+3}{2(3)+5}$$
$$= \frac{6}{11}$$

c) $\frac{1}{4}$

$$\lim_{x \to 5} \frac{\left(\sqrt{x-1}-2\right)\left(\sqrt{x-1}+2\right)}{(x-5)\left(\sqrt{x-1}+2\right)}$$
$$= \lim_{x \to 5} \frac{x-1-4}{(x-5)\left(\sqrt{x-1}+2\right)}$$
$$= \lim_{x \to 5} \frac{x-5}{(x-5)\left(\sqrt{x-1}+2\right)}$$
$$= \lim_{x \to 5} \frac{1}{\sqrt{x-1}+2}$$
$$= \frac{1}{\sqrt{5-1}+2}$$
$$= \frac{1}{4}$$

d) $\dfrac{1}{2}$

$$\lim_{x\to 2} \frac{(x-2)(x+4)}{(x-2)(x^2+2x+4)}$$

$$= \lim_{x\to 2} \frac{(x+4)}{x^2+2x+4}$$

$$= \frac{2+4}{2^2+2(2)+4}$$

$$= \frac{6}{12}$$

$$= \frac{1}{2}$$

e) $-\dfrac{1}{9}$

$$\lim_{x\to -3} \frac{\dfrac{x+3}{3x}}{3+x}$$

$$= \lim_{x\to -3} \frac{x+3}{3x(x+3)}$$

$$= \lim_{x\to -3} \frac{1}{3x}$$

$$= -\frac{1}{9}$$

Lesson 3—Using Limits to Find Slopes of Tangents

PRACTICE EXERCISE
Answers and Solutions

1. a) $= 10$

$$m = \lim_{h\to 0} \frac{f(x+h)-f(x)}{h}$$

$$= \lim_{h\to 0} \frac{(x+h)^2+4-(x^2+4)}{h}$$

$$= \lim_{h\to 0} \frac{(5+h)^2+4-(5^2+4)}{h}$$

$$= \lim_{h\to 0} \frac{25+10h+h^2+4-25-4}{h}$$

$$= \lim_{h\to 0} \frac{10h+h^2}{h}$$

$$= \lim_{h\to 0} 10+h$$

$$= 10+(0)$$

$$= 10$$

b) $= -6$

$$m = \lim_{h\to 0} \frac{(x+h)^2+4-(x^2+4)}{h}$$

$$= \lim_{h\to 0} \frac{(-3+h)^2+4-((-3)^2+4)}{h}$$

$$= \lim_{h\to 0} \frac{9-6h+h^2+4-9-4}{h}$$

$$= \lim_{h\to 0} \frac{-6h+h^2}{h}$$

$$= \lim_{h\to 0} -6+h$$

$$= -6+0$$

$$= -6$$

3. $= 48$

$$m = \lim_{h \to 0} \frac{(x+h)^3 - 3 - (x^3 - 3)}{h}$$

$$= \lim_{h \to 0} \frac{(4+h)^3 - 3 - (4^3 - 3)}{h}$$

$$= \lim_{h \to 0} \frac{64 + 48h + 12h^2 + h^3 - 3 - 64 + 3}{h}$$

$$= \lim_{h \to 0} \frac{48h + 12h^2 + h^3}{h}$$

$$= \lim_{h \to 0} 48 + 12h + h^2$$

$$= 48 + 12(0) + (0)^2$$

$$= 48$$

Practice Test

Answers and Solutions

1. a) 2

b) 1

c) Does not exist

d) 4

e) 4

f) 4

g) The function is discontinuous for $x = 1$ because $\lim_{x \to 1^+} f(x) \neq \lim_{x \to 1^-} f(x)$.

3. a) $= 8$

$$m = \lim_{h \to 0} \frac{f(x+h) - f(x)}{h}$$

$$= \lim_{h \to 0} \frac{(4+h)^2 - 5 - (4^2 - 5)}{h}$$

$$= \lim_{h \to 0} \frac{16 + 8h + h^2 - 5 - 16 + 5}{h}$$

$$= \lim_{h \to 0} \frac{8h + h^2}{h}$$

$$= \lim_{h \to 0} 8 + h$$

$$= 8 + 0$$

$$= 8$$

b) $= 2$

$$m = \lim_{h \to 0} \frac{(1+h)^2 - 5 - (1^2 - 5)}{h}$$

$$= \lim_{h \to 0} \frac{1 + 2h + h^2 - 5 - 1 + 5}{h}$$

$$= \lim_{h \to 0} \frac{2h + h^2}{h}$$

$$= \lim_{h \to 0} 2 + h$$

$$= 2 + 0$$

$$= 2$$

DERIVATIVES AND DERIVATIVE THEOREMS

Lesson 1—Derivatives Using First Principles

PRACTICE EXERCISE
Answers and Solutions

1. a) $= 8x$

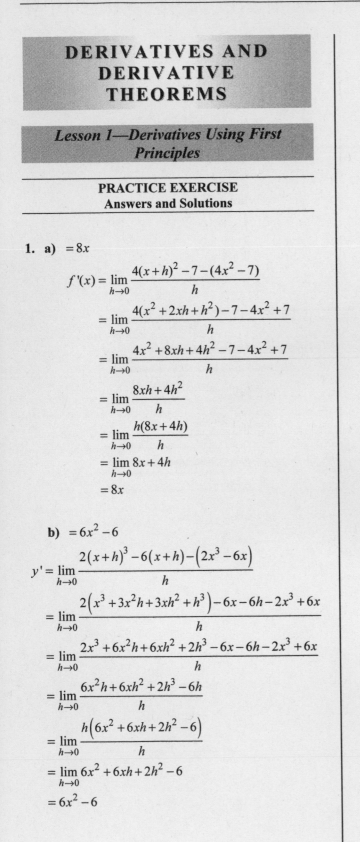

$$f'(x) = \lim_{h \to 0} \frac{4(x+h)^2 - 7 - (4x^2 - 7)}{h}$$

$$= \lim_{h \to 0} \frac{4(x^2 + 2xh + h^2) - 7 - 4x^2 + 7}{h}$$

$$= \lim_{h \to 0} \frac{4x^2 + 8xh + 4h^2 - 7 - 4x^2 + 7}{h}$$

$$= \lim_{h \to 0} \frac{8xh + 4h^2}{h}$$

$$= \lim_{h \to 0} \frac{h(8x + 4h)}{h}$$

$$= \lim_{h \to 0} 8x + 4h$$

$$= 8x$$

b) $= 6x^2 - 6$

$$y' = \lim_{h \to 0} \frac{2(x+h)^3 - 6(x+h) - \left(2x^3 - 6x\right)}{h}$$

$$= \lim_{h \to 0} \frac{2\left(x^3 + 3x^2h + 3xh^2 + h^3\right) - 6x - 6h - 2x^3 + 6x}{h}$$

$$= \lim_{h \to 0} \frac{2x^3 + 6x^2h + 6xh^2 + 2h^3 - 6x - 6h - 2x^3 + 6x}{h}$$

$$= \lim_{h \to 0} \frac{6x^2h + 6xh^2 + 2h^3 - 6h}{h}$$

$$= \lim_{h \to 0} \frac{h\left(6x^2 + 6xh + 2h^2 - 6\right)}{h}$$

$$= \lim_{h \to 0} 6x^2 + 6xh + 2h^2 - 6$$

$$= 6x^2 - 6$$

c) $= -\dfrac{1}{x^2}$

$$y' = \lim_{h \to 0} \frac{\dfrac{1}{x+h} - \dfrac{1}{x}}{h}$$

$$= \lim_{h \to 0} \frac{x - (x+h)}{x(x+h)h}$$

$$= \lim_{h \to 0} \frac{-h}{x(x+h)h}$$

$$= \lim_{h \to 0} \frac{-1}{x(x+h)}$$

$$= -\frac{1}{x^2}$$

d) $= \dfrac{3}{2\sqrt{3x+1}}$

$$f'(x) = \lim_{h \to 0} \frac{\sqrt{3(x+h)+1} - \sqrt{3x+1}}{h}$$

$$= \lim_{h \to 0} \frac{\sqrt{3(x+h)+1} - \sqrt{3x+1}}{h} \times$$
$$\frac{\sqrt{3(x+h)+1} + \sqrt{3x+1}}{\sqrt{3(x+h)+1} + \sqrt{3x+1}}$$

$$= \lim_{h \to 0} \frac{3(x+h)+1 - (3x+1)}{h\left(\sqrt{3x+h+1} + \sqrt{3x+1}\right)}$$

$$= \lim_{h \to 0} \frac{3h}{h\left(\sqrt{3x+h+1}\right) + \sqrt{3x+1}}$$

$$= \lim_{h \to 0} \frac{3}{\sqrt{3x+h+1} + \sqrt{3x+1}}$$

$$= \frac{3}{\sqrt{3x+1} + \sqrt{3x+1}}$$

$$= \frac{3}{2\sqrt{3x+1}}$$

PRACTICE EXERCISE
Answers and Solutions

1. a) $f'(x) = 18x^2$

b) $\dfrac{1}{2\sqrt{x}}$

$y = \sqrt{x}$

$y = x^{\frac{1}{2}}$

$\dfrac{dy}{dx} = \dfrac{1}{2}x^{\frac{-1}{2}}$

$= \dfrac{1}{2\sqrt{x}}$

c) $f'(x) = -\dfrac{4}{x^5}$

$f(x) = x^{-4}$

$f'(x) = -4x^{-5}$

$f'(x) = -\dfrac{4}{x^5}$

d) $\dfrac{dy}{dx} = \dfrac{20}{3}\sqrt[3]{x}$

$y = 5x^{\frac{4}{3}}$

$\dfrac{dy}{dx} = \dfrac{4}{3}\left(5x^{\frac{4}{3}-1}\right)$

$\dfrac{dy}{dx} = \dfrac{20}{3}x^{\frac{1}{3}}$

$\dfrac{dy}{dx} = \dfrac{20}{3}\sqrt[3]{x}$

3. a) $28x - y = 28$

$y' = 14x$

Slope at (2, 28)

$m = 14(2)$

$m = 28$

Equation of tangent

$28 = \dfrac{y-28}{x-2}$

$28x - 56 = y - 28$

$28x - y = 28$

b) $2x - y = 4$

$f(x) = x - 4x^{-1}$

$f'(x) = 1 + 4x^{-2}$

$f'(x) = 1 + \dfrac{4}{x^2}$

Slope at (2, 0)

$m = 1 + \dfrac{4}{2^2}$

$m = 1 + 1$

$m = 2$

Equation of tangent

$2 = \dfrac{y-0}{x-2}$

$2x - 4 = y$

$2x - y = 4$

Lesson 3—The Product Rule

PRACTICE EXERCISE
Answers and Solutions

1. a) $\dfrac{dy}{dx} = 105x^6$

$g(x) = x^3$

$g'(x) = 3x^2$

$h(x) = 15x^4$

$h'(x) = 60x^3$

$\dfrac{dy}{dx} = (x^3)(60x^3) + (15x^4)(3x^2)$

$\dfrac{dy}{dx} = 60x^6 + 45x^6$

$\dfrac{dy}{dx} = 105x^6$

b) $f'(x) = 180x^5$

$f(x) = (5x^7)(6x^{-1})$

$g(x) = 5x^7$

$g'(x) = 35x^6$

$h(x) = 6x^{-1}$

$h'(x) = -6x^{-2}$

$f'(x) = 5x^7(-6x^{-2}) + (6x^{-1})(35x^6)$

$f'(x) = -30x^5 + 210x^5$

$f'(x) = 180x^5$

c) $\dfrac{dy}{dx} = \dfrac{495}{2}\sqrt{x^9}$

$y = (5\sqrt{x^3})(9x^4)$

$y = 5x^{\frac{3}{2}}(9x^4)$

$g(x) = 5x^{\frac{3}{2}}$

$g'(x) = \dfrac{15}{2}x^{\frac{1}{2}}$

$h(x) = 9x^4$

$h'(x) = 36x^3$

$\dfrac{dy}{dx} = \left(5x^{\frac{3}{2}}\right)(36x^3) + (9x^4)\left(\dfrac{15}{2}x^{\frac{1}{2}}\right)$

$\dfrac{dy}{dx} = 180x^{\frac{9}{2}} + \dfrac{135}{2}x^{\frac{9}{2}}$

$\dfrac{dy}{dx} = \dfrac{495}{2}\sqrt{x^9}$

d) $f'(x) = \dfrac{7 - 5x^2}{2\sqrt{x}}$

$g(x) = (7 - x^2)$

$g'(x) = -2x$

$h(x) = (\sqrt{x}) = \left(x^{\frac{1}{2}}\right)$

$h'(x) = \dfrac{1}{2}x^{-\frac{1}{2}}$

$f'(x) = (7 - x^2)\left(\dfrac{1}{2}x^{-\frac{1}{2}}\right) + \left(x^{\frac{1}{2}}\right)(-2x)$

$f'(x) = \dfrac{7}{2}x^{-\frac{1}{2}} - \dfrac{1}{2}x^{\frac{3}{2}} - 2x^{\frac{3}{2}}$

$f'(x) = \dfrac{1}{2}x^{-\frac{1}{2}}\left(7 - x^2 - 4x^2\right)$

$f'(x) = \dfrac{7 - 5x^2}{2\sqrt{x}}$

e) $\dfrac{dy}{dx} = \dfrac{25x^2 - 1}{4\sqrt{x}}$

$g(x) = 5x^3 - x$

$g'(x) = 15x^2 - 1$

$h(x) = \dfrac{1}{2}x^{-\frac{1}{2}}$

$h'(x) = -\dfrac{1}{4}x^{-\frac{3}{2}}$

$\dfrac{dy}{dx} = \left(5x^3 - x\right)\left(-\dfrac{1}{4}x^{-\frac{3}{2}}\right) + \left(\dfrac{1}{2}x^{-\frac{1}{2}}\right)\left(15x^2 - 1\right)$

$\dfrac{dy}{dx} = -\dfrac{5}{4}x^{\frac{3}{2}} + \dfrac{1}{4}x^{-\frac{1}{2}} + \dfrac{15}{2}x^{\frac{3}{2}} - \dfrac{1}{2}x^{-\frac{1}{2}}$

$\dfrac{dy}{dx} = \dfrac{1}{4}x^{-\frac{1}{2}}\left(-5x^2 + 1 + 30x^2 - 2\right)$

$\dfrac{dy}{dx} = \dfrac{25x^2 - 1}{4\sqrt{x}}$

f) $f'(x) = 30x^4 - 8x^3 + 99x^2 + 2x - 18$

$g(x) = 3x^2 - x + 18$

$g'(x) = 6x - 1$

$h(x) = 2x^3 - x$

$h'(x) = 6x^2 - 1$

$f'(x) = \left(3x^2 - x + 18\right)\left(6x^2 - 1\right)$

$\qquad + \left(2x^3 - x\right)(6x - 1)$

$f'(x) = 18x^4 - 3x^2 - 6x^3$

$\qquad + x + 108x^2 - 18 +$

$\qquad 12x^4 - 2x^3 - 6x^2 + x$

$f'(x) = 30x^4 - 8x^3 + 99x^2 + 2x - 18$

PRACTICE EXERCISE
Answers and Solutions

1. a) $\dfrac{d_y}{d_x} = \dfrac{-x - 2}{3x^3}$

$g(x) = 1 + x$

$g'(x) = 1$

$h(x) = 3x^2$

$h'(x) = 6x$

$\dfrac{dy}{dx} = \dfrac{3x^2(1) - (1 + x)(6x)}{\left(3x^2\right)^2}$

$\dfrac{dy}{dx} = \dfrac{3x^2 - 6x - 6x^2}{9x^4}$

$\dfrac{dy}{dx} = \dfrac{-3x^2 - 6x}{9x^4}$

$\dfrac{dy}{dx} = \dfrac{-x - 2}{3x^3}$

b) $f'(x) = \dfrac{5x^2 + 20x + 1}{2x^2 + 8x + 8}$

$g(x) = 5x^2 - 1$

$g'(x) = 10x$

$h(x) = 2x + 4$

$h'(x) = 2$

$f'(x) = \dfrac{(2x + 4)(10x) - \left(5x^2 - 1\right)(2)}{(2x + 4)^2}$

$f'(x) = \dfrac{20x^2 + 40x - 10x^2 + 2}{(2x + 4)^2}$

$f'(x) = \dfrac{10x^2 + 40x + 2}{(2x + 4)^2}$

$f'(x) = \dfrac{5x^2 + 20x + 1}{2x^2 + 8x + 8}$

c) $\dfrac{dy}{dx} = \dfrac{\sqrt[6]{x}}{12x}$

$g(x) = x^{\frac{2}{3}}$

$g'(x) = \dfrac{2}{3} x^{-\frac{1}{3}}$

$h(x) = 2x^{\frac{1}{2}}$

$h'(x) = x^{-\frac{1}{2}}$

$\dfrac{dy}{dx} = \dfrac{2x^{\frac{1}{2}} \left(\dfrac{2}{3} x^{-\frac{1}{3}} \right) - \left(x^{\frac{2}{3}} \right) \left(x^{-\frac{1}{2}} \right)}{4x}$

$\dfrac{dy}{dx} = \dfrac{\dfrac{4}{3} x^{\frac{1}{6}} - x^{\frac{1}{6}}}{4x}$

$\dfrac{dy}{dx} = \dfrac{\sqrt[6]{x}}{12x}$

Lesson 5—The Chain Rule

PRACTICE EXERCISE
Answers and Solutions

1. a) $f'(x) = 9\left(5x^3 - x\right)^8 \left(15x^2 - 1\right)$

b) $\dfrac{dy}{dx} = \dfrac{(x-1)}{\sqrt{x^2 - 2x}}$

$y = \left(x^2 - 2x\right)^{\frac{1}{2}}$

$\dfrac{dy}{dx} = \dfrac{1}{2}\left(x^2 - 2x\right)^{-\frac{1}{2}}(2x - 2)$

$\dfrac{dy}{dx} = \dfrac{x - 1}{\sqrt{x^2 - 2x}}$

c) $f'(x) = 3x^2 \left(3x - 1\right)\left(5x - 1\right)$

$g(x) = x^3$

$g'(x) = 3x^2$

$h(x) = \left(3x - 1\right)^2$

$h'(x) = 2\left(3x - 1\right)(3)$

$h'(x) = 6\left(3x - 1\right)$

$f'(x) = x^3 \left(6\left(3x - 1\right)\right) + \left(3x - 1\right)^2 \left(3x^2\right)$

$f'(x) = 3x^2 \left(3x - 1\right)\left[2x + 3x - 1\right]$

$f'(x) = 3x^2 \left(3x - 1\right)\left(5x - 1\right)$

d) $\dfrac{dy}{dx} = \dfrac{-15\left(2x^2 + 1\right)}{2\left(2x^2 - 3\right)^2 \sqrt{5x}}$

$y = \dfrac{(5x)^{\frac{1}{2}}}{2x^2 - 3}$

$\dfrac{dy}{dx} = \dfrac{\left(2x^2 - 3\right)\dfrac{1}{2}(5x)^{-\frac{1}{2}}(5) - (5x)^{\frac{1}{2}}(4x)}{\left(2x^2 - 3\right)^2}$

$\dfrac{dy}{dx} = \dfrac{\dfrac{1}{2}(5x)^{-\frac{1}{2}}\left[10x^2 - 15 - (5x)(8x)\right]}{\left(2x^2 - 3\right)^2}$

$\dfrac{dy}{dx} = \dfrac{-30x^2 - 15}{2(5x)^{\frac{1}{2}}\left(2x^2 - 3\right)^2}$

$\dfrac{dy}{dx} = \dfrac{-15\left(2x^2 + 1\right)}{2\left(2x^2 - 3\right)^2 \sqrt{5x}}$

e) $f'(x) = \dfrac{3x+6}{2\sqrt{x+3}\sqrt{2x\sqrt{x+3}}}$

$f(x) = \left(2x(x+3)^{\frac{1}{2}}\right)^{\frac{1}{2}}$

$f'(x) = \dfrac{1}{2}\left(2x(x+3)^{\frac{1}{2}}\right)^{-\frac{1}{2}}\left[2x\left(\dfrac{1}{2}(x+3)^{-\frac{1}{2}}\right)(1)+(x+3)^{\frac{1}{2}}(2)\right]$

$f'(x) = \dfrac{(x+3)^{-\frac{1}{2}}\left[x+(x+3)(2)\right]}{2\left[2x(x+3)^{\frac{1}{2}}\right]^{\frac{1}{2}}}$

$f'(x) = \dfrac{3x+6}{2\sqrt{x+3}\sqrt{2x\sqrt{x+3}}}$

Practice Quiz

Answers and Solutions

1. $f'(x) = 12x-1$

$f'(x) = \lim\limits_{h\to 0} \dfrac{6(x+h)^2 - (x+h) - (6x^2 - x)}{h}$

$= \lim\limits_{h\to 0} \dfrac{6(x^2 + 2xh + h^2) - x - h - 6x^2 + x}{h}$

$= \lim\limits_{h\to 0} \dfrac{6x^2 + 12xh + 6h^2 - x - h - 6x^2 + x}{h}$

$= \lim\limits_{h\to 0} \dfrac{12xh + 6h^2 - h}{h}$

$= \lim\limits_{h\to 0} 12x + 6h - 1$

$= 12x - 1$

3. $3x + 16y = 14$

$y = \dfrac{1}{x^3}$

$= x^{-3}$

$y' = -3x^{-4}$

$= \dfrac{-3}{x^4}$

So, the slope at $\left(2, \dfrac{1}{2}\right)$ is

$y' = \dfrac{-3}{(2)^4}$

$= \dfrac{-3}{16}$

and the equation of the tangent is

$\dfrac{-3}{16} = \dfrac{y - \dfrac{1}{2}}{x - 2}$

$3x + 16y = 14$

Lesson 6—Implicit Differentiation

PRACTICE EXERCISE
Answers and Solutions

1. a) $\dfrac{dy}{dx} = -\dfrac{x}{y}$

$$8x + 8y\dfrac{dy}{dx} = 0$$

$$8y\dfrac{dy}{dx} = -8x$$

$$\dfrac{dy}{dx} = \dfrac{-8x}{8y}$$

$$\dfrac{dy}{dx} = -\dfrac{x}{y}$$

b) $\dfrac{dy}{dx} = \dfrac{3 - 4y^2}{8xy + 2y}$

$$4x\left(2y\dfrac{dy}{dx}\right) + y^2(4) + 2\left(\dfrac{dy}{dx}\right) = 3$$

$$8xy\dfrac{dy}{dx} + 2\dfrac{dy}{dx} = 3 - 4y^2$$

$$\dfrac{dy}{dx} = \dfrac{3 - 4y^2}{8xy + 2}$$

*Notice the use of the Product Rule in step 1.

c) $\dfrac{dy}{dx} = \dfrac{-2y^4}{x^3 - 4xy^3}$

$$3\dfrac{dy}{dx} - \dfrac{x^2 4y^3 \dfrac{dy}{dx} - y^4(2x)}{\left(x^2\right)^2} = 2\dfrac{dy}{dx}$$

$$3x^4\dfrac{dy}{dx} - x^2\left(4y^3\right)\dfrac{dy}{dx} + 2xy^4 = 2x^4\dfrac{dy}{dx}$$

$$\dfrac{dy}{dx}\left(3x^4 - 4x^2y^3 - 2x^4\right) = -2xy^4$$

$$\dfrac{dy}{dx} = \dfrac{-2xy^4}{3x^4 - 4x^2y^3 - 2x^4}$$

$$\dfrac{dy}{dx} = \dfrac{-2xy^4}{x^4 - 4x^2y^3}$$

$$\dfrac{dy}{dx} = \dfrac{-2y^4}{x^3 - 4xy^3}$$

3. $3x - 2y = 13$

$$3x - y^2 + 6y = x^2 - x$$

$$3 - 2y\dfrac{dy}{dx} + 6\dfrac{dy}{dx} = 2x - 1$$

$$\dfrac{dy}{dx}(-2y + 6) = 2x - 4$$

$$\dfrac{dy}{dx} = \dfrac{x - 2}{-y + 3}$$

Find the slope at the point $(5, 1)$.

$$= \dfrac{5 - 2}{-1 + 3}$$

$$= \dfrac{3}{2}$$

Equation of a tangent at this point.

$$\dfrac{3}{2} = \dfrac{y - 1}{x - 5}$$

$$3(x - 5) = 2(y - 1)$$

$$3x - 2y = 13$$

Lesson 7—Higher Derivatives

PRACTICE EXERCISE
Answers and Solutions

1. a) $f''(x) = 18x - 18$

$$f'(x) = 9x^2 - 18x + 16$$

$$f''(x) = 18x - 18$$

b) $f''(x) = 0$

$$f'(x) = 10$$

$$f''(x) = 0$$

c) $\dfrac{d^2y}{dx^2} = \dfrac{56}{(x-7)^3}$

$\dfrac{dy}{dy} = \dfrac{(x-7)(4) - 4x(1)}{(x-7)^2}$

$\dfrac{dy}{dx} = \dfrac{4x - 28 - 4x}{(x-7)^2}$

$\dfrac{dy}{dx} = \dfrac{-28}{(x-7)^2}$

$\dfrac{d^2y}{dx^2} = \dfrac{\left(x-7^2\,(0)\right) - \left((-28)\left(2(x-7)(1)\right)\right)}{(x-7)^4}$

$\dfrac{d^2y}{dx^2} = \dfrac{56(x-7)}{(x-7)^4}$

$\dfrac{d^2y}{dx^2} = \dfrac{56}{(x-7)^3}$

d) $\dfrac{d^2y}{dx^2} = 90\left(3x^2 - 5\right)\left(3x^2 - 1\right)$

$\dfrac{dy}{dx} = 3\left(3x^2 - 5\right)^2 (6x)$

$\dfrac{dy}{dx} = 18x\left(3x^2 - 5\right)^2$

$\dfrac{d^2y}{dx^2} = 18x\left(2\left(3x^2 - 5\right)(6x)\right) + \left(3x^2 - 5\right)^2 (18)$

$\dfrac{d^2y}{dx^2} = 216x^2\left(3x^2 - 5\right) + 18\left(3x^2 - 5\right)^2$

$\dfrac{d^2y}{dx^2} = 18\left(3x^2 - 5\right)\left(12x^2 + \left(3x^2 - 5\right)\right)$

$\dfrac{d^2y}{dx^2} = 18\left(3x^2 - 5\right)\left(15x^2 - 5\right)$

$= 90\left(3x^2 - 5\right)\left(3x^2 - 1\right)$

Answers and Solutions

1. $= \dfrac{5}{2x^{\frac{3}{2}}}$

$f'(x) = \lim\limits_{h \to 0} \dfrac{\dfrac{-5}{\sqrt{x+h}} + \dfrac{5}{\sqrt{x}}}{h}$

$= \lim\limits_{h \to 0} \dfrac{-5\sqrt{x} + 5\sqrt{x+h}}{h\sqrt{x}\sqrt{x+h}}$

$= \lim\limits_{h \to 0} \dfrac{-5\sqrt{x} + 5\sqrt{x+h}}{h\sqrt{x}\sqrt{x+h}} \times \dfrac{-5\sqrt{x} - 5\sqrt{x+h}}{-5\sqrt{x} - 5\sqrt{x+h}}$

$= \lim\limits_{h \to 0} \dfrac{25x - 25(x+h)}{h\sqrt{x}\sqrt{x+h}\left(-5\sqrt{x} - 5\sqrt{x+h}\right)}$

$= \lim\limits_{h \to 0} \dfrac{-25h}{h\sqrt{x}\sqrt{x+h}\left(-5\sqrt{x} - 5\sqrt{x+h}\right)}$

$= \dfrac{-25}{x\left(-5\sqrt{x} - 5\sqrt{x}\right)}$

$= \dfrac{-25}{-10x\sqrt{x}}$

$= \dfrac{5}{2x\sqrt{x}}$

$= \dfrac{5}{2x^{\frac{3}{2}}}$

3. $9x - 2y = 3$

$\dfrac{dy}{dx} = \dfrac{(x+1)(12x) - 6x^2(1)}{(x+1)^2}$

$= \dfrac{12x^2 + 12x - 6x^2}{(x+1)^2}$

$= \dfrac{6x^2 + 12x}{(x+1)^2}$

The slope at $(1, 3)$ is

$\dfrac{6(1)^2 + 12(1)}{(1+1)^2}$

$= \dfrac{9}{2}$

The equation of the tangent is

$$\frac{9}{2} = \frac{y-3}{x-1}$$

$$9x - 9 = 2y - 6$$

$$9x - 2y = 3$$

5. $\dfrac{dy}{dx} = \dfrac{4x - 3y}{3x + 18y^2}$

$$3x\frac{dy}{dx} + 3y = 4x - 18y^2\frac{dy}{dx}$$

$$\frac{dy}{dx}\left(3x + 18y^2\right) = 4x - 3y$$

$$\frac{dy}{dx} = \frac{4x - 3y}{3x + 18y^2}$$

7. **a)** $a = 6t - 12$

$$v = \frac{ds}{dt}$$

$$v = 3t^2 - 12t$$

$$a = \frac{dv}{dt}$$

$$a = 6t - 12$$

b) $a(35) = 198$

$$a(35) = 6(35) - 12$$

$$a(35) = 198$$

After 35 seconds, the acceleration is $198\,\text{m/s}^2$.

DERIVATIVES OF TRIGONOMETRIC, LOGARITHMIC, AND EXPONENTIAL FUNCTIONS

Lesson 1—Limits of Trigonometric Functions

PRACTICE EXERCISE
Answers and Solutions

1. **a)** $= 1$

$$\lim_{x \to 0} \frac{\sin(4x)}{4x}$$

$$= 1$$

b) $= 0$

$$\lim_{x \to 0} \frac{2 - 2\cos x}{x}$$

$$\lim_{x \to 0} \frac{-2(-1 + \cos x)}{x}$$

$$= -2\lim_{x \to 0} \frac{\cos x - 1}{x}$$

$$= -2(0)$$

$$= 0$$

c) $= \dfrac{4}{3}$

$$\lim_{\theta \to 0} \frac{\sin(4\theta)}{\sin(3\theta)}$$

$$\lim_{\theta \to 0} \frac{\dfrac{\sin(4\theta)}{4\theta}}{\dfrac{\sin(3\theta)}{4\theta}}$$

$$= \lim_{\theta \to 0} \frac{\dfrac{\sin(4\theta)}{4\theta(3)}}{\dfrac{\sin(3\theta)}{4\theta(3)}}$$

$$= \frac{1}{3}\lim_{\theta \to 0} \frac{\sin(4\theta)}{4\theta} \div \frac{1}{4}\lim_{\theta \to 0} \frac{\sin(3\theta)}{3\theta}$$

$$= \frac{1}{3}(1) \div \frac{1}{4}(1)$$

$$= \frac{4}{3}$$

---

d) $= 3$

$$\lim_{x \to 0} \frac{\sin(3x)}{3x^2 + x}$$

$$= \lim_{x \to 0} \frac{\sin(3x)3}{x(3x+1)3}$$

$$= \lim_{x \to 0} \frac{\sin 3x}{3x} \lim_{x \to 0} \frac{3}{3x+1}$$

$$= (1)\left(\frac{3}{0+1}\right)$$

$$= 3$$

e) $= 0$

$$\lim_{\theta \to 0} \frac{1 - \cos(2\theta)}{\theta}$$

$$\lim_{\theta \to 0} \frac{(1 - \cos 2\theta)2}{\theta(2)}$$

$$= -2 \lim_{\theta \to 0} \frac{\cos 2\theta - 1}{2\theta}$$

$$= -2(0)$$

$$= 0$$

f) $= 0$

$$\lim_{x \to 0} \frac{5 \tan x - 5 \sin x}{x \cos x}$$

$$\lim_{x \to 0} \frac{\dfrac{5 \sin x}{\cos x} - \dfrac{5 \sin x}{1}}{x \cos x}$$

$$= \lim_{x \to 0} \frac{5 \sin x - 5 \sin x \cos x}{x \cos^2 x}$$

$$= \lim_{x \to 0} \frac{-5 \sin x (\cos x - 1)}{x \cos^2 x}$$

$$= -5 \lim_{x \to 0} \frac{\sin x}{x} \lim_{x \to 0} \frac{\cos x - 1}{\cos^2 x}$$

$$= -5(1)\left(\frac{1-1}{1^2}\right)$$

$$= 0$$

Lesson 2—Derivatives of Trigonometric Functions
Part 1: Sine and Cosine

PRACTICE EXERCISE
Answers and Solutions

---

1. a) $\dfrac{dy}{dx} = -4 \sin x$

b) $f'(x) = 30x \cos(5x^2)$

$\quad\quad f'(x) = 3 \cos(5x^2)(10x)$

$\quad\quad f'(x) = 30x \cos(5x^2)$

c) $\dfrac{dy}{dx} = \dfrac{\cos 2x(2 \sin x \cos x) - \sin^2 x(-2 \sin 2x)}{\cos^2(2x)}$

d) $f'(x) = 42 \cos^2(7x) \sin(7x)$

$\quad\quad f(x) = -2(\cos(7x))^3$

$\quad\quad f'(x) = -6(\cos 7x)^2(-\sin 7x)(7)$

$\quad\quad f'(x) = 42 \cos^2(7x) \sin(7x)$

e) $\dfrac{dy}{dx} = x \cos x + \sin x$

$\quad\quad y = x \sin x$

$\quad\quad \dfrac{dy}{dx} = x(\cos x) + \sin x(1)$

$\quad\quad \dfrac{dy}{dx} = x \cos x + \sin x$

Lesson 3—Derivatives of Trigonometric Functions
Part 2: Tangent, Cotangent, Secant, and Cosecant

PRACTICE EXERCISE
Answers and Solutions

1. a) $f'(x) = -4\csc^2(2x)$

b) $\dfrac{dy}{dx} = \sec(2x)(\sin x \tan 2x + \cos x)$

$\dfrac{dy}{dx} = \sin x \sec(2x)\tan(2x)(2) + \sec(2x)\cos x$

$\dfrac{dy}{dx} = \sec(2x)(2\sin x \tan 2x + \cos x)$

c)

$f'(x) = \dfrac{\cos x^3 \sec^2(5x-4)(5) - \tan(5x-4)\left(-\sin\left(x^3\right)\left(3x^2\right)\right)}{\cos^2\left(x^3\right)}$

$f'(x) = \dfrac{5\cos x^3 \sec^2(5x-4) + 3x^2 \tan(5x-4)\sin\left(x^3\right)}{\cos^2\left(x^3\right)}$

d) $\dfrac{dy}{dx} = -18x\csc^3\left(3x^2\right)\cot\left(3x^2\right)$

$y = \left[\csc(3x^2)\right]^3$

$\dfrac{dy}{dx} = 3\left[\csc\left(3x^2\right)\right]^2\left(-\csc\left(3x^2\right)\cot\left(3x^2\right)\right)(6x)$

$\dfrac{dy}{dx} = -18x\csc^3\left(3x^2\right)\cot\left(3x^2\right)$

Practice Quiz
Answers and Solutions

1. a) $= 8$

$\displaystyle\lim_{x \to 0} \dfrac{\sin^2(4x)}{2x^2}$

$= \displaystyle\lim_{x \to 0} \dfrac{\sin(4x)\sin(4x)(8)}{2x^2(8)}$

$= 8\displaystyle\lim_{x \to 0} \dfrac{\sin(4x)}{4x}\lim_{x \to 0}\dfrac{\sin(4x)}{4x}$

$= 8(1)(1)$

$= 8$

b) $= 0$

$\displaystyle\lim_{x \to 0}\dfrac{\cos x - 1}{3x}$

$= \dfrac{1}{3}\displaystyle\lim_{x \to 0}\dfrac{\cos x - 1}{x}$

$= \dfrac{1}{3}(0)$

3. $= 16$

$\dfrac{d_y}{d_x} = 8\tan x \sec^2 x$

at $x = \dfrac{\pi}{4}$

$\dfrac{d_y}{d_x}\bigg|_{x=\frac{\pi}{4}} = 8\tan\left(\dfrac{\pi}{4}\right)\sec^2\left(\dfrac{\pi}{4}\right)$

$= 8(1)\left(\sqrt{2}\right)^2$

$= 16$

Lesson 4—Derivatives of Functions with Natural Logarithms

PRACTICE EXERCISE
Answers and Solutions

1. $\dfrac{dy}{dx} = \dfrac{2}{x}$

    $\dfrac{dy}{dx} = \dfrac{1}{x^2}(2x)$

    $\dfrac{dy}{dx} = \dfrac{2x}{x^2}$

    $\dfrac{dy}{dx} = \dfrac{2}{x}$

3. $\dfrac{dy}{dx} = \dfrac{1 - 3\ln x}{x^4}$

    $g(x) = \ln x$

    $g'(x) = \dfrac{1}{x}$

    $h(x) = x^3$

    $h'(x) = 3x^2$

    $\dfrac{dy}{dx} = \dfrac{x^3\left(\dfrac{1}{x}\right) - \ln x\left(3x^2\right)}{x^6}$

    $\dfrac{dy}{dx} = \dfrac{x^2\left(1 - 3\ln x\right)}{x^6}$

    $\dfrac{dy}{dx} = \dfrac{1 - 3\ln x}{x^4}$

5. $\dfrac{dy}{dx} = \dfrac{-y^2}{xy - 1}$

    $x\dfrac{dy}{dx} + y(1) = \dfrac{1}{y}\dfrac{dy}{dx}$

    $x\dfrac{dy}{dx} - \dfrac{1}{y}\dfrac{dy}{dx} = -y$

    $\dfrac{dy}{dx}\left(x - \dfrac{1}{y}\right) = -y$

    $\dfrac{dy}{dx} = \dfrac{-y}{x - \dfrac{1}{y}}$

    $\dfrac{dy}{dx} = \dfrac{-y}{\dfrac{xy - 1}{y}}$

    $\dfrac{dy}{dx} = \dfrac{-y^2}{xy - 1}$

Lesson 5—Derivatives of Exponential and Logarithmic Functions

PRACTICE EXERCISE
Answers and Solutions

1. a) $\dfrac{d_y}{d_x} = 2^x \ln 2$

    b) $\dfrac{dy}{dx} = 8x \ln 5\left(5^{x^2}\right)$

    $\ln y = \ln 4 + \ln 5^{x^2}$

    $\ln y = \ln 4 + x^2 \ln 5$

    $\dfrac{1}{y}\dfrac{dy}{dx} = 0 + 2\ln 5(x)$

    $\dfrac{dy}{dx} = 4\left(5^{x^2}\right)2x \ln 5$

    $\dfrac{dy}{dx} = 8x \ln 5\left(5^{x^2}\right)$

c) $\dfrac{dy}{dx} = 7^{x^3-x} \ln 7\left(3x^2-1\right)$

$\ln y = \ln 7^{x^3-x}$

$\ln y = \left(x^3-x\right)\ln 7$

$\ln y = x^3 \ln 7 - x \ln 7$

$\dfrac{1}{y}\dfrac{dy}{dx} = 3x^2 \ln 7 - \ln 7$

$\dfrac{dy}{dx} = y \ln 7\left(3x^2-1\right)$

$\dfrac{dy}{dx} = 7^{x^3-x} \ln 7\left(3x^2-1\right)$

3. a) $f'(x) = 2^{\sin x} \ln 2\left(\cos x\right)$

Method 1:

$y = 2^{\sin x}$

$\ln y = \sin x \ln 2$

$\dfrac{1}{y}\dfrac{dy}{dx} = \ln 2\left(\cos x\right)$

$\dfrac{dy}{dx} = y \ln 2\left(\cos x\right)$

$\dfrac{dy}{dx} = 2^{\sin x} \ln 2\left(\cos x\right)$

Method 2:

Using $\dfrac{d}{d_x}\left[b^u\right] = \left(b^u\right)(\ln b)\left(\dfrac{d_u}{d_x}\right)$

$f(x) = 2^{\sin x}$

$f'(x) = \left(2^{\sin x}\right)(\ln 2)(\cos x)$

b) $\dfrac{dy}{dx} = 4x\left(1+2\ln x\right)$

$g(x) = 4x^2$

$g'(x) = 8x$

$h(x) = \ln x$

$h'(x) = \dfrac{1}{x}$

$\dfrac{dy}{dx} = 4x^2\left(\dfrac{1}{x}\right) + (\ln x)(8x)$

$\dfrac{dy}{dx} = 4x\left(1+2\ln x\right)$

Answers and Solutions

1. $= \dfrac{25}{2}$

$\lim\limits_{x\to 0} \dfrac{5\sin(5x)(5)}{2x(5)}$

$= \lim\limits_{x\to 0} \dfrac{25}{2}\dfrac{\sin(5x)}{5x}$

$= \dfrac{25}{2} \lim\limits_{x\to 0} \dfrac{\sin(5x)}{5x}$

$= \dfrac{25}{2}(1)$

$= \dfrac{25}{2}$

3. $= 3\sqrt{3}$

$f'(x) = 3(\cos(2x))^2$

$f'(x) = 6\cos(2x)\sin(2x)(2)(-1)$

$f'(x) = -12\cos(2x)\sin(2x)$

$f'(x) = -6\sin(4x)$

slope at $x = \dfrac{\pi}{3}$

$f'\left(\dfrac{\pi}{3}\right) = -6\sin\left(\dfrac{4\pi}{3}\right)$

$= -6\left(\dfrac{-\sqrt{3}}{2}\right)$

$= 3\sqrt{3}$

5. a) $f'(x) = \dfrac{1}{x}\sin\left(2\ln(2x)\right)$

$f'(x) = \left(\sin\left(\ln(2x)\right)\right)^2$

$f'(x) = 2\sin\left(\ln 2x\right)\cos\left(\ln 2x\right)\left(\dfrac{1}{2x}(2)\right)$

$f'(x) = \dfrac{1}{x}\sin\left(2\ln(2x)\right)$

b) $\dfrac{dy}{dx} = 5^{x\sin x}\ln 5\left(x\cos x + \sin x\right)$

Method 1:

$\ln y = x\sin x \ln 5$

$\dfrac{1}{y}\dfrac{dy}{dx} = x\ln 5\cos x + \ln 5\sin x(1)$

$\dfrac{dy}{dx} = y\left(\ln 5\left(x\cos x + \sin x\right)\right)$

$\dfrac{dy}{dx} = 5^{x\sin x}\ln 5\left(x\cos x + \sin x\right)$

Method 2:

Using $\dfrac{d}{dx}\left(b^u\right) = \left(b^u\right)(\ln b)\left(\dfrac{du}{dx}\right)$

$\dfrac{d}{dx}\left(5^{x\sin x}\right) = \left(5^{x\sin x}\right)(\ln 5)\left[x\cos x + \sin x(1)\right]$

EXTREME VALUES AND CURVE SKETCHING

Lesson 1—Intercepts and Zeros

PRACTICE EXERCISE
Answers and Solutions

1. a) $x = 3, y = -6$

$y = 2(0) - 6$

$y = -6$

$0 = 2x - 6$

$3 = x$

b) $x = 0,\ x = 1, y = 0$

$y = x(x-1)$

$= 0(0-1)$

$= 0$

$0 = x(x-1)$

$x = 0,\ x = 1$

c) $x = \dfrac{2}{3},\ x = -4, y = -8$

$y = 3(0)^2 + 10(0) - 8$

$= -8$

$0 = 3x^2 + 10x - 8$

$= (3x-2)(x+4)$

$x = \dfrac{2}{3},\ x = -4$

d) $x = 0,\ x = \pi, y = 0$

$y = 3\sin(0)$

$= 0$

$0 = 3\sin x$

$0 = \sin x$

$x = 0,\ x = \pi$

e) $x = 0$, $x = \dfrac{1}{4}$, $y = 0$

$$y = \frac{4(0)^2 - (0)}{3(0) - 7}$$

$$= 0$$

$$0 = \frac{4x^2 - x}{3x - 7}$$

$$0 = 4x^2 - x$$

$$= x(4x - 1)$$

$$x = 0, \ x = \frac{1}{4}$$

f) $y = \dfrac{3 \pm \sqrt{65}}{4}$, $y = -7$

$$y = 2(0)^2 - 3(0) - 7$$

$$= -7$$

$$x = \frac{3 \pm \sqrt{(-3)^2 - 4(2)(-7)}}{2(2)}$$

$$= \frac{3 \pm \sqrt{65}}{4}$$

Lesson 2—Symmetry of Functions

PRACTICE EXERCISE
Answers and Solutions

1. a) even

$$f(-x) = 4(-x)^2 - 3$$

$$= 4x^2 - 3$$

$$f(x) = f(-x)$$

The function is even.

b) not even

$$f(-x) = 2(-x)^3 + 3(-x) - 1$$

$$= -2x^3 - 3x - 1$$

$$f(x) \neq f(-x)$$

The function is not even.

c) even

$$f(-x) = 4(-x)^4 + 2(-x)^2 - 1$$

$$= 4x^4 + 2x^2 - 1$$

$$f(x) = f(-x)$$

The function is even.

d) even

$$f(-x) = 2\cos(-x) + 3$$

$$= 2\cos(x) + 3$$

$$f(x) = f(-x)$$

The function is even.

3. a) symmetric about the y-axis

$$f(-x) = 3(-x)^2 - 5$$

$$= 3x^2 - 5$$

$$-f(x) = -(3x^2 - 5)$$

$$= -3x^2 + 5$$

$$f(x) = f(-x)$$

The function is even, therefore, is symmetric about the y–axis.

b) symmetric about the origin

$$f(-x) = 2(-x)^3 - 7(-x)$$

$$= -2x^3 + 7x$$

$$-f(x) = -(2x^3 - 7x)$$

$$= -2x^3 + 7x$$

$$-f(x) = f(-x)$$

The function is odd, therefore, is symmetric about the origin.

c) no symmetry

$$f(-x) = (-x)^3 - (-x)^2$$

$$= -x^3 - x^2$$

$$-f(x) = -(x^3 - x^2)$$

$$= -x^3 + x^2$$

$$-f(x) \neq f(-x)$$

$$f(x) \neq f(-x)$$

The function is not even nor odd, therefore, as no symmetry

d) symmetric about the origin

$$y = 4\sin x \cos x$$

$$y = 2\sin(2x)$$

$$f(-x) = 2\sin(2(-x))$$

$$= -2\sin(2x)$$

$$-f(x) = -2\sin(2x)$$

$$-f(x) = f(-x)$$

The function is odd, therefore, is symmetric about the origin.

Lesson 3—Intervals of Increase and Decrease and Maximum and Minimum Values

PRACTICE EXERCISE
Answers and Solutions

1. a) Decreasing: $(-\infty, 4)$

Increasing: $(4, \infty)$

Local minimum at $(4, f(4))$

Minimum value $= f(4) = 7$

$$y = 2x^2 - 16x + 39$$

$$y' = 4x - 16$$

$$0 = 4x - 16$$

$$x = 4$$

Critical value is $x = 4$

Test values:

$$f'(0) = 4(0) - 16$$

$$= negative$$

$$f'(5) = 4(5) - 16$$

$$= positive$$

Decreasing: $(-\infty, 4)$

Increasing: $(4, \infty)$

Local minimum at $(4, f(4))$

Minimum value $= f(4) = 7$

b) Decreasing: $(-\infty, 3) \cup (3, \infty)$

There are no maximum or minimum values.

$$f(x) = \frac{2}{x-3}$$

$$f'(x) = \frac{-2}{(x-3)^2}$$

$f'(x)$ cannot equal zero

$f(x)$ is undefined when $x = 3$

So, 3 is a critical value.

Test values:

$$f'(0) = \frac{-2}{(0-3)^2}$$

$$= negative$$

$$f'(4) = \frac{-2}{(4-3)^2}$$

$$= negative$$

Decreasing: $(-\infty, 3) \cup (3, \infty)$

There are no maximum or minimum values.

c) Increasing: $\left(0, \frac{\pi}{2}\right) \cup \left(\frac{3\pi}{2}, 2\pi\right)$

Decreasing: $\left(\frac{\pi}{2}, \frac{3\pi}{2}\right)$

Maximum value:

$$f\left(\frac{\pi}{2}\right) = 3\sin\left(\frac{\pi}{2}\right) + 2$$

$$= 5$$

Minimum value:

$$f\left(\frac{3\pi}{2}\right) = 3\sin\left(\frac{3\pi}{2}\right) + 2$$

$$= -1$$

$$f(x) = 3\sin(x) + 2, \ 0 < x \le 2\pi$$

$$f'(x) = 3\cos(x)$$

$$0 = 3\cos(x)$$

$$0 = \cos(x)$$

$$x = \frac{\pi}{2} \quad x = \frac{3\pi}{2}$$

Test values:

$$f'\left(\frac{\pi}{3}\right) = 3\cos\left(\frac{\pi}{3}\right)$$

$$= positive$$

$f'(\pi) = 3\cos(\pi)$

$\qquad = negative$

$f'\left(\dfrac{5\pi}{3}\right) = 3\cos\left(\dfrac{5\pi}{3}\right)$

$\qquad = positive$

Increasing: $\left(0, \dfrac{\pi}{2}\right) \cup \left(\dfrac{3\pi}{2}, 2\pi\right)$

Decreasing: $\left(\dfrac{\pi}{2}, \dfrac{3\pi}{2}\right)$

Maximum value:

$f\left(\dfrac{\pi}{2}\right) = 3\sin\left(\dfrac{\pi}{2}\right) + 2$

$\qquad = 5$

Minimum value:

$f\left(\dfrac{3\pi}{2}\right) = 3\sin\left(\dfrac{3\pi}{2}\right) + 2$

$\qquad = -1$

Since the function

$f(x) = 3\sin x + 2$, $0 \le x \le 2\pi$ has a restricted domain, local maximum or minimum values will also occur at the endpoints.

$f(0) = 3\sin(0) + 2 = 2$

Since the function is increasing in the interval $\left(0, \dfrac{\pi}{2}\right)$, 2 is a local minimum

$f(2\pi) = 3\sin(2\pi) + 2 = 2$

Since the function is decreasing in the interval $\left(\dfrac{3\pi}{2}, 2\pi\right)$, 2 is a local maximum.

$f(x) = 3\sin x + 2$, $0 \le x \le 2\pi$, at its endpoints,

$(0, 2)$ *and* $(2\pi, 2)$ to see this:

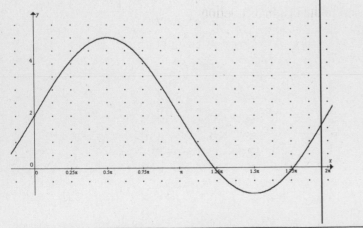

d) Decreasing: $\left(0, \dfrac{\pi}{4}\right) \cup \left(\dfrac{\pi}{2}, \dfrac{3\pi}{4}\right)$

Increasing: $\left(\dfrac{\pi}{4}, \dfrac{\pi}{2}\right)$

Minimum value:

$y = 2\cos^2\left(2\left(\dfrac{\pi}{4}\right)\right)$

$\qquad = 0$

Maximum value:

$y = 2\cos^2\left(2\left(\dfrac{\pi}{2}\right)\right)$

$\qquad = 2$

$y = 2\cos^2(2x)$, $0 < x < \dfrac{3\pi}{4}$

$f'(x) = 4\cos(2x)(-\sin(2x)(2))$

$\qquad = -8\cos(2x)\sin(2x)$

$\qquad = -4(2\sin(2x)\cos(2x))$

$\qquad = -4\sin(4x)$

$0 = -4\sin(4x)$

$0 = \sin 4x$

$x = \dfrac{\pi}{4} \quad x = \dfrac{\pi}{2}$

Test values:

$f'\left(\dfrac{\pi}{6}\right) = -4\sin\left(4\left(\dfrac{\pi}{6}\right)\right)$

$\qquad = negative$

$f'\left(\dfrac{\pi}{3}\right) = -4\sin\left(4\left(\dfrac{\pi}{3}\right)\right)$

$\qquad = positive$

$f'\left(\dfrac{2\pi}{3}\right) = -4\sin\left(4\left(\dfrac{2\pi}{3}\right)\right)$

$\qquad = negative$

Decreasing: $\left(0, \dfrac{\pi}{4}\right) \cup \left(\dfrac{\pi}{2}, \dfrac{3\pi}{4}\right)$

Increasing: $\left(\dfrac{\pi}{4}, \dfrac{\pi}{2}\right)$

Minimum value:

$y = 2\cos^2\left(2\left(\dfrac{\pi}{4}\right)\right)$

$\qquad = 0$

Maximum value:

$y = 2\cos^2\left(2\left(\dfrac{\pi}{2}\right)\right)$

$\qquad = 2$

Lesson 4—Concavity and Points of Inflection

PRACTICE EXERCISE
Answers and Solutions

1. **a)** concave down, negative

    b) concave up, positive

    c) increasing, positive

    d) decreasing, negative

    e) inflection point, zero

    f) local maximum, zero

    g) local minimum, zero

3. **a)** (b, c)

    b) $(0, d)$

    c) $(a, 0)$

    d) $(a, b) \cup (c, d)$

5. **a)**

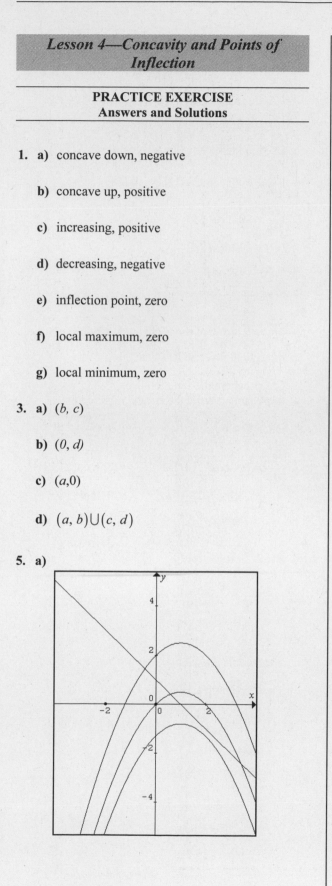

b)

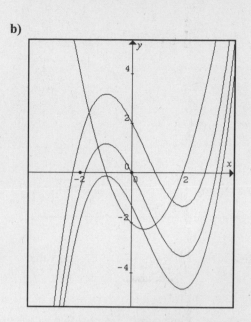

Lesson 5—Optimization Problems

PRACTICE EXERCISE
Answers and Solutions

1. Let a be one number and b be the other number. Let S be the sum and P the product.

    $S = a + b$

    and $P = ab$

    $100 = ab$

    $\dfrac{100}{a} = b$

    So,

    $$S = a + \frac{100}{a}$$

    $$\frac{dS}{da} = 1 - \frac{100}{a^2}$$

    $$0 = 1 - \frac{100}{a^2}$$

    $$\frac{100}{a^2} = 1$$

    $$\sqrt{100} = a$$

    $$10 = a$$

    We ignore the negative square root value.

    Check where the function is increasing or decreasing around the critical number:

    when $a = 1$,

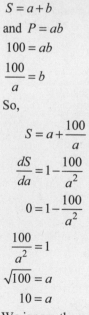

$$\frac{dS}{da} = 1 - \frac{100}{1^2}$$

$$= negative$$

when $a = 20$,

$$\frac{dS}{da} = 1 - \frac{100}{20^2}$$

$$= positive$$

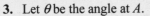

decreasing   increasing

     –   +

1   10   20

test value   critical   test value

           number

Since $\frac{dS}{da}$ changes from negative to positive at

$a = 10$, the original function, $S = a + \frac{100}{a}$,

reaches a local minimum.
When $a = 10$,

$$b = \frac{100}{10}$$

$$= 10$$

The 2 positive numbers whose product is 100 and whose sum is a minimum are 10 and 10.

3. Let θ be the angle at A.

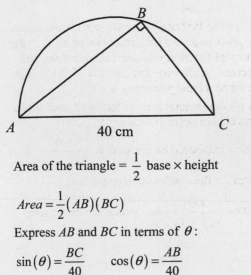

Area of the triangle $= \frac{1}{2}$ base $\times$ height

$$Area = \frac{1}{2}(AB)(BC)$$

Express AB and BC in terms of θ:

$$\sin(\theta) = \frac{BC}{40} \qquad \cos(\theta) = \frac{AB}{40}$$

$$BC = 40\sin(\theta) \quad AB = 40\cos(\theta)$$

$$Area = \frac{1}{2}(40\cos(\theta))(40\sin(\theta))$$

$$= 800\cos(\theta)\sin(\theta)$$

$$= 400(2\cos(\theta)\sin(\theta))$$

$$= 400\sin(2\theta)$$

Use the identity: $2(\sin A)(\cos A) = \sin(2A)$

$$\frac{dA}{d\theta} = 400(\cos(2\theta))2$$

$$\frac{dA}{d\theta} = 800\cos(2\theta)$$

$$0 = 800\cos(2\theta)$$

$$0 = \cos(2\theta)$$

$$\theta = \frac{\pi}{4}$$

Since θ is one of the acute angles in the right

triangle, it must be less than $\frac{\pi}{2}$.

Check where the function is increasing or decreasing around the critical number:

when $\theta = 0$,   when $\theta = \frac{\pi}{2}$,

$$\frac{dA}{d\theta} = 800\cos(2(0)) \qquad \frac{dA}{d\theta} = 800\cos(2(90))$$

$$= 800\cos(0) \qquad\qquad = 800\cos(180)$$

$$= positive \qquad\qquad = negative$$

increasing   decreasing

   +   –

0         $\frac{\pi}{4}$ $\frac{\pi}{2}$

So, there is a local maximum when $\theta = \frac{\pi}{4}$.

The maximum area is:

$$A = 400\sin\left[\left(\frac{\pi}{4}\right)\right]$$

$$= 400(1)$$

$$= 400$$

Therefore, a maximum area occurs when $w = 100$ m.

$$A = 300(100) - \frac{3}{2}(100)^2$$

$$= 30\,000 - 15\,000$$

$$= 15\,000 \text{ m}^2$$

5.

20 cm

$$\frac{20-x}{4}$$

Let x be the length of one portion of wire and $(20-x)$ will be the other.

Let $\frac{x}{3}$ be the side length of the triangle.

Let $\frac{20-x}{4}$ be the side length of the square.

The area of an equilateral triangle is given by:

$A = \frac{\sqrt{3}\,a^2}{4}$, where a is the length of a side.

The combined area, A, of the equilateral triangle and square is:

$$A = \frac{\sqrt{3}\left(\frac{x}{3}\right)^2}{4} + \left(\frac{20-x}{4}\right)^2$$

$$= \frac{\sqrt{3}\,x^2}{36} + \frac{400 - 40x + x^2}{16}$$

$$= \frac{4\sqrt{3}\,x^2 + 3\,600 - 360x + 9x^2}{144}$$

$$= \frac{4\sqrt{3}\,x^2}{144} + \frac{3\,600}{144} - \frac{360x}{144} + \frac{9x^2}{144}$$

Find x and set it to zero.

$$\frac{dA}{dx} = \frac{8\sqrt{3}\,x}{144} + 0 - \frac{360}{144} + \frac{18x}{144}$$

$$0 = \frac{8\sqrt{3}\,x - 360 + 18x}{144}$$

$$0 = 8\sqrt{3}\,x - 360 + 18x$$

$$360 = x\left(8\sqrt{3} + 18\right)$$

$$x = \frac{360}{8\sqrt{3} + 18}$$

$$x \doteq 11.3$$

Test the sign of $\frac{dA}{dx}$ at $x = 11$ *and* $x = 12$.

(Before and after the critical value of 11.3)

At $x = 11$, $\frac{dA}{dx} =$

$$\frac{8\sqrt{3}\,(11) - 360 + 18(11)}{144} \doteq -0.067$$

At $x = 12$, $\frac{dA}{dx} =$

$$\frac{8\sqrt{3}\,(12) - 360 + 18(12)}{144} \doteq +0.155$$

Since the first derivative changed from *negative to positive* across the critical value of 11.3, the original function was decreasing before, and increasing after the critical value of 11.3 and reached a local minimum at $x = 11.3$.

A minimum total area of the equilateral triangle and square occurs when $x = 11.3$ cm.

The wire should be cut so that $\dfrac{360}{8\sqrt{3} + 18}$ cm is used for the equilateral triangle and

$\left(20 - \dfrac{360}{8\sqrt{3} + 18}\right)$ cm is used for the square.

Practice Quiz

Answers and Solutions

1. The function is even and has symmetry about the y-axis.

$$f(x) = \frac{4x^4 - 1}{x^2}$$

$$f(-x) = \frac{4(-x)^4 - 1}{(-x)^2}$$

$$= \frac{4x^4 - 1}{x^2}$$

$$-f(x) = -\left(\frac{4x^4 - 1}{x^2}\right)$$

$$= -\frac{4x^4 - 1}{x^2}$$

Since $f(x) = f(-x)$ and $-f(x) \neq f(-x)$,

the function is even and has symmetry about the y-axis.

3. a) $f'(x) = 3x^2 + 4x - 1$

$f''(x) = 6x + 4$

$0 = 6x + 4$

$x = \dfrac{-2}{3}$

Test values: -1 and 0

$f''(-1) = negative$

$f''(0) = positive$

Concave down: $\left(-\infty, -\dfrac{2}{3}\right)$

Concave up: $\left(-\dfrac{2}{3}, \infty\right)$

Inflection point: $\left(\dfrac{-2}{3}, f\left(\dfrac{-2}{3}\right)\right)$

$= \left(\dfrac{-2}{3}, \dfrac{142}{27}\right)$

b) $f(x) = 2\sin x; \quad 0 < x < 2\pi$

$f'(x) = 2\cos x$

$f''(x) = -2\sin x$

$0 = -2\sin x$

$0 = \sin x$

$x = \pi$

Test values: $\dfrac{\pi}{2}$ and $\dfrac{3\pi}{2}$

$f''\left(\dfrac{\pi}{2}\right) = negative$

$f''\left(\dfrac{3\pi}{2}\right) = positive$

Concave up: $(\pi, 2\pi)$

Concave down: $(0, \pi)$

Inflection point: $(\pi, f(\pi)) = (\pi, 0)$

Lesson 6—Vertical Asymptotes

PRACTICE EXERCISE
Answers and Solutions

1. a) $f(x) = \dfrac{1}{x+1}$

   The function is undefined when
   $x + 1 = 0$.
   $x = -1$ (potential asymptote)

   $\displaystyle\lim_{x\to -1^+}\left(\frac{1}{x+1}\right) = +\infty$

   $\displaystyle\lim_{x\to -1^-}\left(\frac{1}{x+1}\right) = -\infty$

b) $f(x) = \dfrac{2}{x^2 + 2x - 3}$

   The function is undefined when
   $x^2 + 2x - 3 = 0$.
   $(x+3)(x-1) = 0$
   $x = -3$ and $x = 1$ (potential asymptote)

   $\displaystyle\lim_{x\to 1^+}\left[\frac{2}{(x+3)(x-1)}\right] = +\infty$

   $\displaystyle\lim_{x\to 1^-}\left[\frac{2}{(x+3)(x-1)}\right] = -\infty$

   $\displaystyle\lim_{x\to -3^+}\left[\frac{2}{(x+3)(x-1)}\right] = -\infty$

   $\displaystyle\lim_{x\to -3^-}\left[\frac{2}{(x+3)(x-1)}\right] = +\infty$

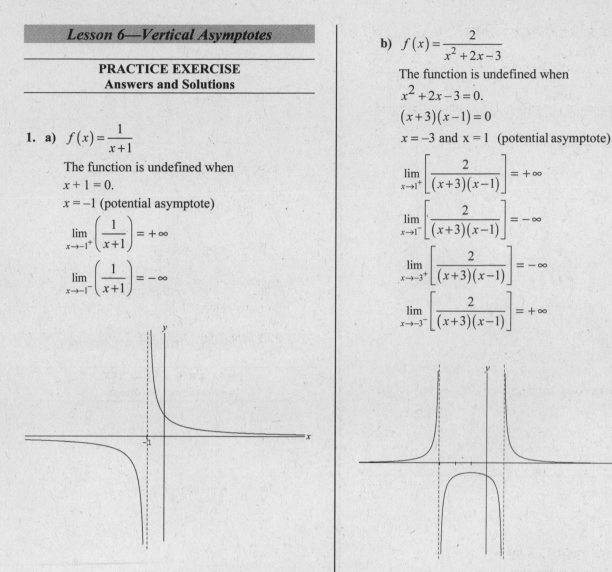

Thus, $x = 1$ is a vertical asymptote.

Thus, $x = -3$ and $x = 1$ are vertical asymptotes.

c) $f(x)\sec x$

$\sec x = \dfrac{1}{\cos x}$

The function is undefined when $\cos x = 0$.

$x = \dfrac{\pi}{2}$ and $x = \dfrac{3\pi}{2}$

$\displaystyle\lim_{x \to \frac{\pi}{2}^+} (\sec x) = -\infty$

$\displaystyle\lim_{x \to \frac{\pi}{2}^-} (\sec x) = +\infty$

$\displaystyle\lim_{x \to \frac{3\pi}{2}^+} (\sec x) = +\infty$

$\displaystyle\lim_{x \to \frac{3\pi}{2}^+} (\sec x) = -\infty$

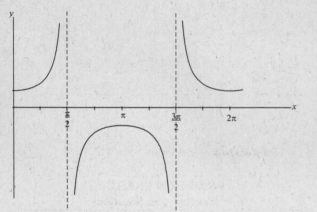

Thus, $x = \dfrac{\pi}{2}$ and $x = \dfrac{3\pi}{2}$ are vertical asymptotes.

d) $y = \dfrac{x+5}{x+4}$

The function is undefined when $x + 4 = 0$.

$x = -4$ (potential asymptote)

$\displaystyle\lim_{x \to -4^-} \left(\dfrac{x+5}{x+4} \right) = -\infty$

$\displaystyle\lim_{x \to -4^+} \left(\dfrac{x+5}{x+4} \right) = +\infty$

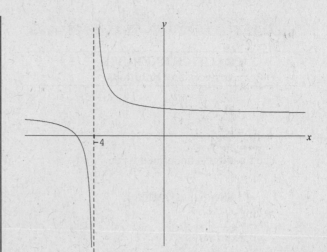

Thus, $x = -4$ is a vertical asymptote.

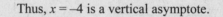
Lesson 7—Horizontal Asymptotes

PRACTICE EXERCISE
Answers and Solutions

1. a) $y = 0$

$$\lim_{x \to \infty} \frac{x^2}{x^3 - 4} = \lim_{x \to \infty} \frac{\dfrac{x^2}{x^3}}{\dfrac{x^3}{x^3} - \dfrac{4}{x^3}}$$

$$= \lim_{x \to \infty} \frac{\dfrac{1}{x}}{1 - \dfrac{4}{x^3}}$$

$$= \frac{\displaystyle\lim_{x \to \infty} \dfrac{1}{x}}{\displaystyle\lim_{x \to \infty} 1 - \lim_{x \to \infty} \dfrac{4}{x^3}}$$

$$= \frac{0}{1 - 0}$$

$$= 0$$

There is a horizontal asymptote at $y = 0$.

b) $y = \dfrac{1}{2}$

$$\lim_{x \to \infty} \frac{2x^2 - x}{4x^2 - 3}$$

$$= \lim_{x \to \infty} \frac{\dfrac{2x^2}{x^2} - \dfrac{x}{x^2}}{\dfrac{4x^2}{x^2} - \dfrac{3}{x^2}}$$

$$= \lim_{x \to \infty} \frac{2 - \dfrac{1}{x}}{4 - \dfrac{3}{x^2}}$$

$$= \frac{\displaystyle\lim_{x \to \infty} 2 - \lim_{x \to \infty} \frac{1}{x}}{\displaystyle\lim_{x \to \infty} 4 - \lim_{x \to \infty} \frac{3}{x^2}}$$

$$= \frac{2 - 0}{4 - 0} = \frac{2 - 0}{4 - 0} = \frac{1}{2}$$

There is a horizontal asymptote at $y = \dfrac{1}{2}$.

c) There are no horizontal asymptotes.

$$\lim_{x \to \infty} \frac{-5x^3 - 4x^2}{3x^2 + x}$$

$$= \lim_{x \to \infty} \frac{\dfrac{-5x^3}{x^2} - \dfrac{4x^2}{x^2}}{\dfrac{3x^2}{x^2} + \dfrac{x}{x^2}}$$

$$= \lim_{x \to \infty} \frac{-5x - 4}{3 + \dfrac{1}{x}}$$

$$= \frac{\displaystyle\lim_{x \to \infty} (-5x) - \lim_{x \to \infty} 4}{\displaystyle\lim_{x \to \infty} 3 + \lim_{x \to \infty} \frac{1}{x}}$$

$$= \frac{-\infty - 4}{3 + 0}$$

$$= -\infty$$

Therefore, there are no horizontal asymptotes.

d) $y = -\dfrac{2}{3}$

$$\lim_{x \to \infty} \frac{-4x^3 + 2x^2 - 1}{6x^3 - x + 5}$$

$$= \lim_{x \to \infty} \frac{\dfrac{-4x^3}{x^3} + \dfrac{2x^2}{x^3} - \dfrac{1}{x^3}}{\dfrac{6x^3}{x^3} - \dfrac{x}{x^3} + \dfrac{5}{x^3}}$$

$$= \lim_{x \to \infty} \frac{-4 + \dfrac{2}{x} - \dfrac{1}{x^3}}{6 - \dfrac{1}{x^2} + \dfrac{5}{x^3}}$$

$$= \frac{\displaystyle\lim_{x \to \infty} (-4) + \lim_{x \to \infty} \frac{2}{x} - \lim_{x \to \infty} \frac{1}{x^3}}{\displaystyle\lim_{x \to \infty} 6 - \lim_{x \to \infty} \frac{1}{x^2} + \lim_{x \to \infty} \frac{5}{x^3}}$$

$$= \frac{-4 + 0 - 0}{6 - 0 + 0}$$

$$= \frac{-4}{6} = \frac{-2}{3}$$

Therefore, the horizontal asymptote is $y = -\dfrac{2}{3}$.

Lesson 8—Oblique Asymptotes

PRACTICE EXERCISE
Answers and Solutions

1. Because the degree of the numerator exceeds that of the denominator by 1, the functions that will have an oblique asymptote are those given in a, c, and d.

   Because the degree of the numerator does not exceed that of the denominator by 1, the functions that will **not** have an oblique asymptote are those given in b, e, and f.

Practice Test

Answers and Solutions

1. a) $(-\infty, a) \cup (0, d)$

b) $(a, 0) \cup (d, \infty)$

c) (b, c)

d) $a, 0$, and d

3. a) $x = -2,\ y = -\dfrac{2}{9}$

x-intercept:

$$0 = \frac{x+2}{x^2 - 9}$$

$$0 = x + 2$$

$$x = -2$$

y-intercept

$$y = \frac{0+2}{0^2 - 9}$$

$$y = -\frac{2}{9}$$

b) The vertical asymptotes are at $x = 3$ and $x = -3$.

Vertical asymptote:

$$x^2 - 9 = 0$$

$$x = \pm 3$$

$$\lim_{x \to 3^-}\left[\frac{x+2}{(x+3)(x-3)}\right] = -\infty$$

$$\lim_{x \to 3^+}\left[\frac{x+2}{(x+3)(x-3)}\right] = +\infty$$

$$\lim_{x \to -2^-}\left[\frac{x+2}{(x+3)(x-3)}\right] = -\infty$$

$$\lim_{x \to -2^-}\left[\frac{x+2}{(x+3)(x-3)}\right] = -\infty$$

The vertical asymptotes are at $x = 3$ and $x = -3$.

c) $y = 0$

$$f(x) = \frac{x+2}{x^2 - 9}$$

$$\lim_{x \to \infty} f(x) = \lim_{x \to \infty} \frac{x+2}{x^2 - 9}$$

$$= \lim_{x \to \infty} \frac{\dfrac{x}{x^2} + \dfrac{2}{x^2}}{\dfrac{x^2}{x^2} - \dfrac{9}{x^2}}$$

$$= \frac{\displaystyle\lim_{x \to \infty} \frac{1}{x} + \lim_{x \to \infty} \frac{2}{x^2}}{\displaystyle\lim_{x \to \infty} 1 - \lim_{x \to \infty} \frac{9}{x^2}}$$

$$= \frac{0 + 0}{1 - 0}$$

$$= 0$$

and $\displaystyle\lim_{x \to -\infty} f(x) = 0$

The equation of the horizontal asymptote is $y = 0$.

d)

$$f'(x) = \frac{(x^2 - 9) - (x+2)(2x)}{(x^2 - 9)^2}$$

$$f'(x) = \frac{-x^2 - 4x - 9}{(x^2 - 9)^2}$$

Critical values:

The numerator will never be zero.

$$-x^2 - 4x - 9 = 0$$

$$x = \frac{4 \pm \sqrt{(-4)^2 - 4(-1)(-9)}}{2(-1)} = \frac{4 \pm \sqrt{-20}}{-2}$$

The denominator is zero when $x = \pm 3$

Test values: $x = -4, -2, 2$, and 4

$$f'(-4) = \frac{-(-4)^2 - 4(-4) - 9}{\left[(-4)^2 - 9\right]^2} = \frac{-9}{49}$$

$$f'(-2) = \frac{-(-2)^2 - 4(-2) - 9}{\left[(-2)^2 - 9\right]^2} = \frac{-5}{25}$$

$$f'(-4) = \frac{-(-4)^2 - 4(-4) - 9}{\left[(-4)^2 - 9\right]^2} = \frac{-9}{49}$$

$$f'(-2) = \frac{-(-2)^2 - 4(-2) - 9}{\left[(-2)^2 - 9\right]^2} = \frac{-5}{25}$$

There are no intervals of increase.

Intervals of decrease:

$(-\infty, -3) \cup (-3, 3) \cup (3, \infty)$

There are no maximum or minimum values.

e)

$$f'(x) = \frac{-x^2 - 4x - 9}{\left(x^2 - 9\right)^2}$$

$$f''(x) = \frac{\left(x^2 - 9\right)^2(-2x - 4) - \left(-x^2 - 4x - 9\right)(2)\left(x^2 - 9\right)(2x)}{\left(x^2 - 9\right)^4}$$

$$f''(x) = \frac{-2\left(x^2 - 9\right)\left[\left(x^2 - 9\right)(x + 2) + \left(-x^2 - 4x - 9\right)2x\right]}{\left(x^2 - 9\right)^4}$$

$$f''(x) = \frac{-2\left[x^3 + 2x^2 - 9x - 18 - 2x^3 + 8x^2 - 18x\right]}{\left(x^2 - 9\right)^3}$$

$$f''(x) = \frac{2\left(x^3 + 6x^2 + 27x + 18\right)}{\left(x^2 - 9\right)^3}$$

Critical values:

The numerator is zero when

$x^3 + 6x^2 + 27x + 18 = 0$

This occurs when $x \doteq -0.796$

The denominator is zero when $x = \pm 3$

Test values: $x = -4$, -2, -1, 0, 2, and 4

$$f''(-4) = \frac{2\left[(-4)^3 + 6(-4)^2 + 27(-4) + 18\right]}{\left[(-4)^2 - 9\right]^3} = \frac{-116}{343}$$

$$f''(-2) = \frac{2\left[(-2)^3 + 6(-2)^2 + 27(-2) + 18\right]}{\left[(-2)^2 - 9\right]^3} = \frac{-40}{-125}$$

$$f''(-1) = \frac{2\left[(-1)^3 + 6(-1)^2 + 27(-1) + 18\right]}{\left[(-1)^2 - 9\right]^3} = \frac{-8}{-512}$$

$$f''(0) = \frac{2\left[(0)^3 + 6(0)^2 + 27(0) + 18\right]}{\left[(0)^2 - 9\right]^3} = \frac{36}{-729}$$

$$f''(2) = \frac{2\left[(2)^3 + 6(2)^2 + 27(2) + 18\right]}{\left[(2)^2 - 9\right]^3} = \frac{208}{-125}$$

$$f''(4) = \frac{2\left[(4)^3 + 6(4)^2 + 27(4) + 18\right]}{\left[(4)^2 - 9\right]^3} = \frac{572}{343}$$

The original function is concave up in the intervals: $(-3, -0.786) \cup (3, \infty)$

The original function is concave down in the intervals: $(-\infty, -3) \cup (-0.786, 3)$

Since the sign of the second derivative changes at $x = -0.786$, a point of inflection exists at

$(-0.786, f(0.786)) \doteq (-0.786, -0.145)$

f)

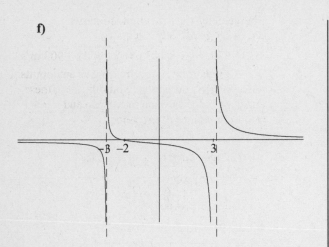

5. Let s be the length of the base and let h be the height of the box.

$SA = 2s^2 + 4sh$

Using the volume formula, we can isolate h:

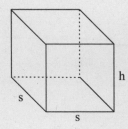

$V = s^2 h$

$h = \dfrac{1\,000}{s^2}$

Substitute:

$SA = 2s^2 + 4s\left(\dfrac{1\,000}{s^2}\right)$

$ = 2s^2 + 4\,000s^{-1}$

$\dfrac{d(SA)}{ds} = 4s - \dfrac{4\,000}{s^2}$

$0 = 4s - \dfrac{4\,000}{s^2}$

$\dfrac{4\,000}{s^2} = 4s$

$4\,000 = 4s^3$

$s = 10$

Test values: 9 and 11

$\dfrac{d(SA)}{ds} = 4(9) - \dfrac{4\,000}{(9)^2}$

$\phantom{\dfrac{d(SA)}{ds}} = 36 - \dfrac{4000}{36}$

$\phantom{\dfrac{d(SA)}{ds}} = negative$

$\dfrac{d(SA)}{ds} = 4(11) - \dfrac{4\,000}{(11)^2}$

$\phantom{\dfrac{d(SA)}{ds}} = 44 - \dfrac{4\,000}{121}$

$\phantom{\dfrac{d(SA)}{ds}} = positive$

Since the first derivative changes from negative to positive at $s = 10$, the surface area function,

$SA = 2s^2 + 4s\left(\dfrac{1\,000}{s^2}\right)$, reached a minimum

value.

Substituting, we find

$h = \dfrac{1\,000}{(10)^2}$

$h = 10$

The dimensions of the box of minimum surface area: a base length of 10 cm and a height of 10 cm.

7. $f'(x) = -3x^2 + 8x + 3$

$f'(x) = -(3x+1)(x-3)$

$0 = -(3x+1)(x-3)$

$x = -\dfrac{1}{3} \quad x = 3$

Test values: −1, 0 and 4

$f'(-1) = negative$

$f'(0) = positive$

$f'(4) = negative$

The function is decreasing on

$\left(-\infty, -\dfrac{1}{3}\right) \cup (3, \infty)$ and increasing on

$\left(-\dfrac{1}{3}, 3\right)$.

There is a local minimum at $\left(-\dfrac{1}{3}, \dfrac{121}{27}\right)$ and a

local maximum at $(3, 23)$.

$f''(x) = -6x + 8$

$0 = -6x + 8$

$x = \dfrac{4}{3}$

Test values: 0 and 2

$f''(0) = positive$

$f''(2) = negative$

The function is concave up on $\left(-\infty, \dfrac{4}{3}\right)$ and

concave down on $\left(\dfrac{4}{3}, \infty\right)$, and there is an

inflection point at $\left(\dfrac{4}{3}, \dfrac{371}{27}\right)$.

y-intercept: 5

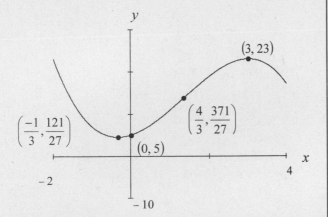

APPLICATIONS OF DERIVATIVES

Lesson 1—Distance, Velocity, and Acceleration

PRACTICE EXERCISE
Answers and Solutions

1. a) $t = 183.676 \text{ s}$

$h = -4.9t^2 + 900t + 2.4$

$t = \dfrac{-(900) \pm \sqrt{(900)^2 - 4(-4.9)(2.4)}}{2(-4.9)}$

$t = 183.676 \text{ s}$

b) Maximum velocity = 900 m/s
Minimum velocity = –900 m/s

$h = -4.9t^2 + 900t + 2.4$

$v = \dfrac{dh}{dt} = -9.8t + 900$

Since this problem involves a restricted domain of $0 \le t \le 183.676$, the endpoints of the velocity-time function must be considered.

The velocity-time function is linear.
$v(0) = -9.8(0) + 900 = 900 \text{ m/s}$
$v(183.676) = -9.8(183.676) + 900 = -900 \text{ m/s}$
Since a linear function cannot have any points where its first derivative would be zero, these endpoint values are the maximum and minimum values of the velocity.

c) $v = 312 \text{ m/s}$ upward

$v = -9.8(60) + 900$

$v = 312 \text{ m/s}$ upward

3. a) Neptune $\quad h = -5.88t^2 - 8t + 200$

$v = \dfrac{dh}{dt} = -11.68t - 8$

$a = \dfrac{dv}{dt} = -11.68 \text{ m/s}^2$

Mars $\quad h = -1.85t^2 - 8t + 200$

$v = \dfrac{dh}{dt} = -3.7t - 8$

$a = \dfrac{dv}{dt} = -3.7 \text{ m/s}^2$

Venus $\quad h = -4.45t^2 - 8t + 200$

$v = \dfrac{dh}{dt} = -8.9t - 8$

$a = \dfrac{dv}{dt} = -8.9 \text{ m/s}^2$

b) Maximum speed = 52.199 m/s

$$0 = -4.45t^2 - 8t + 200$$

$$t = \frac{-(-8) \pm \sqrt{(-8)^2 - 4(-4.45)(200)}}{2(-4.45)}$$

$$t = 5.865 \text{ s}$$

Since this problem involves a restricted domain of $0 \le t \le 5.865$, the endpoint values of the velocity-time function must be considered.

$$v(t) = -8.9t - 8$$

$$v(0) = -8.9(0) - 8 = -8$$

$$v(5.865) = -8.9(5.865) - 8 = -52.199$$

Since a linear function cannot have any points where its first derivative would be zero, these endpoint values are the maximum and minimum values of the velocity.

The object has a maximum velocity of –8 m/s and a minimum velocity of –52.199 m/s.

The absolute value of –52.199 is the value of the object's maximum speed.

c) Difference in speed = 30.3 m/s

Neptune

$$t = \frac{-(-8) \pm \sqrt{(-8)^2 - 4(-5.8)(200)}}{2(-5.8)}$$

$$t = 5.22 \text{ s}$$

$$v = -11.6t - 8$$

$$= -11.6(5.22s) - 8$$

$$= -68.59 \text{ m/s}$$

The maximum speed of the object on Neptune is 68.59 m/s.

Mars

$$t = \frac{-(-8) \pm \sqrt{(-8)^2 - 4(-1.85)(200)}}{2(-1.85)}$$

$$t = 8.458 \text{ s}$$

$$v = -3.7t - 8$$

$$= -3.7(8.458s) - 8$$

$$= -39.29 \text{ m/s}$$

The maximum speed of the object on Mars is 39.29 m/s.

Difference: $68.59 - 39.29 = 30.3$ m/s

Lesson 2—Rate of Change Involving Area and Volume

PRACTICE EXERCISE
Answers and Solutions

1. a) $= 900 \, \text{m}^3/\text{s}$

$$V = s^3$$

$$\frac{dV}{dt} = 3s^2 \frac{ds}{dt}$$

When $s = 10 \, \text{m}$

$$= 3(10 \, \text{m})^2 (3 \, \text{m/s})$$

$$= 900 \, \text{m}^3/\text{s}$$

b) $A = \pi r^2 \quad 15 = \pi r^2, \quad r = \sqrt{\dfrac{15}{\pi}} \, \text{m}$

$$\frac{dA}{dt} = \pi 2r \frac{dr}{dt}$$

When $A = 15 \, \text{m}^2$

$$-1.2 \, \text{m}^2/\text{s} = 2\pi \left(\sqrt{\frac{15}{\pi}} \, \text{m} \right) \frac{dr}{dt}$$

$$\frac{dr}{dt} = \frac{-1.2 \, \text{m}^2/\text{s}}{2\pi \left(\sqrt{\dfrac{15}{\pi}} \, \text{m} \right)}$$

$$\frac{dr}{dt} = \frac{-3}{5\sqrt{15\pi}} \, \text{m/s}$$

3. $\dfrac{40}{49\pi} \, \text{cm/s}$

$$V = \frac{4}{3} \pi r^3$$

$$\frac{dV}{dt} = 4\pi r^2 \frac{dr}{dt}$$

When $r = 3.5 \, \text{cm}$

$$-40 \, \text{cm}^3/\text{s} = 4\pi (3.5 \, \text{cm})^2 \frac{dr}{dt}$$

$$\frac{-40 \, \text{cm}^3/\text{s}}{4\pi (3.5 \, \text{cm})^2} = \frac{dr}{dt}$$

$$\frac{dr}{dt} = \frac{-40 \, \text{cm}^3/\text{s}}{4(12.25 \, \text{cm}^2)\pi}$$

$$= \frac{-40}{49\pi} \, \text{cm/s}$$

Since this rate of change is negative, the radius is decreasing at a rate of $\dfrac{40}{49\pi}$ cm/s .

5. $\dfrac{ds}{dt} = \dfrac{3}{10}$ m/s

$V = s^3$

$SA = 6s^2$

$40\,\text{m}^2 = 6s^2$

$s = \sqrt{\dfrac{20}{3}}$

$\dfrac{dV}{dt} = 3s^2 \dfrac{ds}{dt}$

When $SA = 40\,\text{m}^2$

$6\,\text{m}^3/\text{s} = 3\left(\sqrt{\dfrac{20}{3}}\text{m}\right)^2 \dfrac{ds}{dt}$

$\dfrac{ds}{dt} = \dfrac{3}{10}$ m/s

Lesson 3—Rates of Change Involving Triangles

PRACTICE EXERCISE
Answers and Solutions

1. $\dfrac{dz}{dt} \doteq 2.69$ m/s

$\dfrac{dx}{dt} = 2\,\text{m/s}$

$\dfrac{dy}{dt} = 1.8\,\text{m/s}$

After 5 minutes:
$x = 600\,\text{m}$, $y = 540\,\text{m}$,

$z = \sqrt{600^2 + 540^2}$

$= 60\sqrt{181}\,\text{m}$

$z^2 = x^2 + y^2$

Differentiating implicitly:

$2z\dfrac{dz}{dt} = 2x\dfrac{dx}{dt} + 2y\dfrac{dy}{dt}$

$\dfrac{dz}{dt} = \dfrac{x\dfrac{dx}{dt} + y\dfrac{dy}{dt}}{z}$

$\dfrac{dz}{dt}\Big|_{t=5\min} = \dfrac{600(2) + 540(1.8)}{60\sqrt{181}}$

$= \dfrac{36.2}{\sqrt{181}}$

$= \dfrac{181}{5\sqrt{181}}$

$\doteq 2.69$ m/s

3. $\dfrac{dz}{dt}\Big|_{z=30} = 2\sqrt{3}$ m/s

$\dfrac{dx}{dt} = 4$

$\dfrac{dz}{dt} = ?$

z

x

When $z = 30$ m,

$x = \sqrt{30^2 - 15^2}$

$= \sqrt{675}$

$= 15\sqrt{3}\,\text{m}$

$z^2 = x^2 + 15^2$

Differentiating implicitly:

$2z\dfrac{dz}{dt} = 2x\dfrac{dx}{dt}$

$\dfrac{dz}{dt} = \dfrac{x\dfrac{dx}{dt}}{z}$

$\dfrac{dz}{dt} = \dfrac{x\dfrac{dx}{dt}}{z}$

When $z = 30\,\text{m}$

$\dfrac{dz}{dt}\Big|_{z=30} = \dfrac{\left(15\sqrt{3}\right)(4)}{30}$

$= 2\sqrt{3}$ m/s

5. The base is changing at a rate of –3.6 cm/min

A: area

$$\frac{dA}{dt} = 9 \, \text{cm}^2/\text{m}$$

$$\frac{da}{dt} = 3 \, \text{cm/m}$$

$$\frac{db}{dt} = ?$$

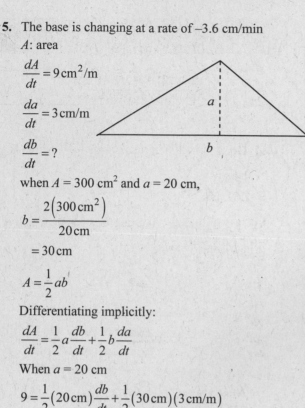

when $A = 300$ cm^2 and $a = 20$ cm,

$$b = \frac{2\left(300 \, \text{cm}^2\right)}{20 \, \text{cm}}$$

$$= 30 \, \text{cm}$$

$$A = \frac{1}{2} ab$$

Differentiating implicitly:

$$\frac{dA}{dt} = \frac{1}{2} a \frac{db}{dt} + \frac{1}{2} b \frac{da}{dt}$$

When $a = 20$ cm

$$9 = \frac{1}{2}(20 \, \text{cm})\frac{db}{dt} + \frac{1}{2}(30 \, \text{cm})(3 \, \text{cm/m})$$

$$\frac{9 - 45}{10} = \frac{db}{dt}$$

$$\frac{db}{dt} = -3.6 \, \text{cm/min}$$

The base is decreasing at a rate of 3.6 cm/min when the altitude is 20 cm and the area is 300 cm^2.

Practice Quiz

Answers and Solutions

1. a) $t \doteq 4.71$

$$t = \frac{-5 \pm \sqrt{(5)^2 - 4(-4.9)(85)}}{2(-4.9)}$$

$$t \doteq 4.71$$

b) Maximum speed: $\doteq 19.5$ m/s

$$v = \frac{dh}{dt} = -9.8t + 5$$

Since this problem involves a restricted domain of $0 \le t \le 4.71$, the endpoint values of the velocity-time function must be considered.

$$v(0) = -9.8(0) + 5 = 5 \, \text{m/s}$$

$$v(4.71) = -9.8(4.71) + 5 = -41.16 \, \text{m/s}$$

Since a linear function cannot have any points where its first derivative would be zero, these endpoint values are the maximum and minimum values of the velocity.

The maximum speed reached by the object is 41.16 m/s.

c) $= -19.5 \, \text{m/s}$

$$v(t) = -9.8t + 5$$

$$v(2.5) = -9.8(2.5 \, \text{s}) + 5$$

$$= -19.5 \, \text{m/s}$$

d)

$$v = -9.8t + 5$$

$$a = \frac{dv}{dt} = -9.8$$

The acceleration is a constant value of $-9.8 \, \text{m/s}^2$.

3.

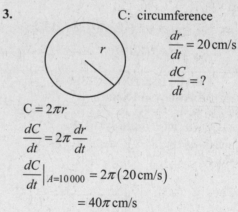

C: circumference

$$\frac{dr}{dt} = 20 \, \text{cm/s}$$

$$\frac{dC}{dt} = ?$$

$$C = 2\pi r$$

$$\frac{dC}{dt} = 2\pi \frac{dr}{dt}$$

$$\left.\frac{dC}{dt}\right|_{A=10\,000} = 2\pi(20 \, \text{cm/s})$$

$$= 40\pi \, \text{cm/s}$$

Lesson 4—Applications in Economics

PRACTICE EXERCISE
Answers and Solutions

1. a) $C'(x) = 4.2 + 0.02x$

b) $= \$24.20$

$$C'(1\,000) = 4.2 + 0.02(1\,000)$$

$$= 4.2 + 20$$

$$= \$24.20$$

c) 1 790 units need to be produced.

$$40 = 4.2 + 0.02x$$

$$x = \frac{35.8}{0.02}$$

$$x = 1\,790$$

1 790 units need to be produced to give a marginal cost of \$40.

3. a) $P(x) = R(x) - C(x)$

$$P(x) = \left(6x - 0.008x^2\right) - \left(55 + 1.9x - 0.009x^2 + 0.000\,08x^3\right)$$

$$P(x) = -0.000\,08x^3 + 0.001x^2 + 4.1x - 55$$

b) $P'(x) = -0.000\,24x^2 + 0.002x + 4.1$

Set $P'(x) = 0$ and solve for x:

$$0 = -0.000\,24x^2 + 0.002x + 4.1$$

$$x = \frac{-(0.002) \pm \sqrt{(0.002)^2 - 4(-0.000\,24)(4.1)}}{2(-0.000\,24)}$$

$$\approx 134.936$$

Test values: $x = 130, 140$

$$P'(130) = -0.000\,24(130)^2 + 0.002(130) + 4.1 = +0.304$$

$$P'(140) = -0.000\,24(140)^2 + 0.002(140) + 4.1 = -0.324$$

Since the value of the derivative function changed from positive to negative, the profit function reached a maximum value

To maximize profit, 135 items should be produced.

Lesson 5—Applications in Biological Sciences

PRACTICE EXERCISE
Answers and Solutions

1. a) Decay function because $k = \dfrac{-\ln 3}{7}$, which is negative.

b) Growth function because $k = \dfrac{1}{4}\ln 2$, which is positive.

3. a) $f'(t) = \dfrac{1\,500\ln 3}{7}e^{\frac{\ln 3}{7}t}$

$$f'(5) = \frac{1\,500\ln 3}{7}e^{\frac{\ln 3}{7}(5)}$$

$$\approx 515.99$$

After 5 hours, the growth rate is 516 bacteria/hour.

b) $f'(t) = 2\,000$

$$2\,000 = \frac{1500\ln 3}{7}e^{\frac{\ln 3}{7}t}$$

$$\frac{28}{3\ln 3} = e^{\frac{\ln 3}{7}t}$$

$$\ln\left(\frac{28}{3\ln 3}\right) = \ln\left(e^{\frac{\ln 3}{7}t}\right)$$

$$\ln\left(\frac{28}{3\ln 3}\right) = \frac{\ln 3}{7}t$$

$$t = \frac{\ln\left(\dfrac{28}{3\ln 3}\right)}{\dfrac{\ln 3}{7}}$$

$$\approx 13.632\text{ h}$$

Lesson 6—Newton's Method

PRACTICE EXERCISE
Answers and Solutions

1. ≈ 3.46

$f(x) = x^2 - 12$

$f'(x) = 2x$

$x_2 = x_1 - \dfrac{f(x_1)}{f'(x_1)}$

$= 2 - \dfrac{(2)^2 - 12}{2(2)}$

$= 2 + 2$

$x_2 = 4$

$x_3 = 4 - \dfrac{(4)^2 - 12}{2(4)}$

$= 4 - \dfrac{1}{2}$

$= 3.5$

$x_4 = 3.5 - \dfrac{(3.5)^2 - 12}{2(3.5)}$

≈ 3.46

3. $x_3 \approx 3.141\,6$

$f(x) = \sin x$

$f'(x) = \cos x$

$x_2 = x_1 - \dfrac{f(x_1)}{f'(x_1)}$

$x_2 = 3 - \dfrac{\sin(3)}{\cos(3)}$

$x_2 \approx 3.142\,5$

$x_3 = x_2 - \dfrac{f(x_2)}{f'(x_2)}$

$x_3 = 3.142\,5 - \dfrac{\sin(3.142\,5)}{\cos(3.142\,5)}$

$x_3 \approx 3.141\,6$

5. $x_3 = 1.0472$

$f(x) = 4\sin^2 x - 3$

$f'(x) = 8\sin x \cos x$

$\quad\ = 4\sin 2x$

$x_2 = 1 - \dfrac{4\sin^2(1) - 3}{4\sin(2(1))}$

$x_2 = 1 - \dfrac{4\sin^2(1) - 3}{4\sin(2(1))}$

$x_2 = 1 - \dfrac{4\sin^2(1) - 3}{4\sin(2(1))}$

$x_2 \doteq 1.0461$

$x_3 = 1.0461 - \dfrac{4\sin^2(1.0461) - 3}{4\sin(2(1.0461))}$

$x_3 \doteq 1.0472$

Practice Test

Answers and Solutions

1. a) Maximum velocity $= -6$ m/s.

Minimum velocity $= -14.52$ m/s.

Maximum speed $= 14.52$ m/s

When $h = 0$:

$0 = -4.9t^2 - 6t + 9$

$t = \dfrac{-(-6) \pm \sqrt{(-6)^2 - 4(-4.9)(9)}}{2(-4.9)}$

$t \approx 0.87$

$V = \dfrac{dh}{dt} = -9.8t - 6$

at $t \approx 0.87$:

The restricted domain for this problem is $0 \le t \le 0.87$. The endpoints of the linear velocity-time function must be considered.

$v(0) = -9.8(0) - 6$

$\quad\ = -6$ m/s

$v(0.87) = -9.8(0.87) - 6$

$\quad\quad\ = -14.52$ m/s

The maximum velocity is -6 m/s.

The minimum velocity is -14.52 m/s.

The maximum speed is 14.52 m/s,

b) $t = 0.41\,\text{s}$

$$-10 = -9.8t - 6$$
$$t = 0.41\,\text{s}$$

3. a) $\left.\dfrac{dh}{dt}\right|_{h=4} = -\dfrac{49}{72\pi}\ \text{m/s}$

Diameter = 6 m

7 m

$r = 3\,\text{m}$

$\dfrac{h}{r} = \dfrac{7\,\text{m}}{3\,\text{m}}$

$\therefore r = \dfrac{3}{7}h$

$V = \dfrac{1}{3}\pi r^2 h$

$= \dfrac{1}{3}\pi\left(\dfrac{3}{7}h\right)^2 h$

$= \dfrac{3}{49}\pi h^3$

$\dfrac{dV}{dt} = -2$

$\dfrac{dh}{dt} = ?$

$r = \dfrac{3}{7}h$

$\dfrac{dV}{dt} = \dfrac{9}{49}\pi h^2 \dfrac{dh}{dt}$

$\dfrac{dh}{dt} = \dfrac{49\dfrac{dV}{dt}}{9\pi h^2}$

$\left.\dfrac{dh}{dt}\right|_{h=4} = \dfrac{49(-2)}{9\pi(4)^2}$

$\left.\dfrac{dh}{dt}\right|_{h=4} = -\dfrac{49}{72\pi}\ \text{m/s}$

b) when $r = 1\,\text{m}$, $h = \dfrac{7}{3}$

$\dfrac{dh}{dt} = \dfrac{49\dfrac{dV}{dt}}{9\pi h^2}$

$\left.\dfrac{dh}{dt}\right|_{h=\frac{7}{3}} = \dfrac{9(-2)}{9\pi\left(\dfrac{7}{3}\right)^2}$

$\left.\dfrac{dh}{dt}\right|_{h=\frac{7}{3}} = -\dfrac{2}{\pi}\ \text{m/s}$

5. a) $= \$5.60\,/\text{item}$

$C'(x) = 3 + 0.026x$

$C'(100) = 3 + (0.026)(100)$

$= \$5.60$

b) $R'(800) = \$34/\text{item}$

$R(x) = xp(x)$

$= x(2 + 0.02x)$

$= 2x + 0.02x^2$

$R'(x) = 2 + 0.04x$

$R'(800) = 34$

c) $x = 71$

$C'(x) = R'(x)$

$3 + 0.026x = 2 + 0.04x$

$1 = 0.014x$

$x = 71.4$

Approximately 71 items should be produced for maximum profit to be reached.

7. a) $= \dfrac{179}{385}$

≈ 0.465

$f(x) = x^3 + 2x - 1$

$f'(x) = 3x^2 + 2$

$x_1 = 1$

$x_2 = 1 - \dfrac{x^3 + 2x - 1}{3x^2 + 2}$

$= 1 - \dfrac{(1)^3 + 2(1) - 1}{3(1)^2 + 2}$

$= \dfrac{3}{5}$

$x_3 = \dfrac{3}{5} - \dfrac{\left(\dfrac{3}{5}\right)^3 - 2\left(\dfrac{3}{5}\right) - 1}{3\left(\dfrac{3}{5}\right)^2 + 2}$

$= \dfrac{179}{385}$

≈ 0.465

b) $= \dfrac{27}{5}$

$f(x) = x^2 - 4x - 5$

$f'(x) = 2x - 4$

$x_1 = 3$

$x_2 = 3 - \dfrac{x^2 - 4x - 5}{2x - 4}$

$= 3 - \dfrac{(3)^2 - 4(3) - 5}{2(3) - 4}$

$= 7$

$x_3 = 7 - \dfrac{(7)^2 - 4(7) - 5}{2(7) - 4}$

$= \dfrac{27}{5}$

ANTIDERIVATIVES AND AREA

Lesson 1—The Antiderivative

PRACTICE EXERCISE
Answers and Solutions

1. a) $y = -x^3 - x^2 + x + C$

$\dfrac{dy}{dx} = -3x^2 - 2x + 1$

$dy = \left(-3x^2 - 2x + 1\right) dx$

$\int 1\, dy = \int \left(-3x^2 - 2x + 1\right) dx$

$y + C_1 = -3\left[\dfrac{x^{2+1}}{(2+1)}\right] - 2\left[\dfrac{x^{1+1}}{(1+1)}\right] + 1x + C_2$

$y = -x^3 - x^2 + x + C$

b) $p = 3\ln|z| + \dfrac{3}{z} - \dfrac{1}{z^2} + C$

$\dfrac{dp}{dz} = \dfrac{3}{z} - \dfrac{3}{z^2} + \dfrac{2}{z^3}$

$dp = \left(\dfrac{3}{z} - \dfrac{3}{z^2} + \dfrac{2}{z^3}\right) dz$

$\int 1\, dp = \int \left(\dfrac{3}{z} - \dfrac{3}{z^2} + \dfrac{2}{z^3}\right) dz$

$\int 1\, dp = 3\int\left(\dfrac{1}{z}\right) dz - 3\int\left(z^{-2}\right) dz + 2\int\left(z^{-3}\right) dz$

$p + C_1 = 3\ln|z| - 3\left[\dfrac{z^{-2+1}}{(-2+1)}\right] + 2\left[\dfrac{z^{-3+1}}{(-3+1)}\right] + C_2$

$p = 3\ln|z| + 3z^{-1} - z^{-2} + C$

$p = 3\ln|z| + \dfrac{3}{z} - \dfrac{1}{z^2} + C$

c) $y = \tan x + C$

$\dfrac{dy}{dx} = \sec^2 x$

$dy = \left(\sec^2 x\right) dx$

$\int 1\, dy = \int\left(\sec^2 x\right) dx$

$y + C_1 = \tan x + C_2$

$y = \tan x + C$

d) $u = \dfrac{1}{2}y^2 - \sin y$

$\dfrac{du}{dy} = y - \cos y$

$du = (y - \cos y)\,dy$

$\int 1\,du = \int (y - \cos y)\,dy$

$u + C_1 = \dfrac{1}{2}y^2 - \sin y + C_2$

$u = \dfrac{1}{2}y^2 - \sin y + C$

3. a) $\int (5x-3)^{12}\,dx = \dfrac{1}{65}(5x-3)^{13} + C$

Let $u = 5x - 3$

$\dfrac{du}{dx} = 5$ or $dx = \dfrac{du}{5}$

$\int (5x-3)^{12}\,dx$

$= \int (u)^{12}\left(\dfrac{du}{5}\right)$

$= \dfrac{1}{5}\int (u)^{12}\,du$

$= \dfrac{1}{5}\left[\dfrac{u^{12+1}}{(12+1)} + C_1\right]$

$= \dfrac{1}{65}(u)^{13} + C$

$= \dfrac{1}{65}(5x-3)^{13} + C$

b) $\int \left(\sqrt{4x^2 - 10x}\right)(4x-5)\,dx =$

$\dfrac{1}{3}\left(4x^2 - 10x\right)^{\frac{3}{2}} + C$

Let $u = 4x^2 - 10x$

$\dfrac{du}{dx} = 8x - 10$ or $du = (8x-10)\,dx$ or

$dx = \dfrac{du}{(8x-10)}$

$\int \left(\sqrt{4x^2 - 10x}\right)(4x-5)\,dx$

$= \int (u)\dfrac{1}{2}(4x-5)\left(\dfrac{du}{8x-10}\right)$

$= \int (u)\dfrac{1}{2}(4x-5)\left(\dfrac{du}{2(4x-5)}\right)$

$= \dfrac{1}{2}\int (u)\dfrac{1}{2}\,du$

$= \left[\dfrac{1}{2}\dfrac{u^{\frac{1}{2}+1}}{\left(\dfrac{1}{2}+1\right)} + C_1\right]$

$= \dfrac{1}{2}\left[\dfrac{2}{3}u^{\frac{3}{2}} + C_1\right]$

$= \dfrac{1}{3}\left(4x^2 - 10x\right)^{\frac{3}{2}} + C$

c) $\int \left[\cos^4(8x)\right]\left[\sin(8x)\right]dx =$

$-\dfrac{1}{40}\cos^5(8x) + C$

Let $u = \cos(8x)$

$\dfrac{du}{dx} = -8\sin(8x)$

$dx = \dfrac{du}{-8\sin(8x)}$

$\int \left[\cos^4(8x)\right]\left[\sin(8x)\right]dx$

$\int (u)^4\left(\sin(8x)\right)\dfrac{du}{-8\sin(8x)}$

$= -\dfrac{1}{8}\int (u)^4\,du$

$= -\dfrac{1}{8}\left[\dfrac{u^{4+1}}{(4+1)} + C_1\right]$

$= -\dfrac{1}{40}\cos^5(8x) + C$

d) $\int \left(e^{\ln(4x)}\right)\left(\dfrac{1}{x}\right)dx = e^{\ln(4x)} + C$

Let $u = \ln(4x)$

$\dfrac{du}{dx} = \left(\dfrac{1}{4x}\right)(4) = \dfrac{1}{x}$

$dx = \dfrac{du}{\dfrac{1}{x}}$

$$\int \left(e^{\ln(4x)}\right)\left(\frac{1}{x}\right)dx$$

$$= \int \left(e^u\right)\left(\frac{1}{x}\right)\left(\frac{du}{\frac{1}{x}}\right)$$

$$= \int \left(e^u\right)du$$

$$= e^{\ln(4x)} + C$$

Lesson 2—Differential Equations with Initial Conditions

PRACTICE EXERCISE
Answers and Solutions

1. a) $a(t) = t + 1$

$$\frac{dv}{dt} = t + 1$$

$$v = \frac{t^2}{2} + t + C \qquad\qquad v(0) = 0$$

$$v = \frac{t^2}{2} + t$$

$$\frac{ds}{dt} = v$$

$$\frac{ds}{dt} = \frac{t^2}{2} + t$$

$$\qquad\qquad\qquad s(0) = 0$$

$$s = \frac{t^3}{6} + \frac{t^2}{2} + C$$

$$s = \frac{t^3}{6} + \frac{t^2}{2}$$

To be complete, $s(t) = \frac{t^3}{6} + \frac{t^2}{2}$ for all $t \geq 0$.

Note that we use the $s(t)$ (displacement as a function of time) notation instead of our usual s notation because the question gives acceleration as a function of time.

b) $a = 3\sin t$

$$v = \int (3\sin t)dt$$

$$v = -3\cos t + C_1$$

Assigning initial velocity information gives the velocity function.

$$1 = -3\cos(0) + C_1$$

$$1 = -3(1) + C_1$$

$$C_1 = 4$$

$$v = 4 - 3\cos t$$

$$s = \int (4 - 3\cos t)dt$$

$$s = 4t - 3\sin t + C_2$$

Use initial conditions for displacement:

$$1 = 4(0) - 3\sin(0) + C_2$$

$$C_2 = 1$$

$$s = 1 + 4t - 3\sin t$$

c) $\dfrac{d^2 y}{dx^2} = x - 1$

$$\frac{dy}{dx} = \int (x-1)dx$$

$$\frac{dy}{dx} = \frac{1}{2}x^2 - x + C_1$$

Using $(0, 1)$

$$1 = \frac{1}{2}(0) - (0) + C_1$$

$$C_1 = 1$$

$$\frac{dy}{dx} = \frac{1}{2}x^2 - x + 1$$

$$y = \int \left(\frac{1}{2}x^2 - x + 1\right)dx$$

$$y = \frac{1}{6}x^3 - \frac{1}{2}x^2 + x + C_2$$

Using $(1, 2)$

$$2 = \frac{1}{6} - \frac{1}{2} + 1 + C_2$$

$$C_2 = \frac{4}{3}$$

$$y = \frac{x^3}{6} - \frac{x^2}{2} + x + \frac{4}{3}$$

d) $v = 2t - 1$

$s = \int (2t - 1)\, dt$

$s = t^2 - t + C$

It is important to note that this result relates displacement and time.

At $t = 3$, we find that

$s(3) = 6 + C$, and at $t = 5$, we find that

$s(5) = 20 + C$.

Since the object did not change direction in the time interval (3, 5), the distance traveled in that interval is $s(5) - s(3) = 14$ m.

e) $y = A \sin 4x + B \cos 4x$

$1 = A \sin 2\pi + B \cos 2\pi$

$B = 1$

$y' = 4A \cos 4x - 4(1) \sin 4x$

$1 = 4A \cos 2\pi - 4 \sin 2\pi$

$A = \dfrac{1}{4}$

$y = \dfrac{1}{4} \sin 4x + 1 \cos 4x$

f) First, we find k from Hooke's Law $(F = ks)$.

The spring is stretched from 0.1 m to 0.2 m by applying 10 N.

So, $10 = k(0.1)$ or $k = 100$.

Set up the equation for the second differential:

$s'' + \dfrac{k}{m} s = 0$

Since we know mass is 0.5 kg,

$s'' + 200s = 0$

$s = A \sin \left(\sqrt{200}\, t \right) + B \cos \left(\sqrt{200}\, t \right)$

$(0.3 - 0.1) = A \sin (0) + B \cos (0)$

$B = 0.2$

$s' = \sqrt{200} A \cos \left(\sqrt{200}\, t \right) - \sqrt{200} B \sin \left(\sqrt{200}\, t \right)$

From this equation, we note that at time zero, the displaced spring is held at rest. So, this derivative equals zero (at time zero). This gives:

$0 = \sqrt{200} A \cos (0)$

$A = 0$

$s = 0.2 \cos \left(\sqrt{200}\, t \right)$

(from the original equation)

g) Let y = the number of rabbits present at any time, t, in years.

For continuous exponential growth:

$y = A e^{kt}$

Using (0, 100):

$y = 100 e^{kt}$

Using (2, 900)

$900 = 100 e^{2k}$

$9 = e^{2k}$

$\ln 9 = \ln e^{2k}$

$\ln 9 = 2k$

$k = \dfrac{\ln 9}{2} = 1.099$

$y = 100 e^{\left(\frac{\ln 9}{2} \right)}$

At $t = 3$:

$y(3) = 100 e^{\left(\frac{\ln 9}{2} \right)(3)}$

$y(3) = 2\,700$

Practice Quiz

Answers and Solutions

1. $\int \left(x^2 - 3\right) dx = \dfrac{2x^3}{3} - 3x + C$

3. $f(x) = 3x - 3\ln|x| + C$, where $x \neq 0$

5. $F(x) = \dfrac{x^2}{2} - 1$

$F(x) = \int (x)\, dx$

7. $\int \left(\cos^3 x\right) dx = \sin x - \dfrac{1}{3}\sin^3 x + C$

$\int \left(\cos^3 x\right) dx$

$= \int \left(\cos^2 x\right)\left(\cos x\right) dx$

$= \int \left(1 - \sin^2 x\right)\left(\cos x\right) dx$

$= \int \left(\cos x - \cos x \sin^2 x\right) dx$

$= \int \left(\cos x\right) dx - \int \left[\sin x\right]^2 \left(\cos x\right) dx$

Let $u = \sin x.\ \dfrac{du}{dx} = \cos x\ \ or\ \ dx = \dfrac{du}{\cos x}$

$\int \left(\cos x\right) dx - \int \left[\sin x\right]^2 \left(\cos x\right) dx$

$= \int \left(\cos x\right) dx - \int [u]^2 \left(\cos x\right)\left(\dfrac{du}{\cos x}\right)$

$= \int \left(\cos x\right) dx - \int \left(u^2\right) du$

$= \left[\sin x + C_1\right] - \left[\dfrac{1}{3}u^3 + C_2\right]$

$= \sin x - \dfrac{1}{3}\sin^3 x + C$

Lesson 3—Signed Area

PRACTICE EXERCISE
Answers and Solutions

1. a) Signed area $\doteq$ .1.

$f(x) = \dfrac{1}{x}$

The general antiderivative function is

$A(x) = \ln|x| + C$

The signed area in the interval $[1, 3]$ is:

$A(3) - A(1)$

$= \left[\ln 3 + C\right] - \left[\ln 1 + C\right]$

$= \ln 3 - \ln 1$

$\doteq 1.1$

b) Signed area $= 2$

$f(x) = \sin x$

The general antiderivative function is:

$A(x) = -\cos x + C$

The signed area in the interval $[0, \pi]$ is:

$A(\pi) - A(0)$

$= \left[-\cos \pi + C\right] - \left[-\cos 0 + C\right]$

$= [1] - [-1]$

$= 2$

c) Signed area $= \dfrac{32}{3}$

$f(x) = 2x^2 - 2$

The general antiderivative function is:

$A(x) = \dfrac{2}{3}x^3 - 2x + C$

The signed area in the interval $[2, 3]$ is:

$A(3) - A(2)$

$= \left[\dfrac{2}{3}(3)^3 - 2(3) + C\right] - \left[\dfrac{2}{3}(2)^3 - 2(2) + C\right]$

$= [12] - \left[\dfrac{4}{3}\right]$

$= \dfrac{32}{3}$

d) Signed area = $\dfrac{28}{9}$

$$f(x) = \frac{2}{3}x^{\frac{1}{2}}$$

The general antiderivative function is:

$$A(x) = \frac{2}{3}\left(\frac{x^{\frac{1}{2}+1}}{\left(\frac{1}{2}+1\right)}\right) = \frac{2}{3}\left(\frac{2}{3}x^{\frac{3}{2}}\right) = \frac{4}{9}x^{\frac{3}{2}}$$

The signed area in the interval [1, 4] is:

$$A(4) - A(1)$$

$$= \left[\frac{4}{9}(4)^{\frac{3}{2}} + C\right] - \left[\frac{4}{9}(1)^{\frac{3}{2}} + C\right]$$

$$= \left[\frac{32}{9}\right] - \left[\frac{4}{9}\right]$$

$$= \frac{28}{9}$$

e) Signed area = -9

$$f(x) = x^2 - 4x$$

The general antiderivative function is:

$$A(x) = \frac{1}{3}x^2 - 2x^2 + C$$

The signed area in the interval [0, 3] is:

$$A(3) - A(0)$$

$$= \left[\frac{1}{3}(3)^3 - 2(3)^2 + C\right] - \left[\frac{1}{3}(0)^2 - 2(0)^2 + C\right]$$

$$= [-9] - [0]$$

$$= -9$$

f) Signed are = $e - 1$

$$f(x) = e^x$$

The general antiderivative function is:

$$A(x) = e^x + C$$

The signed area in the interval [0, 1] is:

$$A(1) - A(0)$$

$$= \left[e^1 + C\right] - \left[e^0 + C\right] \quad A(x) = e^x + C$$

$$= e - 1$$

Lesson 4—The Definite Integral

PRACTICE EXERCISE
Answers and Solutions

1. Approximate signed area = 2

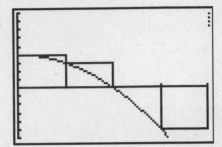

Each rectangle has its left edge contacting the function $f(x) = 4 - x^2$

The width of each rectangle is $\dfrac{4 - 0}{4} = 1$

The height of the first rectangle is $f(0) = 4$

The height of the second rectangle is $f(1) = 3$.

The height of the third rectangle is $f(2) = 0$.

The height of the fourth rectangle is $f(3) = -5$.

The total signed area of the 4 rectangles is:

$$(1)(4) + (1)(3) + (1)(0) + (1)(-5) = 2$$

3. a) $p(x) = \dfrac{1}{2}x^2 + x$

$$p(x) = \int_{-2}^{x}(t+1)\,dt = \left(\frac{1}{2}t^2 + t + C\right)\Bigg|_{-2}^{x}$$

$$p(x) = \left[\frac{1}{2}x^2 + x + C\right] - \left[\frac{1}{2}(-2)^2 + (-2) + C\right]$$

$$p(x) = \frac{1}{2}x^2 + x$$

b)

$$p(-2) = \frac{1}{2}(-2)^2 + (-2) = 0$$

$$p(3) = \frac{1}{2}(3)^2 + (3) = \frac{15}{2}$$

$$p(-3) = \frac{1}{2}(-3)^2 + (-3) = \frac{3}{2}$$

5. $x = 5$ or -2

$$\int_2^x (2t - 3)\,dt = 12$$

$$\left(t^2 - 3t + C\right)\Big|_2^x = 12$$

$$\left[x^2 - 3x + C\right] - \left[2^2 - 3(2) + C\right] = 12$$

$$x^2 - 3x + 2 = 12$$

$$x^2 - 3x - 10 = 0$$

$$(x - 5)(x + 2) = 0$$

7. 7

Using the property

$$\int_a^b [f(x)]\,dx = -\int_b^a [f(x)]\,dx$$

$$\int_2^4 [f(x)]\,dx = -\int_4^2 [f(x)]\,dx = -10$$

and

$$\int_4^5 [f(x)]\,dx = -\int_5^4 [f(x)]\,dx = -(-17) = 17$$

Substitute: $a = 2$, $b = 4$, $c = 6$

$$\int_2^6 [f(x)]\,dx = \int_2^4 [f(x)]\,dx + \int_4^6 [f(x)]\,dx$$

$$\int_2^6 [f(x)]\,dx = -10 + 17$$

$$\int_2^6 [f(x)]\,dx = 7$$

Lesson 5—Area Between Curves

PRACTICE EXERCISE
Answers and Solutions

1. a) Area = $\dfrac{2}{3}$

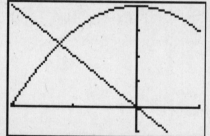

Area =

$$\int_0^1 (1 - x^2)\,dx = \left(x - \frac{1}{3}x^3 + C\right)\Big|_0^1 = \left[1 - \frac{1}{3}\right] - [0] = \frac{2}{3}$$

b) Area = $\dfrac{4}{3}$

$$\int_{-1}^1 (1 - x^2)\,dx = \left(x - \frac{1}{3}x^3 + C\right)\Big|_{-1}^1 = \left[1 - \frac{1}{3}\right] - \left[-1 + \frac{1}{3}\right] = \frac{4}{3}$$

c) Area $= 2.79$

We need to find the intersection points for $y = -x^2 + 4$ and $y = -2x$.

Solving $-x^2 + 4 = -2x$ using the quadratic formula yields the roots $1 \pm \sqrt{5}$.

Enclosed area $= \displaystyle\int_{1-\sqrt{5}}^0 \left(-x^2 + 4 + 2x\right)\,dx$

$$= \left(-\frac{1}{3}x^3 + 4x + x^2 + C\right)\Big|_{1-\sqrt{5}}^0$$

$$= [0] - \left[-\frac{1}{3}\left(1 - \sqrt{5}\right)^3 + 4\left(1 - \sqrt{5}\right) + \left(1 - \sqrt{5}\right)^2\right]$$

$$\doteq 2.787$$

d) Area $= \dfrac{32}{3}$

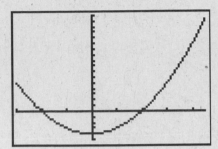

The quadratic function $y = x^2 - 4$ will intersect the x-axis at ± 2. This function will also intersect the line $x = 4$ at the point $(4, 12)$.

Enclosed area $= \displaystyle\int_2^4 \left(x^2 - 4 \right) dx$

$= \left[\dfrac{1}{3}(4)^3 - 4(4) \right] - \left[\dfrac{1}{3}(2)^3 - 4(2) \right]$

$= \left[\dfrac{16}{3} \right] - \left[-\dfrac{16}{3} \right]$

$= \dfrac{32}{3}$

e) Area $= \sqrt{2} - 1$

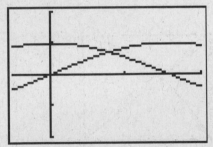

The functions intersect when $\sin x = \cos x$.

The root we use is $\dfrac{\pi}{4}$.

Enclosed area $= \displaystyle\int_0^{\frac{\pi}{4}} \left(\cos x - \sin x \right) dx$

$= \left. (\sin x + \cos x + C) \right|_0^{\frac{\pi}{4}}$

$= \left[\sin \dfrac{\pi}{4} + \cos \dfrac{\pi}{4} \right] - \left[\sin 0 + \cos 0 \right]$

$= \left[\dfrac{\sqrt{2}}{2} + \dfrac{\sqrt{2}}{2} \right] - \left[0 + 1 \right]$

$= \sqrt{2} - 1$

f) Area $= \dfrac{45}{4}$

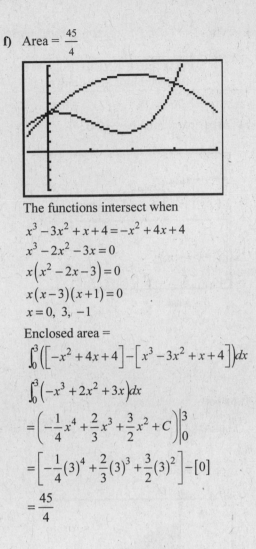

The functions intersect when

$x^3 - 3x^2 + x + 4 = -x^2 + 4x + 4$

$x^3 - 2x^2 - 3x = 0$

$x\left(x^2 - 2x - 3 \right) = 0$

$x(x - 3)(x + 1) = 0$

$x = 0, \ 3, \ -1$

Enclosed area $=$

$\displaystyle\int_0^3 \left(\left[-x^2 + 4x + 4 \right] - \left[x^3 - 3x^2 + x + 4 \right] \right) dx$

$\displaystyle\int_0^3 \left(-x^3 + 2x^2 + 3x \right) dx$

$= \left. \left(-\dfrac{1}{4}x^4 + \dfrac{2}{3}x^3 + \dfrac{3}{2}x^2 + C \right) \right|_0^3$

$= \left[-\dfrac{1}{4}(3)^4 + \dfrac{2}{3}(3)^3 + \dfrac{3}{2}(3)^2 \right] - \left[0 \right]$

$= \dfrac{45}{4}$

Lesson 6—Area Using Numerical Methods

PRACTICE EXERCISE
Answers and Solutions

1. a) Area approximation = 0.863 4

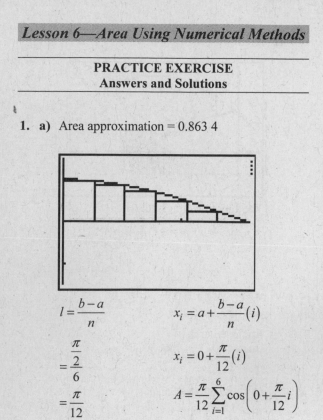

$$l = \frac{b-a}{n} \qquad\qquad x_i = a + \frac{b-a}{n}(i)$$

$$= \frac{\frac{\pi}{2}}{6} \qquad\qquad x_i = 0 + \frac{\pi}{12}(i)$$

$$= \frac{\pi}{12} \qquad\qquad A = \frac{\pi}{12}\sum_{i=1}^{6}\cos\left(0 + \frac{\pi}{12}i\right)$$

$$A \approx 0.863\ 4$$

b) Signed area = 1

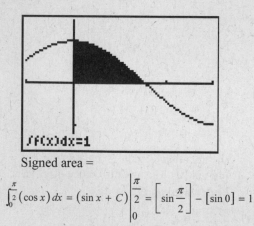

∫f(x)dx=1

Signed area =

$$\int_0^{\frac{\pi}{2}} (\cos x)\, dx = (\sin x + C)\Big|_0^{\frac{\pi}{2}} = \left[\sin\frac{\pi}{2}\right] - [\sin 0] = 1$$

The actual area under the curve is 1 unit squared. So, our approximation is not too far off, considering that we use only 6 rectangles.

3. a) $\dfrac{b-a}{n} = \dfrac{1}{2}$

$$0 \rightarrow \frac{1}{2} \rightarrow 1 \rightarrow \frac{3}{2} \rightarrow 2$$

$$A = \frac{1}{2}\left(\frac{1}{2}\right)\left[1 + 2(1.5) + 2(3) + 2\left(\frac{11}{2}\right) + 9\right]$$

$$A = \frac{30}{4}$$

$$A \approx 7.5$$

Using the formula and $f(x_i)$, our approximation is 7.5 units squared.

b) $f(x) = 2x^2 + 1$

$$\int_0^2 (2x^2 + 1)\, dx = \left(\frac{2}{3}x^3 + x + C\right)\Big|_0^2 = \left[\frac{16}{3} + 2\right] - [0] = \frac{22}{3}$$

Our approximation in (a) above is not too far off for only 4 trapezoids.

Practice Test

Answers and Solutions

1. a) $\int\left(\dfrac{e^{-x}}{2} + 2\cos x\right)dx = \dfrac{e^{-x}}{2} + 2\sin x + C$

b) $\int(\sin x - \pi)\,dx = -\cos x - \pi x + C$

3. Using Hooke's Law, we start with $F = ks$ and apply the given information to find the constant (k).

$F = ks$

$1 = k(0.02)$

$k = 50$

Now (again using Hooke's Law), we set up the second-degree differential equation.

$\dfrac{d^2 s}{dt^2} + \dfrac{50}{0.1} s = 0 \qquad$ and the solution

$\dfrac{d^2 s}{dt^2} + 500 s = 0$

$s = A\sin\sqrt{\dfrac{k}{m}}\,t + B\cos\sqrt{\dfrac{k}{m}}\,t$

$s = A\sin\sqrt{500}\,t + B\cos\sqrt{500}\,t$

We use the initial conditions that at time zero, $s = 0.02$

$0.02 = 0 + B\cos 0$

$B = 0.02$

Differentiate s to obtain $\dfrac{ds}{dt}$ and apply the conditions that at time zero, $\dfrac{ds}{dt} = 0$.

$\dfrac{ds}{dt} = \sqrt{500}\,A\cos\left(\sqrt{500}\,t\right) - \sqrt{500}\,B\sin\left(\sqrt{500}\,t\right)$

$0 = \sqrt{500}\,A\cos(0) - (0)$

$A = 0$

$s = 0.02\cos\left(\sqrt{500}\,t\right)$

5. a) The signed area under function f in the interval

$[0, 3]$ is:

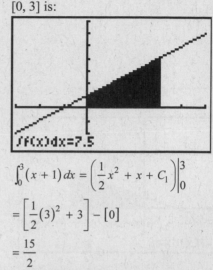

$\int_0^3 (x+1)\,dx = \left(\dfrac{1}{2}x^2 + x + C_1\right)\Big|_0^3$

$= \left[\dfrac{1}{2}(3)^2 + 3\right] - [0]$

$= \dfrac{15}{2}$

The signed area under function g in the Interval $[0, 3]$ is:

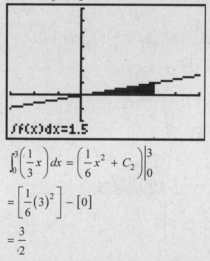

$\int_0^3 \left(\dfrac{1}{3}x\right)dx = \left(\dfrac{1}{6}x^2 + C_2\right)\Big|_0^3$

$= \left[\dfrac{1}{6}(3)^2\right] - [0]$

$= \dfrac{3}{2}$

The area between the 2 functions in the interval $[0, 3]$ is the difference of these 2 calculated areas.

$\dfrac{15}{2} - \dfrac{3}{2} = 6$

b) The difference function, d, (upper – lower) in the interval $[0, 3]$ is:

$$d(x) = f(x) - g(x)$$

$$d(x) = (x + 1) - \left(\frac{1}{3}x\right)$$

$$d(x) = \frac{2}{3}x + 1$$

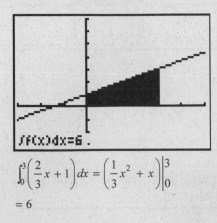

∫f(x)dx=6 .

$$\int_0^3 \left(\frac{2}{3}x + 1\right) dx = \left(\frac{1}{3}x^2 + x\right)\bigg|_0^3$$

$$= 6$$

7. Approximate area $= 25.5$ units squared

The width of each trapezoid is $\dfrac{b-a}{n} = \dfrac{1}{2}$.

Over 8 trapezoids, we get the following intervals:

$$\left[0, \frac{1}{2}\right], \left[\frac{1}{2}, 1\right], \left[1, \frac{3}{2}\right], \left[\frac{3}{2}, 2\right], \left[2, \frac{5}{2}\right], \left[\frac{5}{2}, 3\right], \left[3, \frac{7}{2}\right], \left[\frac{7}{2}, 4\right]$$

$$A \approx \frac{1}{2}\left(\frac{b-a}{n}\right)\left[f(a) + 2f(x)_1 + 2f(x)_2 + \ldots + f(b)\right]$$

$$A \approx \frac{1}{4}\left[\begin{array}{c} 1 + 2\left(\dfrac{5}{4}\right) + 2(2) + 2\left(\dfrac{13}{4}\right) + 2(5) + 2\left(\dfrac{29}{4}\right) \\ + 2(10) + 2\left(\dfrac{53}{4}\right) + 17 \end{array}\right]$$

$$A \approx \frac{1}{4}(102)$$

$$A \approx 25.5$$

This approximation is very close to the exact value of the area under the curve over the given interval. There are two reasons that this approximation is more accurate than the approximation found using a rectangular approximation with four rectangles.

First, we are using more trapezoids, which makes the width of each one less and the difference in $f(x)$ over the sub-interval less. Second, we are using trapezoids, which approximate the curve more more closely than do rectangles.

9. a) $\int_{-2}^{4}\left(3x^2 + 2x - 1\right) dx = 78$

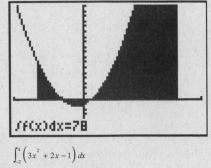

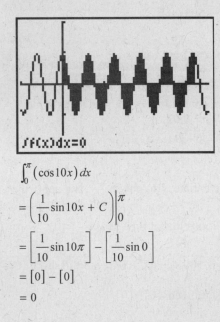

∫f(x)dx=78

$$\int_{-2}^{4}\left(3x^2 + 2x - 1\right) dx$$

$$= \left(x^3 + x^2 - x + C\right)\bigg|_{-2}^{4}$$

$$= \left[4^3 + 4^2 - 4\right] - \left[(-2)^3\,(-2)^2 - (-2)\right]$$

$$= [76] - [-2]$$

$$= 78$$

b) $\int_0^{\pi}\left(\cos 10x\right) dx = 0$

∫f(x)dx=0

$$\int_0^{\pi}\left(\cos 10x\right) dx$$

$$= \left(\frac{1}{10}\sin 10x + C\right)\bigg|_0^{\pi}$$

$$= \left[\frac{1}{10}\sin 10\pi\right] - \left[\frac{1}{10}\sin 0\right]$$

$$= [0] - [0]$$

$$= 0$$

11. 0.70

Using: Average value $= \dfrac{\int_a^b f(x)\,dx}{b-a}$

$\dfrac{\int_{\frac{\pi}{6}}^{\frac{\pi}{3}} (\cos x)\,dx}{\dfrac{\pi}{3} - \dfrac{\pi}{6}}$

$= \dfrac{(\sin x + C)\Big|_{\frac{\pi}{6}}^{\frac{\pi}{3}}}{\dfrac{\pi}{6}}$

$= \dfrac{\left(\sin \dfrac{\pi}{3}\right) - \left(\sin \dfrac{\pi}{6}\right)}{\dfrac{\pi}{6}}$

$= \dfrac{\dfrac{\sqrt{3}}{2} - \dfrac{1}{2}}{\dfrac{\pi}{6}}$

≈ 0.70

METHODS OF INTEGRATION AND APPLICATIONS

Lesson 1—Fundamental Theorem of Calculus

PRACTICE EXERCISE
Answers and Solutions

1. $a = 1,\ b = 3$

3. $F(x) = \dfrac{-1}{x} + C$

5. $-\cos x \big|_0^\pi = -(-1) + (1) = 2$

7. $\cos x\,dx$

$\int (2\cos x)\,dx$

$= \int (\cos x + \cos x)\,dx$

$= \int \cos x\,dx + \int \cos x\,dx$

Lesson 2—Integration by Substitution

PRACTICE EXERCISE
Answers and Solutions

1. a) $\int \cot x\, dx$

Look at integrand:

$\cot x$

$\dfrac{\cos x}{\sin x}$

$u = \sin x$

$du = \cos x\, dx$

$dx = \dfrac{du}{\cos x}$

Now, apply this to original integral:

$\int \dfrac{\cos x}{u} \dfrac{du}{\cos x}$

$\int \dfrac{1}{u}\, du$

$\ln|u| + C$

$\ln|\sin x| + C$

b) $\int \dfrac{2e^{\sqrt{x}}}{\sqrt{x}}\, dx$

$u = \sqrt{x}$

$du = \dfrac{1}{2\sqrt{x}}\, dx$

$dx = \left(\dfrac{2u}{1}\right) du$

$\int \dfrac{2e^u}{u}\left(\dfrac{2u}{1}\right) du$

$\int 4e^u\, du$

$4e^u + C$

$4e^{\sqrt{x}} + C$

3. a) $\ln 4 - \ln 3$

$\int_3^4 \left(\dfrac{1}{x-1}\right) dx$

Let $u = x - 1$

$du = dx$

When $x = 3$, $u = 3 - 1 = 2$

When $x = 4$, $u = 4 - 1 = 3$

$\int_3^4 \left(\dfrac{1}{x-1}\right) dx$

$= \int_2^3 \left(\dfrac{1}{u}\right) du$

$= \left(\ln|u| + C\right)\Big|_2^3$

$= \ln 3 - \ln 2$

$\doteq 0.405$

b) $\int_3^4 \left(\dfrac{1}{x-1}\right) dx$

$= \left(\ln|x-1| + C\right)\Big|_3^4$

$= \ln|4-1| - \ln|3-1|$

$= \ln 3 - \ln 4$

Lesson 3—Integration by Partial Fractions

PRACTICE EXERCISE
Answers and Solutions

1. a) Divide each term by the denominator.

$\int \left(\dfrac{1}{x} + \dfrac{1}{x^2}\right) dx$

$\ln|x| - \dfrac{1}{x} + C$

b) When performing division, set up as follows:

$\dfrac{x^3 - x^2 - 0x - 1}{x+1}$, then divide.

Integrand becomes $\dfrac{x^2 - 2x + 2}{1} - \dfrac{3}{x+1}$

(the quotient and remainder)

Integrate to obtain the final answer:

$\dfrac{x^3}{3} - x^2 + 2x - 3\ln|x+1| + C$

c) $\int \dfrac{1}{2x^2 - 2}\,dx \Rightarrow \dfrac{1}{2}\int \dfrac{1}{x^2 - 1}\,dx$

Work with integrand:

$$\dfrac{1}{x^2 - 1} = \dfrac{1}{(x+1)(x-1)}$$

$$\dfrac{A}{x+1} + \dfrac{B}{x-1}$$

$$A(x-1) + B(x+1) = 1$$

$$A + B = 0$$

$$-A + B = 1$$

$$B = 0.5$$

$$A = -0.5$$

So,

$$\dfrac{1}{2}\int \left(\dfrac{-1}{2(x+1)} + \dfrac{1}{2(x-1)} \right) dx$$

$$\dfrac{1}{2}\left(\dfrac{1}{2}\right)\left(-\ln|x+1| + \ln|x-1| \right)$$

$$\dfrac{-\ln|x+1|}{4} + \dfrac{\ln|x-1|}{4} + C$$

d) $\int \dfrac{x+2}{(x+1)^2}\,dx$

Work with integrand:

$$\dfrac{A}{x+1} + \dfrac{B}{(x+1)^2}$$

$A(x+1) + B = x + 2$ (equating numerators)

This equates to the original, so solve for variables:

$$A = 1$$

$$A + B = 2$$

Solve, substitute and complete:

$$\int \left(\dfrac{1}{x+1} + \dfrac{1}{(x+1)^2} \right) dx$$

$$\ln|x+1| - \dfrac{1}{(x+1)} + C$$

Lesson 4—Integration by Parts

PRACTICE EXERCISE
Answers and Solutions

1. a) $\int (2x+1)e^{-x}\,dx$

First, write out the integration by parts formula, then apply:

$$\int f(x)g'(x)\,dx = f(x)g(x) - \int g(x)f'(x)\,dx$$

$$f(x) = 2x + 1$$

$$f'(x) = 2$$

$$g'(x) = e^{-x}$$

$$g(x) = -e^{-x}$$

Once we identify the separate parts and the left-hand side of the formula is identical to our given integral, we can immediately solve using only the right-hand side of the formula (In some occasions, as seen in previous examples, we re-arrange the original integral).

$$= -(2x+1)e^{-x} - \int -e^{-x}(2)\,dx$$

$$= -(2x+1)e^{-x} + 2\int e^{-x}\,dx$$

$$= -(2x+1)e^{-x} - 2e^{-x} + C$$

$$= -2xe^{-x} - e^{-x} - 2e^{-x} + C$$

$$= -2xe^{-x} - 3e^{-x} + C$$

$$= -(2x+3)e^{-x} + C$$

b)

$$f(x) = x$$

$$f'(x) = 1$$

$$g'(x) = \cos 3x$$

$$g(x) = \dfrac{1}{3}\sin 3x$$

Then, using the formula:

$$= \dfrac{1}{3}x\sin 3x - \int (\sin 3x)\,dx$$

$$= \dfrac{1}{3}x\sin 3x + \dfrac{1}{9}\cos 3x + C$$

c) $f(x) = x$

$f'(x) = 1$

$g'(x) = \sec^2 x$

$g(x) = \tan x$

Now, apply the formula:

$= x \tan x - \int \tan x (1) dx$

$= x \tan x - \left(-\ln|\cos x| \right) + C$

$= x \tan x + \ln|\cos x| + C$

d)

$f(x) = \dfrac{x}{2}$

$f'(x) = \dfrac{1}{2}$

$g'(x) = e^x$

$g(x) = e^x$

$= \dfrac{xe^x}{2} - \int \left(\dfrac{1}{2} \right) e^x dx$

$= \dfrac{xe^x}{2} - \dfrac{e^x}{2} + C$

This answer can be combined as a single fraction, if desired.

e) -4

$f(x) = 2$

$f'(x) = 2$

$g'(x) = \cos x$

$g(x) = \sin x$

$f'(x) g(x) - \int g(x) f'(x) dx$

$= 2x \sin x - \int (\sin x)(2) dx$

$= 2x \sin x + 2\cos x + C$

$\int_0^\pi 2x \cos x \, dx$

$= \left(2x \sin x + 2\cos x + C \right) \Big|_0^\pi$

$= \left[2\pi \sin \pi + 2\cos \pi \right] - \left[2(0)\sin 0 + 2\cos 0 \right]$

$= \left[0 + 2(-1) \right] - \left[0 + 2(1) \right]$

$= -4$

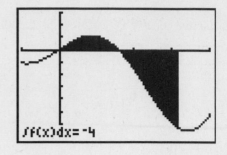

f) $\pi - 2$

Similar to (e) except the limits of integration are changed, so the answer becomes:

$\int_0^{\frac{n}{2}} 2x \cos x \, dx$

$= \left(2x \sin x + 2\cos x + C \right) \Big|_0^{\frac{\pi}{2}}$

$= \left[2\left(\dfrac{\pi}{2} \right) \sin \dfrac{\pi}{2} + 2\cos \dfrac{\pi}{2} \right] - \left[2(0)\sin 0 + 2\cos 0 \right]$

$= \left[\pi + 2(0) \right] - \left[0 + 2(1) \right]$

$= \pi - 2$

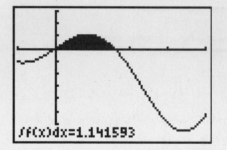

506

Practice Quiz

Answers and Solutions

1. $\dfrac{\pi^2}{2} \doteq 4.935$

$\displaystyle\int_0^\pi (x + \cos x)\,dx$

$= \left(\dfrac{1}{2}x^2 + \sin x + C\right)\Bigg|_0^\pi$

$= \left[\dfrac{1}{2}(\pi)^2 + \sin \pi\right] - \left[\dfrac{1}{2}(0)^2 + \sin 0\right]$

$= \dfrac{\pi^2}{2}$

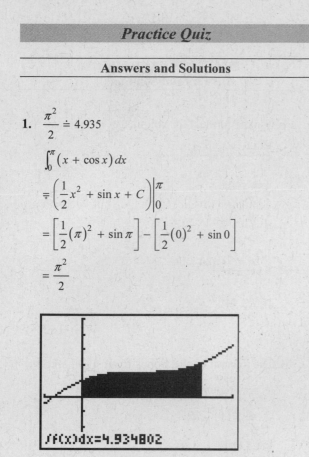

∫f(x)dx=4.934802

3. First rewrite and simplify the function:

$$\int \dfrac{(x^2-1)}{(x^2-1)^2(x-1)}\,dx \Rightarrow \int \dfrac{1}{(x^2-1)(x-1)}\,dx$$

Normally, we would set this up as follows:

$$\dfrac{Ax+B}{(x^2-1)} + \dfrac{D}{(x-1)}$$

But if we tried to solve this using a system, we will find it does not work. The reason for this is that the denominator of our integrand must be rewritten as follows before solving:

$$(x^2-1)(x-1)$$

$$(x+1)(x-1)(x-1)$$

$$(x+1)(x-1)^2$$

This is why the hint was necessary.

Properly applied, the rules of partial fractions suggest we break this up as:

$$\dfrac{A}{x+1} + \dfrac{B}{(x-1)} + \dfrac{D}{(x-1)^2}$$

$$A(x-1)^2 + B(x+1)(x-1) + D(x+1) = 1$$

$$A(x^2 - 2x + 1) + B(x^2 - 1) + D(x+1) = 1$$

$$A + B = 0$$

$$-2A + D = 0$$

$$A - B + D = 1$$

$$A = \dfrac{1}{4}$$

$$B = -\dfrac{1}{4}$$

$$D = \dfrac{1}{2}$$

We can bring a common factor out in front of the integral sign in order to simplify the equation until the final step. We use the rule that says:

$$\int kf(x)\,dx = k\int f(x)\,dx$$

$$\dfrac{1}{4}\int \left(\dfrac{1}{x+1} + \dfrac{-1}{(x-1)} + \dfrac{2}{(x-1)^2}\right)dx$$

$$\dfrac{1}{4}\ln|x+1| - \dfrac{1}{4}\ln|x-1| - \dfrac{2}{(x-1)} + C$$

5. $-\ln\left(e^2-1\right) + \ln\left(e-1\right) \doteq -1.313$

$$\int_1^2 \frac{e^x}{1-e^x}\,dx$$

$$u = \left(1-e^x\right)$$

$$du = -e^x\,dx$$

Determine the new limits of integration,

When $x = 1$, $u = 1 - e$.

When $x = 2$, $u = 1 - e^2$.

$$\int_1^2 \frac{e^x}{1-e^x}\,dx = -\int_{1-e}^{1-e^2} u^{-1}\,du$$

$$= \left(-\ln|u| + C\right)\Big|_{1-e}^{1-e^2}$$

$$= \left[-\ln\left|1-e^2\right|\right] - \left[-\ln\left|1-e\right|\right]$$

$$= -\ln\left(e^2-1\right) + \ln\left(e-1\right)$$

$$\doteq -1.313$$

$\int f(x)dx = ^-1.313262$

Lesson 5—Volumes of Revolution

PRACTICE EXERCISE
Answers and Solutions

1. a) Use the formula for volume:

$$\int_a^b \pi\left[f(x)\right]^2 dx$$

$$\int_2^3 \pi x^4\,dx$$

$$= \frac{\pi x^5}{5}\Big|_2^3$$

$$= \frac{243\pi}{5} - \frac{32\pi}{5}$$

$$= \frac{211}{5}\pi$$

b) The interval in question is from $0 \to \frac{\pi}{4}$.

(Knowing that $180° = \pi$ radians)

$$\int_a^b \pi\left[f(x)\right]^2 dx$$

for $f(x) = y = \sec x$

$$V = \int_0^{\frac{\pi}{4}} \pi \sec^2 x\,dx$$

$$= \pi \tan x\Big|_0^{\frac{\pi}{4}}$$

$$= \pi(1-0)$$

$$= \pi$$

c) $\int_a^b \pi\left[f(x)\right]^2 dx$

$$V = \int_0^3 \pi(2)^2\,dx$$

$$= 4\pi x\Big|_0^3$$

$$= 12\pi$$

Confirm: The original function is just the line at $y = 2$. If we break this up into rectangles, they will all rotate to form a cylinder of radius 2 and a height equal to the interval $0 \to 3$, or 3 units.

The formula for the volume of a cylinder is $\pi r^2 h$.

$$V = \pi r^2 h$$

$V = \pi(4)(3)$

$= 12\pi$

So, it is confirmed.

d) $y = (x-1)^2$

$V = \int_0^1 \pi\left(x^2 - 2x + 1\right)^2 dx$

$= \pi\left(\dfrac{x^5}{5} - \dfrac{x^4}{1} + \dfrac{2x^3}{1} - 2x^2 + x\right)\Bigg|_0^1$

$= \pi\left(\dfrac{1}{5} - 1 + 2 - 2 + 1\right) - 0$

$= \dfrac{\pi}{5}$

e) We can use the preliminary work done in (d) above, and skip to the step where the interval is calculated into the equation.

$= \pi\left(\dfrac{x^5}{5} - \dfrac{x^4}{1} + \dfrac{2x^3}{1} - 2x^2 + x\right)\Bigg|_1^2$

$= \pi\left(\dfrac{32}{5} - 16 + 16 - 8 + 2\right) - \pi\left(\dfrac{1}{5} - 1 + 2 - 2 + 1\right)$

$= \pi\left(\dfrac{2}{5}\right) - \pi\left(\dfrac{1}{5}\right)$

$= \dfrac{\pi}{5}$

Compare and comment: The value obtained for the volume is equal to (d). However, this is not simply because the interval was the same length in each case.

The key to this answer lies in the fact that the original function, $y = (x-1)^2$, is a parabola with a vertex at $(1,0)$. It has a line of symmetry at $x = 1$. So, any volume generated to the left of this line would be the same generated to the right. The interval in (d) is one unit left of the axis of symmetry.

The interval in (e) is one unit immediately to the right of the axis of symmetry.

f) $y = \sqrt{x}$

$V = \int_0^a \pi(x)^1 dx$

The square root is removed since the function is being squared.

$V = \dfrac{\pi x^2}{2}\Bigg|_0^a$

$= \dfrac{a^2 \pi}{2}$

If, $a = 2$, then

$V = 2\pi$

Practice Test

Answers and Solutions

1. $F(b) - F(a)$, F continuous

3. $\int\left[\sqrt{3x^2 - 5}\,(12x)\right]dx$

$u = \sqrt{3x^2 - 5}$

$du = \dfrac{6x}{2u}dx$

$\int u(12x)\dfrac{2u}{6x}du$

$\int 4u^2 du$

$= \dfrac{4u^3}{3} + C$

$= \dfrac{4}{3}\left(3x^2 - 5\right)^{\frac{3}{2}} + C$

5.

$\int 5x \sin x\, dx$

$f(x) = 5x$

$f'(x) = 5$

$g'(x) = \sin x$

$g(x) = -\cos x$

$= 5x(-\cos x) - \int(5)(-\cos x)\,dx$

$= -5x\cos x + 5\int \cos x\, dx$

$= -5x\cos x + 5\sin x + C$

7. For question 2, we used basic integration techniques and the final answer (now a definite integral) is $1+\cos 1$, which is approximately 1.54.

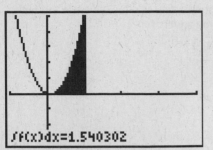

For question 3, we used integration by substitution, but this function has $\sqrt{3x^2-5}$ as part of its original function and its integral. This is only defined if $x^2 \geq \dfrac{5}{3}$, so our limits of integration will not give us an answer with real roots. The function is not continuous over the interval.

For question 4, we used integration by substitution, and the final answer is $\dfrac{\sin^6 1}{2}$ or $\cong 0.177\,5$.

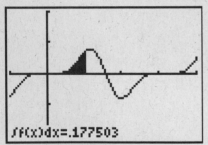

For question 5, we used integration by parts and the final answer is $-5\cos 1 + 5\sin 1$.

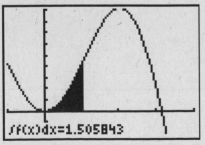

For question 6, we used integration by parts, twice, obtaining a final answer of $e-2$.

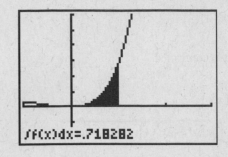

9. a) $\dfrac{Ax+B}{\left(x^2-x-1\right)} + \dfrac{C}{\left(x-3\right)}$

b) $\dfrac{A}{\left(x-2\right)} + \dfrac{B}{\left(x-2\right)^2} + \dfrac{C}{\left(x-2\right)^3} + \dfrac{Dx+E}{\left(x^2+x+1\right)}$

NOTES

NOTES

ORDERING INFORMATION

SCHOOL ORDERS

Schools and school jurisdictions are eligible for our educational discount rate. Contact Castle Rock Research for more information.

***THE KEY* Study Guides** are specifically designed to assist students in preparing for unit tests, final exams, and provincial examinations.

***THE KEY* Study Guides**—$29.95 each plus G.S.T.

SENIOR HIGH		JUNIOR HIGH	ELEMENTARY
Biology 30	Biology 20	English Language Arts 9	English Language Arts 6
Chemistry 30	Chemistry 20	Mathematics 9	Mathematics 6
English 30-1	English 20-1	Science 9	Science 6
English 30-2	Mathematics 20-1	Social Studies 9	Social Studies 6
Mathematics 30-1	Physics 20	Mathematics 8	Mathematics 4
Mathematics 30-2	Social Studies 20-1	Mathematics 7	English Language Arts 3
Physics 30	English 10-1		Mathematics 3
Social Studies 30-1	Mathematics 10		
Social Studies 30-2	Combined		
	Science 10		
	Social Studies 10-1		

Student Notes and Problems (SNAP) Workbooks contain complete explanations of curriculum concepts, examples, and exercise questions.

SNAP Workbooks—$29.95 each plus G.S.T.

SENIOR HIGH		JUNIOR HIGH	ELEMENTARY
Biology 30	Biology 20	Mathematics 9	Mathematics 6
Chemistry 30	Chemistry 20	Science 9	Mathematics 5
Mathematics 30-1	Mathematics 20-1	Mathematics 8	Mathematics 4
Mathematics 30-2	Physics 20	Science 8	Mathematics 3
Mathematics 31	Mathematics 10	Mathematics 7	
Physics 30	Combined	Science 7	
	Science 10		

Class Notes and Problem Solved—$19.95 each plus G.S.T.

SENIOR HIGH		JUNIOR HIGH
Biology 30	Biology 20	Mathematics 9
Chemistry 30	Chemistry 20	Science 9
Mathematics 30-1	Mathematics 20-1	Mathematics 8
Mathematics 30-2	Physics 20	Science 8
Mathematics 31	Mathematics 10 Combined	Mathematics 7
Physics 30		Science 7

Visit our website for a tour of resource content and features or order resources online at
www.castlerockresearch.com/store/

#2410, 10180 – 101 Street NW
Edmonton, AB Canada T5J 3S4
e-mail: learn@castlerockresearch.com

Phone: 780.448.9619
Toll-free: 1.800.840.6224
Fax: 780.426.3917

CASTLE ROCK
RESEARCH CORP

ORDER FORM

THE KEY	QUANTITY	Student Notes and Problems Workbooks	QUANTITY SNAP Workbooks	Problem Solved and Class Notes	QUANTITY Class Notes	QUANTITY Problem Solved
Biology 30		Mathematics 31		Mathematics 31		
Chemistry 30		Biology 30		Biology 30		
English 30-1		Chemistry 30		Chemistry 30		
English 30-2		Mathematics 30-1		Mathematics 30-1		
Mathematics 30-1		Mathematics 30-2		Mathematics 30-2		
Mathematics 30-2		Physics 30		Physics 30		
Physics 30		Biology 20		Biology 20		
Social Studies 30-1		Chemistry 20		Chemistry 20		
Social Studies 30-2		Mathematics 20-1		Mathematics 20-1		
Biology 20		Physics 20		Physics 20		
Chemistry 20		Mathematics 10 Combined		Mathematics 10 Combined		
English 20-1		Science 10		Mathematics 9		
Mathematics 20-1		Mathematics 9		Science 9		
Physics 20		Science 9		Mathematics 8		
Social Studies 20-1		Mathematics 8		Science 8		
English 10-1		Science 8		Mathematics 7		
Math 10 Combined		Mathematics 7		Science 7		
Science 10		Science 7				
Social Studies 10-1		Mathematics 6				
Social Studies 9		Mathematics 5				
English Language Arts 9		Mathematics 4				
Mathematics 9		Mathematics 3				
Science 9						
Mathematics 8						
Mathematics 7						
English Language Arts 6						
Mathematics 6						
Science 6						
Social Studies 6						
Mathematics 4						
Mathematics 3						
English Language Arts 3						

Total Cost

Subtotal 1	
Subtotal 2	
Subtotal 3	
Cost Subtotal	
Shipping and Handling*	
G.S.T	
Order Total	

*(Please call for current rates)

School Discounts

Schools and school jurisdictions are eligible for our educational discount rate. Contact Castle Rock Research for more information.

PAYMENT AND SHIPPING INFORMATION

Name: _____
School _____
Telephone: _____

SHIP TO
School Code: _____
School: _____
Address: _____
City: _____ Postal Code: _____

PAYMENT
☐ By credit card   VISA/MC
Number: _____
Expiry Date: _____
Name on card: _____
☐ Enclosed cheque
☐ Invoice school   P.O. number: _____

CASTLE ROCK
RESEARCH CORP

#2410, 10180 – 101 Street NW, Edmonton, AB T5J 3S4   **Phone:** 780.448.9619   **Fax:** 780.426.3917   **Toll-free:** 1.800.840.6224
Email: learn@castlerockresearch.com   www.castlerockresearch.com